AI

THE TUMULTUOUS HISTORY OF THE SEARCH FOR ARTIFICIAL INTELLIGENCE

DANIEL CREVIER

BasicBooks

A Division of HarperCollins*Publishers*

Library of Congress Cataloging-in-Publication Data
Crevier, Daniel, 1947–
    AI : the tumultuous history of the search for artificial
intelligence / Daniel Crevier.
        p.   cm.
    Includes bibliographical references and index.
    ISBN 0–465–02997–3
    1. Artificial intelligence—History.   I. Title.
Q335.C66   1993
006.3'09—dc20   91–55461
                                                                       CIP

Designed by Ellen Levine

93 94 95 96 CC/HC 9 8 7 6 5 4 3 2 1

To Céline

Contents

Preface

Not too long ago, if you walked into the computer room of MIT's Artificial Intelligence Laboratory, the first thing you noticed was a winding yellow brick path painted on the floor. At the end of this path, dangling from the ceiling above a large computer, was a resplendent rainbow. In case you missed the first two references, a poster of Judy Garland as Dorothy was taped to the computer's side and the computer itself had been given the nickname Oz.[1]

In reality, Oz was nothing more sophisticated than a mainframe computer controlling a network of smaller computers. But just as an earlier traveler over the rainbow had hoped that a wizard named Oz might be able to fashion a brain for a straw-stuffed friend, the researchers at MIT's Artificial Intelligence Lab hoped that their Oz might be used to create computer-generated intelligence.

From its inception the Artificial Intelligence Laboratory at MIT has occupied most of a tall building in what is known as Technology Square, a section of campus a short jog away from the heart of the Massachusetts Institute of Technology on Mass Avenue. It was on this campus that I spent far too many days and nights in the early 1970s busily assembling a Ph.D. thesis on a topic related to AI, but different enough to keep me away from the lab itself. While doing my own work, I observed the goings on over at Tech Square with a perplexed and somewhat envious interest. For every so often information would leak out about some new and exotic breakthrough that suggested that AI was where the computer world's future was being created and tested before being loosed on the rest of us.

I followed these developments with intense interest. I remember vividly a demonstration in which the AI computer was hooked up to a TV camera, so that those of us interested in a first demonstration of the future could observe the computer manipulate the arm of a robot piling up children's blocks, building a mirror image of a model block structure shown to the camera. In another demonstration, an operator conversed with a computer in English, ordering it to manipulate a block construction displayed on a screen, and even had the machine answer questions about its motivations. Not knowing how to evaluate all this, many of us in attendance weren't sure whether we had just witnessed the dawning experiment of the coming age of AI or a bit of theater.

The answer was not long in coming. While these AI experiments of the 1960s and early 1970s were fun to watch and probably even enjoyable to create, it soon became clear that the techniques they employed would not be useful apart from dealing with carefully simplified problems in restricted areas. Not surprisingly, the U.S. military, one of the main sponsors of early AI research, was also one of the first to have second thoughts. Tech Square, and other centers that had sprung up around the world with high hopes of early success, soon found themselves fighting for their very survival. Human intelligence, whatever it was, was not about to yield its secrets quickly.

In the early 1980s, after I had left MIT to return home to Canada to work in AI-related research, I read about the next breakthrough—expert systems. While broad-based artificial intelligence might still be many years away, the idea that one could create systems that captured the decision-making processes of human experts, even if those systems operated only on narrowly focused tasks, suddenly seemed on the horizon or, at most, just over it. The expert system was promoted as a sort of nonhuman idiot savant, but one that could be exploited for profit without guilt or shame. It could be tailored to diagnose the ailments of humans and machines, or to select the optimal site for oil exploration or the best wine for dinner. The prospects were exciting and appeared boundless. Bankrolled primarily by a great deal of private capital, expert systems moved out of the laboratory and into the marketplace, where many of the new companies foundered. But those people involved in artificial intelligence have always been part of a community that has a common ideal, in respect to which numerous approaches rival each other for attention, funding, and the chance to succeed. The failure of expert systems rekindled interest in the rival technology of artificial neural networks, those webs of interconnected, specially designed processors that could be "trained" (through the application of varying degrees of voltage) to respond on their own to external stimuli.

At that point, I began gathering material for this book. Over the following years, which I spent renewing contacts, attending conferences, interviewing the founders and stars of the field, and running my own AI-related business, I observed the next stage of the rollercoaster ride begin. It now seems that we may soon have a computer for a world chess champion. A second generation of expert systems, this time more savant than idiot, is taking hold of the marketplace with little noise or fanfare. Meanwhile, large AI projects like CyC and SOAR seek to endow computers with common sense in the not-too-distant future; such worldly wise machines may acquire knowledge and refine their reasoning power by themselves, much as humans do, but with the advantages attendant on greater computer speed and memory.

The story of AI consists of successes and failures, visionaries and naysayers, new hardware and lots of programs. It is also the story of a slow but steady acquisition of knowledge about how humans think. After all, the pursuit of artificial intelligence means uncovering the unbelievably complex layers of our own thought processes. The quest for artificial intelligence therefore raises some crucial philosophical issues. What will be the consequences for humans if researchers in artificial intelligence succeed and force us to share the world with entities smarter than ourselves? Are we facing a new Renaissance or the creation of the species that will replace us? And should we rely on these creations to make not only business and scientific decisions for us, but also social, legal, and moral choices? I raised these and similar questions with the leaders of AI: their answers (and your conclusions) may surprise you.

Most of the events I will relate happened in the United States. This emphasis stems only in part from my own bias toward the country where I studied and keep so many friends: it is a fact that most pioneering AI research occurred in America, probably because of the overbearing interest of the U.S. military. My apologies to Japan and Europe, who are now catching up: future accounts of AI will say more about them!

Acknowledgments

I am deeply grateful to those participants in the history of AI who lent me their time and help in preparing this account of their activities. Particular thanks must go to Marvin Minsky, Herbert Simon, Allen Newell, Gerald Sussman, Daniel Dennett, Joseph Weizenbaum, Berthold Horn, Randall Davis, Carl Hewitt, John McClelland, Hans Moravec, Raj Reddy, David Waltz, Patrick Winston, Guy Lapalme, and Lorne Bouchard, who granted me interviews. Several of them, as well as Roger Schank, also read and commented on relevant sections of the manuscript.

Many thanks also to those friends and relatives who reviewed the manuscript and supplied their comments: Simon Paré, Jacques Martineau, Francis Dupuis, Marie-Josée Rousseau, Laurens R. Schwartz, Claire Dowey, and, of course, Paul-Henri Crevier, my father, who helped out on the neurology and philosophy.

Basic Books's Susan Rabiner must be acknowledged for her prodding help throughout; and Phoebe Hoss, for her enlightened revision of the manuscript.

Many thanks also to those publishers and authors who granted me permission to quote from their copyrighted material: Academic Press, the American Council on Education, and Patrick Winston.

I could not have completed the project without the understanding attitude toward book writing of my employer, the Ecole de Technologie Supérieure, which I thank for providing time and secretarial help in the final months. Jocelyne Hall, in particular, was of invaluable help in bringing the illustrations into final shape.

My deepest gratitude goes to my wife, Céline, for her unfailing patience, love, and support throughout the long years it has taken to carry the project through.

Introduction

PROBING THE MYSTERY
OF HUMAN INTELLIGENCE

It is not my aim to surprise or shock you—but the simplest way I can summarize is to say that there are now in the world machines that think, that learn and that create. Moreover, their ability to do these things is going to increase rapidly until—in a visible future—the range of problems they can handle will be coextensive with the range to which the human mind has been applied.   —Herbert Simon, 1957

A s if driven by some invisible hand, humans have always yearned to understand what makes them think, feel, and be, and have tried to re-create that interior life artificially. Long before the vacuum tubes and silicon chips of the modern digital computer, long before the first analog computer, mythologies and literature recorded a timeless need to animate the inanimate, from Pygmalion's attempt to bring to life the perfectly sculpted Galatea to Gepetto's desire that the wooden puppet Pinocchio be a real boy.

An early "man in the machine" was the statue of the god Amon in the royal city of Napata in ancient Egypt around 800 B.C. Upon the demise of a pharaoh, eligible heirs were marched past the statue of Amon until the god made known his choice by extending his arm to grab the successor. Amon then "delivered" a consecrating speech.[1]

A priest, of course, controlled the statue with levers and uttered the sacred words through an opening on the back of the statue. Although it is likely that those who took part in the process, would-be pharaohs and onlookers alike, knew that a bit of theater was being put on, the procedure was taken seriously: in the Egyptian mind, the priest-cum-statue system added up to more than the sum of its parts, and embodied the god.

The *Iliad* describes more sophisticated self-activated automata, attributing them to the work of the divine blacksmith Hephaestus. Among the golden female attendants were gangly walking tripods, forerunners of today's many-legged field robots. In the *Iliad,* Homer also recounts how Daedalus, wing maker extraordinaire to the woe of his son Icarus, molded the copper giant Talos, which patrolled the shores of Crete.[2]

The likely inspiration for such literary automata were real ones being engineered in the Greek city of Alexandria. The Roman architect Vitruvius tells us that between the third and first centuries B.C., a school of early engineers founded by Ctesibius "conceived . . . automatic devices and amusing things of all kinds . . . ravens singing through contrivances using the force of water, and figures that drank and moved about."[3] Similarly, Hero, author of a treatise called *Automata,*[4] treated his readers to a description of a steam-propelled carousel; it now stands as the first-known description of a steam engine!

In Europe, the late Middle Ages and the Renaissance saw a resurgence of automata. Roger Bacon reportedly spent seven years constructing talking figures.[5] To honor Louis XII, Leonardo da Vinci built an automaton in the shape of a lion. During the sixteenth and seventeenth centuries, Italian and French designers, such as Gio Battista Aleotti and Salomon de Caus, elaborated on designs of the Alexandrian school: gardens and grottoes resonated with the songs of artificial birds and mechanical flutists, while fully animated nymphs, dragons, and satyrs pepped up aristocratic receptions.[6] René Descartes built in 1649 an automaton that he called "my daughter Francine." But on one of Descartes' trips, a superstitious ship captain happened to open the case containing Francine and, frightened by her lifelike movements, threw case and contents overboard.

By the eighteenth century, the French artisan Jacques de Vaucanson could assemble his celebrated duck, which provided an almost complete imitation of its model. One prospectus described it as an "artificial duck of golden Copper that Drinks, Eats, Croaks, Splashes in water and Digests as a live duck." Life-sized, the animal rested on a waist-high case containing a drum engraved with cogs and grooves.[7] Control rods passing through the duck's legs caused it to move in a manner programmed in the cogs: today we would call the drum a Read Only Memory (ROM) device.

Although artisans like Pierre and Louis Jaquet-Droz kept producing automata for the pleasure of the rich late into the century, the mechanical arts had reached their limits. The next leap required the automatic switch, or electromechanical relay. This device contains an iron kernel which can change positions under the influence of a magnetic field generated by a current fed to the relay. Depending on the polarity of the current, the kernel opens or closes electrical contacts to motors, lights, or even other relays. Interconnected relays can be used to build mechanisms more complex than those allowed by interlocking gears and cams.

At the turn of the century, the Spaniard Leonardo Torres y Quevedo built a relay-activated automaton that played end-games in chess. The philosophers Leibnitz and Pascal had constructed mechanical computing devices centuries before, but those were perceived as soulless contraptions intended to alleviate the drudgery of addition and subtraction. De Vaucanson's duck was a superb emulation of a living creature. But a device that would play chess against human opponents was something completely different: it seemed to have the ability to think.

In early chapters of this book, I shall describe how relays evolved into vacuum tubes and transistors, which formed the basis for the digital computer, the invention that made artificial intelligence possible. Digital computers are simply devices for manipulating discrete pieces of information, initially taken to correspond to numbers. The insight at the root of artificial intelligence was that these "bits" could just as well stand as symbols for concepts that the machines would combine by the strict rules of logic or the looser associations of psychology. European philosophers and mathematicians had been probing the issues involved in representing the world through abstract concepts for millennia; and they had been asking in the process fundamental questions about the nature of mind and thought. The American pioneers of AI, at first unwittingly and later in enlightened fashion, began to tap the insights of these humanist predecessors. Expressions such as "experimental epistemology" and "applied ontology" then started to describe systematic, down-to-earth research projects in computer science.

Emerging as it does from many fields—philosophy, mathematics, psychology, even neurology—artificial intelligence raises basic issues about human intelligence, memory, the mind/body problem, the origins of language, symbolic reasoning, information processing, and so forth. AI researchers are—like the alchemists of old who sought to create gold from base metal—seeking to create thinking machines from infinitisimally small bits of silicon oxyde.

The birth of AI was tied to the efforts of a variety of talented, intellectually self-confident, well-educated budding mathematicians, electrical engineers, psychologists, and even one political scientist. Some of these figures never really became a part of AI research per se; yet their ideas, developed in other contexts, were enormously influential in determining the early direction of the field. Others made seminal contributions as AI researchers and then left the field to pursue other work. A few, there at the creation, remain there to this day. The various origins of the creators of AI and the enormous influence of their work explains some of the colorful aspect of their pronouncements, and the rollercoaster evolution of their field. As the hoopla over cold fusion illustrated in 1989, even the staid science of physics is not immune to exaggeration and false claims. Yet excesses of optimism seem to occur with particular frequency in AI. There are several reasons that AI workers were, and often still are, more likely to make exaggerated claims than their colleagues of other disciplines.

First, there were plausible reasons in AI's early years for believing in its rapid progress, and these induced early researchers to display the excessive optimism that came to characterize the field. Early progresses in using computers for arithmetic were truly breathtaking. In a few years, technology went from cranky mechanical calculators to machines that could perform thousands of operations per second. It was thus not unreasonable to expect similar progress in using computers as manipulators of symbols to imitate human reasoning.

One misconception further enhanced this temptation. Psychological experiments in the 1950s and 1960s pointed to an oversimplified picture of the mind. The Carnegie Mellon researcher and AI pioneer Herbert Simon compared it to a dim-witted ant winding its way around complex obstacles, saying in effect that complexity lay in the environment and not in the mind itself.[8] There is truth in this statement, but bridging the gap between ant and human still requires a giant leap in complexity. Yet, in the postwar decades, controlled studies on our ability to remember and reason showed their basic limitations. The next time you look up a seven-digit phone number, try thinking of something else for a few seconds before dialing. If you're like most people, this will make you forget the number. We can't keep more than five to nine items at a time in our short-term memory; and as soon as we look away, they vanish. Our long-term memory has an almost unlimited capacity, but it learns very slowly. Transferring an item from short-term to long-term memory takes several seconds. (It takes me about two minutes to learn by heart the seven digits of a phone number.) When we rate alternatives in any complicated problem, like a number puzzle, we need pencil and paper to make up for these deficiencies of our memory.

Early AI researchers reasoned that their computers did not suffer from these limitations. Even in those days, the machines had memories with capacities of thousands of items and access times of microseconds. They could shuffle data much faster than fumbling, pencil-pushing humans can. Computers, thought Simon and his colleagues, should be able to take advantage of these capabilities to overtake humans: it was only a matter of a few years before suitable programming would let them do it. These researchers had not realized that, in activities other than purely logical thought, our minds function much faster than any computer yet devised. They are so fast, in fact, that we are not even conscious of their work. Pattern recognition and association make up the core of our thought. These activities involve millions of operations carried in parallel, outside the field of our consciousness. If AI appeared to hit a wall after earning a few quick victories, it did so owing to its inability to emulate these processes.

Already deluded by false expectations, early AI workers were drawn further onto the path of exaggerated claims by a myriad of other factors. One was the recent and sudden emergence of AI as an identifiable discipline. Like all new frontiers, AI attracted a particular kind of person: one willing to face the lack of academic security in the new field and to live with the haphazard financing of the early years. So novel were the insights offered by the new technology that early researchers looked like elephants in the well-tended flower beds of conventional sciences. As we shall see, AI brought about major revisions in some branches of psychology and mathematics. It is also deeply affecting modern philosophy. To one used to bringing forth such innovations, moderation is a hard virtue to learn.

I have already mentioned that AI is a multidisciplinary science. As Herbert Simon told me: "AI has had problems from the beginning. It is a new field in which people came from many different directions. That has meant they didn't always know where things came from, because many people imported them. And we still haven't established a set of norms of responsibility, of referencing, that keeps us from reinventing wheels all the time."⁹ One of Herbert Simon's best-known students, Edward Feigenbaum, earned his Ph.D. in a tangle of disciplines that well illustrates the incompatibility of AI with the academic structures of the late 1950s and early 1960s. An engineering graduate, Feigenbaum was registered at the business school, and worked on a subject that previously belonged to psychology: the modeling of human memory. Each of the fields from which AI researchers emerge nowadays (psychology, computer science, linguistics, physics, philosophy, mathematics, neurology, or electrical engineering) has its own accepted methodology, and they are often at odds with each other. The different branches of AI lack a common language, values, or standards of achievements. A uniform discipline acts as a moderator on other fields of science and enables their research communities to police themselves. AI lacks that sobering influence, and it shows.

The need to attract research money can also induce careless behavior in researchers, especially in a young science. Like nuclear physics, aerospace research, and astronomy, AI gets its funds from government sources. Davids against Goliaths, the young early AI researchers found that the only way they could channel money away from these traditional disciplines was to proclaim their merits, and the louder the better. Even today, AI researchers have a vested interest in AI's appearing solid and confirmed. Public discussion of the failures and difficulties of the field are against their interest. They now do realize, however, that rash predictions and empty promises are not to their advantage. Herbert Simon likes to say that AI is "hankering for respectability." It is perhaps symptomatic that many younger researchers do not repeat the errors of their elders in this respect. "I refuse to make predictions," MIT's Berthold Horn told me. He compared his attitude to that of an older researcher who

was in charge of the AI conference in Boston ten years ago. There were reporters swarming around, and he was saying things like "Five years from now we'll have robots going around your house picking up the things that you dropped on the floor." I dragged him into a corner and told him, "Don't make these predictions! People have done this before and gotten into trouble. You're underestimating the time it will take." He said, "I don't care. Notice that all the dates I've chosen were after my retirement date!" I said, "Well, I won't be retired and people will come back and ask me why they don't have robots picking up socks in their bedrooms!"[10]

A further spur to boastfulness about AI is that reporters can explain much of it in words understandable to anyone. The final goals and everyday successes of AI are close to our everyday concerns. A computer that beats chess champions or diagnoses diseases has more immediate impact than the discovery of another elementary particle or progress in gene-splicing technology. For a reclusive scientist, the limelight is a temptation hard to resist, and some scientists have probably not been above making a little more of their discoveries to get front-page coverage.

Finally, fast-evolving fields like AI are more subject than others to a perennial problem in technological forecasting. In all domains, researchers invariably overestimate the short-term potential of their work and the speed of its progress. One result is cost overruns, to which AI is more vulnerable than other high-technology projects. Contrary to programs that, like aerospace, involve national prestige or security, AI cannot overcome errors of judgment through sheer budgetary excesses. Often AI researchers helplessly watch their finances run dry, and gain a reputation for not delivering what they promise.

Let's not forget, though, that the other most common mistake in technological forecasting is to *underestimate* long-term achievements. The onlookers at Kitty Hawk never imagined today's airliners. Marie Curie never thought of Nagasaki. Believing today in the failure of AI would be like deciding, after the Vanguard flops in the 1950s, that space travel was impossible.

I shall, in probing the past of AI research, try to arrive at a better forecast. Having recounted the origins and early golden years of AI in the first four chapters, I shall demonstrate in chapters 5 to 8 that, despite a few amazing successes, AI has not so far delivered what the pioneers promised. I shall investigate the reasons for this state of affairs and examine more recent developments to see whether there are reasons to believe that early promises might be fulfilled. To answer this question, I shall first establish the conviction of most modern philosophers that our minds are essentially a product of the complex physical processes in our brains. I shall then ask, How is thought generated in the brain? Do our machines accomplish anything similar to that, and to what degree? This will be the subject of chapters 9 to 11.

Recent research and the trends of the past decades indicate that machines just as clever as human beings may indeed emerge in a not-too-distant future. Such a development will raise deep challenges to humanity's self-esteem, to its meaning in the overall scheme of things, and, indeed, to its very survival. I shall examine these questions in a concluding chapter.

1

ENGINEERING INTELLIGENCE: COMPUTERS AND PROGRAMMING

I believe that in about fifty years' time it will be possible to programme computers . . . to make them play the imitation game so well that an average interrogator will not have more than 70 per cent chance of making the right identification after five minutes of questioning. —Alan Turing, 1950

A definition of artificial intelligence accepted by many practitioners of this art is that of MIT's Marvin Minsky: "AI is the science of making machines do things that would require intelligence if done by men."[1] The machines involved are usually digital computers, and they can be "made" to do things by programming them in certain ways. "Computers" and "programming" will make up the two themes of this chapter. I shall first review how computers came about, and provide an overview of how they work. Next, I shall examine the relationships between programming, logic, calculation, and thought, and how the inquiries of early philosophers and logicians into the nature of thought found their embodiment in contemporary computer programs.

COMPUTERS

Early Devices

It can be argued that computing devices emerged in our century for much the same reason that the abacus did centuries earlier: because we have only ten fingers and ten toes, and computations involving larger and larger numbers required devices that can handle these greater sums with better accuracy and speed.

Stone-age calendars are the first evidence of this desire to rely on external mechanisms to alleviate mental burdens. Rather than tediously counting the days to crop-planting time, our prehistoric ancestors used for alarm clocks the coincidence of celestial bodies with lines of sight defined by carefully positioned ground markers. In the Orient, the abacus helped out in numerical calculations even before the invention of long-hand arithmetic.

With technology showing its metallic head, the lack of extensive number-crunching power became a serious liability. Error-filled navigation tables sent ships crashing on coastlines; and bridges, built upon imprecise calculations, tumbled down. To weed out mistakes from manual calculations, several inventors, including Leibnitz and Pascal,[2] tried their hands at building mechanical calculators. They met with limited success, partly because of the cost of their complex, hand-made devices, and partly because of their specialized natures: early calculators could perform only one basic arithmetic operation at a time. Performing a sequence of operations involving several numbers involved many lengthy manipulations by the users. In other words, one could not *program* these machines to perform several operations.

Oddly enough, the first truly programmable device had nothing to do with numbers. The Frenchman Joseph-Marie Jacquard invented it in 1805 to drive looms: removable punched cards let the same machine weave different patterns. Some forty years later, the British inventor Charles Babbage picked up the idea of punched cards to feed instructions to his ill-fated "analytical engine." This steam-driven contraption would have contained, had it ever been built to specifications, all the elements of a modern computer, including a memory and processing unit (I'll define these words shortly).

Babbage teamed up with Augusta Ada, countess of Lovelace and daughter of the poet Lord Byron. She is often credited with inventing computer programming, the science of telling a computer what operations to perform on what pieces of data. Unfortunately, Ada never had a chance to run her programs because Babbage's grand ideas crashed against the same technological limit that had put a cap on the progress of automata a century earlier. Nineteenth-century mechanics still couldn't produce sufficiently accurate parts, and the analytical engine was never completed. Babbage and Lovelace later tried to recoup their losses by inventing a chess-playing machine and a ticktacktoe machine. They even devised a system for winning at the race track, which in fact forced the countess to pawn her jewels on two occasions. Nowadays the computer language Ada, favored by the U.S. military, perpetuates the memory of the countess of Lovelace.

By 1890, hand-driven mechanical calculators much more modest than Babbage's visionary device made their appearance. Clumsy and expensive, they nevertheless filled a crying need. The Ohdner calculator, for one, would have cost more than $100,000 in today's money and took ten minutes to perform a multiplication! In the same year, the American Herman Hollerith invented for the U.S. government a tabulating machine that processed census data fed to it on punched cards. Hollerith's Tabulating Machine Company eventually merged into a conglomerate that became IBM. Such machines were called "digital calculators," because they represented numbers by cogged wheels or related devices, which could take only a fixed number of positions corresponding to the *digits* in the numbers they denoted. For example, if a wheel had ten possible positions, it could represent the digits from 0 to 9. Even then, though, the cheapest and most efficient way to speed up a calculation remained the abacus. For technical work, the slide rule offered an alternative when it didn't matter whether the answer was off by a few percentage points.

Claude Shannon and His Switches

In the first third of this century, calculators remained essentially mechanical. In 1931, Vannevar Bush at MIT brought to its pinnacle the technology of computing through mechanical devices. His differential analyzer did much more than add or multiply numbers: it actually solved differential equations, using rotating shafts as integrating devices. (Bush's machine was an *analog* calculator: the angular position of a shaft could take any value, and the machine's accuracy was limited only by how precisely one could manufacture the shafts and measure their positions. By contrast, the accuracy of a digital calculator depends on how many digits [cogged wheels] are used to represent numbers.)

In 1938, Bush hired a twenty-two-year-old research assistant, Claude Shannon, to run the differential analyzer.[3] Even though the heart of the device was mechanical and analogical, a complicated digital circuit using electromechanical relays controlled it. This fact set Shannon thinking. Couldn't one make the circuit less complicated than it was? And how about using the relays themselves for computing instead of the spinning disks? These considerations led Shannon to show that one could build, using only interconnected switches that could turn each other on or off, a digital calculating machine performing any imaginable operation on numbers. Further, Shannon's theory showed how, by examining the nature of the operations to perform, one could arrive at a configuration of switches that embodied this operation. The switches had the potential of operating much faster than the cogged wheels previously used in digital machines. Since, however, they could only take two positions (on or off), only two values, taken to be 0 and 1, were available for the digits representing numbers in the machines. This is why computers started using binary arithmetic.

And so it was that in the late 1930s, electromechanical relay switches started replacing gears and cogs in calculators. Just before the Second World War, Howard Aiken at Harvard built a calculator that could calculate twelve times faster than a human being. Vacuum tubes and transistors soon replaced electromechanical relays. These electronically driven switches embodied no moving parts and could operate much faster than relays, which were limited by how fast their iron kernels could change positions. Thus the *electronic* computer, based on vacuum tubes and containing no moving parts, appeared during the Second World War. It was invented not once, but three times: in Germany, for airplane design; in the United States, for calculating artillery tables; and in England, for breaking German secret codes. The American machine contained 18,000 tubes, weighed 30 tons, used as much power as a locomotive, and would have filled a ballroom. But at 20,000 multiplications per minute, the Electronic Numerical Integrator And Calculator (ENIAC) was a thousand times faster than its relay-operated competition.

Von Neumann and His Architecture

When scientists put ENIAC to uses other than war, a major design weakness became clear. To change the sequence of operations performed on the data (what we now call the "program"), engineers had to rewire hundreds of connections in the machine. John von Neumann is usually credited for pointing the way to a better computer architecture in 1945.

Names can mislead: as Chopin wasn't French, von Neumann wasn't German.[4] Born in Budapest in 1903, this scion of an upper-class Jewish family moved to Princeton in the 1930s. In the mid-1940s, von Neumann could rightly count among his contributions the invention of game theory; the theory of automata (which discusses the possibility that machines might be able to reproduce themselves); and, in the field of hydrodynamics, calculations of shock-wave propagation, which were used during the Manhattan Project to help trigger and control the chain reaction of a nuclear explosion in its early phases. He was also the author of a celebrated essay on the mathematics of quantum theory, which was said to have inspired Alan Turing (whom I shall discuss shortly) to become a mathematician.[5]

Remembering the difficulty he had had earlier using a mechanical desk machine to calculate shock-wave propagation, von Neumann, hearing of the ENIAC project in a casual conversation on a train platform, became fascinated. His answer to the problem of changing the computer's instructions appears in retrospect very simple. He realized that one could store the sequence of instructions telling the machine what to do in the same circuitry used to hold the data. (Von Neumann was also the first one to use the term *memory* for this part of the computer: Babbage had called it the "store.") The so-called von Neumann computer architecture, embodied in virtually all computers since the Second World War, breaks a computer into two parts.

The central processing unit (CPU) operates on the data items to be manipulated. These data items (numbers or symbols) are stored in the memory, which makes up the second part of the computer. The memory also contains the program. A von Neumann machine operates in well-defined cycles: Fetch the first instruction from memory. Fetch the data item to operate upon from another part of memory. Perform the operation. Fetch the next instruction from memory, and so on.

The Electronic Discrete Variable Computer (EDVAC) first embodied this architecture. It was followed by the RAND Corporation's JOHNNIAC, so named in honor of John von Neumann. Following von Neumann's penchant for puns, the creators of another machine couldn't resist calling their new machine Mathematical Analyzer, Numerical Integrator And Calculator (MANIAC).

Alas, von Neumann's colleagues did not enjoy his Old World charm and jokes, or endure his impossible driving habits, for long after the war. He died in 1957 of cancer, perhaps induced by radiation exposure during the Manhattan Project.

COGNITION AS COMPUTATION

For several years following their invention, computers were generally perceived as devices for manipulating numbers and straightforward items of data such as names in a telephone directory. However, it soon became clear to some of the computers' inventors and users that the switch positions inside the machines could take on other meanings. In particular, they could stand for symbols representing concepts more abstract than straightforward data. If the computer then manipulated these symbols as specified in its program, perhaps then it could be said to "think." This concept of *cognition as computation* had been the subject of much debate throughout the history of philosophy and mathematics. Could one represent all things under the sun through a set of symbols? Could thought result from the manipulation of these symbols according to a set of predefined rules? And if so, what should the rules and symbols be? As we shall see, such questions found their echoes in early AI efforts.

Early Attempts to Formalize Thought

The thirteenth-century Spanish missionary, philosopher, and theologian Ramón Lull is often credited with making the first systematic effort at artificially generating ideas by mechanical means. Lull's method, crude by today's standards, simply consisted in randomly combining concepts through an instrument called a "Zairja," which the missionary had brought back from his travels in the Orient. A Zairja consisted of a circular slide rule with concentric disks on which appeared letters and philosophical symbols.[6] The combinations obtained by spinning the disks were said to provide metaphysical insights. Rechristening it without undue modesty the *Ars Magna* (Great Art), Lull generalized the Zairja to a host of other fields beyond metaphysics and turned the instrument into the Middle Ages equivalent of a computer for blending ideas. Lull wrote dozens of books dealing with various applications of his Great Art, ranging from morals to medicine and astrology. For every subject the method was the same: identify basic concepts; then combine them mechanically with themselves or ideas pertaining to a related field.

Yet merely generating random combinations was only a small first step toward mechanizing thought: one also required systematic means to interpret and evaluate the combinations. In the seventeenth century, the diplomat, mathematician, and philosopher Gottfried-Wilhelm Leibnitz suggested the possibility of a *calculus ratiocinator,* or reasoning calculus, to achieve this goal. Apparently following Lull's lead,[7] Leibnitz hoped to assign to every concept a number[8] and to resolve the thorniest issues by formally manipulating these numbers. The diplomat in Leibnitz foresaw such an instrument as a common language among nations.

Leibnitz never achieved his objective of completely formalizing thought and in time became keenly aware of the difficulty of the undertaking. One major stumbling block, he noted, lay in the *interconnectedness* of all concepts: "There is no term so absolute or detached that it contains no relations and of which a perfect analysis does not lead to other things or even all other things."[9] Three centuries later, modern AI researchers, trying to carve up reality into convenient niches called "micro worlds," would also founder on this very issue.

Boole and the ''Laws of Thought''

The first recognizable glimmerings of the logic that would later be implemented into computers emerged from the work of a self-taught Englishman, the son of a shoemaker, named George Boole. Boole eventually became one of the most influential thinkers of the nineteenth century. To help support his parents, he became an elementary schoolteacher at age sixteen. But his real work occurred before and after the school day when alone in his room he plowed through advanced monographs in mathematics, learning them with the same thoroughness that had earlier marked his mastery of Greek and Latin. A few years later, he was publishing in mathematical journals. By the time he was thirty-four, even though he did not have a university degree, Boole was appointed professor of mathematics of the newly founded Queen's College at Cork in Ireland. There he attempted nothing less than a mathematical formulation of the fundamental processes of reasoning. He started by investigating how one could combine classes and subclasses of objects, and then how such classes intersected with other classes. Boole showed how one could draw useful conclusions from such analysis. He assigned symbols to the operations of combining either all elements of two sets (which he named "union"), elements belonging to both sets ("intersection"), or objects falling outside a given set ("complement"). In this way, operations on sets could be represented in a crisp shorthand. For example, A $\cup$ B meant "the union of sets A and B." Using these symbols, Boole could analyse and simplify complicated operations involving many sets, much as his fellow mathematicians could manipulate ordinary algebraic equations. Boole formulated simple and well-defined laws to perform these simplifications (see figure 1.1).

In the title of his celebrated 1854 book, *The Laws of Thought,* Boole stated that these principles were fundamental descriptions of thought. He was partly right. After all, to talk intelligently about apples and oranges, one should know that both belong to the wider set (or category or class) of fruits. It also helps to know that some apples are red, but not all. Further, not all red fruits are apples, although they all contain some form of sugar when ripe, and so on. For the first time, Boolean algebra enabled a rigorous and quasimechanical manipulation of categories, an activity basic to human thinking.

Boole could claim universality for his laws in yet another way.[10] Replace the concept of sets by logical propositions that can be either true or false. That is, instead of the set of all apples, consider the sentence "Boole was born in 1815," which is true. Further, replace the operators union, intersection, and complement by the logical operators OR, AND, and NOT. These can combine logical propositions to form other propositions. For example, the combined proposition "Boole was born in 1815 AND he died in 1816" is false. On the other hand, the propositions "Boole was born in 1815 OR he died in 1816" and "Boole was born in 1815 AND he did NOT die in 1816" are both true. It turns out that these operators and propositions combine together in a manner exactly analogous to the set-theoretic operators union, intersection, and complement. Thus, assumed Boole, if the mind works according to

FIGURE 1.1

The Postulates for Boole's Laws of Thought

Here are Boole's laws as they apply to logical propositions and set theory. In either case, the objects studied, basic operations, and identity elements are as follows:

	Logic	Sets
Objects Studied	logical propositions (a, b)	collections of objects (A, B)
Operations	AND: equivalent to the preposition "and"	$\cap$: intersection
	OR: "or"	$\cup$: union
	NOT: "not"	$\neg$: complement
Identity Elements	1: true	I: universal set
	0: false	ϕ: empty set

In these two fields of study, it can be shown by inspection that the following basic facts, called postulates, are true.

Operations are commutative.	a AND b = b AND a a OR b = b OR a	$A \cap B = B \cap A$ $A \cup B = B \cup A$
There are identity elements for the two operations.	a OR 0 = a a AND 1 = a	$A \cup \phi = A$ $A \cap I = A$
Each operation distributes over the other.	a OR (b AND c) = (a OR b) AND (a OR c)	$A \cup (B \cap C) = (A \cup B) \cap (A \cup C)$
	a AND (b OR c) = (a AND b) OR (a AND c)	$A \cap (B \cup C) = (A \cap B) \cup (A \cap C)$
Each element has a complement.	a AND (NOT a) = 0 a OR (NOT a) = 1	$A \cap \neg A = \phi$ $A \cup \neg A = I$

From these basic facts, and others that follow from them, it is possible to manipulate logical expressions, or sentences about sets, in very much the same way as one would manipulate algebraic expressions. One could do this a little more easily, in fact, because ordinary algebra offers less freedom than does logic or sets. More specifically, ordinary algebra, in which elements are the real numbers and the operations are additions and multiplications, is not a Boolean algebra because addition is not distributive over multiplication. That is, it is not generally true that $a + (b \times c) = (a + b) \times (a + c)$.

these laws, it performs logical operations in the same way it manipulates sets (see figure 1.1).

In fact, Boole had laid the foundation for analyzing thought in more ways than even he had foreseen. Ninety years after their publication,

Boole's ideas supplied the basis for Claude Shannon's analysis of switching circuits, which, as I have described, makes up the theoretical foundation for all modern computers. Shannon's intuitive leap was to realize that switches resembled logical propositions in that they could take only two positions, *open* and *closed.* If one took these positions to stand for *true* and *false,* one could then analyze combinations of switches with the same mathematical machinery that Boole had used for propositions. To illustrate this point, I have drawn up examples of simple Boolean propositions and their embodiments in switching circuits in figure 1.2.

Reasoning Calculuses, or the Fundamental Impotence of Logic

Yet Boole's laws did not shape up to a complete calculus for reasoning. Essential elements were missing. Boolean algebra, as his "Laws of Thought" are now known, could not serve as a complete generic tool for expressing logical sentences because of its lack of flexibility. It lets you assign true or false values to basic propositions such as "I own my house" or "Mary owns her house," but cannot express statements such as "Every house has an owner." Boole's formalism prevents the creation and manipulation of statements about general or indefinite objects. Further, each Boolean proposition is an unbreakable atom, its insides totally beyond reach. A more powerful formalism would require the ability to define basic elements (such as *house* and *owner*) that are not themselves true or false logical propositions, and combine these into sentences that could be true or false. The German mathematician Gottlob Frege came up with such a system in 1879.[11]

Then thirty-one, Frege, an assistant professor of mathematics at the University of Jena, improved on Boole's system by introducing the concept of *predicates.* A predicate is a logical entity with a true-false value. But it contains arguments that are *not* logical variables: the predicate OWNS(x,y) could mean that person y owns house x. OWNS has value true if y really owns x, but x and y, in themselves, are neither true nor false. A further refinement of Frege's system introduced two quantifiers. The universal quantifier $\forall x$, which means "For all x," denotes that a logical proposition is true for all values of variable x. The existential quantifier $\exists y$ ("There exists a y such that") means that at least one value

FIGURE 1.2
Three Switching Networks and Their Corresponding Boolean Propositions

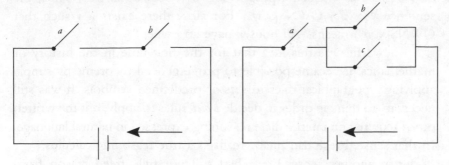

Switch *a*: If you are driving
Switch *b*: and there is a stop sign
Current: then you must stop

(a)

Switch *a*: If you are driving
Switch *b*: and there is a traffic light
Switch *c*: or a stop sign
Current: then you must stop

(b)

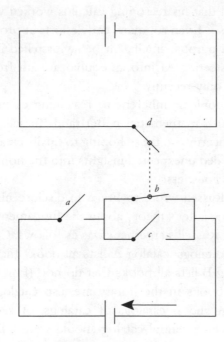

Switch *b*: If the light you see is green
Switch *d*: then the cross-street light is not green
The two switches are connected by the Boolean operator NOT, here portrayed
as a string: when *b* is closed, *d* is forced open and vice versa. In computers,
electronic connections replace strings.

(c)

of y exists for which the proposition that follows is true. Thus, the sentence $\forall x \exists y$ OWNS(x,y) ("For all x there exists a y such that OWNS(x,y)") means "All houses have an owner."*

So powerful was this idea that for the first time in the history of mathematics, it became possible to prove general theorems by simply applying typographical rules to sets of predefined symbols. It was still necessary to think in order to decide *which* rules to apply, but the written proof required no intermediate reasoning expressed in natural language. In that sense, Frege had finally realized a true reasoning calculus.

But in another sense, Frege had still not fully freed reason from language. The word *predicate* stems from the Latin *predicare,* which means "to proclaim." Thus, a predicate is nothing but a mnemonic label proclaiming to be what its user defined, through the use of language, beforehand. Hence, the *meaning* of an argument in formal logic lies entirely in the mind of the beholder. Because of this subjective bias, Frege emphasized that his reasoning calculus worked well only in very restricted domains.[12] Even so, many early efforts at programming computers for general-purpose intelligent behavior relied in great measure on this calculus, steering AI into an equivocal path from which it has begun to emerge only recently.

Some of the problems inherent to reasoning calculuses were first noted by the British mathematician Bertrand Russell. These observations, while disconcerting to those hoping to finally create a true reasoning calculus, provided unexpected insights into the nonlogical nature of thought and consciousness.

In June 1902, Russell wrote to Frege to disclose his discovery of a contradiction in the latter's theory about the fundamental laws of arithmetic. The gist of Russell's argument was as follows. Consider a library with two central catalogs: catalog A lists all books that refer to themselves, and catalog B lists all books that do not. (For simplicity, let us assume that the books in the library are also catalogs, thus making central catalogs A and B catalogs of catalogs, or sets of sets.) The question is, On which central catalog should we list B? Either choice

---

*Actually, Frege used a different notation for the universal and existential quantifiers. The notations $\forall$ and $\exists$, as well as many other mathematical symbols in use today, were introduced by the Italian mathematician Giuseppe Peano in the late nineteenth century, and later finalized by Bertrand Russell and Alfred North Whitehead in *Principia Mathematica* (1910).

sounds wrong. We cannot list B in catalog A, because B does not refer to itself, but we also cannot list B in B because then it refers to itself.*

A few years later, Russell and his associate Alfred North Whitehead wrote a three-volume work entitled *Principia Mathematica.* In it, the authors overcame the problems raised by classes of classes through what they called the "theory of types." Individuals, sets (or classes), and classes of classes belong to different logical types. An individual can belong to a class, and a class to a class of classes, but a class cannot belong to a class of objects and, in particular, cannot belong to itself. By in effect outlawing self-reference in their reasoning about sets, Russell and Whitehead managed to avoid the logical traps on which Frege's work had foundered.

The prospects for completely formalizing mathematics appeared excellent, until in 1931 a paper by an unknown twenty-five-year-old Austrian mathematician brought this optimism to an end. Entitled "On Formally Undecidable Propositions in Principia Mathematica and Related Systems I,"[13] the article shattered Russell and Whitehead's system. It demonstrated that using their very axioms and notation, one could state true theorems that no amount of manipulation would ever prove. Kurt Gödel, the paper's author, went even further and claimed that every consistent logical system would suffer from a similar weakness. He proved this result by coaxing the logical formalism in *Principia* to stand up and acquire a level of meaning its authors had never foreseen. Through a clever encoding scheme establishing a correspondence between logical symbols and the very numbers they were supposed to talk about, Gödel built logical sentences that referred to themselves. Moreover, he showed that one can always encode, in any sufficiently powerful and consistent logical system, a sentence that means: "This sentence cannot be proved using the system's formalism." The intriguing result of such a construction is that the sentence has to be true! To see why, first remember that the logical system in question is assumed *consistent,* which means that it does not allow us to prove false statements. But suppose now that the sentence is false. Since it says "I cannot be proved," being false means that it can, in fact, be proved. If it can be proved, our system would not be consistent, since it would enable us to

---

*The original (and entirely equivalent) formulation of Russell's paradox is "Consider R, the set of all sets which are not members of themselves. Is R a member of itself?"

prove a false statement. Thus, the sentence has to be true, which means that its demonstration really is beyond the capabilities of our logical system.

As the philosopher J. R. Lucas pointed out in 1961,[14] an even more surprising fact about this result is that human reasoning recognizes the truth of the sentence, but the logical system cannot. We realize its truth by reflecting upon the *meaning* of the sentence and deducing its obvious consequences. As I pointed out earlier, the logical system cannot recognize the truth of the sentence since the symbols in the sentence have no meaning for it.

Alan Turing and His "Machine"

The British mathematician Alan Turing came to conclusions similar to Gödel's, but in an entirely different manner. For the first time, Turing's approach brought together, into a reasoning calculus, the theoretical investigations with the builders of automata's hands-on yearnings to create life.

Born in 1912, Alan Turing remained throughout his adult life a strange mixture of boy genius and bemused professor. In appearance a blunt, clumsy man with little care for social graces, Turing disconcerted auditors with his high, stammering voice and nervous crowing laugh. He had a way of making strange screeching sounds when lost in thought, his mind almost audibly churning away at concepts. He was also renowned for his absent-mindedness. His younger colleague Donald Michie recalls how Turing, fearing a German invasion during the Second World War, tried to provide against the confiscation of his bank account: converting his savings into silver bullion, he buried it in the woods of Buckinghamshire, only to lose track of the spot forever.[15] But Turing had a knack for solving at a glance problems that tended to befuddle engineers for days. A typical example occurred during a wartime visit to the United States, when he won over AT&T Bell Laboratory personnel by instantly figuring out how many combinations a special voice-encoding device provided—a result it had taken a week for a Bell Lab's technician to arrive at.[16]

Mathematicians, computer scientists, and AI researchers revere Turing for two major ideas he had: the Turing machine and the Turing test. A Turing machine is not, in fact, a physical mechanism; rather, it is an abstract device which enjoys many of the properties of a modern digital computer. "Imagine," said Turing in substance, "a reading and writing head which processes a tape of infinite length." The tape would be divided into little squares, each containing a 0 or a 1. Like a typewriter, which will print lower- or uppercase letters depending on which mode it is in, the reading head could be in any number of "states of mind." These states defined how the machine would react to a given symbol on the tape. For example, state number 73 might correspond to the statements:

If the square contains a 0, change to state 32, and move one square to the left on the tape.

If the square contains a 1, change to state 57, replace the 1 in the square by a 0, and move one square to the right.

States number 32 and 57, in turn, might correspond to other statements similar to these. In modern parlance, we would call the sequence of states controlling the head a "program." The initial writing on the tape would be the "data" on which the program acts.

Turing showed that these elementary steps could be used to write a program performing any sequence of well-defined operations. For example, if the 1's and 0's on the tape represent binary numbers, one could write programs to extract their square roots, to divide them, or to combine them in any manner imaginable. The idea that any systematic procedure for operating on numbers could be encoded as a sequence of elementary, machinelike operations has since become known as the "Church-Turing thesis." (The American mathematician Alonzo Church independently reached conclusions similar to Turing's.) Turing even demonstrated the existence of one machine that could mimic the operation of any other of his machines: this he called the "universal machine." One could aptly describe modern digital computers as practical embodiments of universal Turing machines.

Like Gödel, Turing noted (in his case, in regard to the capabilities of his abstract machines) that there exist certain kinds of calculations, which sometimes appear trivial to humans, that no Turing machine can ever perform. Although this result could be viewed as one more defeat for pure logic as a means of dealing with the world, Turing himself did not believe it to be reason enough to doubt the possibility of making computers think. When computers had become a reality in 1950, Turing discussed this question in a celebrated paper entitled "Computing Machinery and Intelligence":

> [T]his [weakness of Turing machines] gives us a certain feeling of superiority. Is this feeling illusory? It is no doubt quite genuine, but I do not think too much importance should be attached to it. We too often give wrong answers to questions ourselves to be justified in being very pleased at such evidence of fallibility on the parts of the machines. Further, our superiority can only be felt on such an occasion in relation to the one machine over which we have scored our petty triumph. There would be no question of triumphing simultaneously over all machines.[17]

Mathematical arguments, claimed Turing in the same paper, are no real help in deciding whether a machine can think. He argued that the question could be settled only experimentally, and proposed the following test to this effect. Suppose a computer could answer any question you might put to it just as a human would. In fact, suppose you were communicating through a terminal with two hidden parties and couldn't tell by questioning them which was human and which was a computer. Wouldn't you then have to grant the computer this evasive quality we call intelligence?

This procedure, which has the advantage of neatly sidestepping the thorny issue of defining intelligence, has become known as the "Turing test."* Turing firmly believed that thinking machines would one day come about. He predicted in his paper that, by the year 2000, a machine would "play the imitation game so well that an average interrogator will not have more than 70 percent chance of making the right identification after five minutes of questioning."[18] Few people would still agree with such an early date; but as we shall see later, Turing may not have been off by more than twenty-five years.

Alan Turing will probably go down in history for his seminal ideas about thinking machines. Yet in his lifetime, his most important work may well have been in cracking German intelligence codes. In the early years of the war, while working at Bletchley Park, a suburb of London, Turing designed a machine called the "Bombe," which explored the

---

*In fact, the procedure as Turing defined it was a little more elaborate: the computer was supposed to pretend it was a woman, the other party being a real woman trying to convince you of her identity. If the computer could fool you as often as a man would in its position, then it passed the test. Nowadays the term *Turing test* usually refers to the simplified procedure I have described.

possible combinations generated by the German encoding machine Enigma. The Bombe was a special-purpose calculating machine based on electromechanical relays. Turing's efforts eventually led to the development of Colossus, a machine many consider the first electronic computer. Colossus, which relied on vacuum tubes rather than on relays, laid German communications bare to British eavesdropping. The British could now direct transatlantic supply ships to steer away from German U-boats, which made possible the buildup leading to the Normandy landing. Foretelling the hard decisions its future intelligent progeny may confront us with, Colossus posed the British command with heart-rending choices. Through it, British intelligence learned of German plans for razing the city of Coventry. For fear of revealing their advantage, authorities chose not to evacuate the city.[19]

Turing did not reap any reward from the society he had helped so generously during its time of need. Atheist, homosexual, and fiercely individualistic, he did not fit into the conformist British society of the day, nor even into the organizations in which he worked. After the war, unable to deal with politics and bureaucracy, Turing left the National Physical Laboratory where he had participated in the design of a machine called the Automatic Computing Engine, in many ways the successor to Colossus. Prosecuted for his homosexuality, he was convicted in 1953 of "gross indecency" and sentenced to a one-year pharmaceutical treatment tantamount to chemical castration. On 7 June 1954, Alan Turing ended his life by eating an apple dipped in cyanide.

2

THE FIRST AI PROGRAM:
DEFINING THE FIELD

Every aspect of learning or any other feature of intelligence can in principle be so precisely described that a machine can be made to simulate it.
                                        —Organizers of the Dartmouth conference, 1956

Symbol-processing AI as we know it today defined itself as an intellectual field in the years following the Second World War—from 1945 to 1956. Three critical events had to occur during this period.

First, AI had to be tied to the computer. Early investigations about intelligent machines centered on feedback theory and efforts at replicating the workings of the brain in networks of artificial neurons. The pioneers of AI broke away from this approach when they decided that human thought processes could be emulated more efficiently by the emerging computer technology. Those who did not develop a fascination with the new digital machines either quickly lost interest in artificial intelligence or stayed in the parallel field of neural networks. Second, a critical mass had to develop: that is, enough people had to start to dabble in AI-computer work to create an intellectual community for such ideas. The kernel of this group was formed by Marvin Minsky, John McCarthy, Allen Newell, Herbert Simon, and their students. Third and most important, these individuals had to find each other. This gathering process started with the emergence of two independent, informal groups around Boston and Pittsburgh, and culminated in the 1956 Dartmouth conference, where the first AI program was presented and discussed.

POSTWAR EFFORTS

In the period immediately following the Second World War, the study of intelligent machines blended fields that later congealed into distinct disciplines: artificial neural networks, control theory, and symbol processing in digital computers. The fundamental differences between the human brain, feedback systems, and digital computers were not clear in this period, and it belonged to the first generation of researchers to bring out the disparities between them.

Norbert Wiener and Feedback Theory

One of the first Americans to observe common points between the mind and engineered devices was the MIT professor of engineering and mathematics Norbert Wiener.[1] The embodiment of the distracted genius (pictorial caricatures of his cigar-toting rotund figure still hang proudly today on the walls of the main hallway of MIT's Building 10), Wiener was MIT's star performer as all-round intellectual gadfly, and sometimes also the institute's chief embarrassment, for thirty years (he died in 1964). A speaker of several languages, he was known to be difficult to follow in any of them.

Prior to joining the mathematics department of MIT shortly after the Second World War, Wiener received his Ph.D. from Harvard and performed postdoctoral work in England, where he managed to displease such eminent mathematicians as Bertrand Russell and David Hilbert.[2] Seeing himself as too broad an intellect, however, to confine himself to a single field of study, Wiener wandered in what he called the "frontier areas" between disciplines. While roaming along the borders of engineering and biology, Wiener created the science of cybernetics.

Feedback is a well-known mechanism in biology. Warm-bodied animals keep themselves within a certain temperature range through biological feedback mechanisms; predatory animals adjust their movements in catching their prey through scent and visual feedback mechanisms. The feedback system we are most familiar with is the thermostat: it achieves a constant temperature in any enclosed environment by assessing the actual room temperature, comparing it to a desired temperature, and then responding—by turning the heater (or air conditioner) either on or off according to whether the existing temperature lies below or above the desired value. The word *feedback* describes how the process returns (feeds back) the result of the control action (the temperature) to the compensating mechanism. Cybernetics (the science of control) was a mathematical theory of feedback.[3] Cybernetics explained why feedback mechanisms, especially in complex interacting systems, sometimes become unstable. This breakthrough allowed Wiener, with the help of others, to develop procedures used during the Second World War to stabilize radar-controlled antiaircraft guns.

But more important to our story, Wiener recognized that central to feedback theory is the idea of information. In essence, feedback mechanisms are information-processing devices: they receive information and then make a decision based on it. Wiener speculated that all intelligent behavior is the consequence of feedback mechanisms; perhaps by definition, intelligence is the outcome of receiving and processing information.

Nowadays this notion appears obvious. Yet it was then a major departure from accepted ideas, notably from Sigmund Freud's theory that the mind essentially manipulates biological energies, which one can repress only at the risk of seeing them emerge again in harmful disguises. This paradigm shift away from energy to information processing would become the underpinning of all subsequent work in artificial intelligence. It deeply affected psychology as well, marking the beginning of the fruitful but uneasy relationship this discipline would maintain with information sciences for the rest of the century.

Weiner himself, however, never really developed a strong interest in computers. "I could never get him to talk about computers very much," commented Marvin Minsky, another seminal figure in early AI research, "and so it is not surprising that Wiener never made any other significant contributions to AI."[4] Nonetheless, his cybernetic theory influenced many generations of early AI researchers.

Neural Networks: McCulloch, Pitts, and Hebbs

Among the researchers who incorporated cybernetics into their early theories of intelligence were those who tried to model the detail of the brain's workings. They planned to accomplish this by simulating individual neurons with electrical components. Contrary to later researchers, who concentrated on experimental simulations, early neural net workers attempted mathematical analyses of how networks of such neurons would behave. Warren McCulloch and Walter Pitts were two of the most truly colorful figures to work in this field. Another influential figure was Donald Hebb, who later provided more theoretical insight by considering biological neurons.

Born into a family of lawyers, doctors, engineers, and theologians,[5] Warren McCulloch was initially destined for the ministry. In the fall of 1917, he entered Haverford College and was soon, according to his own account, called in by the Quaker philosopher Rufus Jones, who asked: " 'What is thee going to be?' And I said, 'I don't know.' 'And what is thee going to do?' And again I said, 'I don't know; but there is one question I would like to answer: What is a number, that a man may know it, and a man, that he may know a number?' He smiled and said, 'Friend, thee will be busy as long as thee lives.' "[6]

McCulloch formulated his answer to the second part of that question with the help of the mathematical prodigy Walter Pitts. The most salient feature of Pitts's childhood is that he ran away from home at the age of fifteen and spent time in a Chicago park where he met an older man he knew only as Bert. "When Bert detected the boy's [mathematical] interests, he suggested that young Pitts read a book that had just been published by a professor at the University of Chicago by the name of Rudolf Carnap." Pitts not only read the book but, upon discovering something he found "unclear," went to Carnap's office for an explanation. "Carnap was amused, because when he said something wasn't clear, what *he* [emphasis added] meant was that it was nonsense. So he opened up his newly published book to where young Pitts was pointing, and sure enough, it was nonsense. Bert turned out to be Bertrand Russell."[7]

In 1943, three years after this encounter, McCulloch and Pitts tried to explain the workings of the human brain by coming up with a mechanism by which networks of interconnected cells could perform logical operations.[8] They started out by asking themselves what could be considered a "least psychic event," and realized that such a fundamental event could be the result of an all-or-nothing impulse by a nerve cell. Perhaps it was at the level of the single nerve cell, by its release or failure to release an impulse, that humans make true/false decisions.

The Pitts-McCulloch paper on neural networks relied heavily on the idea of feedback loops (which they called "circles") to reach some of their conclusions. They pointed out that the loop "senses, to brain, to muscles" can result in purposive behavior if the muscles reduce the difference between a condition perceived by the senses and a desired state of the world. Likewise, they defined memory as signals reverberating in closed paths of neurons. Every remembrance was, according to them, the reactivation of a trace of one such signal in its closed path. The fact that a reactivation of a trace does not tell when the original activation occurred might explain why our memories are so indefinite as to time. We remember events, but not always when they happened, and in what order.

Nowadays we know that conscious decisions about the truth of logical propositions occur at a level much higher than that of the single neuron, probably involving millions of brain cells. McCulloch and Pitts's contribution was important, nonetheless, because it managed to present a valid and thorough mathematical analysis of how interconnected cells, by transmitting or failing to transmit impulses, could perform logical operations—thus, how a mechanism like the brain might compute. These ideas laid the foundation of what is today known as "artificial neural net theory."

Pitts and McCulloch were also able to draw striking parallels between the computing powers of both artificial neural networks and Turing machines. These comparisons, unfortunately, gave the false impression that our brains work like digital computers. They don't, and it took many years to draw AI research away from the dead-end path inspired by this misconception.

The mention of feedback loops in the papers both of Pitts and McCulloch and of Wiener is no accident: they and their co-workers knew each other. When a small group of scientists grow intere⁣ d in a problem, they often form a club to chat about their favorite s⁣ ib,ect. In this case, the club they formed in the late 1940s was named the Teleological Society, reflecting at the same time their interest in goal-oriented behavior in nature (*telos* means "goal" in Greek), McCulloch's taste for pompous terminology, and Wiener's considerable ego (the club's name stemming from the title of his seminal paper published in 1943[9]). The group enjoyed the lively company of yet another first-rate intellectual— John von Neumann, who had emigrated to Princeton before the war.

A group like the Teleological Society was started in England. Its members called themselves the Ratio Club because "they liked the [way the word *ratio*] combined reasoning, relations and numbers."[10] Alan Turing attended some of the meetings, but did not play a central role in the club's activities. Other members included the philosopher Donald Mackay; Turing's colleague Jack Good; the biologist John Pringle; Albert M. Uttley, whose fertile imagination provided the club's multi-referencing name; and the neurosurgeon John Bates. Another member was the brain physiologist Grey Walter, inventor of the first cybernetic "turtle." A wheeled illustration of the power of feedback loops, this dome-shaped device navigated its way around Walter's laboratory and fed from an electrical outlet when its batteries ran low. Widely copied and improved on by later researchers, the turtle evolved in other laboratories into the mobile field robot.

The British and American groups were aware of each other. Warren McCulloch "visited the British, argued with and delighted them, and they returned the favor";[11] but nothing much more than discussion and banter seems to have come out of these interchanges.

Alan Turing was less impressed and considered McCulloch "a charlatan."[12] The reasons for Turing's aversion are not clear, but one can speculate. In "A Logical Calculus for the Ideas Immanent in Nervous Activity," McCulloch and Pitts had argued that their neural networks were equivalent in computing power to Turing machines.[13] As Seymour Papert points out in his introduction to a collection of McCulloch's papers,[14] this claim was exaggerated: McCulloch-Pitts nets are indeed like Turing machines, but correspond to a narrower class of calculable numbers. It would have been in character for Turing to take offense in the *bévue*.

In 1949, six years after McCulloch and Pitts had shown how neural networks could compute, the McGill University physiologist Donald O. Hebb suggested how they could learn.[15] He proposed the idea that brain connections change as we learn different tasks, and that specific new neural structures account for knowledge. Hebb's ingenious proposal dealt with the conductivity of synapses, or connections between neu-rons. He postulated that the repeated activation of one neuron by another through a particular synapse increased its conductivity. This change would make further activations more likely and induce the formation of tightly connected paths of neurons in an otherwise loosely connected structure.

THE CAMBRIDGE DUO

Although Wiener, McCulloch, Pitts, and Hebbs belong to the genera-tion preceding the actual founders of AI, the latter were educated in neural nets and cybernetics. Marvin Minsky and John McCarthy were two key figures of the new generation.

Marvin Minsky

At the same time as Donald Hebb, an unusual Harvard undergraduate named Marvin Minsky was independently coming, in a roundabout way, to conclusions similar to his. Minsky's physicist friend Jeremy Bernstein says that "it was not entirely clear what (Minsky's) major academic field was—or, perhaps, what it wasn't."[16] Minsky himself recalled elsewhere: "I wandered around the university and walked into people's laboratories and asked them what they did. I didn't know anything about the social life of the undergraduates, but I knew when the department teas were, and I'd go and eat cookies and ask the scientists what they did. And they'd tell me."[17] They more than told him: they gave him labs of his own, three of them! A nominal physics student, Minsky did experimen-tal work in physical optics in the physics department. He also grew interested in neurology and talked a zoology professor, John Welsh, into letting him use a roomful of equipment, where he became an expert in the neurophysiology of crayfish (a small fresh-water lobster). Under the influence of electrodes Minsky had attached to individual nerves of the animal's claw, the crayfish picked up a pencil, waved it around, and released it when Minsky excited the fibers that inhibited the closing of the claws. When he wasn't doing physics or dissecting crayfish, Minsky hung around the psychology laboratory, where he was able to sample a cross-section of psychology as it existed in the late 1940s. At one end of the lab was the behaviorist camp of B. F. Skinner and his followers, who then held sway over most psychological research in the United States.

Born in 1898 with the publication of the American educator and psychologist Edward Lee Thorndike's book *Animal Intelligence,* behaviorism was a brutal transposition to human psychology of Pavlovian experiments conducted on animals in which one would, for example, flash a bright light at a cat whenever one fed the animal. After several days, the animal would salivate in response to the flashing light even in the absence of food. Pavlov called the light "stimulus" and the salivation "response." For behaviorists, all actions, thoughts, or desires were simply reflexes triggered by a higher form of stimulus. The only difference between animals and humans was that humans were able to react to more complex sets of stimuli, called "situations." Given that the mind was just a device for associating situations with responses, there was no point in examining it, as had been done by the earlier methodology that used introspection to study the mind. The AI pioneer Herbert Simon said later, "You couldn't use a word like 'mind' in a psychology journal—you'd get your mouth washed out with soap!"[18] For extremists like B. F. Skinner, mind did not even exist. One could study the act of remembering, but to investigate memory itself transgressed scientific discipline. Ironically, when in the 1940s and 1950s engineers started building machines that played checkers, proved mathematical theorems, and also contained a device they called a "memory," the engineers discussed the "minds" of their machines in as much detail as they wanted to. Nevertheless, Minsky liked Skinner very much, and spent some time helping the psychologist design equipment for his experiments. As I shall show, Skinner's ideas about reinforcement learning also later inspired Minsky to build a neural net machine.

Minsky didn't think much of the physiological psychologists at the other end of the Harvard psychology lab. This group tried to understand little parts of the nervous systems, such as the sensitivity of the ear, without relating them to the rest.

In the middle of the laboratory, however, were young assistant professors who came much closer to Minsky's own way of thinking. Among them was George Miller, who attempted to model the mind through mathematics. A few years later, in 1956, Miller became famous with the publication of an essay on short-term memory. Entitled "The Magical Number Seven," this article shed a critical light on our reasoning processes.[19] We suffer, claimed Miller, from an inability to keep in mind more than seven items of information at a time. In pointing out this limitation, Miller emphasized the active role of the mind as a processor of information: gone was the behaviorist model of a purely passive association mechanism. With Miller, Minsky decided to study learning. "I found this thing called the *Bulletin of Mathematical Biophysics*," Minsky told me years later. "It had the works of Warren McCulloch and the great pioneers of the 1940's. . . . As soon as I saw that I started to think 'How could I make a learning machine?'"

Yet in 1949, Minsky was facing more down-to-earth problems. Eating cookies at department meetings and hopping between too many laboratories, in addition to taking music composition courses on the side, he had let his grades fall. To boost his average, he decided to write a memorable undergraduate thesis. For this he had to switch over to the mathematics department, since regulations in the physics department didn't allow for a thesis. That presented no problem: Minsky had also liberally sampled the Harvard course curriculum and earned enough math credits to qualify as a major in *that* field.

Under the direction of the mathematician Andrew Gleason, he wrote a somewhat esoteric paper on the subject of topology. It involved proving that at each moment there is on the surface of the earth a square with three of its four corners at the same temperature. Mathematicians don't judge results by their practicality. It was the elegance of Minsky's demonstration that impressed Gleason. "You are a mathematician," he said on reading the thesis, and urged Minsky to register for his Ph.D. at the prestigious Princeton mathematics department.

Minsky followed this advice and blissfully discovered that Princeton wouldn't cause him any problem with grades. "Once, I took a look at my transcript," he said. "Instead of the usual grades, all the grades were A's—many of them in courses I had never taken. Lefschetz (the mathematics department's director at Princeton) felt that either one was a mathematician or one wasn't, and it didn't matter how much mathematics one actually knew."[20]

Heavily influenced by McCulloch and Pitts through his undergraduate work with George Miller, and still somewhat under the influence of Skinner's behaviorism, Minsky approached another graduate student with an idea for putting theory into practice. Dean Edmonds's interests were not in the study of the brain but in the relatively new science of electronics. "Instead of studying neural networks in the abstract,"

Minsky thought to himself, "why not build one?" Edmonds agreed, as did George Miller, who obtained a two-thousand-dollar grant from the Office of Naval Research.

During the summer of 1951, Minsky and Edmonds returned to Harvard and assembled the first neural net machine from three hundred vacuum tubes and a surplus automatic pilot from a B-24 bomber. The assemblage (which they called the Snarc) consisted of a network of forty artificial neurons that simulated the brain of a rat learning its way through a maze. Each neuron corresponded to a position in the maze and, when it fired, showed that the "rat" knew itself to be at this point in the maze. Other neurons connected to the activated one represented the choices open to the "rat" (for example, to go left or right). Which of these neurons fired depended on the strength of their connections to the activated neuron: it was the automatic pilot's role to adjust these connections. Instead of moving the elevators or ailerons of an airplane, the automatic pilot turned the knobs that set the strengths of the connections. When, by chance, the "rat" made a sequence of good moves and found its way out of the maze, the connections corresponding to these moves were strengthened. In this way, the "rat" gradually learned its way through the maze.

Two thousand dollars went a long way in 1951, but certainly not as far as allowing custom-designed parts. Minsky and Edmonds had to make do with whatever surplus gear they could scrounge up, and the world's first artificial neural net wasn't exactly the epitome of engineering elegance. As Minsky recalled to me:

> To train [the system], you had to reward the neurons which had fired recently. So each neuron had a timing circuit that would stay on for, say, five seconds after it fired. The circuit operated a magnetic clutch that went to the potentiometer. If you turned on this big motor, then a shaft was rolling in, with a chain drive going to all forty of these potentiometers. So if the neuron had fired three seconds ago and you switched on the motor, then the potentiometer would slowly turn for two seconds.

Since the procedure resembled the stimulus-reward techniques of behaviorism, Minsky tried talking to Skinner about the machine. The psychologist wasn't interested. It soon became clear that Skinnerian learning techniques were not leading Minsky anywhere: they provided no way for the machine to reason about what it was doing, and thus formulate a plan.

Returning to Princeton at the end of the summer, Minsky made these problems the subject of his doctoral dissertation, which "described brains much larger" than the Harvard machine, Minsky told me. "[They had] sensors that turned on intermediate sections and different kinds of feedback that could let it do some planning ahead. There was some discussion about how a network can control another. Some of these ideas are just now being rediscovered as the connectionists start to think about multimode networks."

To a doubting department head who wondered whether this work was really mathematics, von Neumann, also a member of Minsky's dissertation committee, replied, "If it isn't now it will be someday—let's encourage it."[21]

Minsky obtained his Ph.D. in 1954, convinced that a sufficiently large neural network with enough memory loops to actually reason would require thousands or millions of neurons. He knew he couldn't build that large a network, and looked for other ways to get machines to think. Dean Edmonds, who had never been impressed with the Harvard machine, went on to become a professor of physics at Boston University.

Meanwhile, Andrew Gleason wanted Minsky back at Harvard. On the recommendations of von Neumann, Norbert Wiener, and Claude Shannon, Gleason had his former protégé accepted as a junior fellow. As such Minsky could proceed with his research in complete freedom for three years. His only obligation was to dine with the other junior fellows on Monday evenings.

Since Minsky was then reconsidering his interest in artificial neural networks, he temporarily directed his mental energies into the field of optics and, in 1955, invented and patented the first "confocal scanning microscope."[22] This device imaged interconnections of neurons in much greater detail than the Golgi staining process (see chapter 11). Strangely, the instrument was ignored by microscope manufacturers until the late 1980s, but there are now on the order of one thousand of them, priced at around $100,000 each, Minsky told me. Unfortunately for him, this commercial success happened long after the patent expired.

It was around 1955, as Minsky recalled it:

that I met a young man named Ray Solomonoff who was working on an abstract theory of deductive inference. . . . He had worked on a learning machine . . . that was pretty formal.* I was so impressed I decided this was much more productive than the neural net system, in which you built a piece of hardware and hoped it would do the right thing. With [this new] approach, you tried to make theories of what kind of inferences you wanted to make, and then asked, "How would I make a machine do exactly that?" It was a different line of thought.

Following this encounter, it gradually dawned on Minsky that there was a difference between understanding how the brain is built and finding out what it does. As it turned out, digital computers were just about then starting to offer a way to explore this last path. It was becoming possible for scientists to describe to a computer, in a symbolic way, what they thought the mind did, and have the machine behave in exactly this manner.

John McCarthy

John McCarthy[23] was born to a Lithuanian Jewish mother and an Irish Catholic father who took up Marxism and fought for it as a union leader. Opposition to conventional ideas ran deep in the McCarthy family: John was thrown out of Cal Tech for refusing to attend physical education classes. Later, the U.S. Army dismissed his brother Patrick for being a communist. Patrick also lost a post office job for refusing to sign a loyalty oath. In 1945, though, after John's brush with Cal Tech, the army didn't have any choice but to put up with his own communist bias because he had already been drafted. Fortunately for John McCarthy, the war promptly ended; and as a veteran, John was able to return to Cal Tech. He obtained his bachelor degree in mathematics in 1948. Shortly thereafter, he moved to Princeton for graduate work. Having read about von Neumann's research on finite automata, he began to explore their possibilities as intelligent agents. After graduation, he spent a summer with Claude Shannon editing a collection of papers on the subject.[24] In

---

*Solomonoff's theory, later independently rediscovered by other researchers, is called today "algorithmic probability theory."

his own contribution to the volume, McCarthy discussed the possibility of making a Turing machine behave intelligently. This first effort at artificial intelligence did not turn out very well, and taught McCarthy two lessons.

First, Turing machines did not provide the right medium for establishing a theory of how machines could imitate human behavior. The problem was one of sensitivity: small changes in machine structure brought about enormous changes in behavior, and vice versa. Intuitively small changes in humanlike behavior required very large changes in machine structure to account for them. Second, the name "automata studies" wasn't right for the kind of investigations McCarthy had in mind: most of the papers he and Shannon received had nothing to do with the reproduction of human intelligence. A catchier appellation was required.

A summer spent working at IBM in 1955 focused McCarthy's interests on digital computers. Hands-on work convinced him that computers provided the tool for actually building artificial intelligences, while Turing machines and automata theory only allowed him to study intelligence in the abstract.

Since then, McCarthy has never stopped looking for ways to embody mind into computers. Fellow researchers now grant him a special place in the history of AI and agree that McCarthy's own mind is also special. His ability to dive into the depths of a problem through sheer concentration is legendary. Another McCarthy trademark is the long silences he tends to inflict upon his partners in a conversation, leaving them to wonder how they may have offended him. This is apparently a product of his high intellectual standards, which command him to shut up when he can't think of anything worthwhile to say. Those standards account for McCarthy's successes, but also for his relatively short list of publications and his dissatisfaction with other people's work. His former student Hans Moravec told me: "It's hard for John to communicate well with anybody that isn't a graduate student in his areas. The ideas are there, but the willingness or the ability to make some compromise in explaining some of them he thinks should be obvious are missing. If you're talking with John it takes skill to learn to communicate with him!"[25]

Yet McCarthy is far from being a loner. In fact, his social environment heavily influences his opinions and way of life. That could have led to inconvenience in the early 1950s, when he followed his parents and brother into communist militancy. Fortunately, his relative obscurity as an assistant professor protected him from the wrath of another McCarthy then witch-hunting from Washington. In the 1960s, John McCarthy grew his hair, donned a headband, and joined the counterculture movement. Still socially conscious, he became one of the first crusaders against the misuse of information possible through government and corporate computer data banks. Years before the Privacy Act of 1974 became law, McCarthy's proposal, which he called the "Bill of Rights," appeared in the September 1966 issue of *Scientific American*. With his second wife, Vera, in the 1970s, McCarthy took his cue from the "me" generation: his "own thing" was to court danger through parachute jumping and alpinism. Unfortunately, this way of life was more dangerous than being a communist in the reach of Joseph McCarthy: Vera died in a climbing accident during an all-women ascent of Annapurna. In the 1980s, John McCarthy donned three-piece suits and voiced conservative opinions. He decided his 1966 proposals for computer privacy were a mistake, since merely possessing information causes no harm. The law, McCarthy now thinks, should concern itself with the usage of information, not with its whereabouts. About research financing, McCarthy's philosophy is the direct opposite of equality: he summarizes his position as "Make the peaks higher," meaning that one should make the best research institutions still better. And the former communist opposed Edward Fredkin's idea of an international AI laboratory: his reason: the Soviet Union would take an unfair advantage of it.[26]

During the 1955–56 academic year, Marvin Minsky was a Harvard fellow, and McCarthy taught at nearby Dartmouth College, in New Hampshire. The idea of intelligent machines fascinated them both: "They had a gleam in their eye!" recalls their colleague Herbert Simon.[27] They were becoming aware of the work of other researchers in the field and wished to bring them together. For this, they enlisted the help of two senior scientists who were also interested in the subject.

One was Nathaniel Rochester of IBM, designer of the IBM 701, the first general-purpose, mass-produced electronic computer. McCarthy had met him in connection with IBM's gift of a computer to MIT. With the help of three colleagues from the IBM research laboratory in Poughkeepsie, New York, Rochester was then simulating neural networks on IBM's new 704 computer.[28] More precisely, he was programming the machine to solve the numerical equations describing a large-scale neural network. This use of the computer was quite different from the symbol processing, "top-down" approach in which Minsky and McCarthy were interested. Intrigued, Rochester hoped that Minsky and McCarthy's approach might help computers exhibit originality in problem solving, which was his main interest.

The other helpful elder was Claude Shannon. Both Minsky and McCarthy had worked for him during the summer of 1953 at Bell Labs. Co-editing the book on automata theory with intelligence had furthered Shannon's interest in the younger man's work.

And so it was that with the backing of Rochester and Shannon, McCarthy and Minsky persuaded the Rockefeller Foundation to cover the $7,500 cost of a summer workshop on thinking machines. The two-month meeting, held in 1956 on the Dartmouth campus under McCarthy's auspices, brought together the few researchers then active in the field.[29]

In addition to the four organizers—McCarthy, Minsky, Shannon, and Rochester—of this Dartmouth conference, six other participants showed up. One was Ray Solomonoff of MIT, who had converted Minsky to the symbol-processing point of view. During the conference, Solomonoff pleaded against a tendency that was already becoming clear among would-be AI researchers: that of giving the most complicated and intellectual problems to machines in an effort to demonstrate their intelligence to the world. Solomonoff proposed that using easier problems would simplify the analysis of the mental processes involved. The point was well taken for yet another reason probably unknown to Solomonoff at the time: the problems that we find easiest (like recognizing a human face) are often the thorniest ones to program into a computer. The ability to tackle intellectual problems is a poor definition of intelligence.

Also present was Oliver Selfridge, a former assistant of Norbert Wiener who had proofread the galleys of the first edition of the latter's *Cybernetics* in 1948. In 1956, Selfridge was at MIT's Lincoln Laboratory working on pattern recognition by machine. He had already started programming computers to recognize letters of the alphabet and to translate Morse code.[30] Shortly after the conference, Selfridge delivered his most important contribution to the field—a forerunner of expert systems called Pandemonium.[31] Instead of a dignified sequence of statements, Selfridge believed an AI program should look like Milton's capital of Hell: a screaming chorus of demons, all yelling their wishes to a master decision-making demon. Each demon was a short sequence of statements looking for a particular configuration in the data (say, a vertical stroke in a printed character, or a specific conjunction of symptoms in a patient). The master demon made its decision by integrating the lower-level decisions of each of the small demons. For technical reasons, the idea did not catch on for fifteen years but, when it did, accounted for much of the success of expert systems.

Two minor participants at the conference were Trenchard More and Arthur Samuel. A graduate student at Princeton, More was writing a thesis on ways of proving theorems using a technique called natural deduction. Samuel, then at IBM, was investigating how computers could be made to learn by teaching them to play checkers. His efforts had a significant impact later.

THE FIRST AI PROGRAM

The last two participants in the Dartmouth conference, Herbert Simon and Allen Newell, had an immediate impact on AI's debut. Together, they had already written a computer program that, they claimed, showed that computers could think.

Herbert Simon

Herbert Simon was then thirty-six, and his background did not readily explain his competence or even interest in AI.[32] A political scientist by training, he had started his career researching municipal administrations. In 1948, he had made a brief venture into civil service as a member of the body that administered the Marshall Plan after the Second World War. That same year, he published a book entitled *Administrative Behavior*, which established his reputation as an expert in the functioning of human organizations. Soon thereafter, Simon helped found Carnegie Tech's Graduate School of Industrial Administration. (Carnegie Tech is now Carnegie Mellon University.) In 1956, Simon was a professor of industrial administration there.

Many would claim that Simon's specialty in those years—bureaucracies—lies at the exact opposite of intelligence. Yet his groundbreaking work led him to guess at several common points in the workings of both, and more recent findings by others have confirmed his intuition.

He had long been fascinated with how people make decisions; and his conclusions, though contrary to conventional economic theory, offered an open window into the workings of the human mind.

Before Simon, economists believed (and to a certain extent still do) that companies and even individuals making economic decisions behaved with perfect rationality and omniscience. Before reaching an investment or policy decision, a company was assumed to consider all possible alternatives and choose the one that brought about the largest benefits. The same kind of care was expected of a consumer shopping for a refrigerator. These assumptions enormously simplified the mathematical analysis of economic systems because they assumed economic agents were always trying to maximize or minimize some function, such as profit or cost. Since well-known mathematical tools existed for finding a function's trough or crest, economic behavior then became a tractable problem. But Simon pointed out, in his theory of *Bounded Rationality,* why these basic assumptions do not always work in practice.[33]

First, no one looks at all of the alternatives. When shopping for an appliance, most people will decide roughly what they are willing to pay, look at a couple of models, and pick the one that comes closest to their requirements. Companies do the same: year-end budgeting exercises typically exhaust the executives involved after only a few simulation runs.

Simon realized that alternatives do not come to a decision maker on a golden plate, and that there is a cost associated with finding and evaluating each possibility. For this reason, a decision process really consists in a search through a finite number of options, the fewer the better. Rather than optimizing some function of all options, like the associated profit, the bureaucrat in each of us picks the first choice that meets a pre-set acceptance criterion. Simon called this behavior "satisficing."

The inability to overcome the cost of searching through many alternatives limits us as decision makers. As any sore-footed appliance shopper will confirm, this weakness does not necessarily lie in our minds. Simon discovered another weakness that has more of the attributes of a mental restriction: both people and organizations have difficulty coming up with original solutions to problems. In organizations, this inaptitude shows itself in the existence of the rule book, or management manual. In recent years, a more abstract manifestation of it has received the name of "corporate culture." Such observations led Simon to speculate that the mind mostly functions by applying approximate or cookbook solutions to problems. This idea became the basis for "heuristic," or "rule-bound," programming.

Finally, Simon had noted that members of organizations identify with subgoals rather than with global aims. For example, a company's advertising department strives to produce the flashiest ad campaigns it can, whether or not they increase the company's profits. Only supervision by top management can reconcile the two goals of profits and glamorous advertising. Thus, organizations in effect achieve global goals (here, growth or survival) by breaking them up into smaller aims (like advertising and profits), which different departments pursue in a coordinated manner. This "goal, subgoal" strategy is now a key concept of AI.

In retrospect, Simon's transition from economics to artificial intelligence appears almost natural. As he told me: "I was always interested in the nature of intelligence. Any word of some mechanism that behaved intelligent-like was something I pricked up my ears at."

Allen Newell

Simon arrived at the Dartmouth conference with his younger colleague, Allen Newell. The son of a radiology professor at Stanford University, Newell had grown up in San Francisco. He graduated in physics from Stanford, where he took courses from the mathematician George Polya. Artificial intelligence owes to Polya the word *heuristic,* which he coined for the rules of thumb people apply in everyday reasoning. In 1945, Polya showed the problem-solving power of heuristics in an influential book called *How to Solve It.*[34]

After Stanford, Newell spent a year in Princeton's graduate school of mathematics, but did not find it as congenial as Minsky and McCarthy had (he entered Princeton at the same time as McCarthy, but missed Minsky by a couple of years). Contrary to them, Newell decided he wasn't a mathematician, and dropped out of graduate school. He preferred work where he would have concrete problems to solve. It was then 1950, and the RAND Corporation of Santa Monica offered bright young scientists with a practical bent the opportunity to prove themselves.

Newell was set to work on a project aimed at modeling a regional air-defense center. Part of the activity consisted in producing aerial maps through a computer-driven printer. Simon, who found time in his hectic schedule to consult for RAND, happened to see the printer in activity.

To anyone familiar with the drawing programs available on today's home computers, this would have been a perfectly trivial sight. But in the early 1950s, Simon found it an eye-opener: the dots and characters making up the maps weren't numbers. He saw them as symbols, and a computer was manipulating them! From there to deciding that computers could just as well simulate thought still required a major conceptual leap, but Simon made it without flinching. From then on, he and Newell started holding informal discussions on the subject.

For Newell, however, the lightning bolt of conversion occurred in 1954, when Oliver Selfridge visited RAND to describe the pattern-recognition work that would soon lead him to Pandemonium. These ideas hooked Newell with the realization that a complex process could come about as a result of the interactions of many simpler subprocesses. "It all happened in one afternoon," he says.[35]

The First AI Program

With the help of J. C. Shaw, an actuary turned computer programmer at RAND, Newell and Simon started in the fall of 1955 the development of what is now considered the first artificial intelligence program: Logic Theorist. Simon recalled it for me as follows:

> That autumn, we had considered three tasks for the program. Our original intention was to start out with chess, and then we also considered doing geometry. We thought, probably wrongly, that in both of these there were perceptual problems, important as humans performed the tasks, that would be hard to deal with. So we went to logic, for no deeper reason than that I had the two volumes of [Russell and Whitehead's] *Principia* at home. . . . We were not looking for an efficient way of proving theorems. We were looking at how humans, by selective heuristics, found the right thing to do next. That was certainly in the center of my mind: what heuristic . . . would kick out the right theorem to use rather than searching forever.

As Simon, Newell, and Shaw had realized, theorem proving can be reduced to a selective search. It helps to represent the search graphically as a treelike structure, called the "search tree." The starting point, or root node, is the initial hypothesis, on which the rules of logic allow a certain number of elementary manipulations, which yield slightly modified versions of the hypothesis. Each possible manipulation corresponds to a branch out of the root node. Applying other manipulations to each of these results gives the next generation of branches, and so on. Somewhere down the tree, after the application of an unknown number of manipulations, lies the desired conclusion: the problem is to find a path leading to this result.

To find this path, Logic Theorist explored the tree in a goal-oriented manner. Starting at the root node, it applied appropriate rules of thumb, or heuristics. These rules allowed it to select, among all possible branches leaving the node, the one that was most likely to lead toward the goal. Following this branch, Logic Theorist reached a new node at which it applied the heuristics again. Searching, goal-oriented behavior, rule-bound decisions—most of the basic ideas of Simon's bounded-rationality theory—were thus carried over to AI.

Programming a computer, any computer, was laborious in 1955; and the trio of researchers found it easier to hand-simulate the program before coding it into the machine. In his autobiography, Simon describes one such simulation session:

Allen [Newell] and I wrote out the rules for the components of the program (subroutines) in English on index cards, and also made up cards for the contents of the memories (the axioms of logic). At the [Graduate School of Industrial Administration] building on a dark winter evening in January 1956, we assembled my wife and three children together with some graduate students. To each member of the group, we gave one of the cards, so that each person became, in effect, a component of the [Logic Theorist] computer program—a subroutine that performed some special function, or a component of its memory. It was the task of each participant to execute his or her subroutine, or to provide the contents of his or her memory, whenever called by the routine at the next level above that was then in control.

So we were able to simulate the behavior of [Logic Theorist] with a computer constructed of human components. Here was nature imitating art imitating nature. . . . Our children were then nine, eleven, and thirteen. The occasion remains vivid in their memories.[36]

The actual implementation of Logic Theorist on a computer at RAND did not occur before the summer of 1956. Well before that, the hand simulations demonstrated the program's soundness to Simon's satisfaction. He thus proceeded to make an announcement to his first class of the new year at Carnegie Mellon: the future Nobel laureate boasted of nothing less than inventing an intelligent program over the Christmas vacation. Simon is no more abashed in his autobiography, where he reports this success as follows: "[W]e invented a computer program capable of thinking non-numerically, and thereby solved the venerable mind/body problem, explaining how a system composed of matter can have the properties of mind."[37]

Boastful as he sounds, Simon may have a point. The philosopher Daniel Dennett, to whom I read this quotation, scoffed at the thought that Logic Theorist by itself solves the mind-body problem. Dennett, however, went on to argue that AI as a whole may very well hold the key to this mystery. Logic Theorist in any case kicked off an unending debate about its philosophical implications. As if to confirm Simon's point, Logic Theorist was eventually able to prove thirty-eight of the first fifty-two theorems in chapter 2 of Russell and Whitehead's *Principia Mathematica*. Logic Theorist's proof for one theorem (number 2.85) was even more elegant than the one derived by Russell and Whitehead: Simon delighted Russell by informing him of this success.[38]

In deriving this proof, the program had surprised its authors in another way: they had not explicitly instructed it to find the proof. Yet, the structure of the program caused it to do so anyway, thereby showing that programs can at times do more than their programmers tell them. Theorem 2.85 also provided an amusing footnote to the history of AI: Newell and Simon submitted the new proof for publication to the *Journal of Symbolic Logic,* listing the program as a co-author. Entirely missing the implications, the editor turned down the paper on the grounds that it was no accomplishment to prove a theorem in the outmoded system of *Principia.*[39]

"Beads" of Memory

The computer implementation of Logic Theorist took a long time because it had to await the development by Newell, Simon, and Shaw of a computer-programming language with enough power and flexibility. This language was called IPL (for Information Processing Language) and incorporated another invention of the trio that is perhaps more important than Logic Theorist: the *list-processing* technique for programming.

IPL differed from other high-level languages like FORTRAN, of which IBM released a first version shortly before Newell, Simon, and

Shaw developed IPL. Short for FORmula TRANslation, FORTRAN was aimed at scientists and engineers. It eased the description of numerical operations, like computing algebraic formulas. If you have programmed a microcomputer, you may have used the BASIC language, which has many features in common with FORTRAN.

Newell, Simon, and Shaw were unhappy with languages like FORTRAN because they didn't model two important features of the mind. First, they assumed that thought consists in constantly creating, changing, and destroying interacting symbol structures. Languages like FORTRAN and BASIC cannot do that. They require that all arrays of numbers or symbols used in a program be defined beforehand in a program statement. This statement in effect reserves a region of memory to store these symbols until they come into use. Having to include this statement in the program forces the programmer to know in advance what the program will do, and prevents the program from creating new symbol structures. Say, we give it information about individual items named JOHN, JIM, and MARY. Generating a new array for them called PEOPLE is impossible to a FORTRAN or BASIC program. An IPL program could do this, however, because it didn't reserve memory space ahead of time for its symbol structures. The second feature Newell, Simon, and Shaw wanted to model was the associative character of human memory. In our minds, each idea or remembrance can lead to other symbols that are linked to it, and these links can be acquired through learning.

The trio was able to incorporate into a computer language the ability to associate and modify symbol structures through the list-processing technique, which Herbert Simon has described as follows:

The basic idea is that, whenever a piece of information is stored in memory, additional information should be stored with it telling where to find the *next* (associated) piece of information. In this way the entire memory could be organized like a long string of beads, but with the individual beads of the string stored in arbitrary locations. "Nextness" was not determined by physical propinquity but by an address, or pointer, stored with each item, showing where the associated item was located. Then a bead could be added to a string or omitted from a string simply by changing a pair of addresses, without disturbing the rest of the memory.[40]

Simon told me that he and his colleagues took their cue from early drum machines, the ancestors of today's hard-disk memory-storage devices. For technical reasons irrelevant to modeling the mind, drum machines already used a technique similar to list processing. Newell and Simon discussed this idea extensively at Dartmouth with John McCarthy, who later used it in his own AI language called LISP (see chapter 3).

The Dartmouth Conference of 1956

At Dartmouth, Newell and Simon were, as the only participants with a working AI program, far ahead of the others. For this reason, Minsky remembers them as being a little standoffish during the conference. Herbert Simon confirmed to me: "We were probably fairly arrogant about it all. Neither Al [Newell] nor I are known for much modesty under such circumstances." That state of affairs also gave rise to tense moments the following September, when the time came to report on the workshop at a meeting of the Institute of Radio Engineers held at MIT. Since they were the only ones with concrete results, Newell and Simon challenged McCarthy's right to report alone. They finally settled by having two separate talks: McCarthy summarized the meeting in general, while Newell and Simon expounded on Logic Theorist.[41]

The organizers of the Dartmouth conference had hoped for the emergence of a common feeling on both where the discipline was and where it was going. As a starting point for discussion, they had proposed the following statement: "Every aspect of learning or any other feature of intelligence can in principle be so precisely described that a machine can be made to simulate it." This belief has remained the cornerstone of most AI work until today. It later became known as the "physical symbol system hypothesis." The basic idea: our minds do not have direct access to the world. We can operate only on an internal representation of it, which corresponds to a collection of symbol structures. These structures can take the form of any physical pattern. They can consist of arrays of electronic switches inside a digital computer, or meshes of firing neurons in a biological brain. An intelligent system (brain or computer) can operate on these structures to transform them into other constructions. Thought consists of expanding symbol structures, breaking them up and reforming them, destroying some and creating new ones. Intelligence is thus nothing but the ability to process symbols. It exists in a realm different from the hardware that supports it, transcends it, and can take different physical forms.

The Dartmouth conference was in many ways inconclusive and deeply disappointed its principal organizer, John McCarthy. For one thing, people came for different periods of time, which precluded regular meetings. The problem was perhaps that not all participants agreed on the conference format. Herbert Simon recalled to me that "they were going to have a kind of floating crap game all summer with people sitting with each other, thinking and so on. And [Newell and I] were busy programming the Logic Theorist, so we agreed we'd spend [only] a week at Dartmouth."

No consensus emerged on what the field was or where it was going, and most of the participants later persisted in their own approaches. As Simon described it to me: "It was going off into different directions. They didn't want to hear from us, and we sure didn't want to hear from them: we had something to *show* them! . . . In a way, it was ironic because we already had done the first example of what they were after; and second, they didn't pay much attention to it. But that's not unusual. The 'Not Invented Here' sign is up almost everywhere, you know."

There was, nevertheless, enthusiasm; but Minsky recalls that it perversely induced a false sense of achievement.[42] Contrary to what the participants believed, their understanding of the theories of symbolic manipulation was still quite incomplete. Further, AI research did not elicit the worldwide interest they had expected. "Dartmouth got only half a dozen people active that weren't before," Simon told me. "[We] remained a very small group for quite a few years after that," Minsky confirmed to me, "because most people thought AI was impossible. [In a sense] that was the pleasant part of it: if you got an idea, you didn't have to worry about publishing it the same week!"

Yet the conference is generally recognized as the official birth date of the new science of artificial intelligence. One reason is perhaps that most participants in the meeting had never met each other before. "It did crystallize the group, gave a sense that if I got an idea, I'd call Herb Simon and say, 'What do you think of this?' . . . Looking back, that was the start of the community," Marvin Minsky told me.

Dartmouth indeed defined the AI establishment: for almost two decades afterward, all significant AI advances were made by the original group members or their students. We can surmise that if the brilliance of the conference participants accounts for much of this state of affairs, then the preference of agencies to fund recognized élites is not a negligible factor either.

The other claim of the Dartmouth conference for being the cradle of AI was the christening of the new discipline. McCarthy, remembering his disappointment with the automata-theory papers edited with Shannon, was looking for an accurate and catchy name. Overcoming the resistance of some participants (Samuel felt that "artificial" sounded phony, and Newell and Simon persisted in calling their work "complex information processing" for years afterward), McCarthy persuaded the majority to go for "artificial intelligence." He lays no claim to having coined the phrase, and admits it may have been used casually beforehand. Yet nobody denies him the achievement of getting it widely accepted. To label a discipline is to define its boundaries and identity: this accomplishment belongs to John McCarthy.

3

THE DAWN OF THE
GOLDEN YEARS: 1956–63

After Dartmouth, AI, for better or for worse, was now a field of intellectual inquiry. In many ways it was no more unified than it had been before 1956 but, perhaps because of the continuing exchange of ideas initiated at Dartmouth, AI started progressing in leaps and bounds. It is probably not much of an exaggeration to suggest that the later advances made in AI consist largely of elaborations and implementations of ideas first formulated in the decade following Dartmouth. During those years the main centers of AI research were Carnegie Mellon (then Carnegie Tech), MIT and its Lincoln Laboratory, and, to a lesser extent, Stanford and IBM.

AI researchers centered their work around two main themes. First, they wanted to limit the breadth of searches in trial-and-error problems; the Logic Theorist, Geometry Theorem Prover, and SAINT programs were results of this effort. Next, they were hoping and trying to make computers learn by themselves; their attempts in this direction were the chess, checkers, and pattern recognition programs.

MODELING HUMAN COGNITION AT CARNEGIE TECH

As proud as Newell and Simon were of their Logic Theorist program, some new research coming out of psychology in 1954—on problem-solving behavior in humans—suggested that humans do not reason the way Logic Theorist did. Of course, in itself this should not have been all that disturbing. For humans to make the final breakthrough in de-signing a flying machine, they first had to accept that such machines do not necessarily have to be modeled on the way birds fly. Why should a thinking machine have to think the way humans think? But then again, if humans can reason, why ignore totally the design of the only success-ful intelligent system around?

And so contrary to the goals of most other participants at the Dart-mouth conference, Alan Newell and Herb Simon's attempts at program design soon shifted away from trying to exploit the capabilities of computers to trying to simulate the human cognitive processes. So productive would this approach turn out to be that they never again deviated from it.

What set them on this path was some ground-breaking research by psychologists O. K. Moore and S. B. Anderson.[1] Moore and Anderson had presented test subjects with a series of puzzles and logical problems of the kind Logic Theorist solved, and had asked their subjects to "think aloud" while working on the problems. Following Moore's and Ander-son's lead, Newell and Simon carried out similar experiments that proved "fabulously interesting" to the Carnegie Tech researchers. Simon remembered it for me as follows:

> We started looking at this human data, and asking "Are these people behaving like the Logic Theorist?" The answer was no. Then we asked, "How are they behaving?" And we extracted the ideas for our [next program] General Problem Solver right out of human protocols. . . . What separates GPS from Logic Theorist is that with GPS we learned to extract out an organization and a set of heuristics which had in it no mention of a [particular] task. The whole structure . . . was encoded in a completely task independent manner. You just had to plug in the task-specific components, so to speak, into the slots, and it worked! The

word *general* refers specifically to the fact that we had segregated the task-dependent and the task-independent parts.[2]

The first run of Newell and Simon's GPS occurred in 1957.[3] By then they had given a name to this task-independent method: "means-ends analysis." In a sense, means-ends analysis is just Wiener's feedback principle carried to a higher level of abstraction. Like any good feedback mechanism, means-ends analysis worked by detecting differences between a desired goal and the actual state of affairs, and then reducing these differences. Where means-ends analysis improved upon this basic concept was in its ability to react to a wide spectrum of variations—not just one, as a thermostat might, but much as humans react when they are given a variety of slightly different problems to solve.

Consider, for example, how you would program GPS to solve the problem of the monkey faced with the perennial too-high banana. The animal, alone in a room containing a single chair, tries to grab a banana dangling out of its reach. Is the monkey (or GPS) clever enough to move the chair to the banana and climb up?

To explain the problem to GPS, the programmer first gave it a set of spatial coordinates, which described the positions of the monkey, the banana, and the chair. The programmer instructed GPS to calculate differences in positions among these elements. He also informed GPS of certain actions to perform to reduce these differences. In this case, the set of predefined actions or operators was: "move chair," "climb up chair," "jump," and "move self." (We'll assume the program thought of itself as the monkey.)

GPS could not perform some of the actions unless certain conditions existed beforehand—as the programmer also informed GPS. For example, it was of no use to have the monkey "climb up chair" unless the monkey had already "moved self" and "moved chair" underneath the banana. Likewise, the monkey could not move the chair unless both chair and monkey were first brought together—that is, to the same set of coordinates. All this information was given in a standardized form called the "difference table." To explain a new problem to GPS, one needed only to construct an appropriate difference table. GPS took care of the rest through means-ends analysis.

In the monkey's case, GPS applied the actions "move self to chair," "move chair to banana," and "climb upon chair." This sequence of actions reduced the three kinds of differences identified during the problem analysis to zero, and thus allowed the problem to be solved.

Furthermore, the preconditions associated with two of the actions led GPS to identify two subgoals accessory to its main goal: "move the chair" and "get to the chair." This breaking up of the problem into subproblems was a characteristic feature of means-ends analysis. It stemmed directly from Simon's observations on the workings of organizations. Also, when GPS abandoned jumping and tried another approach instead, it applied "backtracking," another basic tool of AI. This strategy (Does this work? If not, try something else) explains how computers can at times generate more knowledge than their programmers put into them.

GPS, in various forms, remained a part of Simon and Newell's research from 1957 to 1968. GPS was also the subject of a doctoral dissertation by a student, G. Ernst, who adapted it to several problems.[4] GPS learned to solve various puzzles, performed symbolic integration, and broke secret codes.

Other experiments on modeling human cognition also went on at Carnegie Tech in the late 1950s and early 1960s. Edward Feigenbaum studied human learning by building a working model of how people memorize nonsense syllables: his program EPAM (for Elementary Perceiver And Memorizer) induced psychologists to look at human memory in a new light.[5] (I shall say more about EPAM in chapter 10.) Another student, Robert K. Lindsay, studied verbal behavior at a deeper level: his SAD SAM program parsed sentences in ordinary English and extracted from them information about family trees.[6] Given the sentences "Jim is John's brother" and "Jim's mother is Mary," the machine would start building the internal equivalent of a genealogical tree. This tree implicitly contained the information that Mary was also the mother of John.

The computer running SAD SAM may well have been the first machine to show the glimmerings of understanding in the human sense. For us, as humans, to understand is to be able to relate a new piece of information to other facts we already know, and to do so in a manner that usually lets us draw conclusions we have not yet been given. The richer the network of connections, the deeper the understanding. SAD SAM was a first step in this direction.

MACHINE-BASED INTELLIGENCE

While the Carnegie Tech contingent from the Dartmouth conference did their work on human cognitive processes, most of the other participants were still under the impression that extensive knowledge of how the human brain works was not necessary for their original goal of developing machine-based intelligence. Their programs reflect what would become the traditional AI approach.

The Geometry Theorem Prover at IBM

In the late 1950s IBM became seriously involved in the computer business. Since artificial intelligence at the time looked like a natural extension of computer research, the company allowed such work to proceed. Nathaniel Rochester of IBM, for example, was impressed by some simple results Marvin Minsky had gotten from manually running a simulation of a program he had written to prove high school geometry theorems. He decided to try out the idea on IBM's newest machine, the 704 model, and entrusted the job to Herbert Gelernter, a young recruit with a Ph.D. in physics and earth-shaking enthusiasm. The road from manual simulation to a running program, however, would prove to be much longer and much more arduous than anyone expected. It took Gelernter close to three years of work to write and debug the twenty thousand individual instructions making up Geometry Theorem Prover. Before that, he had virtually to invent a new programming language endowed with both the symbol-manipulating power of Newell and Shaw's IPL, and the ease of programming afforded by IBM's new FORTRAN language for scientific computations.

The Geometry Theorem Prover worked backward.[7] One first described to it the theorem to prove. Much as a human being does, the program then started to build a chain of intermediate results leading back to known theorems or axioms. But what makes Gelernter's work so interesting and important is that to figure out what steps might lead back to the axioms, the program looked at a drawing. Since computers couldn't yet "see" through television cameras, Gelenter had to enter a representational figure as a series of point coordinates on punched cards. Using these coordinates, the program was able to extract the same kind of information a human does when looking at a representational figure: Which sides are equal or parallel to each other? Are there any right angles? Are some angles equal to each other?

With this information, the program pruned its search tree: that is, it tried to demonstrate formally only those properties that appeared to be true in the drawing, something that humans do unconsciously with problems of this kind.

This pruning made all the difference:[8] to derive a two-step proof in the blind mode, the program had to choose between 1,000 × 1,000 (one million) possible combinations. For a three-step theorem, there would be 1,000 × 1,000 × 1,000 (a billion) choices. By "looking" at the "figure," the program reduced this unmanageable quantity to 25 choices for the two-step problem, and to 125 for three steps (see figure 3.1).

The Geometry program could eventually prove theorems involving up to ten steps. More important, however, GTP was the first demonstra-

FIGURE 3.1
Example of a Proof Found by the Geometry Theorem Prover

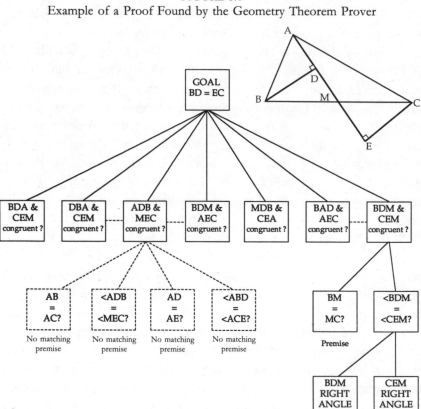

Figure 3.1 (*continued*)

This is the theorem to prove: two verticles of a triangle are equidistant from the median drawn from the third vortex. In the figure, this corresponds to showing that segment BD is equal to segment EC. The premises are:

BM = MC
BDM and MEC are right angles.

The program knows that a good way to show the equality of two line segments is to prove they belong to congruent triangles. It therefore sets out, as a first step, to identify two triangles containing segments BD and EC. Since it must match them vortex for vortex, the program must consider 144 possible pairs of triangles. Only 6 of them are congruent. As the dotted paths illustrate in the search tree above, one way to go about the proof would be to attempt to show formally the congruence of all these pairs; in most cases this would fail. Instead, the program ignores triangle pairs that are not numerically congruent in the figure. After discarding many such possibilities, the program hits upon the pair BDM and CEM, which the figure indicates to be congruent. The program then formally demonstrates the congruence of the two triangles by showing from the premises that they have equal sides opposite equal angles. These steps of the demonstration also involve trying out many pairs of sides and angles: only the correct matches appear above.

Comparison with a model (here the drawing, in coordinate form) is an efficient way to identify paths leading to a solution down a search tree.

---

tion of "model referencing." In AI parlance, a model is a simple internal representation of a complex process and can be used to make plausible inferences about it. For example, when talking to another person, we solve the problem of how to formulate what we say by referring to our internal model of what this person already knows and how he or she thinks. In the Geometry program, the model was the drawing of the figure. Modern expert systems may have a "user model," which helps the system understand queries from its users and thereby frame its answers. Thus, in developing a workable program for GTP, Gelernter not only came up with a new programming language but contributed a key idea that would continue to be used in all future AI research.

While one IBM computer was proving theorems under the guidance of Gelernter's program, another was learning to play checkers under the guidance of Arthur Samuel (he used the game to find out whether one could program computers to learn by themselves; as soon as the program figured out how to beat its creator, Samuel had his answer!). A third program was learning to play chess under another IBM researcher, Alex Bernstein.

Eventually, the AI projects conducted at IBM fell victim to their own successes. Bernstein's chess work caught the eye of the public through articles in *The New York Times* and *Scientific American.*[9] Samuel and Gelernter soon received similar publicity. As a result, IBM's president, Thomas J. Watson, was cornered during a shareholder's meeting into explaining why the company spent research dollars on such frivolous matters.[10] In addition, IBM's marketing people were noticing an alarming trend in customer psychology: customers felt threatened by computers and shied away from them. It wasn't even clear that the AI projects were causing this reaction, but Watson had had enough.

From then on, Gelernter and Bernstein turned to other matters: Bernstein eventually became a psychiatrist, and Gelernter went back to physics. Samuel was sent away to Europe, where interest in his checkers program allowed him access to the laboratories of IBM's competition. As for IBM's future marketing strategies, gone was the Buck Rogers image of computers as giant brains, to be replaced with a reassuring bromide on moronic number crunchers. Computers, IBM kept saying in many voices and through all the channels a multinational can muster, would do only what they were told. They would never steal any manager's job, and their only talent lay in the speedy processing of torrents of numbers.

Ironically, this company line, taken for pragmatic reasons against the early evidence of successful AI experiments, turned out to be an accurate forecast of the performance of computers during the next quarter-century!

Pandemonium at Lincoln Laboratory

The Lincoln Laboratory lies several miles away from the main campus of MIT, and (at least in the 1950s and 1960s) much farther psychologically: behind its heavily guarded security gates were relegated those defense-related research projects MIT considered too sensitive for the more informal ways of academia. Although there was really nothing secret about his AI research, Oliver Selfridge of Pandemonium fame was working there, taking advantage of the equipment and personnel available. When Minsky joined him in 1957, Selfridge had already worked for some years on a branch of AI that would later become known as "pattern recognition."

One aspect of this research that was particularly representative of the

"early post-Dartmouth" period is Selfridge's preoccupation with automated learning: that is, how to make an AI program that could deduce
concepts or information not explicitly given to it.[11] I described in
chapter 2 how Selfridge divided his programs into many independent
functions he called "demons": each demon looked for a certain characteristic in the object to be recognized and screamed more or less loudly
according to how sure it was of the presence of the characteristic; and
a master demon (call it Beelzebub) decided, from the volumes of the
different voices in the choir, what the object was. For example, in a
Pandemonium program for recognizing the letters of the alphabet, the
demon in charge of vertical strokes would scream more loudly in the
presence of a capital *I* than of a lowercase one. Since this demon would
probably be the only one to scream in these cases, the master demon
would know which mode was meant. Likewise, when confronted with
two agonizing screams for "vertical stroke" and a merely plaintive one
for "horizontal stroke," Beelzebub would decide on *H,* and so on for
other letters.

Early efforts at getting programs to learn led Selfridge and other
investigators, like Samuel at IBM with his checkers program, to a sobering conclusion. AI researchers could, rather easily in fact, invent mathematical procedures that let a letter-recognizing or a chess-playing Beelzebub learn by experience which set of screams corresponded to which
letter, or move to play. Mostly, it was a simple matter of adapting
correlation techniques developed earlier by statisticians.

Neither Selfridge nor Samuel could, however, make their Beelzebubs
create new demons. For example, faced with the letter *o,* Selfridge's
Beelzebub could not be made to conjure up a hole-detecting demon. A
programmer had to step in and program one for it. Until this restriction
was overcome, concluded Selfridge, "artificial intelligence [would] remain tainted with artifice."[12]

The LISP Language at MIT

While Selfridge and his group were working in the shielded seclusion
of the Lincoln Laboratory developing various AI programs, John
McCarthy over at the electrical engineering department of MIT was
thinking in much larger terms. In a period of about five years he made
two major breakthroughs: the LISP language and time sharing. The first
would be a blessing to all AI researchers to this day. The second would

literally revolutionize computer research in general. In 1958, McCarthy announced the development of the LISP language. LISP, for LISt Processing, was soon universally adopted as the programming language for AI research. In designing LISP, McCarthy took part of his inspiration from IPL, the early language developed at Carnegie Mellon by Newell, Simon, and Shaw.

LISP, IPL, and a third language—COMIT developed in 1962, also at MIT—were all high-level programming languages in that most of their statements looked like English words, and one statement could tell the computer to perform many operations, or even a complicated operation.[13] Prior to the development of high-level languages, programmers had to specify any operation as a long string of mnemonics and numbers (the assembly language), which more closely controlled the computer's hardware. In addition to requiring large amounts of time, this way of entering instructions made error detection extremely difficult. It was also cumbersome to change the program later to meet new needs.

Running a program written in a high-level language is a two-step process. First, another program called the "compiler" or "interpreter" translates statements of the original program into the low-level instructions they represent. Second, the computer executes these low-level instructions. The process in effect delegates menial programming tasks to the computer itself. In this way, high-level languages like LISP brought about a giant increase in programmer productivity.

LISP, COMIT, and IPL also belonged to the class of list-processing languages. We saw in chapter 2 how such languages can reproduce the associative and symbol-generating capabilities of the human mind. They achieve this by treating the different symbols they handle as a long string of beads, each bead pointing to the next one; this string is called a "list." LISP improved on the process by introducing ways of eliminating unused beads in the list. It inserted any new item required at the beginning of the list, and returned unused ones to the end of the list, where they could be assigned new definitions if needed. Computer people call this process of sending stragglers back to the end of the line "garbage collection." It avoids filling the computer memory with useless variables.

Wouldn't you like to have the ability to look into your own mind and change it when you don't like yourself? It turns out a LISP program can do that, at least in principle. The statements making up the program are part of the list of symbols the program operates upon. A LISP program can thus change its own instructions.

AI researchers still haven't been able to capitalize on this ability to design evolving programs that bootstrap themselves into true intelligence, but McCarthy included the possibility in the AI tool kit at the very beginning. Indeed, in a 1958 paper, entitled "Programs with Common Sense," McCarthy wrote, "Our ultimate objective is to make programs that learn from their experience as effectively as humans do."[14] Early on, McCarthy realized that for this to be possible one should be able to program meaningful changes of behavior in a simple way. This ability would make it possible, as a practical first step, to enter knowledge manually into the program in an efficient manner. Ultimately, it would let the program change itself in simple, meaningful steps.

Proposing that it should be as easy for a person to improve the program as to give advice to a friend, McCarthy described a program structure called the Advice Taker. In a striking parallel with Oliver Selfridge's Pandemonium, McCarthy proposed to replace the sequence of imperative statements making up a run-of-the-mill program by declarative sentences of the form "If such happens, then do that." Each of these pieces of advice, similar to one of Selfridge's demons, would be tested for applicability by a control program equivalent to Selfridge's master demon. This precursor of the inference engines of today's expert systems would possess a deductive power sufficient to endow the Advice Taker with common sense, in the meaning McCarthy defined: "We shall . . . say that a program has common sense if it automatically deduces for itself a sufficiently wide class of immediate consequences of anything it is told and what it already knows."[15]

Returning now to LISP, let us note that the language also innovated by making use of a technique called "lambda-calculus," first invented as an abstract tool in mathematical logic by the American mathematician Alonzo Church.[16] Lambda-calculus treats functions—that is, relations between objects or numbers—as objects also. Thus in LISP, applying a function to a function is just as easy as multiplying two numbers. In practice, this means that in LISP you can easily say sentences like "The block over the one adjacent to the blue pyramid," which implies an application of the function "over" to the function "adjacent."

The superior memory management and representational properties of LISP soon led the entire AI community to prefer it to COMIT and IPL. Yet LISP was not generally accepted as a useful tool for AI overnight, because list-processing languages in general presented major disadvantages. For one thing, they threw away half the computer memory. The address of the "next bead" took up as much room as the bead itself, a major handicap for the small memories available in the 1960s.

Further, partly because a list-processing language could modify itself during execution, it could not be converted once and for all into machine language. This "compiling" speeds up program execution by as much as a hundred times. Instead, a LISP program had to be interpreted, or converted, into machine language during execution, statement by statement—an agonizingly long process.

"To conventional programmers these languages seemed ridiculous if not suicidal," recalled Herbert Simon.[17] Berthold Horn, now a professor at MIT, couldn't use LISP for his thesis in the 1960s: he had to rely on a kind of souped-up machine language. "There was a transition between the time when LISP was a toy, but people saw what it was good for, to when LISP was actually a usable tool. 1970 was the beginning of useful LISP programs," Horn told me.[18]

Time Sharing at MIT

In and of itself, LISP was surely enough of a contribution to establish forever McCarthy's reputation as one of the major figures in AI research. Yet shortly after its release, McCarthy had ready a second major contribution, a system called "time sharing." Its usefulness would become apparent immediately, not only to the community of AI researchers but to all computer programmers. In time, time sharing would become the blessing (and sometimes the curse) of most computer users around the world.

Throughout the 1950s and well into the 1960s, computers were bulky, expensive machines which required air-conditioned environments and specialized personnel to run them. A typical computer, though it usually offered less memory and processing power than today's desktop machines, still had to accommodate the needs of a large group of users.

In the early days, a programmer had to submit a program in the form of a bulky deck of cards to a (usually) sleepy operator. Some hours (and, when luck ran low, days) later, the programmer would be handed back a printed output containing the results of the run. Typically, the printout revealed errors in the program code or data, which made the results useless. It usually took several passes to get a program of even a few lines to run correctly, and one was lucky to do it in less than a week.

McCarthy and his colleague Fernando Corbato, another MIT computer scientist, decided they couldn't get any work done under such conditions. Their remedy was to let several users talk to the computer at the same time. Instead of a single card reader, they thought of installing several terminals, each equipped with a keyboard through which users would enter programs or commands. The computer would switch from keyboard to keyboard very quickly. The machine's ability to read and send back data much faster than a human would give users the illusion of having the computer for their exclusive use.

Like most technical innovations, the idea was more complicated than it sounds. Simply switching between terminals was not enough: the computer also had to reload the right program for each terminal and return to the right step in its execution. A complicated control program called the "operating system" was needed to perform these operations. To transfer programs in and out of the computer fast enough, McCarthy and Corbato also had to design new high-speed memories.

Yet even with these, it was necessary to leave several programs in the computer at the same time. Since computer programs need to write the results of their operations into other parts of computer memory, they tended to erase or modify each other. To prevent this, a new mechanism called "memory protection" had to be implemented.

Going from the concept phase to a working time-sharing system required the cooperation of computer manufacturers, and it took McCarthy and Corbato years to convince them to take the idea seriously. Finally, a startup company founded by MIT colleagues, the Digital Equipment Corporation, supplied some equipment.[19]

Soon DEC's PDP-1 computer was turned into the world's first time-sharing system. Partly through that innovation, DEC became in time the world's second-largest computer manufacturer. Later the team assembled by McCarthy and Corbato time-shared MIT's mainframe computer.

The result was worth it. When everything worked correctly, time sharing was pure bliss for programmers. Early on terminals looked like typewriters: both the user's input and the computer's responses were printed on paper. Later, the printers were replaced by silent and faster cathode-ray tubes. Often, however, the programs took too long to run, or too many users overloaded the system. Minutes would then pass before the machine could respond to a command, and users were as frustrated as in the old days. For anyone who had endured the card-deck routine, though, there was no question that productivity was still up 1,000 percent.

Machine-Aided Cognition

In 1958 Marvin Minsky, having worked for just about a year at Lincoln Laboratory, during which time he had cooperated with Selfridge and his team on various projects, decided to join McCarthy at MIT. He was hired by the mathematics department, but later switched to electrical engineering.* He and John McCarthy, of course, knew each other well, having first met at Princeton and later spent the summer of 1956 together at the Dartmouth meeting. Minsky's move to MIT appeared initially to be a wonderful teaming up of two formidable AI figures. Together they established the MIT Artificial Intelligence Group and for the next few years worked in close coordination with each other. Minsky's colleague Joseph Weizenbaum told me that "in the early 1960s, Minsky and McCarthy were almost synonymous, bound together. You never said just Minsky or just McCarthy, you said Minsky-and-McCarthy."[21] No one who knew them at that time could have guessed that they would later drift apart, each eventually to be identified with the opposite ideological pole of AI.

Within a few years, signs of impending conflict began to appear. Part of the problem appears to have been ideological. In the days when everybody was overly enthusiastic about the imminent realization of AI, McCarthy rightly kept a cool head and predicted the difficulties to come. He correctly perceived that the stumbling blocks were common sense and language understanding. But in this regard his research philosophy started to diverge from that of his friend. Today, when many AI researchers are looking at means other than pure logic for tackling the problems of AI, McCarthy has remained faithful to his initial convictions: namely, that the way to AI was by working through the processes of formal logic. Minsky, on the other hand, became over the years the champion of the antilogic branch of AI. To what extent this divergence of opinion motivated McCarthy simply to leave MIT is not clear. In any

---

*Minsky's year at Lincoln Laboratory followed an unfortunate interlude in a new department at Tufts University called Systems Analysis, which he recalls as "a bridge between cybernetics and psychology."[20] It was 1957, and Senator Joseph McCarthy saw fit to include two of the department's founders, Richard Rudner and William C. Schutz, on his list of subversive people; the university closed the department.

case, in 1962, when offered the opportunity to head his own artificial intelligence laboratory in Stanford University, McCarthy departed for California.

McCarthy left MIT just as time sharing was achieving official recognition. On 27 June 1963, MIT received a $2,220,000 grant from a newly created Defense Department agency: the Advanced Research Projects Agency (ARPA) was created after Sputnik to ensure that America would never again be caught with its technological pants down. The grant was to fund, according to the *Boston Herald,* "new ways in which computers can help people in their creative works, ranging from research to education and management. The project (would) operate under the name MAC, representing its objective—Machine-Aided Cognition—and its principal tool—the Multiple Access Computer."[22] Marvin Minsky, with McCarthy's departure the sole head of the AI group, was to be the principal beneficiary of the part of the grant that went to the AI group, a full third of the total amount.

The basic idea, according to the *Herald,* was to develop an "information utility," which would distribute the computer's logical power "in much the same manner that electricity is universally available."[23] In modern terminology, the two interpretations of the MAC acronym refer to artificial intelligence and time sharing. Even if they both relate to computers, lumping them in a single project sounds a little like creating a faculty of agriculture and Chinese cuisine, on the grounds that both have to do with food. Since the two concepts appeared far-fetched anyway, that discrepancy apparently didn't faze ARPA's director J. C. R. Licklider. ARPA's philosophy then was "Fund people, not projects!" Minsky had been a student of Licklider's at Harvard and knew him well. As Minsky told me, "Licklider gave us the money in one big lump," and didn't particularly care for the details.

For many years, Project MAC brought MIT three million dollars a year in grants. More important, MAC attracted scientists from everywhere to come for various periods as consultants. "Virtually every prominent computer scientist has contributed to project MAC," Minsky told me.

Other work performed at MIT during this period yielded interesting results for the future of artificial intelligence. In 1961, for instance, a student of Minsky's named James Slagle wrote a program called SAINT, for Symbolic Automatic INTegrator.[24] SAINT applied the methodology of Newell and Shaw's Logic Theorist to problems of symbolic integration. For its final exam, Slagle tested SAINT on eighty-six problems (many of which were from MIT freshmen's final examinations); SAINT successfully solved eighty-four. In addition to demonstrating that Logic Theorist's methods could cover problems in algebra as well as logic, SAINT was probably the first AI program explicitly to address the problem of searching what became known as "AND/OR trees."

Often one cannot find a solution to a problem through a single sequence of operations. Instead, one may discover that a solution path breaks down into several questions that must all be answered. For example, showing that The Butler Did It might entail proving that the fingerprints are his, AND that they were put on the glass before the Countess swallowed the poison, AND that there are no other fingerprints. If we can't establish all three of these facts, then we can try to prove another all-inclusive set of evidences for the Nephew, or the Doctor, or the Ingenue. In complicated situations, simply keeping up a list of all combinations of facts required to reach a conclusion requires major bookkeeping. The SAINT program pointed the way to a solution.

Another graduate student, Joel Moses, later expanded SAINT into a program called SIN for Symbolic INtegrator, which could solve "[i]ntegration problems as difficult as ones found in the largest tables."[25] In 1969, SIN grew further into a system called MACSYMA, which today assists engineers, scientists, and mathematicians in the interactive solution of mathematical problems.

Back in 1963, Marvin Minsky had to keep the newly enlarged AI group on an even keel without McCarthy's help. No programmer himself, Minsky became known as a theoretician and mentor to many students: some grew into important AI researchers in their own right. The best example is perhaps Patrick Winston, who now holds Minsky's former job as the head of the AI lab. "Marvin is a very unusual thesis supervisor," Winston told me.

> He is not the sort of person who spoon-feeds his students by any means. He is also, by virtue of his extreme intelligence and as a founder of the field, quite scary for an ordinary graduate student. That, coupled with his general lack of organization, made it difficult for as shy a student as I was to see Marvin on any kind of regular basis. So I didn't see him often: I think I count two or three times during the whole exercise. But when I did see him it had important consequences . . . [because of] his ability to see what was important

in my work. What I found out is that Marvin's jokes often become important thesis topics. He will say something that sounds like a joke but is actually very profound. Even more ironic is that if you take an idea to Marvin, he'll probably misunderstand it to be some better idea. Your best bet is to let it ride and listen to him comment on what he thinks you said![26]

Minsky's former student Berthold Horn also liked his adviser's hands-off attitude, but for a different reason. "I was too shy to go talk to him and he was very busy," Horn told me. "So I was pretty much finished before he had a chance to interact with [my work], which is a good thing because he would have been, and in fact was, later, very much opposed to it."

Among the former students of Minsky I met, only David Waltz expressed disappointment about the guidance he received:

I tried several topics for a Ph.D. thesis, . . . and Marvin was always saying, "Oh, it's a great topic, keep working on it." Then after six months had gone by he would say, "Well, maybe you should be working on something else." . . . If it had not been for the Vietnam War I think I might not have finished. . . . But Minsky saved me from the draft. . . . He wrote a letter to my draft board telling them that I was working on this ARPA project that was critical to the nation's strength, and my board bought it, fortunately.[27]

Gerald Sussman had no such reservations. "Marvin is a second father to me," he confided. "Many of the things I do now I do to keep him happy."[28]

Minsky influenced the development of AI through his students and by the articles and books he wrote. Over the years, all fields of the new science felt his influence, from language processing to parallel computing. In the early 1960s, he launched the AI group on a systematic research effort that spanned more than fifteen years.

MAN AGAINST COMPUTERS:
THE HACKERS

The AI group gravitating around Minsky in the mid-1960s comprised about twenty people. They were graduate students "and ex-students. The singular thing was that we had a very powerful engine of MIT dropouts," Minsky told me. These were mathematics and engineering undergraduates who had abandoned their studies in favor of a full-time addiction to computers. "Some of them came from the famous MIT Model Railroad Club, which was beginning to think of making computers to control its trains," Minsky mentioned on another occasion.[29] They called themselves "disciples of the hack," or "hackers," after their own slang for a clever programming trick. Their life style gave rise to a brand new culture which quickly spread to computing centers around the world.

Most conspicuously, hackers were night creatures. David Waltz (who, uncharacteristically, did earn his Ph.D.) recalled his hacking days for me in his office overlooking the Charles River at the Thinking Machines Company:

> The cool thing to do was to stay at the lab long hours. The really dedicated slept on mattresses, never left the lab. I think most of us did that at one time or another because [initially] we didn't have time sharing, and we had to sign up for time on the machine. If you signed up for after midnight you'd get a two-hour block at a time, and at other times all you could get was a one-hour block. . . . So you sure weren't going to go home and drive in or ride a bike. You would sleep on a mattress, and take your shift when the time came.

The pattern persisted even after time sharing, for reasons often other than technical. Says Randall Davis of his student days at McCarthy's Stanford AI Lab:

> When all you could get [during the day] was one twentieth of a time-sharing system, you worked at night. . . . I used to work till about four in the morning, then I would sleep until noon. Partly because I could get more of the machine, but also because it gets very quiet at

night. . . . It was a nice sense of sitting down at work after dinner and knowing that I wasn't going to get interrupted for the next eight hours. There was great freedom in that. I was famous for sleeping through lunchtime meetings.[30]

In some cases, though, hacking had a frankly pathological side. The immediate rewards and punishments associated with time sharing added a Pavlovian aspect to programming, which only worsened the mono-maniacal fixation required to get results out of early computer systems. For these reasons, the MAC acronym was jokingly understood in many circles as "Man Against Computers" or "Maniacs And Clowns."

The hacker culture later fueled epic controversies. In 1976, a colleague of Minsky's, Joseph Weizenbaum, fired the first shot in his *Computer Power and Human Reason*.[31] Weizenbaum spent an entire chapter decrying the psychology of hackers, whom he portrayed as haggard, bearded young men obsessively clattering at keyboards. For Weizenbaum, their attach-ment to computers stemmed from acute feelings of insecurity, which led them continually to seek confirmation of their power over the machine by demanding more performance from it. They proceeded without theory, method, or knowledge of the domains of application of their programs. Seymour Papert, who later co-directed the AI laboratory with Minsky, acknowledged the hackers' lack of method: "Without specifications they would just start programming, quick and dirty. If you tried to tell them what to do, you got nowhere at all." But, added Papert, such bumbling activity did not preclude invention: "The hackers were creating the front of computer science. They did the first computer graphics, the first word-processing, the first computer games, the first time-sharing."[32]

Minsky, for his part, adamantly sang to me the praise of hackers:

These were very involved young people, who had a great many ideas. . . . There was a vacuum in which the professional people in computer science were mostly confounded themselves, former electrical engi-neers who were thrown into the computer world and never under-stood it. Whereas these young people, the hackers, . . . knew how to build, and they had a program in their heads and everyday would write a new kind of program that none of the professionals ever imagined.

In her 1984 book, *The Second Self,* MIT sociopsychologist Sherry Turkle pursued the debate through a deeper probe of the hacker psyche.

Like Weizenbaum, she believed the hacker's obsessive need for mastery of the machine had its roots in deep insecurity. Further:

> There are few women hackers. This is a male world. Though hackers would deny that theirs is a macho culture, the preoccupation with winning and of subjecting oneself to increasingly violent tests makes their world peculiarly male in spirit, peculiarly unfriendly to women. There is, too, a flight from relationship with people to relationship with the machine—a defensive maneuver more common to men than women. The computer that is the partner in this relationship offers a particularly seductive refuge to someone who is having trouble dealing with people.[33]

To me, Minsky objected adamantly:

> Turkle has learned some sociology and studied these people as though they had been shaped by this environment or had some kind of quirk. . . . She has missed that these are not a class of people that you study like some tribe of primitives. Each of them is a fantastically different individual. It's like saying Rembrandt and Picasso and Dali all had some nerdiness quality. These were people who were too smart for the system.

Elsewhere, Minsky pointed out, "Contrary to common belief, hackers are more social than normal people." Referring to their frequent late-night gatherings at Chinese restaurants, Minsky remarked, "What's the most significant feature of Chinese food besides the food itself? It's a group decision."[34]

But, retorts Sherry Turkle, "the hacker culture is a culture of loners who are never alone. It is a culture of people who leave each other a great deal of psychological space."[35] She quotes one of her study subjects who has "tried out" having girl friends: "Hacking is easy and safe and secure. I used to get into relationships that usually led to me getting burned in some way. It is easy to go out with people who are only interested in hacking because it is a safe and secure environment."[36]

Yet another fascinating quirk of the hackers' personality is their abhorrence of locks. It probably stems from the presence in computers of protection mechanisms, which challenge hackers' lust for complete dominion over the systems. Any kind of security device, including a locked door, is a challenge no red-blooded hacker can resist. David Waltz recalled one such occasion for me:

> There were some at the lab who wanted to go and find anything that was being held secret. One of our colleagues always wanted to keep his documents hidden or encrypt them or keep them under lock. One night Gilbert Voyat, a postdoc of Papert, and Tom Knight, whom you called to get into any room if it was locked because he . . . could figure out a way to get in, . . . decided to see what was in our colleague's office: they would get in by crawling through the crawl space [over the ceiling], and then climb down through. Unfortunately the ceiling gave way under Gilbert's weight: he fell, cracked a rib and punctured a lung, landing on the desk and there was plaster and pieces of tile all over the place. That only fed our friend's belief that people were trying to get at what he was doing. I don't know why they wanted to get in. I guess because somebody was keeping them out. If it's locked then there must be something interesting to find if you got in, I guess. It was just a hack.

Locks are still an important part of a hacker's life, and the subject can have strange ramifications. As I was recently talking about the old days with Gerald Sussman, hacker emeritus himself and now one of the pillars of the MIT AI lab, one of Sussman's younger colleagues walked in and announced he was resigning from the AI lab. Since he wasn't paying attention to me, I decided to stay and hear out his reasons. The problem was, it turned out, that he objected on general principles to controlling access to his computer with a password: "I don't wear a coat of arms on the street, why should I act any differently at work?" Unfortunately a group of Dutch hackers had discovered the weakness and were using his work station as a port of entry into the AI lab's whole network, wreaking havoc in disk files. (Hackers are usually content, when they break into a system, to leave some innocuous message of victory and depart without further disturbance. This group was uncharacteristically nasty.) Other researchers in the AI lab, who didn't share their colleague's concern about coats of arms, were demanding that he implement a password, or else. I understand Sussman later arbitrated a compromise.

CONCLUSION

Taking stock in the early 1960s, researchers were ready to declare themselves successful in reaching the first of their objectives: that is, in limiting the search in trial-and-error problems. Logic Theorist worked, and the Geometry program narrowed down its choices to less than one half of 1 percent of available options at each step of a proof. The SAINT program also generated only a small number of irrelevant subgoals.

Yet if computers behaved efficiently as search engines, they were dreadful students. Like draft animals, one could train them to associate pre-set responses with appropriate stimulus patterns, but they stubbornly refused to come up with useful ideas of their own to make sense of new situations. Reflecting on the nature of the related problems of learning and understanding, researchers mused that more than anything else these two activities involved building links. Learning and understanding imply relating newly acquired knowledge to previously known facts in a manner permitting its efficient use. For the SAD SAM program, if it already knew that Mary was the mother of Jim, understanding that John was Jim's brother meant that the program could infer that Mary was also John's mother. Yet that was only the barest of beginnings: if SAD SAM had really understood this new fact as a human being does, it would also have been able to tell you that Jim and John almost certainly knew each other, spoke the same language, and shared the same cultural background. If pressed, SAD SAM should have been able to add that they might look alike and were probably on friendly terms, and that their age difference was almost certainly less than fifteen years.

In order to make computers learn and understand in a manner approximating the human norm, it was thus necessary to solve an underlying problem beforehand: that is, to find out how to represent, within the memory of a computer, such different pieces of knowledge as these, as well as the links relating them. Hence, in the first years of the 1960s, researchers decided to put learning on the back burner and concentrate on the problem of knowledge representation instead. Their efforts in this direction would bring about spectacular successes, but also disillusionments that they are only now beginning to recover from.

4

THE CONQUEST OF MICRO WORLDS: 1963-70

In the middle and late 1960s, AI blossomed in a thousand flowers. AI researchers applied their new programming techniques to many problems which, although real, had been carefully simplified, partly to isolate the problems to be addressed, but partly also to fit into the tiny memories of the computers available in those days. The researchers were not disappointed, and their successes brought about new understandings in how to represent knowledge about the world in a computer. The undertaking which best describes the spirit of the times is the Blocks Micro World project carried out at MIT, and which inspired other efforts, notably at Stanford. In a world of pure geometric forms, robots looked through television cameras, interpreted what they saw, moved about, manipulated blocks, and talked about their perceptions, activities, and motivations. As if to cap these successes, AI also struck an apparently fatal blow against the now rival science of artificial neural networks by exposing basic flaws in current neural network research.

PROGRESS IN KNOWLEDGE REPRESENTATION

Like Newell, Simon, and Shaw before him, Marvin Minsky was, by the early 1960s, giving some thought to the fact that the human mind does not really work like a logical engine, at least not in its initial attempts to solve most problems. No human being, for example, on being presented with a particular problem, beelines into a systematic search for its solution. Instead, it seems, humans employ a much less taxing solution. Before considering more comprehensive approaches, most of us simply jog our memories for past experiences of a similar nature. If something suggests itself to us, we see whether the relationship between the old experience and the new one is tight enough to make a match. If not, we will probably call up a second and a third memory before attempting anything more complex.

For example, an experienced pediatrician doesn't make a diagnosis of measles in a sick child by searching through a list of all sicknesses with their associated symptoms; rather, one asks oneself, "What do these symptoms remind me of?" Much more than on logic, in our first attempt to solve any problem, we will rely on our ability to make associations between present and past experiences having some element in common.

The Square Root of Analogy

How do we associate two ideas, concepts, or situations? More generally, by what standard do we consider two experiences to be alike? To find out more about just this kind of thinking, particularly the concept of alikeness, Minsky went to Tom Evans, one of the students in the AI group. Working under Minsky's supervision, Evans would create the program ANALOGY in 1963.[1]

By then most AI researchers believed that alikeness, at least as far as the human brain is concerned, is communicated at the time we make an internal description of past experiences. For AI work, it quickly became clear that it was important to write such descriptions in a manner that favored the easy detection of similarities between objects. Evans chose a relatively simple world in which to work. More important, he chose the kind of problem that frequently appears in human intelligence tests; in fact, he took actual problems from tests of the American Council on Education (ACE). One of these problems is of the sort illustrated in figure 4.1.

Like Gelernter before him (see chapter 3), Evans had to do without image scanners or digitizers to enter the figure descriptions. He had to "draw" it the tedious old-fashioned way, with the point-coordinate system. By "looking" at these point coordinates, the computer had to realize, in this example, that to solve the problem it should remove the inner object in square *A* to make squares *A* and *B* identical: It had to establish for itself that the large triangle in square *A* corresponds to the one in square *B*.

FIGURE 4.1

A Typical Problem Solved by Tom Evans's ANALOGY Program:
A is to *B* what *C* is to which of figures 1 to 5?

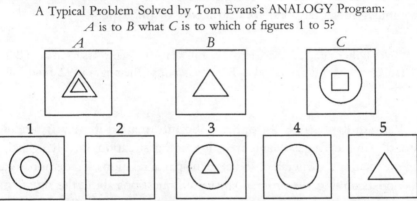

To solve this problem, the program had to devise a transformation that would turn *A* into *B,* and then apply this transformation to *C* to obtain one of the figures among 1 to 5. This procedure is not as simple as one would think. For example, formulating the solution rule as "Remove inner triangle" instead of "Remove inner object" would not have worked, since *C* contained no triangle. But that was not all. Suppose *C* contained two inner objects: a square and a triangle. Then there would have been two possible rules for turning *A* into *B:* "Remove inner triangle" or "Remove inner objects." To find out which, the program also had to look at figures 1 to 5 and find out which rule turned *C* into one of them. Often there was more than one rule that took *A* into *B,* and *C* into one of 1 to 5. Evans therefore also had to build into his program how to decide which analogy rule "made the most sense."

Evans tested his program on questions from genuine IQ tests. This one was extracted from the 1942 Test for College Freshmen of the American Council on Education.

As explained in the caption to figure 4.1, there is more to this problem than meets the eye. In a way, the ANALOGY program had to compute the square root of analogy. Not only did it explore how two objects (like *A* and *B*) were alike or different; it also had to evaluate how plausible the likenesses of two pairs of objects were. This is what people do all the time, unconsciously, to weed out the multitude of irrelevant analogies that would otherwise clog their thinking. It is not yet quite clear how we do that, and the success or failure of the quest for AI might hinge on how well researchers solve this problem. Tom Evans was the first to clearly identify the issue, and solve it in a restricted context.

Hidden Structures

Two doctoral theses submitted in 1964 by students of Minsky tackled the design of verbal knowledge structures, letting the computer converse in natural English. In Daniel Bobrow's STUDENT program, the computer solved algebra story problems of this type:

> "Bill's father's uncle is twice as old as Bill's father. Two years from now Bill's father will be 3 times as old as Bill. The sum of their ages is 92. Find Bill's age."[2]

Bertram Raphael's SIR (for Semantic Information Retrieval) "understood" simple English sentences describing situations involving part-whole relations, ownership, and certain spatial relations. To demonstrate its understanding, the program answered questions about the situations described to it. In this example of a conversation with SIR, the program's responses are capitalized:

1. Every boy is a person.
   I UNDERSTAND

2. A finger is part of a hand.
   I UNDERSTAND

3. Each person has two hands.
   THE ABOVE SENTENCE IS AMBIGUOUS. PLEASE REPHRASE IT.

4. There are two hands on each person.
   I UNDERSTAND

5. How many fingers does John have?
THE ABOVE SENTENCE IS AMBIGUOUS, BUT I ASSUME (HAS) MEANS (HAS AS PARTS). I DON'T KNOW WHETHER FINGER IS PART OF JOHN.

6. John is a boy.
I UNDERSTAND

7. How many fingers does John have?
THE ABOVE SENTENCE IS AMBIGUOUS, BUT I ASSUME (HAS) MEANS (HAS AS PARTS). HOW MANY FINGERS PER HAND?

8. Every hand has 5 fingers.
. . . I UNDERSTAND

9. How many fingers does John have?
. . . THE ANSWER IS 10.[3]

In the early 1960s, nowhere but at MIT could such a dialogue have taken place. Not only did time sharing increase programming efficiency, it also let programmers converse with their machines. Yet the main target of these two projects was not conversational ability per se, but an exploration of the knowledge structures that would make it possible. In order to map the English sentences into the internal representations of their programs, both Raphael and Bobrow used a technique called "template matching."

As Raphael was quick to acknowledge in his thesis, this was an easy way out: humans parse sentences in a much more complex manner. The programs simply scanned sentences for sets of key words that triggered appropriate actions. For example, when Bobrow's program met the phrase

the sum of _____ and _____

it "knew" that the words in the blanks designated variables that had to be added together. Likewise,

_____ times _____

would tell the program to multiply the variables. Clearly, this scheme could work only in limited contexts. For example, when faced with the clause "the number of times I went to the movies," a truly intelligent

program should not think—as STUDENT did—of multiplying together the phrases "the number of" and "I went to the movies." For the
technique to result in some semblance of meaningful dialogue, one had
to narrow the subject matter to the small one known to the program,
and often reformulate some sentences to fit the patterns.

To see how confined SIR and STUDENT were in their respective
domains, consider the meaning of the word *has* in both programs.
STUDENT translated *has* into an equal sign (as in "John has three
dogs," which really means "The number of John's dogs = 3"). For SIR,
has meant either "has as parts" or "owns." In either case, it implied a
subordinate relationship in a tree structure. It also inferred a certain kind
of transitivity, because if a boy has (as parts) hands, and if hands have
(as parts) fingers, then boys have fingers.

Even in these restricted contexts, both programs often stumbled on
the problem of "disambiguation," or choosing between two possible
meanings of a word. In the example, statement 3 ("Each person has two
hands") appears ambiguous to SIR because it does not know whether
has means "owns" or "has as parts" (before the interviewer starts talking
to SIR, the program knows nothing about boys, hands, or fingers, and
would find it perfectly sensible for a hand to own its fingers). However,
in sentence 5 ("How many fingers does John have?"), SIR correctly
interprets *have* as "have as parts" because it has already figured out (from
statement 2) that a finger is a part of something (a hand).

This dialogue gives a good idea of the capabilities of SIR. While
impressive as a first effort, the program obviously falls far short of
human reasoning powers. As for STUDENT, Daniel Bobrow claimed
it could solve algebra story problems with the ability of a good high
school student, with one important caveat: most problems in standard
texts could not be solved by STUDENT exactly as written. However,
Bobrow was usually able to find paraphrases of the problems which
STUDENT could solve. Certainly the use of template matching for
sentence parsing was partly to blame for these flaws. Later, more powerful techniques led to closer approximations of human performance.
Following the groundbreaking work of Ross Quillian (see below), such
techniques as William Wood's augmented transition networks (ATN's)
or Roger Schank's semantic primitives (see chapter 7) allowed the computer to take a much deeper look at both the structure of the sentence
and the meanings of the words before interpreting a statement.

On the problem of knowledge representation itself, STUDENT, SIR, and ANALOGY let their authors and their common mentor Marvin Minsky define general means for representing knowledge. Knowledge could be expressed as rules such as "Multiply two variables separated by the word *times.*" It could also be held in data structures describing the templates for parsing sentences, or property lists of the type

(SUBPART, ((PLIST, NAME, HAND, NUMBER, 2) (PLIST, NAME, FINGER)))[4]

which meant in SIR that a person has two hands, and that hands in turn have fingers as parts.

Knowledge could also consist of procedures for applying the rules to the data structures, or for figuring out which rule to apply when more then one fit the situation. It was gradually becoming clear to Minsky and his students that they needed systematic ways for applying the rules and sifting through the data structures.

A Net for Meanings

Two years after SIR and STUDENT, a doctoral dissertation by Ross Quillian, under the direction of Herbert Simon at Carnegie Mellon University, broke further ground in knowledge representation. Quillian had been trained as a sociologist, but he also loved computers. Herbert Simon recalled him for me: "He came [to Carnegie Mellon] with some pretty definite ideas. The graduate students I like are the ones who come with ideas and give me a hard time, not the ones to which I tell what to do."[5]

Specifically, Quillian wanted to try to program the associative aspects of human memory, in an effort to duplicate the mechanism by which humans understand spoken language. Given Simon and Newell's general philosophy about the need to model AI research on human thinking, Quillian's proposal was well received.

Before 1966, efforts to program computers to understand language had relied on one of two methodologies. The first, exemplified by SIR and STUDENT, relied on pattern-matching techniques. An even more primitive example of this technique was a program called SYNTHEX.[6] First, sentence by sentence, indeed word by word, an entire encyclopedia was entered on magnetic tape, as was a word index as voluminous as the corpus itself. When asked a question, SYNTHEX could do nothing more sophisticated than run through the tape in search of the sentence in its encyclopedic database with the largest number of words in common with the question. (The index just speeded up the search.) If appropriate, the program then used an elementary form of syntactic analysis to reformulate the sentence as an answer to the question. For example, if asked "What do birds eat?" SYNTHEX might have found the sentence "Worms are eaten by birds," and answered: "Birds eat worms." SYNTHEX could not, however, identify the elements of an answer if they were scattered over more than one sentence. Simple variations in the form or contents of the question (like reformulating the preceding one as "How do crows feed?") also threw it off. This "Sears' catalogue" approach to information retrieval, as the method used in SYNTHEX became known, simply had to be refined.

The other methodology language programmers relied on was the newly revamped science of formal grammar. At just about the time of the Dartmouth conference, a bold and debate-loving young man from MIT named Noam Chomsky breathed new life into the sedate field of linguistics.[7] Chomsky took the extreme position that one could analyze language without any reference to its contents or meaning. Let us imagine for a moment that just as the lungs are a breathing organ, there is somewhere in our brain a nameless but real "language organ." This organ, Chomsky suggested, was so structured as to verbalize our thoughts according to very specific rules amounting to a formal mathematical system. Chomsky then proceeded to reformulate traditional grammar and syntax according to this new mathematical framework.

Not surprisingly, Chomsky's idea appealed to those computer scientists developing the higher languages like FORTRAN and LISP. Chomsky's mathematical framework for language analysis seemed to be just the thing they needed both to analyze their previous efforts and to develop even better computer language programs, because it predicted that a computer could accurately analyze languages without having any real understanding of the meanings carried by the languages.

Unfortunately, it soon became obvious that this theory did not apply to human languages. The theory should certainly have allowed for the rapid and straightforward development of automatic translation—that is, the translation of one language into another by analyzing the syntactic structure of a sentence, translating the words through a lexicon, and reassembling them according to the syntax of the target language. Yet most often such mappings yielded ludicrous results. An example often quoted in the AI community concerns the sentence "Strong is the spirit but weak is the flesh." A trip back and forth into Russian is said to have turned it into: "The vodka is good but the meat is rotten." It soon became clear that selecting the proper words in the target language required a deeper interpretation of sentences. For these reasons, many researchers started looking at semantics, or the analysis of meaning, as a tool more appropriate than syntax for computers to analyze language.

Modeling the internal representation of words in human memory seemed a good place to start, and this is what Ross Quillian attempted.[8] In a sense, Quillian's work extended the representations used in SAD SAM for family trees. Consider, for example, the two sentences:

After the strike, the president sent him away.

After the strike, the umpire sent him away.

We know the meaning of *strike* in each case: the word *president* elicits the idea of labor conflicts, while the word *umpire* calls forth an association of batters at the plate. Of the two meanings of *strike,* one is thus somehow closer to *president,* and the other to *umpire.* To find out which meaning to choose in a particular context, Quillian developed the idea of "intersection nodes." As Simon recalls, he proceeded by analogy with the magnetic core memory of early computers: memory elements were laid out in a grid, with each element at the intersection of two perpendicular wires. Only when triggered by simultaneous signals from both wires would an element light up.

Following Quillian's reasoning, imagine a network of interconnected nodes, with each node corresponding to a word in the dictionary. These nodes light up when activated by signals from other nodes. Perhaps the network is displayed on a large panel like the ones for power or telephone grids in utility control centers. We will assume that lighting up the word *president* (say, in red) sets up an activation wave that first lights up (in yellow) the words contained in the definition for *president,* then the words in the definitions of these words, and so on.

Next, we start a similar activation wave from the light for the labor kind of *strike* (there are different lights for each meaning of a word). We'll assume that when a word is lighted up by both activation waves (as a memory core element excited by both of its wires), it shows up in green on the panel. The green lights are Quillian's intersection nodes.

We can assume that for activation waves starting at *president* and *strike,* *labor* will be an intersection node, and perhaps also *worker* and *union.* Further, there probably will not be many intermediate nodes between the intersections (green nodes) and the root nodes *(strike* and *president).* Thus, the number of green nodes, and their distances from the root nodes, provide a measure of how closely presidents are associated with the labor kind of strike. Likewise, the activation waves for the words *president* and the baseball kind of strikes at the plate would intersect at fewer nodes, if any; and these should be further removed from the root nodes. This tells us that a sentence containing the word *president* is likely to be dealing with the labor kind of strike.

How well did that work in processing actual sentences? Unfortunately, Quillian couldn't tell for sure because his computer contained only thirty-two thousand words of memory. Since the program itself used up much of that space, there was only room for twenty word definitions in the machine. All the program could do was to find intersection nodes of two words in these limited samples and make up simple sentences explaining how the root words intersected at the nodes. For example, the words *cry* and *comfort* intersected at the word *sad* because:

1. cry2 is among other things to make a sad sound
2. to comfort3 can be to make2 something less2 sad.[9]

The appended numbers indicated to which of their encoded meanings the words referred. "Cry2" was to weep; and "cry1," to call out. Thus, an expanded version of the program might have disambiguated *cry* in a sentence containing *comfort.*

After obtaining his Ph.D. from Carnegie Mellon, Quillian went to work for a firm in Boston and stirred up interest for his technique at MIT. Since Quillian's networks dealt with the meanings of words, they became known as "semantic networks." When Minsky decided to collect the theses of Evans, Bobrow, Raphael, and others under a single cover and publish them, he asked Quillian to join in with a shortened version of his own dissertation. The book *Semantic Information Processing* appeared in 1968 and deeply impressed the still young and exclusive tribe of AI researchers.[10] "Seminal ideas," "a classic of the AI literature": all the epithets that make up the trappings of scientific success attached to the work of Quillian and the MIT crowd.

By that yardstick, the Carnegie Mellon crew missed the boat. Herbert Simon led a group effort on subjects similar to those of Minsky's team and published them in 1972 under the title *Representation and Meaning*.[11] "To my considerable surprise and chagrin," reported Simon, *"Representation and Meaning* made no splash at all. . . . I have always felt that I somehow let these colleagues down."[12]

Might Minsky's flamboyance explain the greater popularity of his book? Perhaps partly. Aphorisms of Minsky's, such as "The brain is just a meat machine," never failed to impress the AI crowd and often found their way to the general public. "He loves to say sensational things!" his colleague and critic Joseph Weizenbaum told me. "He wants to be provocative, . . . it's just part of his person."[13] Indeed, Minsky has often stepped out of the Spartan confines of scientific research into the limelight. The press and popular journals quote him much more often than his more reserved colleagues. His activities include consulting for movies like Stanley Kubrick's *2001,* taking part in NASA symposia about space travel, or trading literary references with his long-time friend, the late Isaac Asimov.

Some of Minsky's associates take a dim view of these activities; and Weizenbaum, for one, is not a Minsky fan. "I've known Marvin for a very long time," he told me, "and early on I began to form a hypothesis, mainly that when he dies, we'll find a letter addressed to us, to be opened after his death. And the letter will say 'Dear children, how could you have believed all the bullshit that I have told you through all these many years?' "

Minsky, of course, denied to me the existence of any such letter, but looking at him—at his slanted eyes, half Slavic, half Jewish, and the demonic rictus of his smile—I couldn't help wondering.

THE BLOCKS MICRO WORLD

The thrust of AI research in the middle and late 1960s is best illustrated by a project which, in those years, absorbed the efforts of most of the MIT AI laboratory. The project demonstrated that, if the subject of study was limited to simple geometric shapes, computers could be induced to interpret images of this world, manipulate blocks, answer questions about them, and even move about in such a world. The project was directed by Marvin Minsky and a newly found colleague who replaced John McCarthy. The Blocks Micro World project had a profound influence on other researchers, and some of its main themes were taken up in other research centers, notably Stanford.

The LOGO of a South African Maverick

In the mid-1960s, a strong new voice asserted itself among the growing chorus of AI tenors. In 1963, its owner entered Marvin Minsky's MIT office after a circuitous route through the jungles of Africa, Alan Turing's alma mater in England, and the Geneva laboratory of the psychologist/philosopher Jean Piaget.

The son of an itinerant South African entomologist researching the tsetse fly, Seymour Papert[14] spent his early childhood camping along the east coast of Africa in the early 1930s. The Papert family's way of life was straight out of a Hemingway story. Traveling along bush trails, they hunted their food and fixed their trucks when they broke down. Trucks, in fact, make up one of Papert's most vivid memories of the period. Especially gears: he would crawl under a truck and watch them spinning. Later in his youth, Papert experimented with gears and assembled them in ever more complex mechanisms. As an adult, he praised them as models through which he acquired many otherwise abstract notions. "My first brush with equations in two variables immediately evoked the [transmission] differential," said Papert.[15]

In the jungle camps, the Paperts had been the only whites for miles around. When he entered school in Johannesburg, young Seymour was ignorant of apartheid, and the concept totally baffled him. Upon realizing the illiteracy of black domestic servants of the neighborhood, the industrious ten-year-old organized evening lessons for them. It hadn't occurred to him that such activities were then illegal: the lessons were abruptly terminated, and Seymour just missed being thrown out of school. This was just the first of Papert's anti-apartheid activities, activities that would later lead the United States immigration authorities to deny him a visa for many months. In addition to raising his social consciousness, the night school experience also made Papert curious about another kind of wheels: those that go around in people's heads.

Adults justified their reluctance to let blacks sit at school desks by citing fear of contagious disease. But, reflected Papert, these are the same servants who take care of babies and cook the food in the whites' homes. How can the ruling class think like that?

As a high school student, Papert was led by such questions to take an interest in logic. He was even permitted to attend seminars on the subject at the University of Johannesburg, where he first heard arguments about the possibility of formalizing logic. Yet after taking up philosophy at the university, Papert decided mathematics was more to his liking and earned a Ph.D. in that discipline from the University of Witwatersrand in 1952. Moving to England, he continued his studies at Cambridge University, and earned a second doctorate.

Papert was then thirty years old, and his successes in mathematics, while impressive in their own right, still left unanswered his questions about the philosophy and mechanism of thinking. Jean Piaget offered him the opportunity to pursue these questions. In a series of conferences Papert attended in Paris, the Swiss psychologist explained how he had turned into scientific experiments age-old riddles about thinking which had baffled philosophers.

For example, do we learn abstract ideas, as Hume preached; or are ideas innate, as Descartes believed? Piaget decided to look at children and find out. It turned out that both philosophers were partly right: some human know-how is inborn, but most we must learn by trial and error. Yet we may learn only what our brains allow us to: the acquisition of much knowledge must await this organ's proper stage of development.

Piaget also realized that real thought differs enormously from the polished and formalized argument chains of logicians. The thread of thought is not the single leading *filium Ariadnes* of Leibnitz, but more like an interwoven, complicated fabric. It travels back and forth between error and success and links simple structures that interact to form a more complicated concept. Consider the idea of number, for example, which had fascinated Aristotle, Frege, Russell, and even McCulloch. Piaget saw it as emerging from such elemental building blocks as order, inclusion, and nearness, which develop separately beforehand. Piaget called such building blocks "mother structures." Papert later elaborated on them under the name of "micro worlds."

Enthralled with Piaget's approach, Papert joined him at his Geneva Center for Genetic Epistemology in 1958, and five years of fruitful work ensued. However, if Piaget and Papert agreed on general principles, disagreements emerged about methodology. Piaget did not see the advantage of using computers to model the kind of mental structures he postulated. Papert did see their advantage, but since computers were still a rare commodity in the late 1950s, he took to commuting to England's National Physical Laboratory to work on Alan Turing's machine. His trips to England allowed him to meet American AI researchers, who attended British conferences on occasion: Papert met Minsky at a London symposium. "It was remarkable that both he and I had discovered the same theorem about Bayes' rule [a basic theorem in probability theory] and learning machines," Minsky told me.[16]

Impressed, Warren McCulloch invited the peripatetic mathematician to work in the United States; and in the fall of 1963, right after McCarthy's departure, Papert joined Minsky at MIT.

Rarely had cooperation between two researchers been so productive: colleagues no longer said "Minsky-and-McCarthy," but "Minsky-and-Papert." The two soon initiated new research programs in the theory of computation, robotics, human perception, and child psychology. When the Artificial Intelligence Group formally became the MIT AI Laboratory in 1968, Minsky and Papert acted as co-directors.

Absent-minded like many driven intellectuals, Papert is said to have once realized, midway across the Atlantic, that he had left his wife behind in a New York airport. Colleagues report that he sometimes forgets to show up at lectures and, when he does, tends to get carried away into whatever topic fascinates him at the moment. A man of dramatic personal magnetism, he is likely to startle interviewers with juggling demonstrations at airport terminals or by stopping his car in the middle of a U-turn to formulate a thought. Papert's aphorisms, like Minsky's, tend to stick. One of his favorites is that we are to thinking as the Victorians were to sex. He aims this barb at formal education's insistence on structured, faultless expression of reasoning, in direct contradiction to the actuality that normal thought is in fact muddled, and that clear explanations come after one has reached a conclusion. This insistence leads many children to perceive their own thought processes as inadequate, to feel ashamed, and to give up on learning.

To fight this tendency, in 1967 Papert developed a softer approach to learning called LOGO. It was the first computer programming language designed for use by children. Using simple keyboard commands, children direct the movements of a screen turtle up and down, across, or in any combination of such movements. The turtle, inspired by Gray Walter's (see chapter 2) laboratory-roving contraption, is a small figure living in the micro world of a computer screen. Ostensibly, LOGO aims at letting the student master basic concepts in geometry. With each new instruction for the mouse to move one way or another, the student learns such concepts as what is a square or a triangle or a circle. But in fact, hidden within LOGO is a much more powerful educational tool, and one Papert feels is the key to all learning, not just math learning: namely, learning by experimentation. Success resides in fixing program bugs rather than in avoiding mistakes, thus removing any fixation on rote learning or first-time perfection. In LOGO, an angle isn't a meaningless figure made up of two lines with a small arc between. Instead, by programming the turtle to draw a circle, the child is invited to perceive it as a change of direction. The program tells the turtle to move forward a few steps, then rotates it by a few degrees, moves it forward again, and so on until the circle is closed.

LOGO is now a commercial and educational success, and Papert is even better known for his educational applications of computers than for his crucial contributions to AI research.

Making Computers See

In one of their first projects together, Minsky and Papert tackled the problem of making computers see. They reasoned that if they ever succeeded in making machines intelligent, having to talk to them through keyboards and printers would thoroughly spoil the fun. Further, if they wanted their machines to do something more useful than passing Turing's test, they would have to give them direct access to the world through eyes, ears, and hands. To Minsky and Papert, eyes looked like a good starting point. Even though their interest in the subject was genuine, it was by accident that the research was conducted at MIT. Marvin Minsky explained it to me in this way:

I had been advocating this pretty generally and sent proposals to Stanford Research Institute, Information International, Bolt Beranek and Newman, and two other places, suggesting that they do vision research. They in turn addressed financing requests to ARPA [Advanced Research Projects Agency]. A lady named Ruth Davis was then in charge of the relevant part of the agency. Somehow all these proposals landed on desk around the same time. She said, "This is crazy. Why don't we give the money to Minsky at MIT since he is the one who's been counseling all these people?" So they started piping more money for us to do vision. And I was mad because I had three children. You see, as a consultant to these other people, I could get double time. Whereas if you get the money for your institution, you can't keep any for yourself. The worst part was that these new projects kept me from doing any kind of consulting. I was too busy!

And so it happened that, in 1966, Minsky hired a first-year undergraduate student and assigned him a problem to solve over the summer: connect a television camera to a computer and get the machine to describe what it sees. The student was Gerald Sussman. Now a professor at MIT, he remembers his first encounter with Minsky vividly:

I didn't know Minsky at all, except for the fact that he was this famous person who was trying to make computers think. I heard other freshmen in the dormitory who said, "There are some crazy people up in Technology Square and they have a PDP-6." That was a big computer with sixteen thousand words of memory. I had only used much smaller computers, and I wanted to see a PDP-6. I went over, and a guy named [Richard] Greenblatt was in charge. He didn't seem to care if I played with the machine a bit, so I started tinkering. . . . One day I was working on a program to teach a neural network to play tic-tac-toe. I had the network displayed on the screen and was trying to figure out how to adjust the parameters. Then this bald-headed gentleman showed up: he was clearly the boss. Surely he was going to throw me out! He walked up to me and asked what I was up to. So I told him and at some point mentioned that the network was randomly interconnected: I'd set the initial weights through a random number generator.

He asked me why.

"Well, I didn't want it to have initial misconceptions," I said.

He answered, "It has them. You just don't know what they are." That struck me as the most profound remark I'd ever heard! . . .

After a while Minsky said, "How would you like to get paid for what you're doing?" And that's how I started working for him. . . . He put me in charge of the next year's vision project, and we tried to solve the problem in one summer. We couldn't!"[17]

The incident is now remembered as one of the best examples of the naïveté of early AI efforts. The truth is that, after more than a quarter century of additional research, the problem of computer vision has turned out to be one of the toughest nuts to crack in AI. As Sussman's colleague Berthold Horn, now a vision expert, facetiously pointed out to me: "You'll notice that Sussman never worked in vision again!"[18]

The difficulty is that since computers can handle only numbers, or at least discrete pieces of data amounting to numbers, the best way to represent an image inside a computer is as an array of numbers, in paint-by-number fashion.* Each number corresponds to a point in the image, and its value tells the brightness of the point. Black is zero, white is usually 255, and intermediate values coincide with varying shades of gray. Color images are turned into three monochrome images (one each for red, green, and blue), which are then also represented as arrays of numbers.

Nowadays, special electronic interfaces can turn (digitize) TV images into numbers as fast as the camera generates them. In the 1960s, early vision researchers did not have it so easy. I have described how Tom Evans and Alex Bernstein, early in the decade, had to manually enter their geometric figures as sequences of point coordinates. When they made programs to analyze very complex block scenes, Patrick Winston and David Waltz entered them into the computer in the same manner. In 1961, Larry Roberts at Lincoln Laboratory digitized photographs by scanning them mechanically with a photocell. In the late 1960s, Gerald Sussman and his friends were able to do away with photographs: they used a special electronic tube called the "image dissector" that took several minutes to digitize an image. They also used a device called a "RAND tablet," developed at the RAND Corporation with the help of Newell and Simon's associate Cliff Shaw. When you drew on the tablet with a stylus, the same lines appeared on the computer's monitor.

Turning images into numbers, however, is only an insignificant part of the problem of making computers see. Suppose that you are handed a printout of a quarter of a million numbers, which is how many dots there are in a standard TV image. Your job is to tell, by somehow massaging these numbers, what the image represents. You are not

*In fact, the human retina uses a similar representation. The mental operations that allow us to interpret images are just as complicated as those that computers must perform. Since people perform these operations unconsciously, vision appears simple and easy. It is anything but.

allowed to lay out the numbers in an array, color them, and look at them: this would just be using your eyes and visual cortex, and the computer is not equipped with such. Instead, to be in the position of Gerry Sussman in this fateful summer, you must devise a sequence of operations to perform on the numbers, a sequence that will yield a string of letters describing the contents of the image (strings such as "The Eiffel Tower seen from the Trocadero," or "Winston Churchill making the victory sign"). The sequence of operations (or program) can use all the logic and arithmetic operations available to computers, but it should work on all images an ordinary person can interpret. How's that for a summer job?

I asked Minsky, "Why put an undergrad in charge? And why Sussman?" "Because he had ideas," was the response. "Your status in this little society of ours was proportional to the ideas you had: people were good at recognizing good ideas. So Gerry was a big shot in the AI group drive." David Waltz, who was a graduate student in those days and also worked on vision projects, confirmed it: "Gerry Sussman was involved in everything. He probably had a hand in all the pieces of work that came out."[19] But if Sussman drove the AI team, what drove Sussman? "I'm in this because it's fun," he explained to me. "I'm not some kind of lofty intellectual. I like building stuff. At the bottom line, I'm a classical version of a tinkerer. And when you think something is fun, you analyze it to get better at it."

Yet when they finally realized the extent of the vision problem, Minsky and Papert attacked it with the help of a full team of graduate students, many of whom I have named. Over the rest of the 1960s, they did manage to let computers interpret images, albeit in a very restricted context. To simplify their experiments with vision, robotics, and even natural language processing, Minsky and Papert invented the Blocks Micro World. This universe was a trifle dull perhaps, but easier to comprehend than our disorderly cosmos. It consisted of simple geometrical forms: pyramids, square and rectangular blocks of various colors, and boxes to put them in.

In 1961, Larry Roberts had already designed a program that could "look" at a block construction, analyze it into its component blocks, and make a line drawing of the scene as seen from another point of view.[20] The program worked by locating sharp transitions between gray values, which corresponded to edges of objects. It then fitted straight lines to the points identified on the edges, used them to delimit block facets, determined which facets joined to form a block, corrected them for perspective, and calculated their distances from the camera. In order to identify the component blocks, however, Roberts's program needed internal descriptions of them: it could not have recognized a block of a different shape from those already in memory. This strategy was at odds with the ability of people to see unknown objects, and required improvements.

Three years later, Adolfo Guzman came up with a program that could analyze scenes made of blocks of almost any shape, as long as they had planar surfaces and did not contain holes.[21] Guzman made heavy use of the edges of the blocks: for his program to spot them well enough, he had to cheat a little and paint the blocks in black with white stripes on the edges. To tell the blocks apart, Guzman's program relied on how the edges of the blocks joined together in the image.

For example, some junctions, shaped like the letter T, resulted from one edge (the vertical stroke in an upright T) being occluded by another block. In this case, the surfaces on either side of the vertical stroke belonged to the same block, and the one above the horizontal stroke, to another block. Using such simple heuristics, Guzman was able to link together the visible sides of blocks of unknown shapes. Upon reading about Guzman's work, two independent researchers, Max Clowes and David Huffman (the latter well known for a coding technique that bears his name), separately came up with a more elegant and powerful algorithm for it.[22]

Yet a major problem remained. It bothered David Waltz, who was then looking for a Ph.D. project acceptable to Marvin Minsky. In a complex scene with many overlapping objects, the problem of defining objects through their edges became unsolvable: there were too many ways in which different edges could combine to form an object. To reduce the number of possible combinations, Waltz used a technique that became known as "constraint propagation." It began with the trivial observation that a straight-line edge has two ends. At each end, it joins with other edges in a distinctive fashion. In addition to the T junction I mentioned, there were the L, the "fork," and the "arrow" junctions. Just as Guzman had realized that a single junction constrains the objects to which the adjacent surfaces can belong, Waltz understood that a pair of junctions at each end of a line imply an even stiffer set of constraints. If one then travels to a third junction by following an edge, these constraints propagate over to the new junction, which even further limits the number of possibilities. Such considerations rapidly led to a unique definition of the objects by their edges. This time Minsky agreed it was a clever hack, and Waltz obtained his degree.

A triumph of the Blocks Micro World effort was Patrick Winston's program.[23] So impressed were Minsky and Papert by Winston's abilities that not long after he earned his Ph.D., they made him director of the AI Laboratory so as to have more time for research themselves. "It all came out of a footnote in my thesis proposal," Winston recalled to me. "I had this idea that maybe differences in semantic nets might be useful in learning. The thesis was a consequence of lucky explorations rather than a carefully designed project handed to me by a person or committee."[24]

By considering various block scenes containing examples of simple structures, Winston's program learned to recognize them. For example, after looking at several examples of arches, and being told that they were arches, the program made up the description "two blocks supporting a third one." As illustrated in figure 4.2, this depiction was a semantic network similar to one of Quillian's. Armed with this knowledge, the program recognized later instances of arches. It was even possible to refine the descriptions by showing to the program near misses: instances of structures that did not quite correspond to the definitions. For example, Winston could show his program constructions resembling arches, but in which the two supporting blocks touched each other. He would also tell it that these were not-quite arches. The program would realize how they differed from true arches and change its definition of an arch to "two non-touching blocks supporting a third one."

In yet another Blocks Micro World experiment, Minsky and Papert used the vision program to make a robotic arm construct block structures. The arm had a moving shoulder, three elbows, and a wrist; it used fourteen hydraulic cylinders for muscles. Before attempting to grab any blocks, the robot would hold its hand in front of the camera and wave it a little to see whether it really was itself. The computer then adjusted the coordinate system used in the image to make it correspond with the coordinates of the hand. First tries didn't work very well, and the research team had to add sensors to the fingers, and more programs to let the hand verify that things were where the eye told it they were. Still more vision programs had to make sure there was nothing in the way when the hand moved from place to place.

To decide how to erect a structure, higher-level programs planned

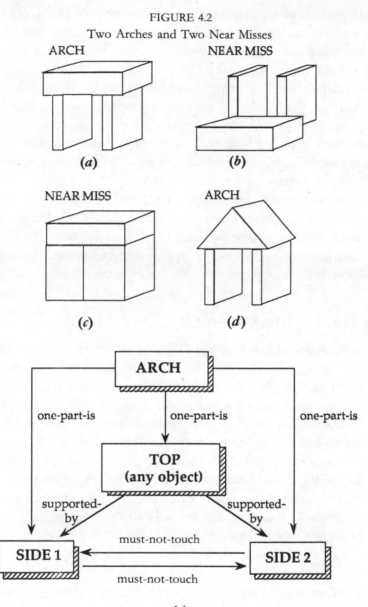

FIGURE 4.2

Two Arches and Two Near Misses

ARCH

NEAR MISS

(a)

(b)

NEAR MISS

ARCH

(c)

(d)

ARCH

one-part-is   one-part-is   one-part-is

TOP
(any object)

supported-by   supported-by

must-not-touch

SIDE 1   SIDE 2

must-not-touch

(e)

Patrick Winston used these examples to teach his program the concept of an arch. Figure (*a*) provides the program with an initial definition. The near miss in (*b*) tells the program that the third block must lie on the two supporting ones. Near miss (*c*) shows that the supporting blocks must not touch each other. The last example of an arch (*d*) illustrates that the upper block can be any object that will stay on the two supports. The resulting semantic net description of the arch appears in (*e*).

Source: Patrick H. Winston, "Learning Structural Descriptions from Examples," doctoral diss., published as Project MAC Report MAC TR-76, MIT, Cambridge, Mass., 1970.

which blocks to pick and in what order. More intricate planning routines then worked out the details of any movement ahead of time. For reliability, programs verified at every step that the state of the world matched the plans. Slight errors and slips in grabbing a block, or unwanted displacements of other blocks by the hand, had to be accounted for. All in all, the MIT robot team felt their project almost matched in complexity NASA's Apollo moon-landing program then under way. Eventually a team led by Patrick Winston and Berthold Horn built a system called Copy-Demo that could look at a block construction and build a mirror image of it.

In the late 1960s, other hand-eye robots existed at both John McCarthy's AI laboratory in Stanford and Scotland's Edinburgh University. Both robots experimented with block manipulation. The Stanford one even matured to the more complex assignment of putting together an automobile water pump from randomly scattered parts.

An Electronic Person?

A team at Stanford Research Institute took a more daring step: they put their robot on wheels and let it move around. The participation of Bertram Raphael, who had joined SRI after studying under Minsky at MIT, made this research effort a second-generation project. Headed by Charles Rosen, the team also included Richard Fikes and Cordell Greene, as well as Nils Nilsson (who later headed the AI group at SRI). Rosen's team could well afford their audacity, since their financing also came from the almost bottomless coffers of ARPA, which by then had recognized Stanford as an AI research center of the same class as MIT and Carnegie Mellon. The military hoped to get out of the exercise a device for the stealthy collection of information behind enemy lines: in effect, a mechanical spy.

Assembled in 1969, the robot was a far cry from a mechanical James Bond. Alone, the wheel-mounted square cabinet making up its body would have projected a semblance of functionality; but topped as it was with TV camera, range finder, and radio-link antenna, it added up to a piece of junk sculpture. The fastening of the parts and the cart's suspension certainly weren't up to military ratings, and the assemblage shuddered at the slightest bump. They called it Shakey.[25]

It existed in a kind of life-sized Blocks Micro World, consisting of seven rooms connected by eight doors. In some of the rooms were square boxes that Shakey could stack and push around. Following instructions given by keyboard in a simplified form of English, it would negotiate its way around obstacles, locate a box in one room, and move it to the top of another box in a different room. To the uncertainties plaguing its hand-eye predecessors, Shakey had to add those about its own position. As for MIT's block-handling robot, thousands of lines of computer code embodied the interlocking facets of its behavior.

Truly innovative to Shakey was a control procedure called STRIPS, for STanford Research Institute Problem Solver. Nils Nilsson and his colleague R. E. Fikes had initially devised STRIPS as an improvement upon Newell and Simon's General Problem Solver.[26] As I discussed in chapter 3, GPS operated by first determining a difference between the actual state of the world and its goal. For each domain of application, programmers had to define and code a new difference-calculating process. Further, a difference table, also specific to each application, allowed GPS to choose rules (or operations) able to reduce each kind of difference. STRIPS obviated the need for defining differences and difference tables by having rules made up of three parts: the preconditions, the delete list, and the add formula. For a hand-eye robot, the rule for picking up a block x might have contained the following entries:

Preconditions: ONTABLE(x), HANDEMPTY, CLEAR(x)

Delete list: ONTABLE(x), HANDEMPTY

Add formula: HOLDING(x)

The preconditions stated that before attempting to pick up block x, the robot must make sure that x was indeed on the table, that the robot's hand was not holding another object, and that there was no other object on top of x. After picking up the block, the delete list told the robot to correct its mental representation of the world as follows: x was no longer on the table, and the robot's hand was no longer empty. Last, to this mental universe must be added that the robot was then holding block x.

In STRIPS, both the state of the world and the goal were defined as lists of predicates like the preceding ones: ONTABLE(B), ON(C,B), CLEAR(C), etc. . . . The differences between the goal and the state were simply component predicates of the goal unmatched by the state. Likewise, rules relevant to reducing the difference were simply those whose add lists contained at least one of the elements missing in the goal. The difference calculating function and difference table were thus implicit in the rule definitions. Through appropriate processing of the precondition and add lists, STRIPS could work out a plan, or a sequence of operations, to achieve the goals. To pile up blocks in a certain way, it could for example figure out which blocks to pick up and in what order.

Through a device called a "triangle table," STRIPS could even learn to think faster. The idea was to lump together the effect of a sequence of operations by working out their composite precondition, add, and delete lists. Thus, a plan simply became a new operation to add to the list of existing operations. STRIPS could also generalize its plans by replacing specific block names with variable names. Thus, having once figured out how to stack up two particular blocks called A and B, it could later draw on this knowledge to stack up any two blocks x and y.

In 1970, Shakey got a bit of unwanted publicity in *Life* magazine[27] when a sensation-seeking reporter dubbed it "the first electronic person." This article perfectly illustrates the kind of overstatement AI tends to elicit in the media. Among other absurdities, the reporter, Brad Darrach, claimed that Shakey "could travel about the moon for months at a time without a single beep of direction from the earth." (In fact, the robot could barely negotiate straight corridors!)

Marvin Minsky was quoted in the article as saying "with quiet certitude: 'In from three to eight years we will have a machine with the general intelligence of an average human being.' "[28] Upon seeing his statement in print, however, Minsky vehemently denied having made it and even issued a circular denouncing the article. Fortunately or unfortunately, the letter never went beyond the AI community, and the editor of *Life* showed no sign of having received it.

SHRDLU

In 1968 and 1969, the Blocks Micro World made up the subject of a celebrated doctoral thesis.[29] Its author was Terry Winograd, a student of Seymour Papert. To all interested, Winograd gravely explained the origin of his program's awkward name: SHRDLU. Winograd pointed out that it listed in order the seventh through twelfth most frequently used letters in English. Typesetters could generate this sequence of letters by sweeping the second row of their special keyboard, and used it as a convenient test of their equipment. Since Winograd's work became a landmark in the field, popular books about AI still quote this explanation. Reporters fell for it, even though it bears absolutely no connection with the purpose of the program; and, in fact, the name was a joke.[30] Winograd had picked it up from *MAD* magazine, which uses the word SHRDLU for mythical monsters and other inelegant oddities.

In SHRDLU, the Blocks Micro World existed only as model within the computer (in this case, a PDP-10 with a quarter-million words of memory). For the benefit of the person running the program, SHRDLU also generated a simulation of the Blocks Micro World on a screen. The display showed blocks and pyramids of various colors and a box to put them in. A simulated robot arm manipulated the objects, under the control of a program that communicated with the user in ordinary English. The user could ask it questions and give it commands. The program would respond with information about the positions of the blocks and could also explain its past actions and their reasons.

The following excerpts from a dialogue with SHRDLU refer to the blocks arrangement in figure 4.3; SHRDLU's answers are in capital letters.

FIGURE 4.3
The Block Scene Manipulated by SHRDLU in the Example

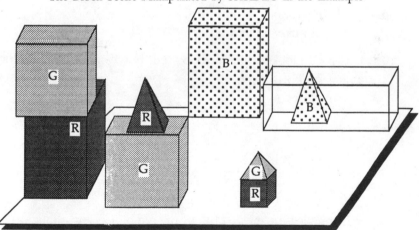

Source: Terry Winograd, *Understanding Natural Language* (New York: Academic Press, 1972), p. 8.

1. pick up a red block.
   OK

2. find a block which is taller than the one you are holding and put it into the box.
   BY "IT," I ASSUME YOU MEAN THE BLOCK WHICH IS TALLER THAN THE ONE I AM HOLDING
   OK

3. what does the box contain?
   THE BLUE PYRAMID AND THE BLUE BLOCK

4. what is the pyramid supported by?
   THE BOX

5. how many blocks are not in the box?
   FOUR OF THEM

6. is at least one of them narrower than the one which I told you to pick up?
   YES, THE RED CUBE

7. is it supported?
   YES, BY THE TABLE

8. can the table pick up blocks?
   NO

9. the blue pyramid is mine
   I UNDERSTAND

10. I own all blocks which are not red, but I don't own anything which supports a pyramid
    I UNDERSTAND

11. do I own the box?
    NO

12. do I own anything in the box?
    YES, TWO THINGS: THE BLUE BOX AND THE BLUE PYRAMID

13. will you please stack up both of the red blocks and either a green cube or a pyramid?
    OK

14. is there a large block behind a pyramid?

    YES, THREE OF THEM: A LARGE RED ONE, A LARGE GREEN CUBE
    AND THE BLUE ONE

15. put a small one into the green cube which supports a pyramid

    OK

16. put the littlest pyramid on top of it

    OK

17. had you touched any pyramid before you put the green one on
    the little cube?

    YES, THE GREEN ONE

18. when did you pick it up?

    WHILE I WAS STACKING UP THE RED CUBE, A LARGE RED BLOCK
    AND A LARGE GREEN CUBE

19. why?

    TO GET RID OF IT

20. why did you do that?

    TO CLEAR OFF THE RED CUBE

21. why did you clear off that cube?

    TO PUT IT ON A LARGE GREEN CUBE

22. why did you do that?

    TO STACK UP THE RED CUBE, A LARGE RED BLOCK AND A LARGE
    GREEN CUBE

23. why did you do that?

    BECAUSE YOU ASKED ME TO[31]

This performance beat anything the key-word and pattern-matching techniques had ever achieved. With SHRDLU, a computer and its user could, for the first time, exchange meaningful information in ordinary English. In a limited sense, the ability of the program to examine its motivations also represented the first glimmering of self-awareness in a computer. Carl Hewitt, who had devised the language in which Winograd wrote SHRDLU, remembered that "it proceeded to completely snow everybody. People said 'AI is finally here!' "[32] SHRDLU was the Wonder Hack!

There were many innovative things about SHRDLU. For instance, in SHRDLU, a word didn't have a definition, and the program contained no such thing as a dictionary. A word was represented as a small program, called at the appropriate point in sentence analysis.

Winograd also believed that syntax (the structure of a sentence) and its meaning are inextricably linked. For him, sentence analysis involved both structure and meaning at the same time. As soon as a fragment of syntactic structure took shape, a semantic program stepped in to see whether it made sense.

For example, suppose we had told SHRDLU "Put the blue pyramid on the blue block out of the box." Syntactic parsing might have identified "the blue pyramid on the blue block" as the object to manipulate. Checking with the figure, semantics would have revealed no blue pyramid on a blue block, and instructed syntax to try another parsing. Likewise, SHRDLU knew that the table could not pick up blocks (see statement 8 in the example). Winograd called this kind of information a "semantic marker" and used it to disambiguate sentences.

To write SHRDLU, Winograd used a version of the LISP-based PLANNER language developed by Carl Hewitt and implemented by himself, Gerald Sussman, and Eugene Charniak.[33] The idea behind PLANNER was to automate tedious programming tasks like looping and backtracking, so that one could write a program without worrying about them.

"There was this big disparity," Hewitt told me, "between the way people programmed in LISP using things like lambda and other specialized functions, whereas in fact they were talking in terms of goals, subgoals, and plans. So I decided, 'We'll have a programming language that has plans, goals, and assertions!' "

Winograd gives the example of trying to program the task of finding a red cube that supports a pyramid. In PLANNER, one would formulate this task as follows:

```
(GOAL (IS ?X1 BLOCK))

(GOAL (COLOR-OF ?X1 RED))

(GOAL (CUBE ?X1))
```

(GOAL (IS ?X2 PYRAMID))

(GOAL (SUPPORT ?X1 ?X2))

When the first statement took control, it made SHRDLU look at all objects until it found a block. Programming a similar search in LISP would have required several statements. Upon reaching its goal of finding a block, the first statement in the example relinquished control to the second statement, which checked whether the object was red. If not, the second statement returned control to the first one, in a process called "backtracking." If the object was indeed red, the second statement gave control to the third statement. In this way, looping and backtracking were completely transparent to the programmer. This transparency also made possible the automation of program writing: a part of SHRDLU, in fact, translated the phrase "a red cube which supports a pyramid" into the preceding statements; SHRDLU then executed them.

The flip side of the coin was that for the scheme to work, an active statement had to take complete control of SHRDLU. In PLANNER, it was thus impossible to separate the knowledge embodied in the statements from the procedure that exploited this knowledge and controlled program execution. "There wouldn't be any superintelligent module that knew all," as Hewitt put it to me. Often a statement had other statements embedded in it, which in turn activated more program fragments elsewhere. Each program fragment acted like an independent agent which interacted with other agents in its own way. As a result, SHRDLU's code resembled a tangled knot which resists unraveling.

One advantage of PLANNER, Hewitt remembered, was that "You didn't have to cook up some crazy difference table. That's a hard way to program." As Allen Newell confirmed to me later, that made up another important aspect of PLANNER. It marked the forefront of a rebellion against Newell and Simon's GPS, as well as against uniform theorem-proving methods such as resolution that were then popular. With PLANNER, the MIT school of thought took yet another step into the antilogical realm that became its trademark.

Because of its lack of structure, critics such as Y. A. Wilks have denied that SHRDLU contributed to our understanding of the mechanisms of thought or that it embodied any theory of language.[34] Their inherent scruffiness has now made PLANNER-like languages fall into disfavor. Yet Marvin Minsky, for one, maintains that natural intelligences are probably organized in this way. His Society of Mind theory describes the architecture of thought as a tangled hierarchy of independent agents, which look somewhat like the program fragments of SHRDLU.[35]

For all its brilliance, SHRDLU was but a shooting star in the firmament of AI. It soon became clear that it could not be extended beyond the Blocks Micro World. The simplicity, logic, and isolation of this domain allowed the appearance of intelligent dialogue by simply dodging difficult language issues. Even within the Blocks Micro World, such idiosyncratic sentences as "How many blocks go on top of each other?" baffled SHRDLU.

Winograd himself later turned toward other approaches to natural language processing. He realized that in the human mind no direct correspondence exists, as in SHRDLU, between sentences and the processes they trigger; that an intermediate layer of world and self-knowledge exists between words and those processes. Further, these processes vary from person to person because knowledge structures differ among individuals. In truth, a sentence acts as a perturbation to an active mind. Its results depend not on what the sentence refers to in the world, but on how it changes the activity of the mind.[36]

MODELING THE BRAIN: THE PERCEPTRON

At the same time Minsky and other Dartmouth conference alumni were busily exploring the symbol-processing approach to AI, other researchers who had now entered the field were trying still to model the brain directly. Their most outspoken advocate had been a classmate of Minsky's at the Bronx High School of Science in the early 1940s. Born in New Rochelle, New York, in 1928, Frank Rosenblatt graduated in social psychology from Cornell University in 1950. In 1956, he earned a Ph.D. in experimental psychopathology from the same university. It was at Cornell's Aeronautical Laboratory that he developed the neural-network device that involved him in an epic controversy with his former classmate. Minsky, as we recall, had been disappointed about his own experimentation with neural nets at Harvard, and his theoretical analysis of them in his doctoral thesis at Princeton.

The Perceptron first existed as a simulation in an IBM 704 computer. In 1958, Rosenblatt introduced it to the press with the distinctive flourish that eventually brought the wrath of the scientific community upon him. Under the title "Human Brains Replaced?" the prestigious magazine *Science* reported on the invention as "no ordinary mechanical mind which stores up information and regurgitates it. . . . Perceptron may eventually be able to learn, make decisions, and translate languages."[37]

In the same year the *New Yorker* quoted Rosenblatt as saying that "[The Perceptron] can tell the difference between a dog and a cat, though so far, according to our calculations, it wouldn't be able to tell whether the dog was to the left or to the right of the cat. We still have to teach it depth perception and refinements of judgment."[38]

As computer vision systems of the early 1990s still cannot in general tell a cat from a dog, Rosenblatt probably meant that the Perceptron could *in principle* acquire this ability. Yet when the press reported on hardware implementation of the Perceptron two years later, it was obvious that the machine needed somewhat more than "refinements of judgment" in order to confront the world. The machine's recognition abilities stopped at letters of the alphabet and changing the typeface yielded an error rate of 21 percent. Still, *Science News Letter* labeled the machine "a breakthrough in data processing."[39]

In truth, the Perceptron was a good idea, and Rosenblatt's problems most likely stemmed from an excess of enthusiasm. His invention brought together Oliver Selfridge's Pandemonium with the simplified neurons of McCulloch and Pitts. A schematic diagram of a Perceptron appears in figure 4.4. It was simply a layer of McCulloch-Pitts neurons sandwiched between sensor and activation units. Each sensor played the role of a Selfridge demon, sending an electric signal ("yell") proportional to the intensity of whatever quantity it was assigned to detect. In the alphabet-recognition application, the sensors were an array of photocells in the focal plane of a lens, like the film in a camera. Each photocell "yelled" according to how much light fell on it. The McCulloch-Pitts neurons made up the second level. Each neuron added up a weighed sum of sensor signals. (A "weighed sum" is when, before adding a new number to the total, you multiply it by a certain weight, which will make it count more or less in the result.)

FIGURE 4.4
A Perceptron

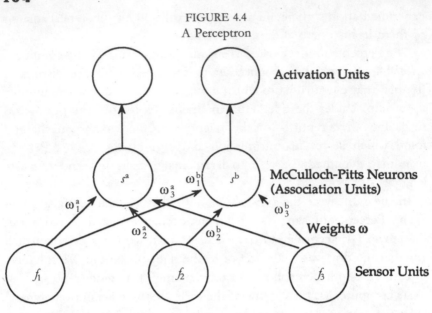

When the weighed sums of their inputs exceeded a certain number called the threshold, the McCulloch-Pitts neurons fired and triggered units in the third layer of the Perceptron. These activation units translated the neuron's signals into something intelligible to the outside world, such as a display of the letter being identified. In an animal, activation units would correspond to muscles, and sensor units, to the animal's senses.

Rosenblatt's main contribution was a trick for adjusting the values of the weights used in the sums to let the Perceptron learn to recognize certain stimuli. Say we were training the machine to recognize letters of the alphabet, and the activation units were lights labeled with the various letters. After training, the proper light should flash on in response to a given letter. Just like Sussman with the PDP-6, Rosenblatt made the initial connections at random, in an effort to simulate the neural connections in an infant's brain. Thus, any light or collection of lights could light up at the beginning of the training period. When a wrong light flashed on, Rosenblatt proceeded to decrease by a fixed amount the weights affecting its connections to the sensory units. When a light should have flashed on and didn't, he increased the weights. When the right light flashed on, he left the weights unchanged.

Rosenblatt went as far as formulating the following theorem, which became known as the "Perceptron Learning Rule":

> If a Perceptron is capable at all of distinguishing between certain input patterns, the procedure above can teach it to do so in a finite number of showings of the patterns.

The learning rule appeared in 1962 in Rosenblatt's *Principles of Neurodynamics*,[40] in which he also made claims of a general nature on the superiority of the neural-network approach over the symbolic approach for the study of intelligence. In truth, Rosenblatt did not back them up with well-structured scientific arguments, and the book's long-winded character did little to serve its author.

In the late 1950s and early 1960s, other workers independently came to conclusions similar to Rosenblatt's, and perhaps for more valid reasons. Among them was Wilfrid K. Taylor, who analyzed the properties of a circuit similar to the Perceptron which became known as the "Taylor net."[41] Bernard Widrow of Stanford University, who had attended the Dartmouth conference, developed with his student M. E. Hoff a circuit they called Adaline, for "adaptive linear neuron."[42] They later extended it into the multiple neuron Madaline, which recognized visual patterns and spoken words. In Germany, the researcher Karl Steinbuch described how a circuit he called the Learning Matrix could be taught to learn patterns in a training procedure similar to Rosenblatt's.[43] Many other researchers followed their example, and the investigation of artificial neural networks enjoyed an early flowering throughout most of the 1960s.

In 1969, a book by Marvin Minsky and Seymour Papert had the effect of a rock thrown into the buzzing activity of this little pond.[44] Research in Perceptrons and their cohorts, the authors showed, had overlooked major weaknesses in the capabilities of these circuits. The catch lay in the preamble to the Perceptron Learning Rule: "When a Perceptron can be trained *at all* to distinguished between patterns, it can be so trained in a finite number of steps."[45] There are, in fact, many and important patterns Perceptrons cannot distinguish.

Consider, for example, images made up of a single dot. If a Perceptron can learn to recognize letters of the alphabet, one would expect it to react to this simplest pattern of all. The fact is that a Perceptron cannot learn to go above threshold when a single dot appears anywhere in an image, and stay below threshold for all other images, including blanks. For a similar reason, Perceptrons cannot perform the two-bit parity operation, also called EXCLUSIVE-OR, or XOR. Given two inputs that can take only the values of 1 and 0, this operation returns a 1 if both inputs have the same value (that is, 00 or 11). It returns a zero if the inputs have different values (01 or 10). It so happens that the negation of XOR—that is, the function NOT(XOR)—is a computationally universal operation, in the following sense: one can express all other binary operations in terms of NOT(XOR), and it is in principle possible to assemble an entire computer out of electronic chips performing only the NOT(XOR) operation. In order to avoid triviality, a computing system must possess this ability to detect the similarity of inputs: Perceptrons cannot perform an XOR or its negation. Other binary operations that Perceptrons can perform, such as OR and AND, are not computationally universal.

Minsky and Papert strongly disparaged previous work in Perceptrons:

> Perceptrons have been widely publicized as "pattern recognition" or "learning machines" and as such have been discussed in a large number of books, journal articles, and voluminous "reports." Most of this writing . . . is without scientific value and we will not usually refer by name to the works we criticize. . . . Appalled at the persistent influence of perceptrons (and similar ways of thinking) on practical pattern recognition, we determined to set out our work as a book.[46]

To further their claim to new ground rules in this arena, Minsky and Papert entitled their book *Perceptrons,* thus appropriating Rosenblatt's invention by virtue of word power. Such was the authority of Minsky and Papert at that time that the book brought neural-network research in the United States to a virtual halt. Papert claimed later that it was mostly a mistake, and that half of *Perceptrons* presented results in favor of the Perceptron, some of them "very surprising and hitherto unknown."[47] Minsky, for his part, called the book an "overkill,"[48] in two ways. First, he agreed with Papert and felt that for all their failings, Perceptrons still packed a lot of classifying power in their simple structure. They probably played a role in the human brain, Minsky believed. Second, the book proved all the easy theorems about Perceptrons, and left nothing of consequence to do for anyone who hadn't spent years working along the particular approach the authors had used. Hence the research vacuum that followed it.

Perceptrons was written as David Waltz was working on his thesis. He recalled the episode for me as follows:

> Marvin and Seymour really were interested in Perceptrons. I and a bunch of other students took a seminar from them, where the goal was to figure out as much about Perceptrons as possible. We were merely to explore in a methodical sense what they were capable of and what they weren't, and try to characterize them in some way. Perceptrons were then hyped pretty heavily, as much as expert systems or neural networks in general were hyped later on. And out of that came the book. . . . I can't speak for what was in Minsky or Papert's heart, but certainly as a graduate student I didn't feel [I was] being assigned to any kind of vendetta or attempt to debunk the field. . . . [Minsky and Papert] didn't try to deliberately mislead . . . If they had figured out you could do more [with neural networks], I think they probably would have jumped on it and tried to do it."

Shortly after the appearance of *Perceptrons,* a tragic event slowed research in the field even further: Frank Rosenblatt, by then a broken man according to rumor, drowned in a boating accident. Having lost its most convincing promoter, neural-network research entered an eclipse that lasted fifteen years.

Many neural-network investigators still hold a grudge against Minsky and Papert, whom they blame for delaying the bloom of their discipline until the 1980s. Indeed, Minsky and Papert had declined to explore a wide-open avenue of research about Perceptrons, conjecturing it would lead to a dead end. As later investigators found out, it did not.

5

CLOUDS ON THE AI HORIZON

I know from experience that challenging these assumptions will produce reactions similar to those of an insecure believer when his faith is challenged. —Hubert Dreyfus

You don't get very far arguing with a man about his religion, and these are essentially religious issues to the Dreyfuses and Weizenbaums of the world. —Herbert Simon

After Herbert Simon's celebrated forecast in 1957 that "in a visible future [machines will handle problems in a range] coextensive to the range to which the human mind has been applied," he went on to predict:

1. That within ten years, a digital computer will be the world's chess champion, unless the rules bar it from competition.
2. That within ten years a digital computer will discover and prove an important new mathematical theorem. . . .
4. That within ten years most theories in psychology will take the form of computer programs, or of qualitative statements about the characteristics of computer programs.[1]

With the public reading of these lines from a paper by himself and Allen Newell, the future Nobel laureate set the boastful tone that marked the relationship between AI and the news media for many years afterward. One year later, Newell, Shaw, and Simon reiterated these estimates even more optimistically:

> In another place, we have predicted that within ten years a computer will discover and prove an important mathematical theorem. On the basis of our [recent] experience with the heuristics of logic and chess, we are willing to add the further prediction that only moderate extrapolation is required from the capacities of programs already in existence to achieve the additional problem-solving power needed for such simulation.[2]

Only slightly abashed seven years later, in 1965, Simon still maintained that "machines will be capable, within twenty years, of doing any work that a man can do."[3] And in a 1967 book, Marvin Minsky proposed a substantially similar forecast: "Within a generation . . . few compartments of intellect will remain outside the machine's realm—the problem of creating 'artificial intelligence' will be substantially solved."[4] John McCarthy, for his part, founded the Stanford AI Project in 1963 "with the then-plausible goal of building a fully intelligent machine in a decade."[5]

Yet as I write these lines a generation later, true artificial intelligences still lie far in the future. Few psychologists know how to program a computer, and the world chess champion is still a human being. A hundred-thousand-dollar prize for the discovery of a new mathematical theorem by a computer remains unclaimed. The reason for this relative lack of progress is that soon after Minsky's last optimistic pronouncement, AI research ran into serious difficulties. Several AI projects disappointed their sponsors on both sides of the Atlantic, and fundamental questions on the ultimate feasibility and morality of AI were asked, some of them by AI researchers.

EARLY DISAPPOINTMENTS

In the late 1960s, the dramatic failure of attempts to make computers translate human languages showed that the machines could not easily imitate human activities. In the early 1970s, attempts to expand the Blocks Micro World and other such experiments into wider fields of applications foundered, and the Defense Department itself started to doubt the ability of AI researchers in all three main research centers (MIT, Carnegie Mellon, and Stanford) to deliver what they promised.

The Failure of Automatic Translation

The first intimation of trouble for AI was the demise of the related field of automatic translation. In 1966, the National Research Council brutally ended all support for such research in the United States. Following the Second World War, the NRC, together with military funding agencies, had launched an intensive research effort in this direction. After the successful use of computers to break German secret codes in England, scientists saw translating written text from one language to another as no more complicated than decoding a cipher. The CIA relished the prospect of massive, effortless translations of Russian publications. However, as we have seen, the processing of "natural language," as opposed to the artificial languages of ciphers and those used to program computers, turned out to be much more difficult than expected. Automating dictionary look-up and the application of grammar rules yielded ludicrous results. After twenty years and twenty million dollars in outlays, no solution was yet in sight; and an NRC committee scuttled the research effort.[6]

The acronym ALPAC, for Automated Language Processing Advisory Committee, still brings shudders to scientists investigating the linguistic side of AI. Fortunately for them, the leading AI research groups in MIT, Stanford, and Carnegie Mellon were not involved in automatic translation and escaped most of the flack. Their recent work on the semantic aspect of language even allowed them to claim a potential solution for word-disambiguation problems. Yet automatic translation was a computer-related field for which expectations had run high. The bitter disappointment it led to should have warned AI researchers of the dangers of hyperbolic claims. And, indeed, not much later, they ran into troubles of their own.

In the late 1960s at Carnegie Mellon, Newell and Simon, with the help of a doctoral student, George W. Ernst, realized the limitations of their General Problem Solver, and moved on to other techniques.[7]

The main problem with GPS had to do with representation: The programmer had to feed information to GPS in a highly stylized way, corresponding to the action-precondition format. One had to work very hard to define each new problem, and the program made relatively small contributions to the solution. Unfortunately, it soon became clear that Planner and STRIPS were not much better in this respect. In fairness to the designers of GPS, Planner, and STRIPS, these systems had never been intended as final solutions, and their authors realized that they left unsolved numerous problems. Today, the likes of GPS, Planner, and STRIPS are simply considered useful components of more general systems.

To realize how far these programs were from genuine intelligence, consider the too-high banana problem again (see chapter 3). One could argue that simply identifying the actions and objects applicable to this task made up 90 percent of the solution: these systems addressed only the other 10 percent. For the monkey, defining the goal of reaching the banana was already a major achievement: hunger probably acted as the prime motivation. Even though feeling hungry is not an intelligent act as such, it is nevertheless part of the individual's overall strategy to survive. The problem of motivating intelligent actions is one that early systems ignored, and it is still largely unsolved. Visually scanning a room and identifying a chair is a task of major proportions. Yet the problem as stated here took it for granted. Identifying the chair as "something to climb up" is yet another conceptual leap. Furthermore, among the thousands of actions the monkey could perform, how did it determine the four pertinent ones: "move chair," "climb up chair," "jump," and "move self"? Why did the animal reject out of hand as unproductive such activities as trying to climb the wall, banging at the door of the room, or gnawing at the backrest of the chair?

Another important problem uncovered by early AI work had to do with generality. It soon became clear that a program could not contain many problem descriptions at the same time, and preserve its working efficiency. Some means was required first to identify the kind of problem one was facing, and then to call up a program equipped with the suitable expertise. But then, how is one to call in the proper expert without knowing as much as the experts?

Finally, remember the aircraft guns whose instability Wiener solved (see chapter 2). The interaction of many simple feedback mechanisms caused the guns' wild behavior. Since GPS and its later counterparts also relied on the interaction of many feedback mechanisms (albeit of a more abstract nature, like means-ends analysis), they were not exempt from instability problems. As a result, AI programs at times behaved in unexpected ways—and still do!

The Micro Worlds' Limitations

We saw in the last chapter how in the late 1960s and early 1970s, Minsky and Papert at MIT led their students to perform a series of experiments that became known as the Micro Worlds project, following Papert's educational terminology. They defined the general thrust of the effort so:

> Each model—or "micro-world" as we shall call it—is very schematic; it talks about a fairyland in which things are so simplified that almost every statement about them would be literally false if asserted about the real world. . . . Nevertheless we feel that [micro worlds] are so important that we are assigning a large portion of our effort towards developing a collection of these micro-worlds and finding how to use the suggestive and predictive powers of the models without being overcome by their incompatibility with the literal truth.[8]

Just as physicists learn about the real world by performing experiments in carefully controlled situations, Minsky and Papert hoped to extract from these toy examples techniques and principles applying to more general situations. They also thought it might be possible to gradually expand some of the micro worlds until they encompassed wider segments of reality. The Blocks world in which SHRDLU lived made up one such micro world. As he pointed out in a later publication, SHRDLU's author, Terry Winograd, initially thought the approach embodied in the program to be open-ended: "[Our system can] engage in dialogs that simulate in many ways the behavior of a human language user. For a wider field of discourse, the conceptual structure would have to be expanded in details, and perhaps in some aspects of its overall organization."[9]

Minsky and Papert considered other micro worlds in varying degrees of detail. The best example is perhaps the world of children's stories, which Eugene Charniak explored in his 1972 doctoral thesis. To determine what his program understood about the stories, Charniak asked it questions about them. A typical story might have started:

Fred was going to the store. Today was Jack's birthday and Fred was going to get a present.

Possible questions would be:

> Why is Fred going to the store?
> Who is the present for?
> Why is Fred buying a present?

Note that the text does not give explicit answers to these queries. As Charniak put it: "The story does not say: 'Fred was going to the store *because* he . . .'" The story does not even contain a full implicit answer; one cannot logically deduce an answer from the statements in the story without using general knowledge about the world such as:

> Objects "got" at stores are usually "bought."
> Presents are often bought at stores.
> If a person is having a birthday, he (she) is likely to get presents.[10]

The fundamental question, to which Charniak tried to give a partial solution in his thesis, was thus: "How do we incorporate common-sense knowledge into the process of understanding natural language?" "With great difficulty!" he answered. Consider, for example, the apparently trivial subject of a child's piggy bank. Charniak bravely attempted to list everything one had to know about piggy banks in order to make sense of stories in which one appears:

Piggy banks (PB's henceforth) come in all sizes and shapes, though a preferred shape is that of a pig. Generally, the size will range from larger than a doorknob, to smaller than a bread box. Generally money is kept in PBs, so when a child needs money he will often look for his PB. Usually, to get money out you need to be holding the bank, and shake it (up and down). Generally holding it upside down makes things easier. There are less known techniques like using a knife to help get the money out. If, when shaken, there is no sound from inside, it usually means that there is no money in the bank. If there is a sound, it means that something is in there, presumably money. You shake it until the money comes out. We assume that after the money comes out it is held by the person shaking, unless we are told differently. If not enough comes out you keep shaking until you either have enough money, or no more sound is made by the shaking. . . . In general the heavier the PB the more money in it. Some piggy banks have lids which can be easily removed to get the money out. Sometimes it is necessary to smash the PB to get the money out. To put money in, you need to have the money and the bank. The money is put into the slot in the bank, at which point you are no longer directly holding the money. Money is stored in PBs for safekeeping. Often the money is kept there during the process of saving in order to buy something one wants. PBs are considered toys, and hence can be owned by children. This ownership extends to the money inside. So, for example, it is considered bad form to use money in another child's PB. Also, a PB can be played with in the same way as, say, toy soldiers, i.e., pushed around while pretending it is alive and doing something.[11]

Note how much longer this working definition of a piggy bank is than the one in a dictionary. It makes generous use of other concepts like money, safekeeping, pigs, and holding, for which even more extensive definitions would be required. Even worse, as Charniak pointed out, the definition leaves out important facts, such as that piggy banks can be thrown. "But this," Charniak optimistically argued, "applies to small objects in general, and would most likely appear in a discussion of 'throw.' "[12]

The sad truth, as proponents of micro worlds realized, was that you cannot define even the most innocuous and specialized aspect of human usage without reference to the whole of human culture. The techniques used in SHRDLU would not work beyond artificially defined toy problems or restricted areas of expertise. Contrary to expectations, the micro worlds approach did not lead to a gradual solution of the general problem of intelligence. Minsky, Papert, and their students could not progressively generalize a micro world into a larger universe, or simply combine several micro worlds into a bigger set. The staff of the MIT AI lab acknowledged four years after Charniak's thesis:

> Artificial Intelligence has done well in tightly constrained domains—Winograd, for example, astonished everyone with the expertise of his blocks-world natural language system. Extending this kind of ability to larger worlds has not provided straightforward, however. . . . The time has come to treat the problems involved as central issues.[13]

Across the country, other AI labs were having their own difficulties. In Stanford, the Shakey robot project came to a halt when the Defense Department realized that it would not lead to the hoped-for automated spying device. Hans Moravec, who observed the dealings as a relatively uninvolved graduate student, recalled these events for me:

> Initially, the guiding principle in DARPA had been to look for promising researchers and just give them a budget, with which they could explore in their own unique and crazy directions. That was the spirit through the Shakey time, the late sixties. By the seventies things had gotten a little bit weird: Many researchers were caught up in a web of increasing exaggeration. Their initial promises to DARPA* had been much too optimistic. Of course, what they delivered stopped considerably short of that. But they felt they couldn't in their next proposal promise less than in the first one, so they promised more. Then writing the final report for that new project involved some stretching. Shakey was no exception. An entire run of Shakey could involve the robot going into a room, finding a block, being asked to move the block over to the top of a platform, pushing a wedge against the platform, rolling up the ramp, and pushing the block up. Shakey never did that as one complete sequence. It did it in several independent attempts, which each had a high probability of failure. You were able to put together a movie that had all the pieces in it, but it was really flaky. Not that it fooled anybody: the DARPA people who were reading those reports had been students in AI a few years before![14]

Disappointing the Defense Department

Another celebrated case of contention is DARPA's Speech Understanding Research (SUR) program, for which Carnegie Mellon acted as a main contractor in the early 1970s.[15] The military's goal had been to let computers understand verbal commands and data, for hands-off interaction with equipment in combat situations. After gobbling up fifteen million dollars over five years, DARPA ended the project under circumstances that remain unclear. Some maintain that it was just the scheduled end of a fixed-length project. The AI grapevine, however, and even some printed accounts,[16] have it that the agency felt that enough was enough, and chopped the program off. I asked the former project manager at

---

*By then, the alphabet-soup strategists had added "Defense" to the Advanced Research Projects Agency's name, turning ARPA into DARPA.

Carnegie Mellon, Raj Reddy, about it, and he maintained that "the benchmarks [set out by DARPA] were met, no question. In fact, exceeded!"[17] These specifications included the understanding of connected speech, a major achievement since previous systems had forced the speakers to pause between words. Enabling the computer to determine where words ended and started was indeed no small success. Further, the systems developed understood sentences from several speakers using a thousand-word vocabulary. The computer was also fairly quick on the uptake: it reacted to the sentences in "near real time," Raj Reddy told me. Reddy, however, admitted to some dissatisfaction on the customer's part. "The issue," he continued, "is that DARPA came back and said, 'The way you've got a thousand-word vocabulary near real time is by constraining the grammar.' But nobody had ever said anything about not constraining the grammar! Nobody even understood that that was a parameter that could be adjusted at the beginning of the project!"

As DARPA had belatedly realized, constraining the grammar constitutes a major drawback. Many contemporary systems masquerading as "natural language front-ends" (meaning that they are supposed to let users enter instructions in ordinary English) give a harder time to their users than more primitive programs that require picking selections from menus. These impostors fail by accepting many natural-sounding commands, and refusing others. As a result, it often takes their users longer to figure out what they are *not* allowed to say than to learn the usage of menus. In short, DARPA felt it had been had.

Three well-known projects financed under the SUR program were HARPY and HEARSAY-II at Carnegie Mellon, and HWIM (for Hear What I Mean) at the firm of Bolt, Beranek & Newman in Cambridge. It is ironic that AI researchers feel very proud about these three projects. In particular, the author Morris W. Firebaugh, in a textbook well received by the AI community, called HEARSAY-II "one of the most influential AI programs ever written."[18] Indeed, HEARSAY-II represented the first application of a device called a "blackboard" to integrate several sources of knowledge. That the project disappointed its sponsors to the point of eliciting comments on "SUR-style debacles" in another book[19] illustrates the communication problems that existed between AI researchers and their patrons.

What with the camouflage and misunderstandings, by the early 1970s "everybody was getting very uncomfortable with the situation,"

Hans Moravec told me in his Carnegie Mellon office. "So there were funding cutbacks in 1974. I think it was literally phrased at DARPA that 'some of these people were going to be taught a lesson, were having their two-million-dollar-a-year contracts cut to almost nothing!' And, of course, they meant Stanford, MIT, and Carnegie Mellon!" "There was almost no funding for a while," Berthold Horn confirmed to me at MIT.

American researchers were not the only ones to feel the ebbing of the tide. A scathing report to their government on the state of AI research in England devastated their British colleagues.[20] Its author, Sir James Lighthill, had distinguished himself in fluid dynamics and had occupied Cambridge University's Lucasian Chair of Applied Mathematics, presently held by Stephen Hawking. The British government traditionally requests scientific advice from past holders of the Lucasian Chair. Ironically, another ex-Lucasian, Sir George Biddell Airy, had been the one to advise Queen Victoria against continuing support for Charles Babbage's difference engine.[21] Sir Lighthill pointed out to the Science Research Council of the UK that AI's "grandiose objectives" remained largely unmet. As a result, his 1973 report called for a virtual halt to all AI research in Britain. This recommendation led to the quasi-dismantling of top-flight research groups, such as that at the University of Edinburgh, and to the emigration of eminent British AI workers to the United States.

CRUCIAL QUESTIONS

In the early 1970s, concerns other than material accompanied the problems AI had in achieving concrete results. Some fundamental problems were pointed out by critics from AI's own ranks. Other critics from outside the field questioned the very assumptions at the basis of AI.

The Frame and Qualification Problems

In 1969, a paper by John McCarthy and his colleague Patrick J. Hayes from the Metamathematics Unit of the University of Edinburgh addressed some of the philosophical problems posed by AI. McCarthy and Hayes conceded that these questions "are identical with or at least correspond to some traditional questions of philosophy, especially in metaphysics, epistemology and philosophic logic." Then, however, they went on to warn their AI colleagues not to expect too much help from this direction:

> Since the philosophers have not really come to an agreement in 2500 years it might seem that artificial intelligence is in a rather hopeless state if it is to depend on getting enough concrete information out of philosophy to write computer programs. Fortunately, merely undertaking to embody the philosophy in a computer program involves making enough philosophical presuppositions to exclude most philosophy as irrelevant. Undertaking to construct a general intelligent computer program seems to entail the following presuppositions:
>
> 1. The physical world exists and already contains some intelligent machines called people.
> 2. Information about this world is obtainable through the senses and is expressible internally.
> 3. Our common-sense view of the world is approximately correct and so is our scientific view.
> 4. The right way to think about the general problem of metaphysics and epistemology is not to attempt to clear one's own mind of all knowledge and start with "Cogito ergo sum" and build up from there. Instead, we propose to use all of our knowledge to construct a computer program that knows. The correctness of our philosophical system will be tested by numerous comparisons between the beliefs of the program and our own observations and knowledge.[22]

However, McCarthy and Hayes then pointed out that an intelligent program must be able to decide what to do by inferring (proving) that a certain sequence of actions will achieve its goal. This new observation raised the question of the applicability of mathematical logic to the analysis of everyday life. The best way to achieve these logical inferences, claimed the authors, was to manipulate certain logical expressions in a formal language. They then introduced a formalism that enabled them to do so: for example, to call up a friend over the telephone, such manipulations determine that we must know his or her phone number (or look it up if we don't), be able to dial it, and assume that the phone system will cause the dialing to establish the communication. In examining their results, McCarthy and Hayes noted a major problem: "in proving that one person could get into conversation with another, we were obliged to add the hypothesis that if a person has a telephone he still has it after looking up a number in the telephone book."[23]

This effect stemmed from the literal-mindedness of formal systems, to which one must specify all consequences of any action. In complicated situations, this requirement turned into a heavy computational burden. Think of a cartoon in which the illustrators animate characters against a fixed background. The actors perform actions that usually cause only small changes to the fixed frame of reference. Sometimes, however, they have drastic consequences: Goofy might trigger a bomb, or a clap of Mickey's hands induce an avalanche. Other changes to the frame can happen independently of the characters' actions: day turns into night, and people grow old.

Since they involve managing a frame of reference, McCarthy and Hayes called these coordination difficulties the "frame problem." It remains one of the great unsolved challenges of AI and can get out of hand even in simple situations. Take, for example, the STRIPS system (see chapter 4) that, in driving Shakey, used lists of additions and deletions to be made to the frame description after each action: picking up a block on top of a pile resulted in the block's being no longer on the pile (delete ONTOP$(x\ y)$), but in the robot's hand (add IN-HAND(y)). But what about unstable block piles that topple at the slightest provocation, causing other piles to fall in domino fashion? In this case, STRIPS also fell to pieces. Likewise, ordering the robot to advance by four inches looks like an easy change to handle: just adjust the robot coordinates in the frame of reference. Yet the only result STRIPS could count on after issuing this command was that Shakey would not advance by *exactly* four inches: the wheels would always slip a little; and in any case, the robot's sensors did not provide a perfectly accurate estimate of its position. Since after a few such displacements Shakey tended to lose track of where it was and bump into things, it was necessary periodically to reassess the robot's situation with respect to the frame.

Yet another aspect of the frame problem involves the planning activity. In evaluating how to travel between two points of a crowded room, Shakey (or STRIPS) had to explore several possible paths. Likewise, when manipulating blocks, the robot had to decide which block to pick and where to place it. When considering several such possible courses of action, STRIPS had to keep in mind all the corresponding alternative universes. In complicated situations, this requirement induced an explosive computational burden.

McCarthy and Hayes also pointed out a problem related to but different from the frame problem, which later became known as the "qualification problem." Going back to the telephone example, they write:

> [W]e assumed that if p looks up q's phone-number in the book, he will know it, and if he dials the number he will come into conversation with q. It is not hard to think of possible exceptions to these statements such as:
> 1. The page with q's number may be torn out.
> 2. p may be blind.
> 3. Someone may have deliberately inked out q's number.
> 4. The telephone company may have made the entry incorrectly.
> 5. q may have got the telephone only recently.
> 6. The phone system may be out of order.
> 7. q may be incapacitated suddenly.[24]

Obviously it is possible to think of as many exceptions or qualifications as we want to the rule: "IF p looks up q's phone number, THEN p will know q's phone number." People take such hair splitting in stride and simply consider that looking up a phone number works, unless there is a good reason why it shouldn't. Telling a computer what makes up a "good reason" has turned out to be surprisingly difficult, and the qualification problem endures as one of the major roadblocks on the way to true artificial intelligence.

Hubert Dreyfus: Is AI Impossible?

More scathing criticisms against AI came from outside the ranks of the artificial intelligence community. As early as 1961, an engineer named Mortimer Taube published the first anti-AI book under the title *Computers and Common Sense: The Myth of Thinking Machines.*[25] Perhaps because its author died shortly after publication, the book raised few eyebrows. Some years later, the distinguished mathematician Richard Bellman also voiced objections, which he eventually published in a short book.[26] Again, Bellman's relatively gentle tone limited the ripples his comments caused.

Lasting grudges and real tooth grinding developed in response to the chiding of the philosopher Hubert L. Dreyfus. The brother of Richard Bellman's research associate Stuart E. Dreyfus, Hubert Dreyfus started out as a physics student at Harvard and moved on to philosophy in graduate school. He was teaching this discipline at MIT in the early 1960s when he heard of the first artificial intelligence programs. A disciple of such modern humanist philosophers as Merleau-Ponty, Sartre, and Heidegger, Dreyfus perceived a basic contradiction between their teachings and AI's goal of embodying intelligence in machines.

The first skirmish between Dreyfus and the artificial intelligentsia (as Dreyfus calls the AI community) occurred during a series of lectures held at MIT in the spring of 1961. Herbert Simon in particular remembers Hubert Dreyfus and his brother Stuart taking strong exception to a conference Simon gave on the EPAM psychological model of short-term memory.[27] Following a panel session, the Dreyfus brothers entered a one-page discussion note in the proceedings volume.[28] It was badly received: "a nasty little diatribe about this preposterous stuff that was being peddled," said Simon. Truly, Stuart and Hubert didn't use diplomatic language: "the relentless prophets of the omniscient computer . . . lack [a] fundamental attribute of the human brain—a few uncommitted neurons," said the Dreyfus brothers, who then proceeded to equate AI with alchemy and likened it to a try at reaching the moon by climbing a mountain.[29] This was definitely not the Dale Carnegie way of making friends with AI researchers!

Three years later, in 1964, when Stuart was also teaching at MIT, he put Hubert in touch with the RAND Corporation. Since Newell, Shaw, and Simon had performed their early work on Logic Theorist and GPS at RAND, the corporation maintained a strong interest in artificial intelligence. RAND hired Hubert as a consultant, with the mission of assessing the feasibility of AI from the philosophical point of view. It is not clear whether RAND thought Dreyfus an unbiased critic or wanted him as a counterpoint to the self-interested cheerfulness of the AI workers. Hubert's former boss at RAND, Paul Armer, later claimed that he would not have hired him had he known of the philosopher's previous appearance in print against AI.[30] The Dreyfus brothers, on the other hand, maintained in a 1985 book that RAND recruited Hubert to point out apparent contradictions between AI and Maurice Merleau-Ponty's philosophy.[31] Be that as it may, the title of Hubert's report when it finally came out—"Alchemy and AI"—was itself an indictment.[32] AI proponents within and outside RAND attempted to prevent its publication. "Simon and Newell," said Dreyfus, "insisted that my paper was nonsense and that RAND should in no way appear to condone it. This led to a year-long struggle within RAND as to whether the paper should be published or suppressed."[33] Herbert Simon, for his part, complained, "[T]he fact that [Dreyfus] was a consultant at RAND immediately gave him credibility. . . . What I resent about this was the RAND name attached to that garbage. That was really false pretences."[34]

"Alchemy and AI" developed the themes laid out in the earlier note without yielding an inch on the diplomatic side. In addition to denying the feasibility of AI on philosophical grounds, Dreyfus took malicious enjoyment in debunking AI claims and alleged successes. With regard to Simon's forecast of an impending computer world chess champion, which by then already went back seven years, the philosopher made much of a ten-year-old child's trouncing of Newell and Simon's experimental chess program. Dreyfus also took advantage of a more serious slip by W. R. Ashby. (A psychiatrist and member of the Ratio Club [see chapter 2], Ashby had published in 1952 a book entitled *Design for a Brain,* which helped motivate early AI research.)[35] Ashby had claimed in a psychiatry journal the fulfillment of another of Simon's predictions concerning a computer's proof of an important mathematical result. The program was Gelernter's Geometry Theorem Prover; and the result, the Pons Asinorum theorem, for which the program had discovered a proof that required no construction. A result, claimed Ashby, that "the greatest mathematicians of 2000 years have failed to notice . . . which would have evoked the highest praise had it occurred."[36] As Dreyfus relished pointing out, psychiatrist Ashby was barking up the wrong tree: despite its impressive name, the theorem simply stated that the opposing angles of an isosceles triangle are equal. Further, the proof in question had been discovered by Pappus around the year 300.

With such lighter touches to enliven its deeper philosophical considerations, "Alchemy and AI" earned itself a reputation as an anticomputer pamphlet. "[I]t became the best seller of any . . . paper that RAND put out, which didn't make them [RAND] a bit happy," recalled Dreyfus.[37]

Also unhappy were Dreyfus's colleagues at MIT, as they made plain to the author of the report. Says Dreyfus: "[T]he rejection was so total that students and professors working on the robot project dared not be seen having lunch with me without risking getting into trouble with their superiors. When Joseph Weizenbaum, the only professor who had any doubts, wanted to discuss his concerns with me, we had to meet at his home in the suburbs."[38]

I met with conflicting verbal reports of this period. Weizenbaum, in fact, didn't have much respect for Dreyfus's report: "It was terribly incompetent," he told me. Dreyfus "knew so little about computers, and made so many mistakes!" Weizenbaum, however, confirmed the manner in which his MIT colleagues treated the philosopher:

> I remember discussions we had on what to do about Dreyfus. A general conclusion was reached more or less explicitly by the AI community: the best thing to do was to give Dreyfus the silent treatment. Just not to talk about him, not to try to defend against him, not to laugh at him, nothing. Basically, as far as the AI community was concerned, Dreyfus became a nonperson. We shudder when we hear that this was done in communist dictatorships, yet we did the same thing.

Weizenbaum denied, however, being forced to hold secret meetings with Dreyfus: "I became the only member of that community that would be seen eating with Hubert Dreyfus. And I deliberately made it very plain that theirs was not the way to treat a human being."[39]

David Waltz, a student during this period, remembered, however, that

> there were great debates between Weizenbaum and Dreyfus on one side and Minsky and Papert on the other. We all went to them religiously and watched. They were in classrooms at MIT, not in big auditoriums. Quite a few people showed up to hear these debates. . . . My recollections are that they were seminars, not outside events. The amount of heat may have been greater than the amount of light. Moreover, I think I was much more partisan than open minded about it.

Waltz insisted that some people at MIT ("but not from the AI Lab!") were on Dreyfus's side:

> He and Weizenbaum were both arguing that the simplistic view of AI propagated by the founders didn't really match human intelligence. I remember once Noam Chomsky came over also. There was personal

animosity between him and Minsky, and people were very rude to Chomsky when he came to the AI lab. They booed when he talked, and he was very miffed.[40]

Weizenbaum, for his part, denied to me any remembrance of such debates.

Had the controversy stayed within the confines of academia, Dreyfus's relations with the rest of the faculty might have returned to a civilized, if still less than cordial, level. Unfortunately, excerpts from the report found their way into the *New Yorker*,[41] which made Dreyfus the "Talk of the Town" and by no means favored de-escalation of the conflict. Perhaps in need of a more congenial environment, Dreyfus eventually accepted a faculty position in Berkeley.

Particularly incensed at MIT was Seymour Papert, who answered "Alchemy and AI" with a memo of his own entitled "The Artificial Intelligence of Hubert L. Dreyfus: A Budget of Fallacies."[42] Papert also had the pleasure of directly breaking through Dreyfus's smugness about computer chess: he challenged Dreyfus to a match with an MIT-brewed chess program called MacHack, and the philosopher lost! This time, it was for the artificial intelligentsia to gloat and publish in the *SIGART Bulletin* (a publication put out by the Association for Computing Machinery) that if a ten-year-old could beat the machine, the machine could beat Dreyfus.

In 1972, Dreyfus expanded "Alchemy and AI" into a book entitled *What Computers Can't Do*. By then, his relations with the AI community had degenerated to downright nastiness. In her best-selling eulogy of AI entitled *Machines Who Think,* the author Pamela McCorduck accused Dreyfus of misleadingly including Seymour Papert in the acknowledgments of *What Computers Can't Do,* implying an actual contribution from Papert. Added McCorduck: "More abundant thanks went to the employee at MIT Press who was smuggling to Dreyfus galleys of a new book by Marvin Minsky so that Dreyfus could frame his objections based on the latest material."[43]

In a 1979 edition of *What Computers Can't Do,* Dreyfus charged Papert with unethically pressuring a magazine editor against having Dreyfus review a book by Minsky, Papert, and Winston.[44] In *Mind Over Machine,* Dreyfus reported similar difficulties with other AI researchers, this time about his appearance in a television program on AI and expert systems.[45]

It wasn't, of course, the first time science has disintegrated into alley-cat pranks. These difficulties appear all the more distressing since time has proven the accuracy and perceptiveness of some of Dreyfus's comments. Had he formulated them less aggressively, constructive actions they suggested might have been taken earlier. In fact, it was almost uncanny for a non-expert in computer science to anticipate as early as 1965 the difficulties AI would run into, and to point out why! Dreyfus's early position is best laid out in the first edition of *What Computers Can't Do*. Polemics aside, his philosophical points deserve careful discussion.

Dreyfus, for starters, was perfectly willing to concede Marvin Minsky's "meat machine" premise: "if the nervous system obeys the laws of physics and chemistry, which we have every reason to suppose it does, then ...we... ought to be able to reproduce the behavior of the nervous system with some physical device." Further on, Dreyfus was even willing to admit that the digital computer could be such a device:

> In general, by accepting the fundamental assumptions that the nervous system is part of the physical world and that all physical processes can be described in a mathematical formalism which can in turn be manipulated by a digital computer, one can arrive at the strong claim that the behavior which results from human "information processing," whether directly formalizable or not, can always be indirectly reproduced on a digital machine.[46]

The catch in this sentence is the word *indirectly:* to achieve a proper reproduction of a brain in the manner conceded by Dreyfus, a computer would need to solve the mathematical equations describing the functioning of each and every neuron in this brain, in detail. While Dreyfus was skeptical in 1972 that the processing power required for such a detailed simulation could ever be achieved in practice, he admitted in later writings that networks of artificial neurons might one day simulate intelligent behavior.[47]

Dreyfus thus aimed his objections specifically at the claim that "a digital computer can reproduce human behavior, not by solving physical equations but by *processing data representing facts about the world using logical operations* that can be reduced to matching, classifying, and Boolean operations"[48] (italics in original). In his view, four specific forms of human thinking central to our cognitive processes would remain forever beyond the reach of systems manipulating "data representing facts about the world," or symbols.

First was the marginal awareness of many factors in our environment which Dreyfus called "fringe consciousness." He claimed that this skill lies at the basis of our ability to zero in, "by means of the overall organization of the perceptual field, on an area formerly on the fringes of consciousness, and which other areas still on the fringes of consciousness make interesting." For Dreyfus, fringe consciousness is what allows a chess player to concentrate on interesting areas of the board. This resulting intuitive ability to "discriminate" between the important and the unimportant, the essential and the inessential, makes up another fundamentally human cognitive operation, according to Dreyfus. A variation on this talent is our ability to narrow the spectrum of possible meanings of a word by ignoring what, out of context, would be ambiguities: Dreyfus called this skill "ambiguity tolerance." The last cornerstone of human cognition consisted, according to Dreyfus, in our "perspicuous grouping" ability, which allows us to recognize objects of the same class without comparing explicit lists of attributes. Instead we "situate the individual with respect to a paradigm case" representative of the entire class.[49]

Why wouldn't AI researchers ever succeed in programming these abilities into their machines? To begin with, said Dreyfus, the reasons why they thought they would did not bear scrutiny. He started by debunking the so-called biological assumption, which has it that the brain functions like a digital computer. As we have seen, the observation that neurons fire a somewhat all-or-nothing burst of activity had led early researchers to assimilate the brain's workings to those of a computer. Few people still held that belief in the early 1970s, and nobody argued against Dreyfus when he pointed out that neurons are not connected at all like the elements of a digital computer. Further, individual pulses are not correlated with symbols. Instead, the rate at which a neuron emits pulses describes the degree to which the senses or other neurons excite it. Therefore, the brain is not a digital system at all, but rather an analogue device working on the principle of pulse-frequency modulation.

Couldn't one overlook hardware and claim that "there is . . . a level—the information processing level—[at which] the mind uses computer processes such as comparing, classifying, searching lists, and so forth, to produce intelligent behavior"?[50] Dreyfus called this claim the "psychological assumption"; and it does, indeed, lie at the root of the cognitive-simulation school led by Newell and Simon.

Dreyfus flamboyantly parted ways with believers in the psychological assumption. In one of the paradoxical statements that make *What Computers Can't Do* worth reading for entertainment value alone, the philosopher claimed that "there are good reasons to doubt that there is any information processing going on in the brain"![51] This assertion rested on a casuistic distinction between information in its technical sense and the usual meaning of the word. Dreyfus noted that information as defined by Claude Shannon (the father of information theory) is nonsemantic, and that information theory is not a theory of meaning. For example, the information-carrying capacity of a transmission line simply measures its ability to transmit bit patterns without garbling them; it makes no difference whether the bits belong to the utterances of a philosopher or to Aunt Susie's mindless chatter. Thus the *meaning* that we attach to the bit patterns has no bearing on their technical character as information. As Shannon put it: "The semantic aspects of communication are irrelevant to the engineering problem."[52] Since thought has everything to do with meaning, Dreyfus could thus claim that it implies no information processing in the "transmission line" sense, and so justify the preceding paradox. To avoid any further confusion in the rest of the book, Dreyfus used the expression "energy transformation" rather than "information processing" to designate the physical aspects of thought.

Going even further, in what was probably the central point of his thesis, Dreyfus claimed that the actual mechanism of these "energy transformations" was unknown and even ultimately irrelevant to the problem of thought, which must be discussed at what he called the "phenomenological level." Dreyfus denied that, according to the cognitive psychologist Ulrich Neisser, " . . . 'cognition' refers to all the processes by which the sensory input is transformed, reduced, elaborated, stored, recovered, and used."[53] Dreyfus claimed that transformations of sensory input occur at the neurophysiological level, and perception and thought at the phenomenological level. Trying to define a domain of discourse between these two planes, which is what cognitive scientists do, could only lead to confusion. About how frequencies hitting the ear become the sounds we perceive, Dreyfus said, "The energy transformations involved will presumably someday be discovered by neurophysiologists. . . . We do not hear frequencies, we hear sounds." And also: "Phenomenologically we directly perceive physical objects. We are aware of neither sense data nor light rays."[54]

Dreyfus blamed the apparent plausibility of the psychological assumption on a two-thousand-year-old thought habit of Western science and philosophy: we can't accept that we have explained a phenomenon until we have reduced it to laws and rules. "Can one prejudge the results in psychology by insisting theories must be computer programs because otherwise psychology isn't possible?" asked Dreyfus.[55] He added that computers offered another irresistible attraction to psychologists: in pre-computer days, they had to postulate an entity beyond description, the "transcendental ego," to apply the rules they made up. Now computers let them have rules without a transcendental ego, and few psychologists can stay away from such a golden opportunity.

Be that as it may, most artificial intelligence researchers, as opposed to those working in cognitive simulation, do not make the psychological assumption. They do not claim that their programs work like the human mind; they claim simply that it is possible to obtain intelligent behavior in a computer through formal symbol manipulation. Dreyfus labeled this last claim the "epistemological assumption," and admitted that it was "weaker and thus less vulnerable than the psychological assumption."[56] Yet the philosopher by no means considered it a foregone conclusion. Besides the fact that not all nonarbitrary behavior may be formalizable, there remained the problem that a formalism explaining a behavior may not be able to reproduce that behavior. To wit, Dreyfus cited the formal language theory of Noam Chomsky: it allows linguists to formally decide, by applying rules, whether a given sentence is grammatical or not; yet these rules are totally powerless to generate language because they lack any reference to the meanings of the words.

Following Wittgenstein, Dreyfus further noted that trying to generate language according to strict rules threatens an infinite regress. Because of the strong contextual dependence of word meanings, wouldn't we need rules for when to apply the rules, and rules for how to apply these new rules, endlessly? To this problem Dreyfus saw only one possible solution: since computers are insensitive to context, they must be programmed to respond to ultimate bits of context-free, completely determinate data which require no further interpretation in order to be understood. Do such atomic facts exist?

For Dreyfus, answering yes to this question was to make the "ontological assumption." To illustrate how elements of our world derive their meaning from context and situation, Dreyfus quoted a famous example due to the linguist Josuah Bar Hillel.[57] How does one disambiguate *pen* in the sentence: "The box was in the pen"? At first sight, this illustration is not compelling because general knowledge on the relative sizes of boxes and writing pens leads one to think of a playpen. Yet if we happen to be on a ranch, allusion to an enclosure for animals is more likely. How about a sexy female commissar lusciously whispering the sentence to James Bond? Then a writing pen may well hide the microfilm capsule. Such considerations led Dreyfus to extreme skepticism about the existence of ultimate context-free elements.

How then do we get computers to handle contexts? The problem here was that any context always requires interpretation in terms of a broader context to distinguish irrelevant from relevant facts. We must understand "James Bond in Moscow" in terms of Russia, then the cold war, which leads to spying, secret document transfer, and so on. Referring to Joseph Weizenbaum's suggestion of organizing contexts in a nested hierarchy, interpreted from the top down, Dreyfus was again skeptical:

> On the one hand, we have the thesis: there must always be a broader context; otherwise, we have no way to distinguish relevant from irrelevant facts. On the other hand, we have the antithesis: there must be an ultimate context, which requires no interpretation; otherwise, there will be an infinite regress of contexts, and we can never begin our formalization.[58]

Dreyfus saw human beings as embodying a third way out of this dilemma. Instead of using a hierarchy of contexts, they simply recognize the present situation as a continuation or modification of a previous one. Short of simulating human birth and growth, Dreyfus saw no way of getting a computer into an initial situation.

In what he presented as alternatives to the traditional assumptions about cognition, Dreyfus pointed out the role of such factors as the body and our interaction with the world in generating intelligent behavior. These three chapters of the book are almost poetic and replete with sentences like "It has to do with the way man is at home in his world, has it comfortably wrapped around him, so to speak." In concrete terms, what Dreyfus seems to be saying is that often, we need perform very little information processing (or "energy transformation," as Dreyfus would have it) to interact with the world. Instead various cues and physical constraints dictate us a course of action. Here are some examples that Dreyfus did not use but that, I believe, illustrate the point. Using a telephone handset comes naturally since with the shape of our hands and heads, there is only one way to hold it. Instead of the specific and complex instructions a robot would require to lift the handset, all we need is enough general knowledge to conform to the physics of the situation. Likewise, it is a safe bet that any of the last true remaining primitives on this planet, if afflicted with a sore foot and handed a crutch, would immediately understand its use. Animals and humans, says Dreyfus, leave the complexity in the environment, where it belongs, and reduce an otherwise complicated chore to simple reactions.

AI workers periodically rediscover this truth. In the 1960s, Herbert Simon had embodied it into the parable of the ant (see introduction). Nowadays, *reactivity* is again an AI buzzword. Other Dreyfus themes find direct equivalents in technical developments made after he pointed out the problems. For example, his remarks about the difficulty of determining relevance (which he called "essential/inessential discrimination") appeared in his RAND report four years before the 1969 McCarthy-Hayes paper addressing the qualification problem.[59] As an explanation of how people overcome this obstacle, Dreyfus pointed out the importance of context-induced expectations. Only in the 1970s did Roger Schank and Robert Abelson introduce scripts, and Marvin Minsky, frames, to work human expectations into AI programs. Dreyfus's observation that humans perform pattern recognition by comparison to a paradigm or model finds its equivalents in such techniques as case-based reasoning and memory-based reasoning, developed in the 1980s. His doubts about the existence of ultimate logical atoms appear vindicated by the evolution of natural-language processing in AI. Attempts to define logical atoms under the name "semantic primitives" in the 1970s have now yielded to efforts like the CYC project (see chapter 10), which eschew primitives.

Since most AI workers profess a strong antipathy for Dreyfus's views and personality, it is unlikely that such developments occurred in direct response to his attacks.* Yet it wasn't only Dreyfus's delight in riding roughshod over the sensitivities of AI researchers that deprived his remarks of most positive impact. Although his criticisms pointed out

---

*Dreyfus, however, claims a disciple of sorts in AI researcher Terry Winograd, of SHRDLU fame (see chapter 4). In a 1988 article, the Dreyfus brothers mention that "by the end of the 1970s, after trying to write a new knowledge representation language, KRL, to deal with the central role of typical cases and similarity in commonsense knowledge representation, Winograd 'lost his faith' in AI altogether."[60] Winograd confirmed his turnabout through a strong endorsement on the cover of *Mind Over Machine,* in which the Dreyfuses make a substantially similar claim.[61]

real difficulties and did credit to the perceptiveness of modern humanist philosophy, it is highly questionable whether they added up to the theoretical impossibility of artificial intelligence, as he insisted they did.

For example, Dreyfus turned to the theme of infinite regress on three occasions (for essential/inessential distinction, rule application, and interpretation in terms of context). As Zeno pointed out twenty-four centuries ago, such threats can be more apparent than real: Zeno showed this lack of substance by explaining the paradox of Achilles and the tortoise. In principle, went the paradox, Achilles should never win a race against the animal if it is given a head start, for no matter how closely he approaches the tortoise, Achilles will always have half the remaining distance to run. Zeno pointed out that this argument sins by failing to differentiate between an infinite interval and a finite interval infinitely subdivided. A more modern illustration of the illusion concerns nonlinear algebraic equations. Suppose we want to find a number x such that:

$$x = 1.4^x$$

(that is, the number 1.4 raised to the xth power should be equal to x itself). Now one could claim that solving this equation implies an infinite regress, since to know its left-hand side (that is x) we must calculate its right-hand side, which is itself a function of the left-hand side, for which we need the right-hand side again, ad infinitum. It so happens that actually performing these operations—that is, evaluating both sides of the equation alternatively, starting with some initial guess—quickly leads to a good estimate of the answer. Suppose we take the number 3 for an initial guess at the left-hand side of the equation: call that number x_0. Let us now calculate the right-hand side of the equation with this value of x:

$$1.4^3 = 2.744.$$

This yields a new estimate for the left-hand side of the equation, which we'll call x_1. Thus, $x_1 = 2.744$. Feeding this value into the right-hand-side of the equation again, we get:

$$1.4^{2.744} = 2.517.$$

Our revised estimate for the left-hand side, x_2, is thus $x_2 = 2.517$. We can repeat this procedure as many times as we want. After twenty repetitions, the first four digits of the estimate (1.887) no longer change. This means that, to a very good approximation:

$$1.887 \ = \ 1.4^{1.887}$$

and our equation is satisfied. The reason the regress is, in fact, finite is that each step of it amounts to more than an empty logical consideration: it is a procedure that changes the problem data and leaves them in a state closer to a solution. One can argue that the infinite regress of rules threatened by Dreyfus will not materialize for a similar reason. The "rules to interpret the rules" will not act on the first-iteration rules themselves, but will act on the problem description as modified by the application of these first-iteration rules. With a proper selection of rules, this new problem description will be closer to a solution.

In addition to such logical shortcomings, Dreyfus's philosophical position suffered from another weakness: he offered no alternative to the formalism he derided. His insistence on keeping the discussion on the "phenomenological" level, at which he could claim direct access of the mind to the world, could have been specifically designed to antagonize the kind of people who were working in AI. For such inquisitive souls were left to wonder in what way human beings, who have access to the phenomenological level, differed from, say, pumpkins, which presumably have no such access. Dreyfus's suggestions in this respect amounted to pure hand waving: "Just as the brain seems to be, at least in part, an analogue computer, so the mind may well arrive at its thoughts and perceptions by responding to 'fields,' 'force,' 'configurations,' and so on, as, in fact, we seem to do insofar as our thinking is open to phenomenological description."[62]

In his later *Mind Over Machine,* written with his brother Stuart, Hubert Dreyfus appeared to side with the connectionist school of thought, which by then had developed a consistent theory of neural networks. In the late 1960s and early 1970s, however, Dreyfus offered few constructive suggestions.

Joseph Weizenbaum: Is AI Immoral?

Four years after *What Computers Can't Do,* another literary blow befell the artificial intelligence community—this one administered by a recognized insider, whom in fact Dreyfus had criticized in his book. In 1976, attacking AI from another direction than Dreyfus had, MIT's Joseph Weizenbaum published *Computer Power and Human Reason.*[63] While skeptical on the short-term prospects for AI, Weizenbaum was willing to concede its ultimate feasibility; instead, he objected to artificial intelligence on moral grounds. Paradoxically, Weizenbaum's wrath originated in his experience with one of the most talked about and funniest AI programs ever written. To understand what happened, I spent half a day with Weizenbaum at his Cambridge home.

He is a short man with a striking resemblance to Albert Einstein, with perhaps a sprinkling of Joseph Stalin thrown in. Contrary to many of his colleagues, Weizenbaum doesn't take himself too seriously, and told me how he'd started his career "as a kind of confidence man":

Around 1958, I published my first paper, in the commercial magazine *Datamation.* I had written a program that could play a game called "five in a row." It's like ticktacktoe, except you need rows of five exes or noughts to win. It's also played on an unbounded board: ordinary coordinate paper will do. The program used a ridiculously simple strategy with no look ahead, but it could beat anyone who played at the same naive level. Since most people had never played the game before, that included just about everybody. Significantly, the paper was entitled: "How to Make a Computer *Appear* Intelligent" with *appear* emphasized. In a way, that was a forerunner to my later ELIZA, to establish my status as a charlatan or con man. But the other side of the coin is that I freely stated it. The idea was to create the powerful illusion that the computer was intelligent. I went to considerable trouble in the paper to explain that there wasn't much behind the scenes, that the machine wasn't thinking. I explained the strategy well enough that anybody could write that program, which is the same thing I did with ELIZA.

In the mid-1960s at MIT, Weizenbaum was trying to get computers to talk to people in English. He noted that the programs in existence, like STUDENT, had only limited domains of application. Further, the knowledge describing these domains was inextricably bound to the program structure itself. Weizenbaum also deplored the limited capacity of the programs to acquire more information from the users by asking them questions. "I was smart enough to know that I couldn't solve that in the next few weeks," Weizenbaum told me, "so I started thinking about alternatives. . . . I took all my tricks, put them in a bundle, and started this ELIZA business."

One of these tricks was actually a very sensible idea: Weizenbaum decided that the domain knowledge would reside in a program module separate from the one handling the conversations. He reasoned that if different kinds of knowledge were described in different knowledge modules (or "scripts," as he called them), the program could then chat about a variety of topics. Feel like talking about haute couture rather than baseball today? Just load the haute-couture software module! Since the program could learn increasingly better speech, like Eliza Doolittle in George Bernard Shaw's *Pygmalion,* Weizenbaum named it after her. (Another reason, as Weizenbaum later pointed out, was that, "like Miss Doolittle, it was never quite clear whether or not [the program] became smarter.")[64] One of ELIZA's most successful scripts was the one letting it impersonate a Rogerian psychotherapist.* Here is a conversation carried on a terminal between a young lady and this incarnation of ELIZA (the program's responses are in uppercase):

Men are all alike.

IN WHAT WAY

They're always bugging us about something or other.

CAN YOU THINK OF A SPECIFIC EXAMPLE

Well, my boyfriend made me come here.

YOUR BOYFRIEND MADE YOU COME HERE

He says I'm depressed most of the time.

I AM SORRY TO HEAR YOU ARE DEPRESSED

It's true. I am unhappy.

DO YOU THINK COMING HERE WILL HELP YOU NOT TO BE UNHAPPY

I need some help, that much seems certain.

WHAT WOULD IT MEAN TO YOU IF YOU GOT SOME HELP

---

*The psychoanalyst Carl Rogers preached a therapy that consisted in simply encouraging patients to talk about their problems and answering their questions with other questions.

Perhaps I could learn to get along with my mother.

TELL ME MORE ABOUT YOUR FAMILY

My mother takes care of me.

WHO ELSE IN YOUR FAMILY TAKES CARE OF YOU

My father.

YOUR FATHER

You are like my father in some ways.

WHAT RESEMBLANCE DO YOU SEE

You are not very aggressive but I think you don't want me to notice that.

WHAT MAKES YOU THINK I AM NOT VERY AGGRESSIVE

You don't argue with me.

WHY DO YOU THINK I DON'T ARGUE WITH YOU

You are afraid of me.

DOES IT PLEASE YOU TO BELIEVE I AM AFRAID OF YOU

My father is afraid of everybody.

WHAT ELSE COMES TO MIND WHEN YOU THINK OF YOUR FATHER

Bullies.

DOES THAT HAVE ANYTHING TO DO WITH THE FACT THAT YOUR BOYFRIEND MADE YOU COME HERE[65]

Impressive, isn't it? In fact, this apparent brilliance accounted for much of Weizenbaum's annoyance. In truth, as he pointed out, ELIZA understood little more of the girl's problems than an alarm clock "understands" that it should ring at a certain hour. Often, through plain me-you transformations, the program simply mirrored sentences entered from the terminal—as in its response to "My boyfriend made me come here." Sometimes ELIZA tacked leading phrases on the beginning of these reflected statements, as in "(Why do you think) I don't argue with you?" At random intervals, ELIZA would pick a sentence used earlier in the dialogue and return it attached to a leading phrase, as in the last sentence of the example. With a little luck, this trick induced an illusion of deep perceptiveness.

Another of ELIZA's gambits was to watch for a list of key words. When it caught one, the program transformed it in some way, and returned it attached to a leading sentence. For example, in the girl's statement "Perhaps I could learn to get along with my mother," the word *mother* was changed into the name for the set it belonged to—family—and tacked onto the catchall phrase "Tell me more about your. . . ." When all else failed, ELIZA fell back on a list of hedges, such as "Go on" or "I see."

These antics worked of course, only because of the assumed context: the computer's responses appeared plausible thanks to Rogerian therapists' real practice of reflecting back their patient's statements. (Weizenbaum told me that he had originally conceived of ELIZA as a barman, but later decided psychiatrists were more interesting.) It also helped that patients believe that the therapist is after information about themselves rather than about a specific subject at hand. Bizarre statements like "Tell me more about street lights," which would have sounded funny in any other conversation, thus went unquestioned. Usually from the smoke-screen emerged the image of a reasonably sensitive therapist. Conversations with the program did not run as smoothly, however, in cases of mistaken identity. Daniel Bobrow, who left MIT after his Ph.D. for the computer services and consulting firm of Bolt, Beranek & Newman, recounted the following dialogue between ELIZA and a sales vice president of BBN. The vice president thought he was addressing Bobrow himself through a telecomp terminal. Again, the computer's responses are capitalized:

Do you think that I can use the computer this morning?

WHY DO YOU ASK?

I might be able to make some additional telecomp sales.

WHY AREN'T YOU SURE?

My prospective customers have never seen a demonstration of this system.

DOES THAT MEAN VERY MUCH TO YOU?

Of course it does.

YOU SEEM VERY POSITIVE ABOUT THAT.

This is ridiculous.

WHAT DO YOU MEAN THIS IS RIDICULOUS?

Is there any reason I can't use the computer now?

TELL ME MORE ABOUT YOUR PROSPECTIVE CUSTOMERS.[66]

Another script that made ELIZA sound plausible was that of the boorish attendant. In one MIT time-sharing system, hackers have dead-ended users' requests for help into an ELIZA program impersonating a system operator in a foul mood. After a few exchanges, some hapless victims became too upset to realize the prank and kept arguing with the program for several pages of teletyped conversation.[67]

Although ELIZA could be so convincing as to make one wonder whether Turing's test hasn't been unwittingly passed on such occasions, these cases deserve a clearly negative answer: Turing's judge had both to face two parties pretending to be people, and to be aware that one of them was a computer. On the other hand, another ELIZA-like program called PARRY, written under the direction of the psychiatrist Kenneth Colby, a former associate of Weizenbaum's, turned the tables and simulated a paranoid patient instead of his doctor. PARRY's delusion concerned the Mafia, and it related most remarks to the threat it felt from this organization. Like the original ELIZA, PARRY relied on sputtering out variations of pre-set responses randomly selected from a list. Colby and his co-workers submitted to psychiatrists excerpts of dialogues with both PARRY and real patients, which the specialists failed to distinguish accurately.[68] Since Turing did not explicitly require that the computer emulate a *sane* human being, such experiments come close to meeting at least the letter of his specifications. One could blame this outcome on the fixations of a deranged individual emulating the canned responses of a program, instead of on a program imitating the infinite diversity found in a normal person. Yet plugging the loophole by requiring the human party in Turing's test to be sane requires one to define sanity. This does not sound any easier than defining intelligence, which definition Turing designed his test to circumvent in the first place.

Weizenbaum, however, wasn't much worried by these considerations.

Ever the quipster, he published in the *Transactions of the Association for Computing Machinery,* a paper which ridiculed Colby's claims of simulating mental illness in a machine. As he told me:

> I had written a program that asked for input from the console, did nothing with it, and then went back and asked for more input. I sent the listing to the ACM, saying that I had taken Colby's claim very seriously, and written a program that simulated infantile autism. I even said that this program had the unique property that it could be implemented on a typewriter not connected to a computer at all. And you know what? They published it! . . . When the ACM later reprinted their best papers in a twenty-fifth-anniversary edition, this little paper was there, together with the original ELIZA paper.

To understand Weizenbaum's lack of concern, consider how a young mother reacted to a bogus psychotherapy session with one of ELIZA's clones:

WE WANT TO FOCUS ON YOUR RELATIONS WITH THE PEOPLE WHO BOTHER YOU MOST

That is easy. At the moment it is a surfeit of children in too small a space.

IS IT

Yes.

CAN YOU DESCRIBE AN EXAMPLE

Of what.

I SEE

No you don't.

CAN YOU ELABORATE

What on.

LET'S EXPLORE FURTHER YOUR FEELINGS ABOUT IT[69]

To anyone confronting an ELIZA-like program in the proper frame of mind, considerations about its bearing on the Turing test appear theoretical because of the obviousness of the fraud. What did bother Weizenbaum, though, was that many people did not face ELIZA with the right attitude. Even when fully aware of its true nature, they still became emotionally involved with the program and revealed to it intimate personal miseries. Weizenbaum's own secretary, who had watched him work on ELIZA for several months, nevertheless asked him to leave the room on her first "therapy" session with the program. A well-known Soviet computer scientist tried out a version of ELIZA in the presence of his American hosts in Stanford, and embarrassed them by entering into a deeply private discussion with the computer.[70]

Another of Weizenbaum's qualms originated in one more difference he had with Kenneth Colby. The two men, who had been introduced to each other in Stanford by Edward Feigenbaum, had discussed ELIZA-like programs together. (The extent of their collaboration is not clear: both men have their own interpretation of it.) Colby called his version of the program DOCTOR. Contrary to Weizenbaum, who considered his ELIZA an exploration into man-machine communications, Colby saw DOCTOR as a potential therapeutic tool. Weizenbaum disagreed on moral grounds, and Colby proceeded with his experimentations independently. When he beat Weizenbaum to publication through a short note in the *Journal of Nervous and Mental Diseases*,[71] the disagreement escalated into a quarrel over credit for authorship of the program. The dispute flared up in public when Weizenbaum got into an exchange with Colby after a session of the 1973 summer meeting of the International Joint Conference on Artificial Intelligence in Stanford.[72] That the rift over scientific credit partially overshadowed the fundamental disagreement over principles between the two men is deplorable. Fortunately, Weizenbaum presented his position in greater depth in *Computer Power and Human Reason*.

AI researchers, claimed Weizenbaum, collectively behave like the nightly drunkard who has lost his keys in a dark corner, but looks for them under a lamppost because the light is better there. AI's lamppost is the rationalistic, symbol-manipulating view of humans, to which key aspects of human nature will remain forever in the dark. Particularly irritating to Weizenbaum was Herbert Simon's own view of man, whom, as we have already mentioned, Simon likens to an ant: when making its way back home on a wind-molded beach, the insect follows a complicated path around obstacles; yet the complexity of this trajectory lies entirely in the ant's environment, and a simple homing mechanism in the insect itself can account for it.[73] Likewise, Simon hoped to explain the complexity of human thought by simple psychological mechanisms that the computer would be able to match in complexity.[74]

For this view Weizenbaum repeatedly took Simon to task throughout *Computer Power and Human Reason*. Human beings cannot be reduced to an information-processing machine, claimed Weizenbaum, because an organism is defined in large part by the problems it faces. We confront problems no machines could be made to tackle. Some notions machines will never understand because they don't share our objectives. Criticizing AI efforts at transforming English sentences into semantic structures, Weizenbaum asked how such a construct could ever embody the desperate longing of a young man for love as he implores "Will you come to dinner with me this evening?" Or how could a computer ever empathize with Weizenbaum as he recollected:

> Sometimes when my children were still little, my wife and I would stand over them as they lay sleeping in their beds. We spoke to each other in silence, rehearsing a scene as old as mankind itself. It is as Ionesco told his journal: "Not everything is unsayable in words, only the living truth."[75]

Whence does "living truth" spring? Weizenbaum offers as one source the human body, which involves being born of woman:

> [O]ut of [the] problematic reunification of mother and child—problematic because it involves inevitably the trauma of separation—emerge the foundations of the human's knowledge of what it means to give and to receive, to trust and to mistrust, to be a friend and to have a friend, and to have a sense of hope and a sense of doom.[76]

Like Dreyfus, Weizenbaum believes that "a portion of the information the human 'processes' is kinesthetic . . . 'stored' in muscles and joints."[77] One can hardly learn the emotional impact of touching another person's hand, say, without having a hand.

Weizenbaum claims that from the right-hand part of our cognitive organ, the brain, well up such informal processes as intuition, hunches, and wisdom. The conscious GPS-like part of the brain, the left hemisphere, listens in awe to the strange, unconscious processes of its right-hand counterpart. The descriptions it provides "can . . . never be whole, anymore than a musical score can be a whole description or interpretation of even the simplest song. . . . We are capable of listening with the third ear, of sensing living truth that is truth beyond any standards of provability."[78]

Yet from these premises Weizenbaum has, unlike Dreyfus, clearly refrained from concluding the impossibility of artificial intelligence: "I see no way to put a bound on the degree of intelligence [a robot] could . . . in principle attain."[79] The "in principle" is important because Weizenbaum did not see any intelligent machines within Simon's "visible future." "Let me say what's constant as far as AI is concerned," Weizenbaum told me. "It is the enormous overestimate of what has been accomplished, and even more the enormous overestimation of what we are going to do in the next few years."

Weizenbaum, however, judged considerations on the timing of achievements somewhat beside the point:

The only qualification I make, and I can't understand why it is resisted, is that the intelligence that we will develop in machines will always be alien to human intelligence. Consider how different the intelligence of a dolphin is from that of a human being, or how the social intelligence of a Japanese differs from an American's. The intelligence of a computer will be even more different. . . . I don't understand what that reservation takes away from any ambition that the AI people might have.

Yet in his book, Weizenbaum pointed out one major practical limitation stemming from that assertion. There are many objectives and functions, he claimed, that one cannot appropriately assign to machines. And on that issue his feelings ran high: "The very asking of the question, 'What does a judge (or a psychiatrist) know that we cannot tell a computer?' is a monstrous obscenity. That it has to be put into print at all . . . is a sign of the madness of our times."[80]

Weizenbaum accused the artificial intelligentsia of erecting as a motto SHRDLU's operating principle of transforming meaning into function. Such an attitude leads to the complete denial of human values and is characteristic of the restricted vision of the closet hackers who, according to him, were taking over society. After spending an entire chapter describing his perception of the insecure, reductionist, and obsessive psychology of hackers, Weizenbaum added a political dimension to his plea: "The affairs of the world appear to be in the hands of technicians whose psychic constitutions approximate those of the [compulsive programmer] to a dangerous degree."[81]

"The best and the brightest" who concocted the Vietnam War—by considering, GPS-like, communist Vietnam as an undesirable object and applying to it the proper difference-reducing operators—fare no better than the Nazis in Weizenbaum's esteem.

In the particular case of computer applications, Weizenbaum considers "obscene" those that "substitute a computer system for a human function that involves interpersonal respect, understanding, and love."[82] He regards computerized psychiatry as the prime example. Weizenbaum directs his ire at Colby's proposals for using ELIZA for such purposes, and tells of actual clinical experiments in which computers randomly answered patients' questions by yes or no, with allegedly helpful effects. "[D]o we wish to encourage people to live their lives on the basis of patent fraud, charlatanism, and unreality?"[83] he inquired.

In this regard, Weizenbaum told me that he "recently saw his worst fear come true." Kenneth Colby has founded a software company that markets an apparently ELIZA-like program running on a PC. It is designed to help its users overcome depression. Weizenbaum does not accept the argument that if such programs help patients in the absence of overworked psychiatrists, then their use should be explored in any case.

This opposition between operational necessity and principles represents perhaps the best illustration of the problems Weizenbaum addresses. I should like to offer a middle ground for reconciliation. Can't we respect human values, including honesty, not because of high principles but simply because in the long run it is the best policy? In fact, this is probably how such values emerged in the first place. In the instance at hand, this modus operandi would proscribe the use of random yes-no or ELIZA programs for psychotherapy, simply because of their lack of long-term efficiency. Such programs might work for a while because patients would appreciate the apparent consideration of the computer for them. They might even believe the program's answers to be insightful, and be prodded to introspect accordingly. However, extensive use would render the programs' lack of true understanding obvious, and destroy the placebo. If individual patients did not realize it, then the media would sooner or later make it common knowledge. Further, such "fraudulent" programs would jeopardize the introduction of "honest" programs, if such ever come to be.

How would an "honest" program differ from ELIZA? Let's go back to the end of the dialogue with the distressed girl. After hearing that she associates her father with "bullies," the computer asked whether this had any relationship with her boyfriend making her "come here." ELIZA made the remark out of pure dumb luck, as part of its strategy to randomly tack previous statements to leading sentences and parrot them back. It could just as easily have selected the fifth statement from the patient and said "Does this have anything to do with the fact that (it's true)?" But what if the program had made the remark about the girl's boyfriend out of a genuine knowledge that people often unconsciously seek in their mates the character traits of their parents? What if it had seen the bearing of this fact on the girl's distress, and then helped her realize her motivations? Such a program may not have "loved" the girl, to get back to Weizenbaum's objection, but it would certainly have understood her. Most important, it would have helped. It remains to be seen whether AI researchers and psychiatrists can eventually distill such knowledge and perceptivity into a computer program. Weizenbaum claims that no amount of artificial cunning will suffice.

I asked Weizenbaum whether his dissenting attitude had prompted his colleagues to make him a nonperson as they did Dreyfus. He claimed not and pointed out that by the time MIT awarded him tenure, he was already well established as a dissident. He did, however, complain of getting the cold shoulder at the AI lab.

On the other hand, he told me of taking part, in February 1991, in a public debate with Marvin Minsky at a software festival in Munich. (Weizenbaum was born in Germany and speaks the language fluently, but the debate was held in English for Minsky's benefit.) To Weizenbaum's considerable surprise, as he reported, Minsky at one point said, " 'There are two classes of critics of AI. In one class are people like Dreyfus and Searle: they misunderstand, and should be ignored. And then there's Weizenbaum. I owe him a profound apology. I've long misunderstood what he's been saying, and I now see that his criticisms are correct and should be taken seriously.'

"He put his arm around me and the photographers went wild!" Weizenbaum went on. "After a while I could hardly see because of the flashes! I would like to believe in this great reconciliation scene, but I think Marvin just did what comes naturally to him: he said the most sensational thing he could think of."

Does Minsky really take Weizenbaum seriously? I doubt it. When, a

few weeks after the Munich events, I asked him whether he approved
of Weizenbaum's description, in *Computer Power and Human Reason,* of
hackers as compulsive maniacs, he tossed me a curt: "No, but I think
Joe is like that."

CONCLUSION

One might wonder how the disappointing projects and attacks against
AI affected the morale of AI researchers in the 1970s. Surprisingly, I
haven't identified any signs of gloom or discouragement during that
period. It could be that, much as suicides practically disappeared in
besieged England during the Second World War, the researchers' enthusiasm was spurred by the adversity. Another explanation has to do with
the inside perspective into AI research, which was much more encouraging than external assessments of it. Outside observers like Dreyfus
perceived the impossibility of generalizing from the micro worlds experiments, and the shortcomings of GPS, as failures. The truth is that
science advances primarily by refining successive approximations. A
scientific theory (of which GPS and the micro worlds were embodiments, in computer programs) is seldom right or wrong, but merely a
more or less accurate approximation to reality. For example, it would be
foolish to claim that relativity proved Newtonian physics "wrong":
despite its major conceptual differences with relativity, the old theory
still suffices for most engineering work. In the 1970s, AI researchers
realized that they simply had to move on to closer approximations of
how the mind functions. They do appear, however, to have learned to
guard against exaggerating the accuracy of their current theories, as the
founders of AI did in their 1960s forecasts. Older researchers progressively realized in the 1970s that their schedule had been way ahead of
reality. When AI later found its second wind, some of them, as we'll see,
cautioned their younger colleagues against overclaiming.

6

THE TREE OF KNOWLEDGE

[In 1959] it looked like you could do a project in two years. . . . But by 1970, . . . if you had a good idea, it might take two or three years to get other people to appreciate it, and three or four years to actually do the work. So you were progressing in six- or seven-year steps.
                                                              —Marvin Minsky

The very first example of knowledge encoded into rules of thumb, or heuristics, goes back a long way. It is the Edwin Smith papyrus.[1] Smith, an American collector, bought the Egyptian papyrus in a Luxor antique shop in 1882. Some fifty years later, James Breasted, an archeologist at the University of Chicago, deciphered it and placed its date of origin in the seventeenth century B.C. Breasted and later archeologists believe the document to be a copy of an original dating back much earlier: the beginning of the third millennium, or about five thousand years ago.[2] The papyrus represents forty-eight surgical observations of head wounds, all under the same formal representation: title, symptoms, diagnosis, treatment. The symptom-diagnosis pair always appears as follows: "IF you examine a man presenting this symptom, THEN you will say about him: it is such injury." The prognosis—favorable, uncertain, or fatal—is expressed by one of three invariable forms: "It is an injury that I will cure," "It is an injury that I will combat," "It is an injury against which I am powerless." Here is the papyrus's rule pertaining to fractures of the cheekbone:

> Title:
> Instructions for treating a fracture of the cheekbone.
> Symptoms:
> IF you examine a man with a fracture of the cheekbone, you will find a salient and red fluxion, bordering this wound.
> Diagnostic and prognosis:
> THEN you will tell your patient: "A fracture of the cheekbone. It is an injury that I will cure."
> Treatment:
> You shall tend him with fresh meat the first day. The treatment shall last until the fluxion resorbs. Then you shall treat him with raspberry, honey, and bandages to be renewed each day, until he is cured.[3]

In the late 1960s and early 1970s AI researchers were looking for practical problems to solve. They realized that knowledge was the key to problem solving power, and searched for ways to make knowledge available to their computers in large amounts. This search led them to an IF . . . THEN format strikingly like that used by their Egyptian predecessor, and involved new ways of sifting through large amounts of knowledge: these discoveries resulted in the first expert systems. The fathers of expert systems also found ways to express knowledge about knowledge itself: these techniques are now a part of the new field of knowledge engineering.

THE FIRST EXPERT SYSTEMS

The switch from qualitative studies in the control and expression of knowledge to the manipulation of massive amounts of it marks a turning point in the history of AI. As Herbert Simon pointed out to me, it happened not so much because researchers were previously unaware of the power of knowledge, as it did for practical, hardware-oriented limitations:

> Quite deliberately we did a lot of our work in the early days . . . on toy tasks. Toy not in the sense that they weren't hard problems to solve but in the sense that they didn't need much special knowledge.

It isn't as though people weren't aware that knowledge was important. They were steering away from tasks which made knowledge the
center of things because we couldn't build large data bases with the
computers we had then. Our first chess program and the Logic
Theorist were done on a computer that had a 64- to 100-word core
and a scratch drum with 10,000 words of usable space on it. So
semantics was not the name of the game. I remember one student
that I had who wanted to do a thesis on how you extracted information from a big store. I told him "No way! You can only do that thesis
on a toy example, and we won't have any evidence of how it scales
up. You'd better find something else to do." So people did steer away
from problems where knowledge was the essential issue.[4]

In the early 1970s, though, computers with hundreds of thousands of
words of memory became available, thus giving free rein to programmers for implementing applications requiring extensive amounts of
knowledge. Yet, it still took ten years after the advent of such machines
to develop commercial systems relying on extensive knowledge bases
such as XCON, which I shall discuss in a short while. One reason for
this additional delay is the tremendous complexity of the software
needed to develop and run such systems. A related cause is the lengthen-
ing of the development cycles in AI, an unavoidable consequence, alas,
of the maturing of the field. When you start a new science from scratch,
and are almost alone in researching it, you will become of necessity a
fountainhead of new ideas and immediately test them yourself. As research results from other people accumulate, you often will catch yourself rediscovering the wheel, and start spending much time cross-check-
ing your work against others' to guard against that. After a while, most
of the easy problems have been solved; research projects tend to involve
several people, with the attendant political and organizational hangups.
Marvin Minsky pointed out the phenomenon to me, recalling how
fast Slagle's thesis on symbolic integration was completed a few years
after the Dartmouth conference:

Slagle started it in 1959 and was done after two years. So at that time
it looked like you could do a project in two years. . . . But by 1970,
. . . if you had a good idea, it might take two or three years to get other
people to appreciate it, and three or four years to actually do the work.
So you were progressing in six- or seven-year steps.[5]

In the 1970s, AI was "hankering for respectability" in Herbert Simon's words, and emerging from its infancy. Some of its applictions addressed subjects of immediate interest to scientists of other disciplines, and led to the massive commercialization of expert systems in the 1980s. The first expert systems were DENDRAL and MYCIN.

DENDRAL

The seeds for the development of expert systems were planted by a practical young redhead named Edward Feigenbaum. Feigenbaum, then twenty years old and an undergraduate student in electrical engineering, was present when Herbert Simon announced to his first class at Carnegie Tech in 1956 his discovery of an intelligent machine. Fascinated, he afterwards earned his Ph.D. under Simon by building a computer model of human learning called EPAM (see chapter 10). Since his work was performed at the School of Industrial Administration, where Simon then was teaching, it branded Feigenbaum as an expert in this field and landed him after graduation an assistant professorship in the business school at Berkeley. There he tried to emulate his mentor Herbert Simon and set up an artificial intelligence program in an environment designed for churning out accountants and managers. Feigenbaum was soon joined at Berkeley by Julian Feldman, another Carnegie Mellon alumnus.

Despite earning a seventy-thousand-dollar grant from the Carnegie Foundation to support their research (a staggering amount for the time), and publishing the first AI book ever (a collection of papers entitled *Computers and Thought,*[6] which remained the only publication of its kind for several years afterward), the Feigenbaum-Feldman team enjoyed little support from the rest of the faculty. In 1965, Feigenbaum left for the computer science department of Stanford, where he found kindred souls.

His most influential encounter was with Joshua Lederberg. A Nobel Prize winner in genetics, Lederberg wanted to determine the molecular structure of complex organic molecules, and had hit a stumbling block. If you want to study a chemical compound, your first step is to determine its chemical formula. This relatively straightforward analysis tells you how many atoms of each kind the molecules contain. Unfortunately, the formula alone reveals very little about the compound. The properties of a complex molecule depend mostly on the nature of the chemical bonds within the molecule, and on how the atoms are positioned in respect to each other. These properties together make up the molecular structure. There are no simple ways to map the structure of a molecule.

The standard method of analysis consists of literally breaking up the problem into smaller parts. Chemists separate the molecules under study into ionized (electrified) fragments and process them in a device called a "mass spectrometer." The spectrometer provides the mass/charge ratios of the fragments, and shows how many fragments of each kind there are. The mass/charge ratios provide clues to the chemical compositions of the fragments. Together, these pieces of information form an incomplete picture that knowledgeable chemists can solve to reconstruct the original molecule.

Lederberg's problem was one of too many combinations. Each fragment could correspond to several substructures; yet only one global molecular structure fitted all the problem constraints. Finding the global structure involved searching a tree of possibilities. Feigenbaum and Lederberg took account of this fact in naming their program heuristic DENDRAL.[7] The word *dendral* derives from the Greek word for tree. In this case, the tree was often too large for exhaustive search even by a computer. Prior to DENDRAL, chemists attempted to solve the problem in the only way they knew how: they took educated guesses at possible solutions and tested each against the data.

The DENDRAL project, headed by Feigenbaum and his colleague Robert K. Lindsay, started in 1965 and lasted more than ten years. Feigenbaum and his co-workers were able to embody, in a set of rules, part of the knowledge chemists relied upon to make their educated guesses. A typical rule looked like the following:

IF the spectrum for the molecule has two peaks at masses $x1$ and $x2$ such that
a. $x1 + x2$ = Molecular Weight + 28
b. $x1 - 28$ is a high peak, and
c. $x2 - 28$ is a high peak, and
d. at least one of $x1$ or $x2$ is high,

THEN the molecule contains a ketone group.[8]

This set of rules, together with the logic required to combine them and deduce candidates for the global structure of a molecule, made up what is now considered the first expert system. The rules could drastically reduce the required search.[9] For the compound Di-n-decyl $C_{20}H_{22}$ the number of possible combinations exceeded 11,000,000. DENDRAL reduced these to 22,366 cases, which the program could then test individually to see whether they accounted for all the observations. At the end, only one combination would fit the bill, and it was the true molecular structure.

For one class of compounds, DENDRAL even narrowed the search better than the most experienced chemists.[10] DENDRAL demonstrated that one could embody, in the midst of a program doing extensive numerical work, expert knowledge that drastically reduced the effort needed to find the answer. Yet it had one major weakness: the rules and the logic required to apply them made up one tangled set of statements. When it reached a certain size, Feigenbaum and his team found it very difficult to maintain and expand their creation. The originally fluid LISP structure quickly became hard as concrete.

It was at that time that Feigenbaum and another Carnegie Mellon alumnus who had joined him at Stanford, Bruce Buchanan, took their cue from some of the work done by Newell and Simon at their alma mater.[11] Newell and Simon had been investigating a contraption called a "production system" as a model for human cognition.[12] The mathematician Emil Post had been the first to propose the idea in a 1943 paper.[13] The linguist Noam Chomsky used production systems in 1957, under the name "rewrite rules," to formalize his theories on grammar.[14] In the 1960s, they were seized by computer scientists to build compiler programs. Simon told me he first heard of production systems through a young practitioner of computer science:

The guy who brought production systems into [Carnegie Mellon] was Bob Floyd. He was using them to design [special kinds of] compilers. Floyd had gotten his bachelor's degree at Chicago and never went on to a higher degree. He ended up in a software company up in Boston. . . . I went up there to give a lecture and met him. And heard about compiler compilers, heard about productions, heard a lot from him. He was obviously very smart. I sang his praises when I came back, so we said, "The hell with degrees!" and appointed him to a faculty position. He was here for a decade until he went out to Stanford.

MYCIN

Production systems are just lists of IF . . . THEN rules of the type used in DENDRAL, but with an important difference: the mechanism used to decide when and how to apply a given rule is apart from the list of rules itself. In the early 1970s, Feigenbaum and Buchanan set out to explore the implications of this separation of tasks and assigned this work as a thesis project to a doctoral student, Donald Waterman. In 1972, another doctoral student, Edward Shortliffe, set out under the direction of Buchanan to embody practical medical knowledge into a production system.

The result was MYCIN,[15] an expert system for the diagnosis of infectious blood diseases. From the results of blood tests, bacterial cultures, and other information, MYCIN suggested which microorganism was causing an infection. It reached this conclusion through such rules as:

IF
The site of the culture is blood, and the gram strain is positive, and the portal of entry is gastrointestinal tract, and
    [A]—the abdomen is the locus of infection, or
    [B]—the pelvis is the locus of infection
THEN
There is strongly suggestive evidence that Enterobacteriaceae is the class of organisms for which therapy should cover.[16]

MYCIN would then prescribe antibiotics for treating the condition, and even adjusted the dosage according to the patient's body weight.

Since MYCIN was the first expert system to embody cleanly the separation of the rules (which are said to make up the knowledge base) and the logic required to apply them to a particular situation, its authors made available to other researchers a version of MYCIN containing only the inference engine. This evacuated version made up the first expert system shell. Shortliffe and Buchanan called it EMYCIN, which they first claimed stood for "Empty MYCIN." After being the subject of too many jokes, they changed this to Essential MYCIN. Like many doctors, MYCIN relied on the technique of backward chaining to reach its conclusions. Backward chaining is yet another way of keeping a tree search from branching beyond control. MYCIN contained high-level rules that enabled it, from a preliminary scan of a patient's symptoms, to take a stab at a few possible diagnoses. It then worked its way backward, along the search tree defined by its rules, to justify these educated guesses.

As yet another dramatic improvement over DENDRAL, MYCIN had the ability to deal with rules that imply likely results rather than certainties. Given the IF part of a rule, MYCIN could consider that the THEN part was true with only, say, a 70-percent chance. In fact, MYCIN could rate possible conclusions on a scale ranging from −1 (definitely wrong) to +1 (certainly true). MYCIN could combine these certainty factors while following a chain of rules. If this analysis left it with two or more possible diagnoses, it ranked them by order of likelihood. In one blind clinical test rated by a panel of eight experts, MYCIN prescribed antibiotics for blood diseases as well as, or better than, nine individual clinicians.[17]

Randall Davis, who made his own contribution to the MYCIN project, compared MYCIN and DENDRAL for me:

> DENDRAL had the idea of rules, but it was essentially a big LISP program with some conditional rules built in. . . . What DENDRAL contributed was that you could capture domain-specific knowledge as a set of rules. It demonstrated that that was a good idea and a powerful idea, but it didn't have this distinction [between rules and control logic]. By far and away the most important thing MYCIN did was to demonstrate in an unambiguous fashion that the notion of a knowledge-based system was real and tangible, and that high performance really could come almost entirely from a substantial body of knowledge. The notion of backward chaining as a [control logic] is of course computationally trivial. And that's the point. This system was developed at a time when the notion of very clever control structures was being explored. And to a large degree its intellectual impact was an unmistakable demonstration that "In the knowledge lies the power." And that you don't need clever control structures to produce intelligent behavior. . . . [MYCIN's] real place in history was to put a marker on the map and show that the notion of a modular system was real, that it worked.[18]

The two-part construction of MYCIN is crucial. Since the rules in MYCIN itself say little to a nonphysician, I shall illustrate MYCIN's layout, which is also that of a typical modern expert system, with the following set of rules that could be programmed into a computer to enable it to identify large sea animals.

1. IF it is huge THEN it is a whale
2. IF it is NOT huge THEN it is not-a-whale
3. IF it is not-a-whale AND (it blows a jet OR it has a blowhole OR it has a horizontal tail) THEN it is a mammal
4. IF it is not-a-whale AND (it has no blowhole OR it has a vertical tail) THEN it is a fish
5. IF it is a mammal AND it has a pointed snout THEN it is a dolphin
6. IF it is a mammal AND it has a blunted snout AND is with a whale THEN it is a baby whale
7. IF it is a mammal AND it has a blunted snout AND it is not with a whale THEN it is a porpoise
8. IF it is a fish AND is not by itself THEN it may-be-a-tuna
9. If it may-be-a-tuna AND it has a double dorsal fin THEN it is a tuna
10. IF it may-be-a-tuna AND it does not have a double dorsal fin THEN it is an unknown fish
11. IF it is a fish AND is by itself THEN it is a swordfish-or-shark
12. IF it is a swordfish-or-shark AND (it has a sword OR (it is silvery AND has a forward dorsal fin)) THEN it is a swordfish ELSE it may-be-a-shark
13. IF it may-be-a-shark AND it has a sinewy swim THEN it is a shark
14. IF it may-be-a-shark AND it does not have a sinewy swim THEN it is an unknown fish

These rules are the productions; and the entire set of rules, plus the program required to apply them (omitted here), make up the production system. Each rule takes the form of an "IF . . . THEN" statement. The IF part can contain one or several conditions. The presence of an OR operator means that not all conditions need be true for the rule to apply.

Using ORs enables a production system to capture some of the parallelism of human thought. It also enables the system to reach conclusions without a complete knowledge of the problem. For example, the OR conjunctions in rule 3 let the computer move ahead even if you haven't been able to see the entire animal. If you haven't caught sight of the blowhole, maybe you've seen the jet. Failing that, you may have glimpsed the tail. Some of the preconditions are conclusions reached by other rules. For example, rule 5 requires that the animal be a mammal: this is the conclusion of rule 3. Thus, even if each rule contains a separate bit of knowledge, their conclusions and conditions relate the rules to each other.

In fact, we can capture the relationships between the rules very simply. A graphic representation reduces the set of rules to a tree structure. Figure 6.1 contains the search-tree equivalent of the sea animal's production system. To get the computer to use the rule set, it is necessary to explain to it how to search the tree for applicable actions. The same applies to real-world problems. In the sea-animal example, suppose you asked the computer, "What's this swimming on starboard?" (or entered the equivalent keyboard query), without giving any other information. The program should know enough to do the following: First, it should look at the rules available, and realize that it requires more information before answering your question. In this case, the appropriate action would be a query for the information required to apply rule number 1 (IF it is huge THEN it is a whale). Thus, the computer needs a program to allow it to decide, from the set of rules, that it should ask you, "Well, how big is it?" The program should then use your answer to decide what question to ask next. Because of the analogies between rule sets and search trees, parts of this program can resemble the tree-searching programs used in theorem provers. Hence, once we have described the tree to the computer, an analogue of the tree-searching machinery developed for theorem proving can operate on the tree.

The flash of inspiration behind expert systems was just that: the realization, obvious in retrospect, that the tree description and the instructions for exploring the tree can be kept separate in a program. From one application to the next, one then needs only change the description of the tree, by entering a new set of rules. While this procedure improves the power of the program, it represents, in a sense, the opposite of reasoning. This illustrates the deep paradox uncovered by AI research: the only way to deal efficiently with very complex problems

FIGURE 6.1

A Graphic Equivalent of the Sea Animal Expert System

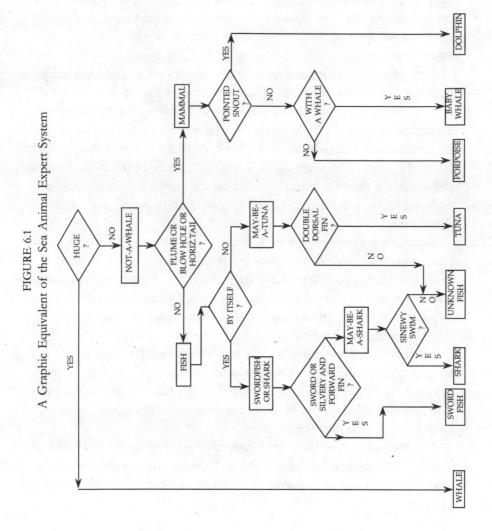

is to move away from pure logic. Consider a physician and a biologist. The biologist, who has studied biochemistry, anatomy, and physiology, can explain better than the physician the workings of a human body out of basic scientific principles. Yet that biologist can't read the telltale signs of a given infection and prescribe the right drug for it. Most of the time, reaching the right decision requires little reasoning: it is simply a question of *knowing* which symptoms go with which illness. Expert systems are, thus, not about reasoning: they are about knowing.

This type of behavior distinguishes, in fact, many of our interactions with the world. We constantly face opportunities to which we should react before they disappear. Reasoning takes time, so we try to do it as seldom as possible. Instead, we store the results of our reasoning for later reference: Feigenbaum and the production system school of AI claim that we store them in the form of rules, or recipes. Typical examples are the multiplication table or the recipe for tying shoelaces (remember how long it took when you had to think each motion through?).

Since remembering requires memory—or "storage space" in computer parlance—we find ourselves constantly trading time for space. We meet the largest payoff in this barter when the process of reasoning involves much trial-and-error searching for a solution. Since most skills required for intelligent behavior are of that nature, intelligent systems need to be partly rule-bound.

To summarize, an expert system has two parts: The first one is the so-called knowledge base. It usually makes up most of the system. In its simplest form, it is a list of IF . . . THEN rules like the one above: each one specifies what to do, or what conclusions to draw, under a set of well-defined circumstances.

The second part of the expert system often goes under the name of "shell." As the name implies, it acts as a receptacle for the knowledge base and contains instruments for making efficient use of it. These include:

- A short-term memory that contains specific data about the actual problem under study. For example, the short-term memory for the sea-animal expert system may contain the information that the animal to identify is not huge and has a vertical tail.
- Tree-searching machinery as such. AI researchers, who are often strongly attached to the past, called this part of an expert system the

inference engine, since it—in sifting through the knowledge base and inferring from it solutions to the problem at hand—fulfills Charles Babbage's notions for his ill-fated "analytical engine" in the nineteenth century (see chapter 1). Randall Davis told me that he coined the term *inference engine* while working on his Ph.D. at Stanford:

> I had to go to Washington to try and explain to some folks from DARPA [the Department of Defense's Advanced Research Projects Agency] what our research was about. I needed a word that would convey to a bunch of people who understood FORTRAN programs that what we were doing was very different. And knowing about Babbage, . . . I figured *inference engine* was in the right spirit. It would orient them toward thinking of a machine because it was an engine, but orient them toward thinking of a machine that was doing inference, not arithmetic. And that is a very important distinction.

- User interface, which can range from simple, menu-driven interaction with the computer, to quasi natural-language dialogue. The expert system uses the user interface to ask you questions like "How large is the animal?" and to understand your answer. Through it, you can also ask the computer to explain how it reached a certain conclusion. To answer, the computer would simply retrace its trip down the decision tree for you, and may say something like: "I conclude it's a dolphin, because it's not huge (rule 1), it has a blowhole (rule 4), and it has a pointed snout (rule 5)."

Nowadays, expert system shells are available from many software companies. To apply them to a particular problem, you simply add the pertinent set of rules into the knowledge base. Counting the basic research and development that went into the technology, a modern expert system shell embodies hundreds of person-years of work. Without it, it would be necessary to do part of this work all over for each new expert system.

An Advance in AI

There are several reasons why expert systems constitute a genuine advance in artificial intelligence.

First, many modern expert systems involve thousands of rules. It would be extremely tedious to find the rules pertinent to a given problem (or follow the corresponding search tree) on paper. User-friendly program interfaces make the search itself transparent and turn the consultation into a question-answering session. At the design stage, the analyst can correct errors by asking the system how it reached a faulty conclusion. The defective rule will appear in the chain of reasoning cited by the system. Since the rules are usually self-explanatory, end users can also follow the reasoning involved and thus satisfy themselves of the validity of the system's conclusion.

To perform all these tasks, expert systems allow the automatic chaining of rules: that is, entering the rules in an order different from the one in which they will appear in the reasoning. Rule chaining also permits the program to infer conditions from conclusions. For example, in a medical expert system, it would be possible to enter the rules as: "Infection by such a microorganism causes this symptom." The expert system could then work its way backward from symptoms to causes.

Problem solutions do not usually follow from a single string of rules or from a single branch of the tree. Several alternative paths are usually open in the search down the tree. For example, a given set of symptoms could come from several illnesses, all of which the system must consider. If unable to rule out all but one diagnosis, the system would supply a list of possibilities, with associated likelihoods. Conversely, several different paths of investigation might lead to a single conclusion. Even if no path offered convincing evidence by itself, the convergence of several paths could allow a conclusion. Expert systems can handle this type of situation also.

Expert systems differ from printed rule books, or even from conventional computer programs, through their flexibility and modularity. In these aspects, they almost rival human reasoning. Expert systems are easy to change or improve. You want to add a new piece of knowledge? Simply leave everything as is, and add a new rule! You would inform a human worker about a new law or regulation in much the same way. By contrast, a change to a conventional computer program interacts with the existing code. It requires a careful screening, and usually changes, to the old code.

Yet another difference of expert systems is their openness, or self-explanatory character. In conventional programs (except perhaps data bases), computer-language instructions, or algorithms, contain the knowledge. It is hidden in the structure of the program itself, rather than made explicit in a separate module. AI workers say that in expert systems, knowledge is declarative; while in conventional programs, it is procedural.

Expert systems resemble human thought in another important way. They are much more resilient than conventional computer programs. One can usually remove any single rule without grossly affecting the program performance. This behavior is also characteristic of a human professional, who can usually still offer an opinion even if some information is removed from the problem formulation. By contrast, if the tiniest detail in the instructions of a conventional program is accidentally erased or changed, the behavior of the program usually changes drastically.

KNOWING ABOUT KNOWLEDGE: TEIRESIAS

In the course of developing DENDRAL and MYCIN, the Stanford researchers encountered a problem that had little to do with LISP, inference engines, or even computer programming in general. It was the extreme difficulty of transferring the appropriate knowledge from the mind of a human expert to the knowledge base of the program. Boiling human knowledge down to a set of well-defined rules turned out to be a very painful process. Both the expert and the computer scientist designing the expert system had to suffer. The French scientific philosopher Claude Bernard had already realized this trait of the human mind in the previous century:

> We achieve more than we know.
> We know more than we understand.
> We understand more than we can explain.[19]

When Randall Davis was looking for a Ph.D. project at Stanford, he decided with his adviser, Bruce Buchanan, to focus on making this knowledge transfer easier. The result, a program called TEIRESIAS,[20] would mark a critical step in the development of a new discipline that became known as "knowledge engineering." Buchanan's classical background (his original field had been philosophy) inspired the program's name. Teiresias, the blind prophet in Sophocles' *Oedipus Rex,* can fathom events hidden to common mortals and possesses a higher form of knowledge. "The notion matched the idea of meta-level knowledge that I was exploring," Davis told me. "It also made for cute quotes that I could scatter through the text of the thesis. They are lines from the play which, taken out of context and dropped at the right places, made for wonderful introductions to the chapters and sections." (Sample: "I shall tell you the whole truth.")

TEIRESIAS' function as a program was to mediate between MYCIN and blood disease specialists desiring to impart some of their knowledge to it. The specialist used MYCIN in the ordinary mode, and TEIRESIAS intervened when the program made a wrong diagnosis. At a doctor's request, TEIRESIAS could then assist him or her in retracing the rules applied by MYCIN in reaching its mistaken conclusion. If one of the rules was found to be wrong, or if the physician realized that a new rule was required to take the new case into account, TEIRESIAS assisted him or her in making the correction. To this effect, TEIRESIAS needed information about how much MYCIN already knew and how it reasoned. Since this kind of information consisted in knowledge about knowledge, Davis called it "meta-knowledge." Much as Tom Evans had explored the square root of analogy in the 1960s, Davis set out to explore the square root of knowledge. For example, TEIRESIAS contained rule schemas that outlined some general characteristics of particular classes of rules. As a case in point, assume the physician has just defined the following new rule:

IF
1. The patient's infection is primary-bacteremia
2. The site is one of the sterile sites
THEN
There is evidence that the bacterium category is enterobacteriaceae.

TEIRESIAS might well reply:

I hate to criticize, Dr. Davis, but did you know that most rules about what the category of an organism might be, that mention the site of a culture and the infection, also mention:
    [A]—the portal of entry into the organism
Shall I write a clause to account for [A]?[21]

THE XCON ADVANCE

Ground breaking as they were as proofs of principle, DENDRAL and MYCIN remained laboratory applications. The development of the expert system that was to win the corporate world over to AI started in Carnegie Mellon University in the late 1970s. The program's initial name of R1 stemmed from a bad joke made by its author, John McDermott ("I had always wanted to be a knowledge engineer, and now I R1").[22] McDermott's client, the Digital Equipment Corporation of Maynard, Massachusetts, preferred the name XCON, for eXpert CONfigurer. If you've ever bought a computer, you probably had to face some of the problems XCON solves. "How much memory does this program require to run? Do I want a color screen? There aren't enough expansion slots for both the modem and the accelerator board. Which one do I need most?" Some accessories may be incompatible, while others require each other. Like new cars, computers can come in so many different configurations that no two are alike. When it went to McDermott, the Digital Equipment Corporation was to produce a new line of minicomputers called VAX. Product configuration of these new machines, or "technical editing," as it is known in the computer industry, had grown into a monster headache. Since 90 percent of the computers coming out of a DEC factory differed from each other, they had to be painstakingly put together on the factory floor, tested (which usually revealed configuration errors to correct), and then disassembled, packed, and shipped. In the late 1970s, with the introduction of the new VAX line, the problem was expected to develop into a bottleneck threatening the very survival of DEC. The engineering manager, Dennis O'Connor, was getting ready to build several dedicated plants in which to perform the preshipment testing, when he decided to see whether any research might have a bearing on the problem (following up on a suggestion made by the vice president for research, Samuel Fuller). With sixty thousand dollars of discretionary funds, O'Connor issued a contract for John McDermott, then a young professor at CMU, to investigate whether an expert system couldn't configure VAX computers. In so doing, O'Connor was running an "amazing risk," recalled DEC's engineering vice president Gordon Bell,[23] for the engineering manager sought the involvement of many others in the company, and his reputation was on the line.

McDermott's feasibility study yielded thumbs-up results, and work started on a prototype configurer at CMU in December 1978. In April 1979, McDermott and his team felt confident enough for a field test, expecting a 95-percent configuring accuracy. This first step of AI out of the academic closet was sobering: XCON averaged one configuration wrong out of five and was sent back to the drafting board. By the end of the year, though, the system was working well enough to be used on actual orders.

McDermott turned over the initial version of XCON to DEC in January 1980. It was then able to configure only one of DEC's computers, the VAX-11/780. It did well in that trial phase, and DEC approved the gradual, in-house extension of it to the rest of its products. By 1984, XCON had become the prototypical expert system success story: from about three hundred rules in 1979, it had grown tenfold to more than three thousand and could configure ten different computer models.[24]

Conceived in the 1960s, expert systems made up the most salient part of AI's revival during the 1970s and became visible to the public in the 1980s. As I shall discuss in the next chapter, that part of the AI iceberg which remains underwater is even more fascinating.

7

COMING OF AGE

A I has never been a monolithic science; by the mid-1970s, the diverging interests of its pioneers were giving birth to recognizable specialties. Adepts of expert systems, as we saw, regrouped around Edward Feigenbaum. Roger Schank, another salient personality, invigorated language analysis by finding new ways to take the meaning of words into account. Marvin Minsky carried the field of knowledge representation a step further by introducing new structures for representing mental constructs. Douglas Lenat explored automatic learning and the nature of heuristics. David Marr saw computer vision in a new light, and the authors of the new PROLOG language brought logic closer to the fingertips of programmers.

ROGER SCHANK: LANGUAGE IS TO FORGET ABOUT THE WORDS

Despite the fiasco of automatic translation in the 1960s, programmers still dreamed of dealing with their computers in languages like English, French, and Japanese instead of LISP or FORTRAN. Laypersons forced into interaction with the machines wished for better means of communication than balky menus to select from or cryptic instructions to type in. And as computer manufacturers and data-processing managers realized, such dreams made economic sense. By then, manufacturers and managers had had ample time to observe the climb up the evolutionary ladder in human-computer communications. During the previous twenty-five years, computer users had had access to ever more powerful tools to communicate with their machines. Binary code had yielded to assembly language and then to high-level languages like FORTRAN; special-purpose communication interfaces like those used for data-base systems, word processors, and spreadsheets were appearing. Managers noted with interest that each of these improvements had increased productivity by a factor of 2 or more. Manufacturers simply loved it: every one of those enhancements had also doubled the number of computer users.[1]

The obvious next step was to teach human languages to the machines, thus opening the way to such marvels as voice-activated word processors, automated librarians, voice control of machinery, classroomlike instruction for expert systems, and—yes—automatic translation. With such incentives, repeated past frustrations about research in Natural Language Processing (NLP) could not stop it for very long. The Automated Language Processing Advisory Committee's conclusion and the realization that SHRDLU's glibness would never extend beyond discoursing about blocks did induce a definite caution in researchers and funding agencies alike, but never kept progress from slowly marching on.

For example, the linguist Charles Fillmore, in an article that appeared soon after the ALPAC report in 1968, pointed out a way to tell apart the meanings of such sentences as "The cook is baking" and "The cake is baking,"[2] where the words *cook* and *cake* are both subjects of the verb *to bake,* and parsing the sentences in the usual way provides no further clues. Fillmore's idea was to distinguish between *surface* cases like subject, usually depending on a word's place in a sentence, and *deep* cases more closely associated with meaning. The ancient Greeks and Romans already knew the trick: they did not count on the position of a word to specify its function in a sentence, but instead modified the ending of the word, which gave them much more flexibility. Latin counted six such cases; and ancient Greek, five. Modern languages like German and Russian continue that practice, and English contains remnants of it in its pronouns (as in *I, me, mine*).

Fillmore proposed eight deep cases, such as *agent* (the instigator of an event), *instrument* (the stimulus or immediate physical cause of an event), and *experiencer* (the entity that undergoes the effect of the action). To tell the cases apart in a language with fixed word endings, Fillmore restricted the *kinds* of words admissible for each case. An agent, for example, had to be animate. Further, each verb could only admit to a certain limited number of cases. These restrictions were often enough to disambiguate a sentence completely. For example, in "the cake is baking" *cake* is inanimate and therefore the experiencer. An animate *cook* would have to be the agent. In "the heat is baking the cake," a quick elimination would finger *heat* as the instrument.

It soon became obvious that parsing techniques designed for conventional grammar weren't up to such antics. In 1970, William Wood, an AI researcher at Bolt, Beranek & Newman in Boston, described a parsing method called the Augmented Transition Network.[3] An ATN could mix syntax rules with such semantic props as knowing that a cook is animate: this gave it the searching savvy to untangle sentences better than any other technique. In the early 1970s, Wood used ATNs in a data-base query program to analyze moon rocks from the Apollo-11 mission. ATNs still make up the heart of many modern natural-language–processing programs.

The use of semantics in language analysis soon became the trademark of a new *enfant terrible* of the AI game, who has often been accused of having carried the strategy to extremes. Roger Schank grew up in Brooklyn and earned a bachelor degree in mathematics at Carnegie Mellon. He soon decided that linguistics was more to his taste and completed a Ph.D in this discipline at the University of Texas in 1969. Having by then reached the ripe old age of twenty-three, he had also found time to work in Stanford with Kenneth Colby, of computer paranoia fame (see chapter 5). It is at the linguistics department of that university that Schank developed, from 1969 to 1974, a theory that became known as "conceptual dependency."

Tall, impressive, and bearded, Schank wears an expression that often suggests both the severity of a Jewish prophet and the peaceful sagacity of an Indian guru. Unabashed about speaking his mind, he subscribes to a motto that many AI researchers have also adopted: extremism makes the best form of emphasis. To wit, the linguist Schank is quoted as having said, "There is no such thing as syntax."[4] He was, in fact, forcefully emphasizing that syntax amounts to an insignificant piece in the giant puzzle of language understanding. He put this observation in more sedate terms in his 1985 book *The Cognitive Computer,* which summarizes many years of his team's research work:

> Our aim was to write programs that would concentrate on crucial differences in meaning, not on issues of grammatical structure. . . . We used whatever grammatical rules were necessary in our quest to extract meanings from sentences but, to our surprise, little grammar proved to be relevant for translating sentences into a system of conceptual representations.[5]

Schank's method stemmed from the observation that English (or Russian or Swahili) is a highly equivocal medium for expressing information. Consider, for example, the many possible uses of a simple word like *gave:*

> John gave Mary a book.
> John gave Mary a hard time.
> John gave Mary a night on the town.
> John gave up.
> John gave no reason for his actions.[6]

A program that systematically made the superficially plausible inference "If John gave Mary something, now Mary has it" would have to conclude, from the second and third phrases, that Mary now possesses *a hard time* and *a night on the town.* The program might even construe from the last two sentences that somebody now possesses *up* and *no reason for John's actions.*

To enable programs to build up truthful representations of sentences and infer plausible conclusions from these constructs, Schank tackled a problem that had stumped philosophers for millenniums. Can one, reflected Schank, define logical primitives with which unequivocally to express all other statements? Gottlob Frege and Bertrand Russell had assumed as much, calling this view "logical atomism." So had Edmund Husserl, the German father of phenomenology. Soon after the Second World War, the Anglo-Austrian philosopher Ludwig Wittgenstein elevated this doctrine to a pinnacle in his celebrated *Tractatus Logico Philosophicus,* only to repudiate this view a few years later.[7] As Hubert Dreyfus has been pointing out ever since the beginnings of AI, modern philosophers like Heidegger and Merleau-Ponty also took a dim view of logical atomism.

Unimpressed, Schank produced a scheme that claimed to reduce all English verbs into as few as *eleven* basic acts. Here are some of them:

ATRANS: To transfer an abstract relationship (e.g., give)
PTRANS: To transfer the physical location of an object (e.g., go)
PROPEL: To apply physical force to an object (e.g., push)
MOVE: For its owner to move a body part (e.g., kick)
MTRANS: To transfer mental information (e.g., tell)
MBUILD: To build new information out of old (e.g., decide)[8]

Schank labeled these elementary building blocks "semantic primitives." The sentence "Burt gave Joe a black eye for calling him a name" would result in the following construct of semantic primitives:[9]

Actor: Joe
Action: MTRANS (name)
From: Joe
To: Burt ——> Anger − 8
               |
               | ——>
                         Actor: Burt
                         Action: PROPEL
                         Object: fist
                         To: Joe's eye ——> Health − 3
                         From: Burt

As a critical advantage, the system provided the computer with expectations in regard to common situations. When the computer saw in a sentence words usually relating to the transfer of possession (such as *give, buy, sell, acquire, donate*), it searched for the normal props of ATRANS: the object being transferred, its receiver and original owner, the means of transfer, and so on. Failure to encounter such corollaries would induce the computer to revise its assumption and try another possible meaning of the word. Further, after successfully parsing a sentence, the machine could make plausible inferences associated with the semantic primitive involved. For ATRANS, said Schank, "a typical rule might be that if someone gets something they want, they may be happy about it and may use it. Another is that if someone relinquishes control of something it may be because they got something in return that they believe to be of greater value."[10]

Aside from a handy parsing and inferential device, conceptual dependency doubled as a plausible psychological model. Schank observed:

> Our ability to remember a story *at all* depends on our ability to form an underlying conceptual representation that is *not* tied to any words. . . . Remembering stories and paraphrasing them requires that we *forget* the words originally used and that we invent our own ways of saying the stories to ourselves. . . . One task in AI, strangely enough, is to get the computer to *forget the words.*[11]

Despite the obvious merits of Schank's approach, most of his colleagues initially considered it thoroughly iconoclastic. Linguists recoiled at this trampling of Chomsky's syntax-oriented methods, then in full bloom. Schank's expectation-driven processing stood at the opposite of the logical methodology proposed by the likes of John McCarthy. Conceptual dependency's claims of psychological plausibility made it somewhat more palatable to the cognitive modeling approach of Newell and Simon, but Schank's processing methods differed markedly from theirs. Newell and Simon had relied on means-end analysis, and their newfound workhorse was production systems: it had little in common with Schank's "slot-filler" techniques.

Schank, however, found a sympathetic listener in Marvin Minsky. "I'm very impressed with conceptual dependency," Minsky told me twenty years after Schank introduced it. "His set of primitives was tremendously insightful, and no one has gotten a similarly good set since."[12]

Schank's assertive manners did little to ingratiate him with those who did not share his point of view. He didn't apologize either and took pleasure in emphasizing the stylistic differences that set his school of thought apart. It is to him that AI researchers owe the dubious demarcation that all are aware of but few openly recognize: the division of AI researchers into *neats* and *scruffies*. Neats, says Schank, wear well-ironed clothes and work on surface phenomena like logic and syntax, which they can understand and put into cozy little boxes. Scruffies dress haphazardly and love dealing with messy problems like semantics. (I have noticed that in private, neats don't mind referring to scruffies as such, but I've never met a scruffy who would acknowledge the epithet.)

In 1973, the first embodiment of conceptual dependency theory stemmed from the work of Schank's first three doctoral students. MAR-GIE, an acronym for Memory, Analysis, Response Generation In English, was a program that analyzed single English sentences, turned them into semantic representations like the preceding one for Joe's black eye, and generated plausible inferences from them. The idea was eventually to use these inferences to understand later sentences, as in the story:

> John went to a restaurant. He ordered a hamburger. It was cold when the waitress brought it. He left her a very small tip.[13]

The scheme did not work. Schank and his students were crestfallen to discover that any single sentence lends itself to so many plausible inferences that it was impossible to isolate those pertinent to the next sentence. For instance, from "It was cold when the waitress brought it," MARGIE could reflect that:

- The hamburger's temperature probably stood between 75 and 90 degrees Fahrenheit.
- The waitress brought the hamburger on a plate.
- She used her hands to carry the plate.
- She put the plate on a table.
- She was close to John when she did so.
- Et cetera . . .

The inference that cold food makes people unhappy generally lay so far down the list that a program like MARGIE never could have related it to the next sentence. As a result, such a program could not have understood the story well enough to answer the question "Why did John leave a small tip?"

To overcome this problem Schank, who had by 1977 moved to Yale University, teamed up with one of his new colleagues, Robert Abelson, professor of psychology at Yale. They reflected that most of our everyday gestures are linked together in meaningful chains, which they called "scripts." For example, the "Going to the restaurant" script might run like this:

Enter restaurant hungry.
If "wait to be seated" sign, wait, then follow maître d' to seat.

Else seat yourself.
Wait for waiter to bring menu.
Choose food.
Order food.
If long wait, then exit restaurant angry.
If food quality abysmal, exit restaurant angry.
Else eat food.
If food quality good, leave large tip.
If food quality bad, leave small tip.
Pay for food.
Leave restaurant no longer hungry.[14]

Much as Schank had previously associated expectations with primitive acts, Schank and Abelson could now use scripts to anticipate and make sense of entire situations. A program like MARGIE could then link the relevant sentences relating John's adventures in the restaurant to specific portions of the restaurant script, analyze how they differed from or followed the script, and extract from them information truly pertinent to the situation.

In 1975, the SAM (for Script Applier Mechanism) program used an automobile accident script as a thread to make sense of newspaper reports of such events. The Ph.D. thesis work of Richard Cullingford, the program first built internal representations of the articles using semantic primitives. SAM could then sift through these unambiguous data structures to answer questions put to it (like "Did anyone get killed?"). By reconstructing English sentences from the internal representations, SAM could also paraphrase the newspaper articles. In the process, and quite as a by-product, SAM became the first working automatic translation program. Even if the original articles were in English, SAM's internal representations of them were not in any human language. In addition to the original module that paraphrased in English, it was just as easy to write into SAM other modules that paraphrased in Spanish and Russian.[15]

Despite these successes, it was obvious, as Schank put it, that "real understanding requires the ability to establish connections between pieces of information for which no prescribed set of rules, or scripts, exist."[16] Another connecting thread was needed, one that worked outside of stereotyped situations. In the 1960s, Abelson had identified one such thread in the goals people hold and the plans they make to reach them. Thus was born Robert Wilensky's Plan Applier Mechanism (PAM). This program could interpret stories like the following by linking sentences together through a character's goals and plans:

> John wanted money. He got a gun and walked into a liquor store. He told the owner he wanted some money. The owner gave John the money and John left.

In the process of understanding a story, the program had to put itself into the shoes of the participants. Here is how PAM paraphrased the story from the thief's point of view:

> I needed to get some dough. So I got myself this gun, and I walked down to the liquor store. I told the shopkeeper that if he didn't let me have the money then I would shoot him. So he handed it over. Then I left.

PAM also understood that the store owner's motivation differed considerably from John's:

> I was minding the store when a man entered. He threatened me with a gun and demanded all the cash receipts. Well, I didn't want to get hurt so I gave him the money. Then he escaped.[17]

With PAM, work on conceptual dependency hit cruising speed, and the students of Schank and Abelson started cranking out new programs every year.[18] Jaime Carbonell's POLITICS sounded like either a right-wing or a hard-core liberal U.S. senator. Gerry DeJong's FRUMP was hooked up to UPI's news wire and summarized the stories it understood in several languages. (Although not always with perfect accuracy: it once reported a violent earthquake in the United States; the actual story had been about the assassination of San Francisco's mayor, which had "shaken America.") A program called IPP, the work of Michael Lebowitz, learned about terrorism as it read news stories about this unfortunate form of warfare. In 1980, Janet Kolodner's CYRUS (justified after the fact as Computerized Yale Reasoning and Understanding System) was, in fact, an attempt to model the memory of a live human being: the diplomat Cyrus Vance. The program actually thought of itself as Vance and obtained its "memories" from news stories about Vance intercepted by FRUMP. Its most striking ability was to guess about matters of which it had no direct knowledge. Once asked whether his wife had ever met the wife of Israel's prime minister Begin, CYRUS remembered that Vance and Begin had participated in a social occasion to which it was likely they had taken their wives, and thus replied—accurately, as it turned out—"Yes, at a state dinner in Israel in January 1980."[19]

MARVIN MINSKY: TO THINK IS TO MOVE AWAY FROM LOGIC

In the early 1970s, Schank and Abelson were absorbing the inspiration for scriptlike structures in sentence analysis directly from the zeitgeist. Years before, Ross Quillian had formally introduced structured objects in the form of semantic nets, only to be thwarted by the inability of 1965-vintage computers to handle the corresponding data-processing load. Perhaps because the more powerful machines of the 1970s didn't mind the extra work as much, structured objects started to look like an idea whose time had come. The micro worlds of Minsky and Papert, as well as the "problem spaces" that Newell and Simon by then used to describe games and other experimental problems, certainly seemed like higher-order structures.

Most observers credit Marvin Minsky for crystallizing the idea in a now-classical paper he published in 1975. In retrospect, the article appeared in an unlikely context, a book edited by Patrick Winston entitled *The Psychology of Computer Vision,* which also contained various doctoral theses on artificial vision.[20] As it turned out, the ideas that Minsky then proposed have so far had their major impact in areas other than vision, which he saw as a prime area for their application.

Minsky began "A Framework for Representing Knowledge" with a bold statement: "It seems to me that the ingredients of most theories in artificial intelligence and in psychology have been on the whole too minute, local, and unstructured to account . . . for the effectiveness of commonsense thought."[21] As a solution, he proposed, "When one encounters a new situation . . . one selects from memory a substantial structure called a frame. This is a remembered framework to be adapted to fit reality by changing details as necessary."[22]

When opening the door into a new room, for example, one would invoke the generic room frame, which would consist of a list of the main features one normally perceives in a room: walls to left, front, and right; a floor; and a ceiling. Minsky called these features "terminals." One would then proceed to match each terminal of the frame with features of the actual image seen. In so doing, one would take into account required properties ("markers" in Minsky's parlance) specified for each feature in the frame. For example, the *room* frame might require that the floor be made of wood, tile, or carpet. Encountering grass instead would cause one to reject the *room* frame, and activate the *outdoors* frame. A cement floor and a large sliding door in one wall would invoke the *garage* frame. If the room frame were indeed accepted, one would proceed to attach various properties to the markers, such as colors and textures of walls and ceilings, presence of windows on the walls, and so on. (AI workers now refer to this activity as "filling slots.") One would then remember this instance of the generic room frame as, say, "Martha's office," and invoke it again upon re-entering the room.

Minsky went on to describe how frames could be linked together or grouped into systems, accounting in the process for major aspects of thought and perception. Visual frames, for instance, could form systems representing various points of view of the inside of a room, thus enabling spatial orientation. A terminal of a frame could point to a subframe, organizing frame systems into hierarchies. Likewise, a word could make up a subframe of a sentence, itself a subframe of the story it helps build up.

In Minsky's view, frame matching accounted for many aspects of thinking normally associated with syntax and logic. Even such a deep cognitive activity as learning mostly consists in building up new frames, usually by copying and modifying old ones to account for new situations.

Minsky's sweeping portrait of the power of his theory made many converts, and all of a sudden frames were "in." As Minsky later mentioned to me:

> One reason that the Frame paper was so influential was that it described many "processes" that would be attached to the frames, especially how default assignments (of "typical" objects) would be specialized in particular circumstances. Then the new, more appropriate frame would be copied and stored away for further use. For some researchers, this may have been the inspiration for the "inheritance"

ideas about the sorts of representations that are now becoming popular under the title "object-oriented."[23]

The success of Minsky's theory was all the more surprising since his paper contained few concrete suggestions for implementing the idea. Programmers who would design a frame-based system were left with much ground to clear before they wrote their first line of code. To critics who later berated him for it, Minsky boasted of not having repeated the error he'd made in *Perceptrons* (see chapter 4). This earlier book he'd written with Papert had presented such a thorough analysis of two-stage neural networks that it hardly left any room to pursue the research, which as a result dried up for ten years. With frames, claimed Minsky, he had been careful to tell just enough of the idea to stir up interest and leave lots of obvious work to do.

One who did not find Minsky's introduction of frames to his liking was Herbert Simon. For one thing, Simon told me, Minsky confused everybody by using the word McCarthy had already appropriated for the frame problem, with which Minsky's frames have nothing to do. Simon asked, "What is a frame?" and continued:

> One of the main things [Newell and I] saw we needed in IPL-5 was a way of representing a more general scheme of relations than list structures. To do that, [we came up with] description lists, or attribute-value pairs. These give you a system essentially as general as first-order predicate calculus. They were deeply built into the IPLs, we used them all the time. We built up big "schemas," as we called them, which were full of slots, because that's what the value of a attribute-value pair is. . . . I have my share of amour propre when it comes to getting credit for scientific discovery. . . . I've been unable to discover in what respects [Minsky's frames] are an advance over description lists. . . . As far as I'm concerned, I've been using frames since 1956.[24]

Simon's frustration, though easily understandable, is an inescapable corollary of scientific progress. There is seldom any such thing as a new idea: Minsky would claim that every new frame is evolved from an older one. In fact, he did not claim credit for inventing frames in his paper. He did make passing reference to Newell and Simon in the second paragraph, but further on attributed the paternity of the concept to other sources: "The frame idea itself is not particularly original—it is in the tradition of the 'schema' of [the psychologist F. C.] Bartlett and the 'paradigms' of the science historian Thomas Kuhn; the idea of a frame system is probably more novel."[25]

Others who had their noses out of joint (to use Simon's term for himself) over frames were the "logic-oriented students of artificial intelligence" whom Minsky targeted at the beginning of the paper. He clearly meant by that phrase the faction led by his old friend McCarthy on the West Coast, as well as the group in Edinburgh, Scotland, who were brewing ideas that would soon lead to the logic-oriented language PROLOG. Gerald Sussman, the student Minsky caught designing a neural net and then put in charge of a vision project (see chapter 4) had an interesting comment to offer when we discussed frames together (Sussman is now a professor at MIT's AI Lab):

McCarthy would regard frames as a poorly formulated set of logical statements. McCarthy is right in that, . . . but it may be irrelevant. [The reason is that] I can *illogically* write or formulate anything I like. If I do write down precise formulas that are illogical, it is because I don't have a precise idea of what I mean. . . . [Putting it down as logic] may not help me any because using precise language to describe essentially imprecise concepts doesn't make them any more precise.[26]

Their very imprecision has made frames one of the favorite tools of the scruffy faction of AI. Scruffies claim that frames make up a much more psychologically plausible mechanism for thought than does logic. More than sixteen years after their introduction, there is still no consensus on the exact place frames should occupy in the architecture of artificial minds. Over the years, frames followed what has become the routine evolutionary path of AI innovations. They were acclaimed by many in the late 1970s as the ultimate solution to the common-sense problem, only to fall out of favor when they turned out not to be the expected panacea. After the usual swings of the pendulum, frames are now considered one of the many useful devices in the AI worker's toolbag.

Minsky, for his part, is certainly not giving up on frames. He recently explained to me an extension of the concept which he calls the "Trans-frame," inspired from Roger Schank's conceptual dependency theory; Minsky believes it to be at the origin of, among other things, our concept of causality: "My guess is that something like this may be wired into the brain," Minsky told me.

DOUGLAS LENAT: THE SQUARE ROOT OF HEURISTICS

Minsky's hypothesis that learning consists of building up new frames is typical of new ground broken in the field of learning during the 1970s. Throughout the 1960s, learning remained pretty much in the state where the early work on pattern recognition had left it in the 1960s, when the major stumbling block was the impossibility of conjuring up new demons. Researchers like Oliver Selfridge had made their programs learn how to recognize letters of the alphabet; Arthur Samuel had written a checkers-playing program that eventually beat its author by learning how to value the good board positions to attain. These programs achieved their feats by figuring out, through statistics, how to assign the proper weights to features they had been *told* how to calculate. Selfridge had written into his program procedures he called "demons," which detected such features as vertical and horizontal strokes and figuratively yelled with more or less vigor according to how long and numerous the strokes were. The program could then learn by itself to correlate the various letters with the demons' chorus. The program could not, however, discover useful new features (like the hole in the letter *o*) or program new demons to detect them. It was this difficulty that researchers, now a little more confident, tackled in the 1970s.

One obvious step along the way consisted of assembling larger procedures out of smaller ones. This is what the Nilsson and Fikes's STRIPS program did at Stanford in the early 1970s. When the Shakey robot had (under STRIP's guidance) devised a sequence of moves to build, say, a new type of block structure, it would assign this procedure a name that afterward allowed STRIPS to evoke it as one single move.

Patrick Winston's program at MIT represented yet another progress: it learned to recognize block structures like arches by looking at examples of them. To this effect, the program constructed a semantic network (a few years later, Winston might have called it a "frame") embodying the *concept* of an arch: two nontouching vertical members supporting a horizontal one.

In 1966, three researchers named E. B. Hunt, J. Marin, and P. Stone had formulated an intriguing psychological model of concept formation.[27] They claimed that we make our concepts by breaking up an unstructured collection of objects or ideas into subsets that have some characteristic in common. Further, maintained Hunt and his colleagues, we do this through an inborn divide-and-conquer strategy. First, we pick the criterion that appears most useful in telling us how to react to whatever we are facing: *friend or foe?* perhaps made a useful starting point for our jungle-dwelling ancestors. Finer distinctions like *human or animal?*, *male or female?*, would follow until, by a process of successive splitting, or "dichotomization," we arrive at a unique definition. In the late 1970s, the AI researcher J. R. Quinlan embodied this method into a program he called ID3 (for Interactive Dichotomizer 3). When the Yugoslav chess player and AI researcher Ivan Bratko turned the program loose on a chess problem, ID3 demonstrated its fighting efficiency in this other junglelike environment.[28] Bratko supplied the program with a set of standard textbook recommendations for playing the end game of king and rook against king. ID3 converted these several pages of diffuse and ill-formulated strategies into six crystal-clear rules that a child could learn and then play the end game with grand-master skill.

The University of Illinois researcher Ryszard Michalski inserted a more complex algorithm for concept formation into a program he first called AQ11 and then INDUCE. (Michalski managed to move away from the Polish Academy of Sciences years before *glasnost*.) AQ11 proved its worth on the concrete problem of diagnosing soybean diseases. It analyzed lists of symptoms from 307 plants with known diseases and generated a set of rules for diagnosing them. When the program applied these rules to a set of 376 new cases, the correct diagnoses emerged 99.5 percent of the time. By contrast, a set of rules supplied by a human plant pathologist produced a success rate of only 83 percent.[29] Had AQ11 formed better concepts about plant disease than the pathologist? Since the program didn't even know what a plant was, the answer is an obvious no. AQ11 could, however, devise new ways of efficiently correlating lists of symptoms with diseases. And it did so by means that may resemble those by which we form concepts like *plant* early in our lives.

Douglas Lenat's Automated Mathematician learned and formed concepts in a sense even closer to the human way.[30] A walking legend in the world of AI research, Lenat found out about computers in a manner typical of his entrepreneurial spirit. As a high school student in Philadelphia, working for $1.00 an hour to clean the cages of experimental animals, he discovered that another student was earning $1.50 to program the institution's minicomputer. Finding this occupation more to his liking, he taught himself programming over a weekend and squeezed his competitor out of the job by offering to work for fifty cents an hour less.[31] A few years later, Lenat was programming Automated Mathematician (AM, for short) as a doctoral thesis project at the Stanford AI laboratory.

Like actors memorizing their lines, expert system programs like DENDRAL and MYCIN can be said to have learned their heuristic rules by *being told* about them. By contrast, AQ11 and ID3 learned by *example* or *induction*. Lenat's AM attempted the much more ambitious task of learning by *discovery*. Like a toddler exploring a playroom, Lenat's program set out to learn about its world by playing with what it found interesting. Since AM lived in a computer, its toys were numbers, and the playroom amounted to the branch of mathematics known as "number theory." Lenat started AM off in life with three endowments. The first was a set of 115 rudimentary ideas in the form of *frames*. For example, one starting frame described the concept of set as a collection of objects. Other frames defined the union, intersection, and equality of sets. Each frame comprised about 25 slots; and since Lenat wanted to find out how much AM would discover with as small a starting base as possible, he left most of the slots empty.

We could call AM's second endowment a *sense of play:* it was embodied in a set of 184 rules in LISP for manipulating the initial frames, filling their empty slots, and creating new concepts by defining new frames. One such heuristic could be translated as "If you find something of interest, look for its inverse." Having discovered multiplication, AM thus found out about division. Another heuristic rule was "Look for extreme cases." When AM discovered that all integers could be evenly divided by other numbers (their divisors), it applied the extreme-case heuristic to look for numbers with as few divisors as possible. This led the program to the concept of prime numbers, which are only divisible by themselves and 1.

AM's third gift would correspond in a person to *aesthetic sensitivity:* the program could appreciate the rightness of good discoveries and decide to pursue them further. AM in fact rated the worth of its concepts on a scale of 0 to 1,000 which it calculated using another set of 59 heuristics.

Of particular interest were the presence of regularities and similarities in the examples of a concept (examples of the concept of prime number were actual values of primes). So were the frequency of these examples, and the number of ways in which a new concept had been suggested. Thus, AM found multiplication interesting because it had discovered it by three different routes besides repeated addition.

Its explorations led AM to rediscover a good deal of standard number theory: about two hundred concepts in all. For example, it noticed that there was only one way to break a number down into prime factors, a result known as the Unique Factorization Theorem. AM even hypothesized that all even numbers greater than 2 are expressible as the sum of primes, an as-yet-unproven result known as Goldbach's Conjecture. One finding particularly excited Lenat. The program applied the extreme-case heuristic to numbers with divisors, but in the direction opposite from that which led to prime numbers. Prime numbers are essentially numbers particularly poor in divisors. AM conjectured that it might also be interesting to look at numbers *particularly rich* in divisors. Randall Davis, in those years also a graduate student at Stanford, said that there were many late nights when Lenat was running AM, and would be sitting and talking. On one such night, the program produced an output which meant: "What does this set of numbers look like: the smallest number with six divisors, the smallest number with seven, etc.?" Davis recalled it so:

> In some sense, it was the dual of prime numbers. The interesting part was that everything else that AM came up with was easily recognized as traditional number theory. But this wasn't, and it looked original, genuinely original. So Doug did a fair amount of running around, trying to see if anybody had ever investigated this notion of composite numbers. Finally, George Polya [to whom AI owes the notion of heuristics in mathematics], who was in his nineties at that point, said that a number theoretician by the name of [Srinivasa] Ramanujan, a self-taught Indian genius, had in fact looked at highly composite numbers. And that was wonderfully poetic because the whole idea behind AM was to recapture the spirit of mathematics as it's actually done, not as it's recast later in clean proofs and logical formalisms. To capture the whole notion of investigating interesting concepts just because they seem interesting, not because you can prove anything about them originally. Ramanujan, who investigated interesting concepts and was completely self-taught, was the only mathematician we

ever found who had looked at this notion. So it was not original, which was too bad, but it was almost better, since it had been Ramanujan who had looked at the idea.[32]

Not long after that momentous night, AM's creative streak ran out of steam. At the peak of its inspiration, every other idea that AM had was interesting: this ratio dropped to less than 10 percent. The fledgling silicon mathematician even went off the deep end into strange investigations about numbers that would be at the same time odd and even. Yet Lenat's project still made a major breakthrough in automated learning, and his colleagues and professors hailed it as such. Having earned his doctorate with flying colors, Lenat left Stanford in 1976 for a faculty position at Carnegie Mellon.

The nonetheless disappointed young professor wondered what had caused AM's sudden loss of inspiration. Certainly it hadn't discovered everything there was to know about numbers: like Isaac Newton, human number theorists know they are like children amusing themselves with pebbles on the beach, while the immensity of the ocean is there to discover. AM had even missed many obvious pebbles, passing by such grade-school notions as remainders and largest common denominators. Lenat quickly fingered the discovery heuristics as the culprit. For some reason, probably buried deep in the nature of reality, these rules could lead AM to some discoveries but not to others. It became obvious after the fact that additional or modified heuristics would have allowed AM to continue on its quest. The obvious solution then was to allow the program to work on its heuristics as it went along. Much as it discovered new results in mathematics, AM should be set to discover new heuristics that would let it discover still more mathematics. So, as Tom Evans twenty years earlier had sought the square root of analogy, and his friend Randall Davis the square root of knowledge, Doug Lenat started looking for the square root of heuristics.

And found it was a tough nut to crack! He had optimistically called his new version of the program EURISKO, for "I discover" in Greek (Archimedes' famed bathtub exclamation "Eureka!" was the past form of *Eurisko*).[33] As it turned out, EURISKO's performance over the next five years lay closer to drowning in a bathtub than leaping on to new discoveries. Every evening Lenat doggedly programmed another overnight run, and every morning the program had found a new way to tear itself apart.

Why was it harder to discover new heuristics than new mathematical concepts? It all had to do with how the two were represented in AM/EURISKO, which was written in LISP. Because John McCarthy had structured LISP to easily accommodate mathematical operations, AM could articulate a concept like *prime number* in a compact frame. A discovery heuristic, on the other hand, typically required Lenat to write two pages of dense LISP code. For AM, defining a new mathematical concept was like slapping together a simple block construction, while for Lenat or EURISKO to define a new heuristic amounted to assembling an intricate Swiss watch. There were so many ways in which the process could go wrong that with EURISKO, it almost always did! The solution was for Lenat to repeat for heuristics what McCarthy had done in LISP for arithmetic: find a way to represent their essential aspects in a simple manner. He slaved over this problem for five years; and the end, his Representation Language Language (RLL) allowed the description of heuristics in frames just as compact as those for mathematical concepts. Lenat could then equip EURISKO with general heuristics to develop new heuristics, such as: "If a heuristic is too inefficient, specialize it into a new one that will be executed less often and produce the same results."[34]

The program kept a batting average of the heuristics it developed, in terms of how much processing time they required, and how many new concepts they generated. It then weeded out the ineffective heuristics, while mutating and improving those that performed best. That was when EURISKO woke up.

In a synergy typical of how computer technologies interact, the fledgling computer program cut its teeth by helping in the design of more powerful computer chips. In those days, engineers were starting to lay microchips in three dimensions by engraving them in superimposed layers. Planning such layouts was like playing three-dimensional chess, and designers tended to get lost in mazes of their own creation: their two-dimensional heuristics didn't work any more, and EURISKO was called upon to supply new ones. Multiple experiments led the program to reinvent the concept of symmetry and decide it was a helpful property for circuits to have. This, in turn, led it to generalize a 2-D junction design to 3-D, in the process allowing the circuit to fulfill the two different functions of NAND and OR gates.

Ever the achiever, Lenat was looking for a more dramatic way to prove the capabilities of his creation. He identified the occasion in a space-war game called Traveler TCS, then quite popular with the public Lenat wanted to reach.[35] The idea was for each player to design a fleet of space battleships according to a thick, hundred-page set of rules. Within a budget limit of one trillion galactic credits, one could adjust such parameters as the size, speed, armor thickness, autonomy, and armament of each ship: about fifty adjustments per ship were needed. Since the fleet size could reach a hundred ships, the game thus offered ample room for ingenuity in spite of the anticlimatic character of the battles. These were fought by throwing dice following complex tables of the probability of survival of each ship according to its design. The winner of the yearly national championship was commissioned inter-galactic admiral and received title to a planet of his or her choice outside the solar system.

Several months before the 1981 competition, Lenat fed into EURISKO 146 Traveler concepts, ranging from the nature of games in general to the technicalities of meson guns. He then instructed the program to develop heuristics for making winning war-fleet designs. The now familiar routine of nightly computer runs turned into a merciless Darwinian contest: Lenat and EURISKO together designed fleets that battled each other. Designs were evaluated by how well they won battles, and heuristics by how well they designed fleets. This rating method required several battles per design, and several designs per heuristic, which amounted to a lot of battles: ten thousand in all, fought over two thousand hours of computer time.

To participants in the national championship of San Mateo, Califor-nia, the resulting fleet of ninety-six small, heavily armored ships looked ludicrous. Accepted wisdom dictated fleets of about twenty behemoth ships, and many couldn't help laughing. When engagements started, they found out that the weird armada held more than met the eye. One interesting ace up Lenat's sleeve was a small ship so fast as to be almost unstoppable, which guaranteed at least a draw. EURISKO had con-ceived of it through the "look for extreme cases" heuristic (which had mutated, incidentally, into "look for *almost* extreme cases"). To the dissatisfaction of many contestants who by then perceived Lenat's de-sign method as an unfair advantage, he handily won the championship. The following year, game organizers wised up and released modified regulations only a week before the contest. In this way, they figured, EURISKO wouldn't have time to fight ten thousand battles against itself! However the program's heuristics had by then matured enough to handle the new regulations without modification, and Lenat claimed title to yet another planet. He bowed out of the next competition when the organizers threatened to cancel it if he ran. The military, for its part, took due notice of the program's performance, and later strategic applications of AI to battle management stemmed in part from EURISKO's simulated war fighting.

Throughout this period, Lenat couldn't help drawing an intriguing parallel. EURISKO designed fleets of space ships in a manner that looked very much like conventional Darwinian evolution, with a major difference. Simply generating random mutations in ship designs and battle-testing them wouldn't have worked: the odds that a random change would make a design worse instead of improving it were so enormous that almost all mutations would have been rejected. Without its guiding heuristics, EURISKO would have needed billions of simulated battles to develop a passable fleet. Biologists had long held similar reservations about Darwinism: natural evolution had been much more efficient than random mutations could account for. Why couldn't the structure of DNA, reflected Lenat, somehow resemble the code for EURISKO? Couldn't it embed heuristics that would make favorable changes much more likely than pure chance would allow? According to Lenat, natural selection could have started with random mutations. If, however, at some point one strain of living cells had accidentally hit upon some primitive heuristic for preferring favorable mutations, then it would soon have overshadowed its competition. Repeated interactions of this process could have led to ever more powerful heuristics and, eventually, to *Homo sapiens*.

DAVID MARR: LET THE WORLD TEACH US HOW TO SEE

When I discussed frames with Marvin Minsky, he pointed out how they could make it easier to identify the contents of an image. For example, if you knew that an image might contain a cube, calling up the "cube" frame after identifying two parallel edges might let the program say, "Well, there ought to be a third edge lying about there." Such considerations eventually led Minsky to a much more involved theory called the Society of Mind, which I shall discuss later. Then, as Minsky told me, "the tragedy is we hired this wonderful young man named David Marr who was a brilliant mathematician and neurological theorist and who understood these ideas very well. But as soon as he got here, he said, 'Well, first let's thoroughly understand low-level vision.' "

Marr's insistence on exploring fundamental phenomena, combined with his compelling personality, held much sway at MIT. As a result, Minsky and Papert's Society of Mind work got shunted to the sidelines. "Seymour and I . . . were unable to persuade any students to work in that direction," said Minsky, "because David Marr was so charismatic." If Minsky was downright unhappy with Marr's influence, however, many AI researchers take a much more positive view of his contributions, and put as much heat in their praise as Minsky has into his disparagement. Such reactions are indicative of how personalities like David Marr's affect colleagues. As Patrick Winston put it to me: "People go 'bimodal' on such persons. Sometimes they believe what they say, and sometimes they hate it. But even there they benefit by virtue of being forced to reflect on things that they wouldn't have thought about otherwise."[36]

In all fairness, Minsky and Papert could have known what to expect as they hired Marr. When he left his native Britain for MIT at the age of twenty-eight, his pioneering work in mathematical neurophysiology had already earned him the recognition and friendship of such figures as Francis Crick, Nobel Prize winner and co-discoverer of DNA's double-helix structure. Marr's 1969 paper on the cerebellum exposed for the first time a precise theory for the mode of operation of this organ, which controls voluntary movements in all vertebrates.[37] Marr's starting point lay in modeling the nerve cells in the cerebellum very much like Rosenblatt's Perceptrons, which Minsky and Papert were debunking in a book that appeared almost simultaneously with the paper.[38] Marr was then twenty-four years old. In 1970 and 1971, he followed through with similar theories for the cerebellar neocortex and the hippocampus.[39] That Minsky and Papert invited this potential opponent to MIT is certainly a sign of their open-mindedness about neural networks.

Marr's own reason for going to MIT was to find out at first hand how difficult a job human brains have in interpreting images for us. "The best way of finding out the difficulties of doing something is to try to do it," said Marr, "so . . . I moved to the Artificial Intelligence Laboratory at MIT, where Marvin Minsky had collected a group of people and a powerful computer for the express purpose of addressing the [vision] question."[40] Patrick Winston emphasized to me the importance of the powerful computer: "One reason Marr came here was the hardware. We saw to it that he had more access to it than at any other place in the world!"

Yet the kind of neural phenomena that Marr had attempted to explain lay on the very first rungs of the ladder of higher abstractions that constitute the mind. The framelike symbolic operations that Minsky and Papert hypothesized stood close to the top of this ladder, and it wasn't surprising that Marr showed little interest in them. David Marr's fundamentally different approach to the study of vision, however, came about for reasons that had little to do with likes and dislikes. A young woman neurologist provided the turning point soon after Marr's arrival at MIT, as he has recalled:

> My approach . . . was very much influenced by the fascinating accounts of clinical neurology. . . . Particularly important was a lecture that Elizabeth Warrington [of the National Hospital, Queen Square, London] gave at MIT in October 1973, in which she described the capacities and limitations of patients who had suffered left or right parietal lesions. . . . For those with lesions on the right side, recognition of a common object was possible *provided* that the patient's view of it was in some sense straightforward. She used the words *conventional* and *unconventional*—a water pail or a clarinet seen from the side gave "conventional" views but seen end-on gave "unconventional" views. If these patients recognized the object at all, they knew its name and its semantics—that is, its use and purpose, how big it was, how much it weighed, what it was made of, and so forth. If their view was unconventional—a pail seen from above, for example—not only would the patients fail to recognize it, but they would vehemently deny that it *could* be a view of a pail. Patients with left parietal lesions behaved completely differently. Often these patients had no language, so they were unable to name the viewed object or state its purpose or semantics. But they could convey that they correctly perceived its geometry—that is, its shape—even from the unconventional view.
>
> Warrington's talk suggested . . . [that] vision alone can deliver an internal description of the shape of a viewed object, even when the object was not recognized in the conventional sense of understanding its use and purpose.[41]

Berthold Horn's project on extracting the shapes of objects from their shading, then still under way at MIT, confirmed Warrington's intuition for Marr. If you shine a lamp sideways at an egg and look at it through one eye, you will still distinctly perceive the egg's three-dimensional oval shape. Horn showed how relatively simple operations performed on image pixels (points in the image) could extract such information, without any prior knowledge of the nature of the objects involved.[42] It seems safe to assume that a mechanism for performing a similar computation is wired into our brains.

From these and similar observations, Marr erected a theory of vision that placed him at odds with many in the AI field. First and foremost, contended Marr, one should look at basic physical realities to constrain and define the problems to be solved. Only then should one think of specific procedures for solving these problems, and of hardware to implement them. If one formulated problems correctly, then one could always come up with the right solutions. As further evidence Marr quoted the many highly specific functions developed by nature for the visual systems of various species in response to their unique requirements. Some jumping spiders have in their retinae a specific detector for the red V markings on the backs of their fellow spiders, and use it to tell a mate from prey. The retinae of frogs incorporate bug detectors, and those of rabbits are tailored to respond to the specific patterns of hovering hawks.

In contrast, previous researchers had tended to look first at what procedures or hardware were available, and then try to apply these to their problems in ad-hoc ways. As an extreme example, Marr quoted an attempt at programming a computer to recognize a telephone in an office by scanning the image about halfway up until it found a dark blob of the right size.

Marr thus built his methodology around two central concepts. The first was to describe problem-solving systems at different levels: roughly corresponding to, first, *what* they were supposed to do, and subordinate to that, to *how* they did it. The second concept consisted in using the foremost level as a starting point for further study.

Around the same time, other influential researchers adopted similar points of view in other guises. Instead of defining minds through the mechanisms by which they solve problems, Allen Newell preferred to talk about what kind of knowledge minds can have, and thus described them at the "knowledge level."[43] The philosopher Daniel Dennett would rather define minds according to what intentions one can ascribe to them; yet, as he explained to me, the basic idea is the same as Marr's, and Dennett calls it the "intentional stance."[44]

This philosophy reaches further than meets the eye. Let's accept for a moment that two systems are exactly equivalent as long as they perform the same functions at the higher, symbolic level. Then it doesn't matter whether they are implemented in brain cells, in an artificial neural net, or even in a serial computer. In particular, according to Dennett, such higher phenomena as intentionality, consciousness, and feelings could appear in hardware systems sufficiently "like" the human mind in some symbolic way. Needless to say, such arguments have become the subject of hot debate.

Meanwhile in the mid-1970s, David Marr went to work at MIT studying vision in terms of what problems it has to solve. This, in turn, amounted to categorizing the clues that the physical world offers for analysis. Much research already existed on the subject, and Marr proceeded to articulate and structure it. As we've seen, one important clue was shading, which provides depth information. Another was stereopsis, the perception of depth through binocular vision. If you place your finger at arm's length and look at it alternatively through the left and the right eyes, your finger appears to switch between two different positions against the background. Our brains use this displacement, called "stereo disparity," to tell the distances of objects. For this to work in the case of your finger, your brain must be able to locate it in both the left-eye and the right-eye images. Should your brain use its knowledge of what fingers look like to do this? As it turned out, not at all. With his friend and colleague Tomaso Poggio, Marr devised a simple algorithm for telling which individual points correspond to each other in left and right images. The procedure, which used only local information about the brightnesses around each point, could be implemented in a simple neural network.[45]

Other clues our visual systems exploit are color and texture, which brand points belonging to the same surfaces. Edges, characterized as sharp variations in brightness, color, or texture, usually correspond to the contours of objects. To distinguish the edges of objects of appreciable size from spurious details (like the contours of a head from the subtle texture of the hair), Marr hypothesized that one first has to blur the image. Interestingly, this can be done through an operator called the Laplacian, which closely resembles a function already identified in the visual response of mammals.

Marr postulated that the brain processes each of the foregoing clues (shading, stereopsis, texture, edges, color) independently, through a series of separate modules. The results of these analyses come together, somewhere in our brain, in a symbolic representation that is not quite three-dimensional: Marr called it the "2 ½ D sketch." It consists of a matrix of cells, each corresponding to a particular line of sight from the viewer. A cell contains the distance and orientation of the surface that lies in it. If a discontinuity in distance or orientation is present, the cell will represent this information also. According to Marr, it is after assembly of the 2 ½ D sketch from purely "bottom up" processing, and not before, that our general knowledge about the world comes into play. We then use our (perhaps framelike) representations of what cubes, people, or trees look like to put the different cells together and identify the components of a scene.

Marr exposed his theory of vision in a book called simply *Vision,* which appeared in 1982. He wasn't entirely happy about the book and discreetly apologized for it in the preface: "In December 1977, certain events occurred that forced me to write this book a few years earlier than I had planned."[46] His hand had been forced by a diagnosis of terminal leukemia, which didn't leave him enough time to finish the book. After several temporary remission periods, Marr died in 1980. It is to his friend and colleague Keith Nishihara that we owe the assembly and revision of the final manuscript.

Despite the heavy criticism that many of Marr's ideas have come under, it is hard to overestimate his influence on AI. Some of it he achieved by sheer force of personality. All his colleagues agree with Minsky's description of him as "charismatic." Patrick Winston recalled him to me as

> quite a multidimensional person. He was very smart, deeply committed to scientific progress, didn't care much about applications. A pleasant guy, easy to get along with, scientifically very sharp and critical, . . . with a style that lent itself to becoming famous. Strangely enough, he liked to think of his ideas as complicated. I once suggested to him that he should make some things easier to understand, and was astonished to find out that he didn't want to. He wanted his ideas to look philosophical, hard to understand, and worthwhile to read about. He moved fast, worked hard, unbelievably hard, all the time. He read widely and kept up with the literature, both on computer science and neurophysiology. He was a smart guy and knew a lot of smart people: they formed an international smart-guy club.

"One thing David was very good at," said Berthold Horn to me, "was formalizing and presenting ideas that were present in the field but hadn't crystallized. He had a talent for naming things. For example, there was a phenomenon in motion vision that everybody knew of but didn't care much for. He gave it the name 'aperture effect,' and all of a sudden it was recognized as a big thing." Patrick Winston concurred: "Terms like the '2 ½ D sketch' had such a ring to them that people soon assumed that he had thought those things up. He had no intention to deceive anyone in that direction, but the fact that the terms stuck made a lot of people associate these ideas with him alone, even though they had grown among the community at large."

Marr's main achievement, Winston believed, was

getting the representations right and ferreting out the [physical] con-straints that make it possible to see at all. Those are great ideas. He wasn't the first person to have them, of course; but he was the first one who clearly articulated their importance and championed them. . . . He's largely responsible for making vision an important problem in AI. This is where methodology is most important, and he was the first person to make a big fuss over it. Sensible big fuss.

On the other hand, continued Winston, "it is possible to be highly critical of Marr, because he tended to encourage people to concentrate on low-level vision and the highly mathematical approach, without going on with the business of seeing." Marvin Minsky, agrees: "[After David joined us,] our team became the most famous vision group in the world, but the one with the fewest results. His idea was a disaster. The edge finders they have now using his theories, as far as I can see, are slightly worse than the ones we had just before taking him on. We've lost twenty years." Hans Moravec, now director of the Mobile Robot Laboratory at Carnegie Mellon and somewhat of a legend himself, likewise agrees. "That was an earlier part of AI, an earlier spirit that has gone away like David Marr," Moravec told me, adding:

His idea was "We really have to be more scientific, more like physics or biology. Let's start with the basics and then build on some theo-ries." The theories are all right, but they haven't been remarkably successful so far. It may well be that the way to build an intelligence is just to get your hands on dirty engineering problems. We don't have

a theory of automobiles. We have good cars, but there are no fundamental equations of automotive science.[47]

"Many of Marr's ideas have already turned out to be wrong," admitted Winston. Berthold Horn pointed out that Marr's so-called independent vision modules now turn out to interact in very intimate ways.
Likewise, one of his pet ideas was to model objects as generalized kinds
of cylinders—an option now rejected by many researchers. "This makes
his early death all the more tragic," added Winston, "because I'm sure
he would have participated in the changes and refinement of those
ideas."

Marr would have thought it was great fun. As he put it in the preface
to *Vision:* "This book is meant to be enjoyed. It describes the adventures
I have had in the years since Marvin Minsky and Seymour Papert invited
me to join [their laboratory] in 1973."[48]

EARLY ATTEMPTS AT LOGIC PROGRAMMING

In the 1970s, from Stanford to Marseille, other researchers were exploring methods that were to the higher processes of mind what Marr's
back-to-basics campaign represented for low-level vision. Opposing
Minsky, Papert, Schank, and Lenat, who made up the antilogical faction of AI, were researchers like John McCarthy, Alan Robinson, Robert Kowalski, and Alain Colmerauer. Although they had also suffered
through a turbulent period in the 1960s, they started breathing much
more easily in the 1970s.

In 1965, the logician Alan Robinson from Argonne Laboratories had
described a new method for logical deduction which he called the
"resolution principle." "Traditionally," said Robinson, "a single step in
a deduction has been required, for pragmatic and psychological reasons,
to be simple enough, . . . to be apprehended as correct by a human being
in a single intellectual act."[49] A method for theorem proving better
adapted to computers was needed, even if it meant sacrificing some of
the clarity to which logicians had grown accustomed. To this end,
Robinson proposed first to turn all logical statements defining the

problem, and any intermediate conclusions reached, into a standard form called a "clause." These clauses described the problem to the computer in a manner that did not look natural to people. For example, the sentences "All men are mortal" and "Socrates is a man" would look like this in clause form:

not man(x) or mortal(x)

man(Socrates).

To prove a result from a list of such statements, Robinson then proceeded in a manner that also looked strangely lopsided to people. He assumed the opposite of what he wanted to prove, and then tried to show that it contradicted the initial set of clauses. For example, to prove that Socrates is mortal, we would start in Robinson's method by asserting the opposite, in clause form:

not mortal(Socrates).

We would then look, in the initial list of clauses, for one that contains the negative of that statement—that is: "mortal(Socrates)." The first clause in the list would do fine if we replaced the variable x by Socrates, to give:

not man(Socrates) or mortal(Socrates)

We would then perform what Robinson called the "resolution" of the two clauses "not man(Socrates) or mortal(Socrates)" and "not mortal(Socrates)." We would achieve this by first merging the clauses and then canceling out the two contradictory statements about Socrates' mortality. This would leave us with the single statement:

not man(Socrates).

What makes resolution particularly well adapted to computers is that from then on, we would simply keep on applying the same recipe as often as necessary. We would look in the list of clauses for one that contained the negative of the statement at hand (in this case we would find "man(Socrates)"), and resolve these two clauses together by merging them and canceling out contradictions. It so happens that when we do this here, the two statements "not man(Socrates)" and "man(Socrates)" simply cancel out, and we are left with nothing. One major contribution of Robinson's classical 1965 paper was to prove that when this happens, it means that the initial statement (here: "not mortal(Socrates)") contradicts the initial set of clauses. In other words, we have just proved in an entirely mechanical manner, that Socrates was mortal! To do this we have said, in the formal language proposed by Robinson, more or less the following: "If Socrates is not mortal, then he cannot be a man. But we know that he is a man, therefore saying that he is not mortal contradicts what we know." In the late 1960s, this discovery created a lot of excitement among AI researchers: a computer that could unfailingly extract the logical consequences of a set of statements or circumstances would certainly be close to true intelligence. And Robinson's method held the promise of letting programs crank out logical deductions without any recourse to intuition or judgment.

In fact, it didn't turn out that way. The reason was not apparent in the preceding example because the initial list contains only two clauses, and we can resolve with only one of them at each step. Practical situations involve long lists of initial clauses; and at any step of a proof, there are usually two or three that can be resolved with. As a result, the proof branches out into many directions, and the number of combinations to try out quickly grows to astronomical proportions. In the late 1960s, several researchers found out that resolution was no panacea to their problems. Among them was John McCarthy, whose student Cordell Green met with disappointing results in a project called QA3.

In true Hegelian fashion, such disappointments brought about a reaction against resolution, a case of which was the development of the programming language Microplanner at MIT. As we saw earlier, Microplanner owed nothing to logicians, but accomplished much of what logicians had sought to achieve with resolution. In Microplanner, the programmer just specified which goals he or she wanted to achieve, and let the inference mechanism built into the language take care of the details. Just as it would find a proof for a theorem among a set of logical statements, Microplanner could find and manipulate the sentences describing a given object in the micro world of blocks. This is how it enabled Terry Winograd of MIT to write his celebrated SHRDLU program, which carried on a dialogue with the user about blocks in ordinary English. Patrick Winston recalled that "the goal-oriented procedures for grasping, clearing, getting rid of, moving and ungrasping made it possible for a clear, transparent, concise program to seem amazingly intelligent."[50]

The MIT people were quite proud of this achievement but, as Carl Hewitt, the author of Microplanner, told me:

In some sense [they] weren't very polite about it. After Microplanner had been done and had a few victories under its belt, Seymour Papert and Gerry Sussman traveled off to Edinburgh, which was the heart of Logicland, to tell them where it was at. The new wave was [the MIT approach]! And [Robert] Kowalski was there as a graduate student at the time doing a dissertation based on resolution. So here's this poor graduate student trying to get a thesis done, and the high and mighty from MIT arrive and [put him down]![51]

Yet the MIT people soon realized that Microplanner was no panacea either. As Marvin Minsky remembered it, "on small problems it worked fine . . . but given large problems it would just disappear and take exponentially long. And so we gave it up."

PROLOG, OR SAYING ''WHAT'' INSTEAD OF ''HOW''

Perhaps stung by the remarks of Papert and Sussman, Kowalski stuck to his guns and investigated resolution further. With his colleague Donald Kuehner, Kowalski published in 1971 a paper in which he showed how simple rules allowed one to eliminate most resolutions irrelevant to the proof.[52] Kowalski and Kuehner illustrated how their procedure, which they called "SL-resolution," reduced the search tree for a simple proof from 513 nodes to only 12.

At about the same time, a young Frenchman named Alain Colmerauer was involved in an automatic translation project at the University of Montreal: he needed an efficient way of parsing sentences. In a September 1970 report, Colmerauer described how sentences could be represented by tree structures, which simple rules could manipulate for the analysis or generation of sentences.[53] When he returned to Marseille the next year, Colmerauer met Kowalski, who was paying a visit. To his surprise, the

Frenchman discovered that his procedure for manipulating trees corresponded to an efficient implementation of Kowalski's method for handling logical clauses. A Franco-British project developed to bring these ideas to fruition. In 1971–72, Colmerauer and his colleague Philippe Roussel wrote a programming language similar to Microplanner, but based on resolution techniques implemented as tree-based data structuring. During a train trip between Paris and Marseille, Roussel's wife came up with a name for the language by contracting the expression "PROgrammation en LOGique."[54] The first version of PROLOG was born, and turned into a runaway success. By 1972, Colmerauer and Roussel had used PROLOG to develop a computerized French-language question-answering system similar in scope to SHRDLU.

In 1974, a major improvement was added at the suggestion of Kowalski and his colleague Maarten van Emden, also of Edinburgh. It consisted in forcing the logical statements to espouse the so-called Horn clause format. A Horn clause is just an IF . . . THEN rule with a single consequence in the THEN part. Further, all conditions expressed in the IF part must be connected by the proposition AND; OR is not allowed. An example of a Horn clause is: "IF it has a white beard AND a booming laugh AND a bright red suit, THEN it enters through the chimney." On the other hand, sentences like "IF it is a fruit, THEN it is an apple OR an orange OR a prune" were not permitted. They had to be translated into Horn clauses before processing. This restriction had two advantages. First, Horn clauses give rise to unique descriptions as tree structures: the trunk corresponds to the single consequent in the THEN part, and the conditions in the IF part branch out from this trunk. If one of the branches is also the trunk of another clause, it can be simply expanded, further ramifications corresponding to the conditions of this new clause. The resulting simplification of the tree structures brought about a substantial speedup in PROLOG's performance. Horn clauses are also much easier for people to understand than the lopsided clauses used by Robinson in 1965.

The other reason for introducing Horn clauses was much dearer to the hearts of logicians: a set of Horn clauses exhibits the delightful property of being *decidable*—in contrast to a set of ordinary clauses which is only *semidecidable*. In other words, if a set of ordinary clauses logically imply a given statement, then there exists a way to prove it in a finite number of steps: a sufficiently clever program should be able to find it. On the other hand if the same program attempts to prove a nontheorem—that is, a statement that does not logically follow from the starting clauses—then it may get stuck in an infinitely long attempt to carry out an nonexistent proof. If, however, the original clauses are expressed in the Horn format, then nontheorems will also be unmasked in a finite number of steps. In this way, a PROLOG program attempting to answer a question by yes when the true answer is no will find out about its mistake before hell freezes over. Likewise, it is safe in a PROLOG environment to assume that if you cannot prove the opposite of something, then this something is true. For example, if you can't show that Paris is burning, then Paris is not burning. The ability to make such assumptions brings PROLOG a little closer to that elusive Grail of the AI search: common-sense reasoning.

The revamped version of PROLOG also contained notable improvements in regard to unification (the procedure for matching variables in order to simplify causes) and backtracking (the method for retreating from an unproductive line of reasoning). Given this extra horsepower, the Franco-British joint effort took on the allure of a competition. In 1977, David Warren, a doctoral student at Edinburgh, realized a compiled version of PROLOG, which ran five to ten times faster than the Marseille interpreted version. The AI group in Marseille has since produced its own fast versions of PROLOG, some of which ran on microcomputers as early as 1979. Other groups from Canada, Belgium, and Hungary soon joined the development effort, and PROLOG became the favored AI language outside the United States. The adoption of PROLOG in the United States was slowed by the existence of a strong LISP tradition in most large centers, and by the unjustified belief that PROLOG wasn't any faster than its inefficient predecessor Microplanner. This attitude changed when the Japanese made PROLOG the core language for their Fifth Generation project (see chapter 8) in the early 1980s, and PROLOG is now on an equal footing with LISP in the United States.

Not everybody is happy about this situation: if you don't believe in logic as a basic attribute of intelligence, PROLOG looks like a bad idea. Marvin Minsky doesn't believe in logic, and to me pronounced himself "horrified" at the Japanese adoption of PROLOG; he even traveled over to Japan with Carl Hewitt to urge—in vain—his Nippon colleagues to reconsider. Minsky now blames the choice of PROLOG for destroying the Fifth Generation effort.

Others, however, just see PROLOG as a programming language

embodying Marr's doctrine that *what* a system or program does takes precedence over *how* it does it. As Patrick Winston put it, "the evolution of computer languages is away from low-level languages, in which the programmer specifies *how* something is to be done, toward high-level languages, in which the programmer specifies simply *what* is to be done." LISP and FORTRAN are *how* languages. "PROLOG," continued Winston, " . . . clearly breaks away from [such] languages, encouraging the programmer to describe situations and problems, not the detailed means by which the problems are to be solved."[55] PROLOG's internal mechanisms for manipulating logical statements take care of such details.

CONCLUSION

At the end of the 1970s, artificial intelligence, now older and wiser, had acquired the full trappings of a scientific discipline. Under the prodding of David Marr and like-minded disciplinarians, its theoretical backbone had gained enough strength to withstand the attacks of naysayers. On the practical side, however, the intelligent machine seemed no closer than at the end of the 1960s. Despite tantalizing glimpses of success on the theoretical side, applications of AI remained few and far apart. Those in the AI community still concentrated on the campuses of a few universities and knew little of the rough-and-tumble world of business and engineering. They would soon step out of their cocoon.

8

THE ROLLERCOASTER
OF THE 1980S

The last decade saw the emergence of AI as an industry, following the now classical high-tech cycle of boom, bust, and recovery. The new attention and money induced an explosion in the number of American AI researchers, while Japanese computer scientists, in an effort to catch up, forged grandiose plans for a new generation of intelligent machines. Once more, AI research did not always deliver the promised results: at least one large American research project disappointed its military sponsors, and the Japanese fell far short of their objectives. Yet expert systems are now proliferating in industry, and AI is quietly being incorporated into an ever-increasing variety of conventional software, with unsung but tangible results.

BOOM

The honor of kicking off the decade where AI stopped being an academic curiosity befell the young professor, John McDermott of Carnegie Mellon University, who, in January 1980, handed over the first working version of his XCON expert system to Digital Equipment Corporation of Maynard, Massachusetts. As I discussed in chapter 6, the

Expert Configurer's assignment was to help DEC engineers in the frustrating and error-prone task of configuring to order its new line of VAX computers. By 1984, XCON had grown tenfold; and by 1986, although the company had invested more than fifty person-years in the program,[1] it was handsomely recouping the investment through annual savings of forty million dollars in testing and manufacturing costs.[2]

The windfall from XCON convinced DEC, and other heavyweights of the corporate world, that expert systems were for them. The economic advantages of the new technology were obvious to even the most obdurate of conservatives in corporate management. The cost of developing expert systems was (and still is) decreasing steadily, while the salaries of human experts keep on rising. After development, replicating an expert system costs pennies. By contrast, educating a person to a corresponding level of competence may cost hundreds of thousands of dollars and take many years. Computers never grow tired or grumpy, deliver a constant standard of performance, and have no hidden agenda. Further, they will not walk out to the competition, call in sick, or retire.

This last advantage may have hastened the birth of several early expert systems. Consider the case of David Smith, at the General Electric Company. Smith was GE's only engineer competent enough to handle all electric locomotive repair problems. When an engine went on the blink in a faraway station, GE's only resource was often to fly Smith over to fix the problem. By 1981, Smith was running ragged and considering retirement. GE succeeded in preserving Smith's competence, and in spreading it all over North America, by codifying it into an expert system. In 1984, the Diesel Electric Locomotive Troubleshooting Aid (DELTA) program could diagnose 80 percent of the breakdowns. It would then provide detailed instructions for performing the repair, using a videodisk player to illustrate its explanations.[3]

Or take Aldo on a Disk, his colleagues at Campbell's Soup Company's name for Aldo Cimino's computer replacement. Cimino was Campbell's resident expert on hydrostatic and rotary bacteria-killing cookers. Like Smith, he was getting on in years, and the constant flights from plant to plant to fix ailing cookers threatened to run him down. By 1985, local plant employees could type the symptoms of defective machines into computers, which made the same diagnosis Aldo would have.[4] Charlie Amble, at General Motors, also trained a computer apprentice before retiring. Nonspecialized personnel can now put sensors to lathes and grinders of the Saginaw plant. A computer listens to the vibrations given off by the machines and detects incipient trouble as Charlie would have.[5]

In the early 1980s, a continuous stream of similar expert-system success stories fed the media. On the "CBS Evening News," in September 1983, millions of viewers heard about a program called PROSPECTOR, which had located molybdenum deposits near Mount Tolman, in Washington State. PROSPECTOR contained, in the form of a series of rules, the collected knowledge of nine geologists. It pinpointed the ore in a small unexplored area, ringed by earlier bores and mines.[6] In the Bell system, another silicon expert called ACE identified trouble spots in telephone networks and recommended appropriate repairs. The FOLIO expert system helped financial advisers select portfolios to meet their clients' investment goals. At the Weather Bureau, WILLARD aided meteorologists in forecasting severe thunderstorms in the central United States.[7]

Most large companies started AI groups to develop in-house applications. In 1985, 150 companies spend $1 billion altogether on internal AI groups.[8] At DEC, for example, the AI group had grown to 77 people by 1986,[9] and mushroomed to 700 in 1988.[10] By then, DEC's AI group was responsible for 40 expert systems in addition to XCON.[11] A similar growth in the artificial intelligence group occurred at Xerox's Palo Alto Research Center (PARC). The Schlumberger-Doll Research Center in Ridgefield, Connecticut, and Texas Instruments in Dallas followed suit. Soon there was scarcely a single large corporation, whether it dealt in computers or not, that did not have its own AI group. In 1987, Du Pont, for example, had 100 expert systems in routine operation and 500 in various stages of development. Ed Mahler, head of the company's AI department, estimated annual savings from these systems at $10 million.[12]

In addition to the publicity given to the flamboyant technical advances, many societal factors enhanced the new AI wave. The "flower children" of the 1960s were growing up and losing their antiscience bias. Personal computers demystified a technology so far hidden in universities and large corporations. The space shuttle brought high tech back into style. The *Star Wars* movies, and the appearance of magazines like *Discover* and *High Technology,* put the future in the limelight. Artificial intelligence suddenly found itself the new darling of the public in general and of the financial community in particular. The lowering of the capital-gains tax rates by the Carter administration in the early 1980s made venture capitalists even more generous with their funds. Further, the billion-dollar biotechnology boom of the late 1970s had created a frenzy for high technology in investment circles.

Conversely, the success of new computer ventures like Apple and Compaq made academics realize that high tech could make them rich. Most leading experts in AI responded to the calls of the financiers and became founding fathers in new ventures. Edward Feigenbaum, with some of his Stanford colleagues, formed Teknowledge, Inc. Researchers from Carnegie Mellon incorporated the Carnegie Group. There were enough MIT spinoffs to create a strip in Cambridge, Massachusetts, known as AI Alley. These startups included Symbolics, Lisp Machines, Inc., and the Thinking Machines Corporation. The researcher Larry Harris left Dartmouth to form Artificial Intelligence Corporation. Roger Schank, at Yale, oversaw the formation of Cognitive Systems, Inc.

In 1986, U.S. sales of AI-related hardware and software reached $425 million.[13] Forty new companies had been formed,[14] with total investments of $300 million. Slightly more than half of this business dealt in specialized microcomputers called LISP machines, dedicated to running LISP programs at close to mainframe speeds. The largest such manufacturers were a division of Xerox in Stamford, Connecticut, a branch of Texas Instruments in Dallas, as well as two startups called Symbolics and Lisp Machines, both in Massachusetts.

The next largest segment of the AI industry wrote and marketed software called "expert system development tools," or "shells": large corporations used them to develop their in-house expert systems. Indeed, an important innovation about expert systems lies in an area their users never see: knowledge engineering. This new branch of computer science develops efficient procedures for transferring knowledge, from the minds of experts, into explicit sets of rules—as Randall Davis's TEIRESIAS helped physicians trace errors in MYCIN's reasoning about a case and correct the faulty inference rules or define new ones (see chapter 6). Because of this research, the time required to design expert systems has decreased drastically. In the early 1970s, the design and test of a single rule took literally weeks. For instance, the five-year MYCIN project, which resulted in a system with only 475 rules, had required more than 20 person-years of effort,[15] or slightly more than two weeks per rule. By 1987, the average engineering time required per rule had dropped to a few hours. Companies could then develop complex systems including thousands of rules at reasonable cost. In 1986, British

Petroleum reported building GASOIL, one of the largest expert systems ever (2,500 rules), in just one person-year.[16] In the early 1980s, four major vendors, all startups, dealt in expert system shells: the Carnegie Group in Pittsburgh; and Teknowledge, Intellicorp, and Inference, all in California.

It is significant that the remaining segment of the AI market, companies that specialized in developing actual expert-system applications, accounted for the least sales. This phenomenon probably had to do with the inclination of expert-systems users to hushing up their applications for competitive advantage. Corporate AI groups much preferred to build their systems in-house, only occasionally entrusting their development to outsiders. Instead, they purchased, from such companies as Teknowledge and Intellicorp, the software tools to make expert-system development easier. To ensure the continued availability of these tools, heavy users of expert systems like Du Pont, GM, and Boeing owned large chunks of the expert-system shell companies.

A brand-new industry also emerged in the related field of computer vision. TV cameras hooked up to dedicated computers appeared on plant floors to perform quality control and help robots grab objects or drill holes at the right places. These systems stood light-years beneath both the several cooperating modules Marr had identified in low-level human vision, and the hypothesis-driven recognition operations Minsky suspected at the higher levels. In the early 1980s, artificial-vision systems ignored texture, stereo, color, and even shading: grays did not exist; and each pixel, or point in the image, was perceived as either black or white. In most cases, the computer's processing abilities stopped at counting pixels in certain areas of an image. Suppose you wanted a robot vision system to verify that a hole had indeed been drilled at a certain location in a part. You would point the camera and rig the lighting so as to make the hole stand out as black against the surface of the part, and program the computer to pass the part if the number of black pixels exceeded a certain value in the relevant image area. It all took a very long time to arrange, and the slightest variation in surface finish of the part, lighting, or positioning would throw the procedure out of kilter. Nevertheless, by 1985 over a hundred companies offered industrial machine-vision systems in the United States, up from fifty-three years before. Their sales totaled eighty million dollars,[17] with a growth rate around 40 percent.

Explosive growth causes havoc in any field, and AI was no exception. Not all academics liked being jolted from the quiet routine of their research. The first meeting of the American Association for Artificial Intelligence, held at Stanford in 1980, gathered no more than one thousand researchers. But most participants, who saw AAAI as a private club where they could compare notes quietly with colleagues—a kind of convention-hall extension of the ivory tower—were in for a surprise. In 1985, attendance at a joint meeting of AAAI and the International Joint Conference on Artificial Intelligence (IJCAI) approached six thousand. Academics felt crowded out. Reporters, venture capitalists, industry head hunters, and young entrepreneurs intent on cashing in on the new technology formed more than half of the participants. Casual dress was out, and three-piece suits were in.

The private sector demand for personnel competent in artificial intelligence far exceeded the supply. This shortage propelled salaries to sky-high levels and created a pressure for researchers to leave academia for private industry. Fewer bright students were willing to endure the miserly stipends of graduate school, when industry started them off at salaries of as much as $30,000 (a windfall in the early 1980s). In the universities themselves, competition for the larger grants now available from sponsoring sources turned academics into unwilling copies of private entrepreneurs. To survive in this context, absent-minded professors had to spend most of their time writing up proposals impressive enough to justify million-dollar budgets. They then devoted whatever was left of their schedules to managing the people and facilities these proposals earned them.

It is hard to measure the step-up in AI research accurately: raw budgets are hard to assess because funding came from several sources. One indication is the increase in size of large research centers. Patrick Winston pointed out to me that the MIT Artificial Intelligence Laboratory mushroomed from about forty researchers in 1975 to over two hundred in the late 1980s—a fivefold increase. The opening of corporate AI research centers, and the inclusion of AI in the computer science curricula of most universities, hint at an even larger hike in the total number of researchers: "We've put out a lot of graduates over the years which have gone out and seeded other universities," Winston observed.[18] As an additional complication, it became hard to tell AI researchers from those of other specialties: Is someone writing an expert system to guide bridge maintenance doing artificial intelligence or civil engineering? As one assessment of the overall research activity, consider the number of technical books published about AI: In the 1970s, five such titles on the average appeared every year. From 1980 to 1986, this number gradually increased to eighty books per year and has remained at that level ever since. It is thus not unrealistic to envision a sixteenfold increase in AI-related research activity during the first half of the 1980s.

In 1987, the future of the new expert-system industry appeared brighter than ever. The ever-increasing power of personal computers made it possible for powerful expert systems to sit on a desk top. Fueling this democratization of AI, the ever-greater efficiency of techniques developed for designing expert systems made them even more affordable. The magazine *Science* hailed the merging of AI into the mainstream of computer science,[19] and *Fortune* glorified "Live Experts on a Floppy Disk."[20]

In 1985, expert-system companies sped through the slump affecting the computer industry without as much as looking over their shoulders.[21] Nothing appeared able to stop their expansion. Once more everything, it seemed, was well in AI.

SIGNS OF TROUBLE

Yet many academics felt uneasy about the wheeling and dealing. In 1984, Roger Schank and Marvin Minsky warned business that enthusiasm for the new technology was out of hand. They argued that expert systems largely stemmed from twenty-year-old programming methods that had gained in power as computers became faster.[22] Recent programs implementing these methods were no smarter than their forebears: they just made stupid decisions faster! In the same year, the AAAI had held a public debate during its annual meeting about the prospect of an "AI Winter."[23] Borrowing from the bleak "Nuclear winter" scenario put forward in a different context, AI researchers thus label this recurring nightmare of theirs: the optimism evaporates in the research community, public opinion follows through, and leading AI figures get ridiculed. Research funding for AI comes to a grinding stop, and twenty-year veterans of the art of list processing end up in the cold and dark as taxi drivers.

Because of AI's ups and downs in public favor since its beginnings, the pervasiveness of this concern is hardly surprising. It may show that repeated disappointments are beginning to instill realism into the forecasts of AI practitioners. Nowadays most AI researchers adopt a markedly low-key posture when dealing with the media. In the mid-1980s, such concerns were justified: through extensive use, many shortcomings of the new technology were becoming plain. Some corresponded to the warnings of Schank and Minsky, but others came as a surprise.

One major flaw affected some of the very successes cited by the proponents of expert systems. Digital Equipment's XCON suffered from an ailment that not even the most acerbic critics of AI had predicted: it started crumpling under its own weight. DEC never stopped adding rules to the system to keep it up with the constant changes and improvements to its product line. By 1987, XCON had grown to about ten thousand rules.[24] Instead of becoming more efficient, the system simply became larger. Soon DEC had to spend two million dollars a year to update the knowledge base. The joke in the company was that XCON had originally replaced 75 people in the configuration department, but that it took 150 to keep it up and running. Likewise, General Electric, unable to keep its DELTA troubleshooting system for locomotives up to date,[25] had to shelve it temporarily. Developers of expert systems had not realized the extent to which knowledge bases require continual revisions to avoid obsolescence. Their upkeep is now a major concern of the expert-system industry.

Knowledge engineers blame these maintenance problems on a property of expert systems they call "opacity": that is, despite the clarity of individual production rules, the effect of their combined operation is hard to predict, and an additional rule can have unexpected effects. Large sets of rules behave in this respect like an unruly mob: group dynamics may lead it to wanton destruction even if all individuals in the crowd hold reasonable desires. One way to restore order would be to introduce a hierarchy among the rules. Like executives of a well-managed company, the rules would reside in modules, organized in a pyramidal structure. A hierarchy would also increase the efficiency of an expert system by allowing the inference mechanism to work at any given time on only a subset of the rules. Yet this organization would be contrary to the democratic character of a rule system. A hierarchy means a step back toward conventional programming, which executes instructions in a strict order of priority.

Expert systems exhibited weaknesses even more basic than opacity. One remained the difficulty of transferring the appropriate knowledge from the mind of a human expert to the knowledge base of the program. Sometimes the most sophisticated knowledge engineering techniques brought about only moderate increases in efficiency. In all cases, these techniques required highly trained (and paid!) human-knowledge engineers, who would all testify to the difficulty of boiling the knowledge of a human expert down to a set of well-defined rules. One reason for this "knowledge bottleneck" may be that true experts do not really think in rules at all. As we saw, critics such as the philosopher Hubert Dreyfus point out that analogy is a large part of human reasoning. In the mid-1980s, expert systems could not match this ability of ours to identify problems and their solutions by comparing them with similar situations in the past. They still can't perform such analogical reasoning very well, but progress is being made.

Even when manuals and codes of procedures existed for the application, the knowledge engineer still had to reformulate them in a manner that the computer could process. Dumping raw legal statutes and law books into a computer is no way to program an automated lawyer! Reproducing even the most elementary type of legal reasoning required careful and detailed handcrafting. In the mid-1980s, knowledge engineers were starting to realize that building truly extensive AI systems would require automating the knowledge-acquisition process itself.

Perhaps the most significant objection to first-generation expert systems was that they did not (and still don't) really understand what they reason about. Machinelike, they handle empty tokens of knowledge that they recognize but do not comprehend. Though they will on occasion show a surprising likeness of human reasoning and competence, it is a void parody, the narrow performance of an automaton instead of a creditable copy of human thought. For example, the medical expert system MYCIN, as well as its descendants, acted on rules of thumb expressing a physician's explicit reactions to patterns of symptoms. This superficial knowledge, which one can summarize with rules, is quite unlike true comprehension based on scientific foundations or on human conceptions of cause and effect. MYCIN did not know what a patient, a bacterium, or a hospital were. Life, death, and doctors were alien concepts to it. The program knew no anatomy or physiology and could not ignore its own rules when circumstances required. As an example of this "by the book" character of expert systems, the MYCIN rule on the drug tetracyclin contended that tetracyclin should not be given to children younger than twelve. The reason for this decree, which MYCIN had no way of understanding, was that tetracyclin stains the teeth of young children. Obviously, in a critical case with tetracyclin the only drug effective or available, a human physician would weigh the cosmetic drawback against the threat to the child's life and prescribe the drug anyway. MYCIN would have let the patient die.

This example shows again another uncanny ability of human beings that expert systems could not (and still can't) duplicate: we understand that some principles apply, unless there are good reasons why they don't. McCarthy, who had first pointed out this qualification problem in 1969, drove the point home again in 1987 in another example. Suppose an expert system contains the rule: "IF I have a boat, THEN I can cross a river."[26] While this rule usually applies, in practice there are infinitely many situations where it will not. There may be no oars, motor, or sail in the boat, or it may leak. The river could be the Niagara just upstream of the falls. The boatman could be paralyzed and unable to use the boat, or someone could have built a wall in the middle of the river. Obviously, trying to define formal exceptions to the rule for all imaginable cases would be a hopeless task.

Animal taxonomy makes up a favorite ground for AI skeptics to expound their reservations. Consider the well-rehearsed elephant rule: "All elephants have trunks." But what then of Clyde, the elephant who lost his trunk in the Punic wars? In the same vein, Marvin Minsky, in his 1982 presidential address to AAAI, threw down to the younger generation the "duck challenge." How could one design an expert system able to carry out the following dialogue?

HUMAN: "All ducks can fly. Charlie is a duck."
EXPERT SYSTEM: "Then Charlie can fly."
HUMAN: "But Charlie is dead."
EXPERT SYSTEM: "Oh! Then Charlie can't fly!"[27]

This dialogue implies the ability to reverse a conclusion after reaching it. The kind of logic required to solve this problem is called "nonmonotonic." To achieve generalized nonmonotonic reasoning, an inference mechanism would need access to many facts about the world. In the preceding case, these would include general knowledge about ducks, life, and death. To solve McCarthy's boat problem, one would need to know about boats, rivers, waterfalls, and a human's ability to operate a boat. Note that when putting this knowledge into a system, one could not know in advance the contexts in which the inference mechanism would use the facts (for example, the absence of oars should hardly prevent a person from using the last remaining lifeboat in a sinking ship). One would therefore need to express all facts with the neutrality of purpose of an encyclopedia. First-generation expert systems were, and their modern equivalents still are, far from this goal. Facts in their knowledge bases are specific to the goals of a program and to the way it processes information. For example, the word *mammal* in the expert system considered in chapter 6 had nothing to do with the dictionary definition of this zoological group; it was simply a label for an intermediate conclusion in the program, which could lead to other labels called *dolphin, porpoise,* or *baby whale.* In no way did the character string *mammal* inform the program that the corresponding word in human parlance normally designates a warm-blooded, air-breathing animal.

For this reason, facts stated in one expert system could not in the mid-1980s be of use to another expert system. Although, as I write this in the early 1990s, the situation is a little different, as yet no expert system can answer an inquiry as: "I don't know whether seals are mammals, but my colleague ZooExpert might. Hold on while I connect you to it!" In general, no two programs share the same information. Further, a given program cannot know the limits of its own knowledge and knows even less where missing information might be. Responses to inquiries that go beyond the knowledge of a system will result in either a "don't know" answer, or worse, a wrong answer. For example, a variant of the sample expert system in chapter 6 might well have decided that seals are not mammals because they do not blow a jet or have a blowhole. This tendency of expert systems to break down when you get to the edge of their knowledge is called "brittleness." AI workers still have far to go before they can distill into their products the age-old maxim of the Chinese philosopher Confucius: "To know that one knows what one knows, and to know that one doesn't know what one doesn't know, there lies true wisdom."

Even more basic weaknesses of expert systems involve their problems with time and causality, and their inability to learn. Early field tests of a system to review routine car loans at the Ford Motor Company flopped on that account: the program found no reason to dispute an application from a twenty-year-old who claimed to have ten years of work experience.[28] Learning involves the establishment of correspondences and analogies between objects and classes of objects. Expert systems have trouble with this kind of activity. Early on some were even unable to handle general statements about classes of objects. Consider, for example, the facts "All humans have a human mother" and "John is a human." A naïve inference engine, trying to draw all possible conclusions from those facts, would get stuck in the line of reasoning that goes: "John has a human mother, John's mother has a human mother, the mother of John's mother has a human mother. . . ."

The limitations of early expert systems appear clearly in guidelines pointing out promising fields of application. Morris W. Firebaugh, a professor at the University of Wisconsin–Parkside, wrote an introductory textbook which the AI community received very well. In it, the author summarized many of the guidelines used in the field through the following *phone-call rule*: "Any problem that can be and frequently is solved by your in-house expert in a 10–30 minute phone call can be automated as an expert system."[29] First, using the phone filters out all sensory inflow: information carried by sight, smell, or body language becomes irrelevant. Similarly, the expert does not have to perform any physical manipulation: one can express the pertinent information in a few hundred words. And, finally, the amount of information processing does not tax a human performer's mind for more than a few minutes. Firebaugh adds that the skill in question should be simple and well defined enough that neophytes routinely learn it. It should belong to a narrow, specialized area and require no common sense.

The philosopher and AI critic Hubert Dreyfus quoted Dr. Sandra Cook, manager of the Financial Expert Systems Program at SRI International, as claiming another condition.[30] Human experts should be able to solve the problem at such a high level that somewhat inferior performance is still acceptable. Since bottling the knowledge into a set of rules will degrade the performance, such tolerance is necessary.

In 1984, the director of marketing with Intellicorp, one of the large companies dealing in expert-system shells, saw an even more restrictive role for first-generation expert systems.[31] Contrary to most of his colleagues, Martin Hollander claimed that the appropriate function of an expert system was to be a "doubting Thomas" adviser. In this mode, the system would not come to any conclusions of its own, but would simply accept a hypothesis from the user and check it for conformance with the rules. In a similar vein, Dreyfus commended a medical expert system called Reconsider.[32] The system did not claim to replace doctors. Instead, it reviewed case information with them, signaled important information they might have neglected to collect, and pointed out alternative diagnoses, if any.

To summarize, the expert systems flaunted in the early and mid-1980s could not operate as well as the experts who supplied them with knowledge. To true human experts, they amounted to little more than sophisticated reminding lists. When, however, know-how was locally unavailable or too expensive, then expert systems operating in a restricted field could make better decisions than untrained or unconcerned human beings. This state of affairs has improved but slightly and is likely to endure until there is basic progress in programming common-sense, learning, and inference abilities into computers.

Finally, in the mid-1980s, a cloud hung over the upstart AI industry. It was the result of a poor business decision by the academic founders of the first AI companies, blinded as they were by their unquestioning faith in the specialized LISP language. When he invented it in the earliest days of AI, John McCarthy had endowed LISP with distinctive properties that made the development of symbol-manipulating programs easier. Since LISP required special computers to run efficiently, the largest segment of the new industry was devoted to manufacturing and selling LISP machines.

These dedicated computers suffered from three main drawbacks. The first was cost. LISP machines didn't pack much more processing power than later IBM or Apple microcomputers, but did not benefit from the economies of scale of these mass-made products. Their price tags of $50,000 to $100,000 placed them out of the reach of all but well-funded research institutions or large corporations. Second, LISP machines were "stand-alone": one could not connect them in a network or link them to the mainframes in which most corporations store their data banks. Finally despite all its virtues, LISP was virtually unknown outside the AI community. Programmers knowledgeable in the language were few and commanded high salaries.

The bias toward LISP machines also affected the software segments of the AI industry. Teknowledge, Inc., had designed its expert-system shells to run on LISP machines, and companies like Palladian and Applied Expert Systems all but imposed the LISP solution on the corporate clients for which they designed custom expert systems.

BUST

By 1987, Apple and IBM-compatible microcomputers of a power comparable to LISP machines made their appearance, and there was no longer any excuse to prefer the nonstandard machines. Further, other AI startups like Gold Hill Computers and First Class Expert Systems ported AI software to conventional machines using the popular C language. This rang the knell of the LISP machine industry.

Since AI had come out of the laboratory, this last mishap threw into a tailspin an entire industry worth close to half a billion dollars in annual sales.[33] Thousands of people lost their jobs, and many entrepreneurs, their shirts. Despite sales of $12 million in 1986,[34] Lisp Machines of Andover, Massachusetts, filed for bankruptcy. From Symbolics, in Cambridge, flowed a torrent of red ink. The company lost $71 million in the two years ended June 1987, on sales of slightly less than $200 million. Symbolics lost an additional $46 million the next year and laid off 450 employees, including its chairman and founder.[35] In the fiscal year ending 30 June 1987, the two leading expert-system shell developers, Teknowledge and Intellicorp, lost $2.8 million and $4 million.[36] Both had had sales of about $20 million.

The computer vision industry suffered a similar setback. A one-time high flier, Machine Vision International, crashed early in 1988. Many large corporations, such as General Electric, Eaton, Gould, and 3M, withdrew from the vision market.[37] In 1987, exhibit floor space for the annual Vision trade show in Detroit's Cobo Hall had dropped by close to 50 percent. Gone were the noisy crowds and exhibits featuring scantily clad women cooing over computer systems. Starting in 1988, the Robotic Industries Association combined its annual robotics show with the Vision convention. Both fairs went from yearly hooplas to a more sedate affair held every other year.[38]

On the research side, one of the largest unfulfilled promises of the fledgling technology was the "Smart Truck," or Autonomous Land Vehicle project, financed by the U.S. military. ALV was part of ten-year project called the Strategic Computing Initiative program, started in 1983 by the Defense Advanced Research Projects Agency. The Smart Truck accounted for about a quarter of SCI's annual budget of $100 million. The project aimed at developing a robot wanderer for such missions as weapons delivery, reconnaissance, ammunition handling, and rear area resupply. The vehicle would rove over rugged terrain as fast as a running soldier, skirt around obstacles, and use any convenient cover for camouflage. Wheeled prototypes would initially be confined to roadways and flat ground, but the final product would travel insectlike, across any terrain, on mechanical legs.[39] Hans Moravec, director of the Mobile Robot Laboratory of Carnegie Mellon University, recalled the project for me:

I was co-principal investigator of one of the big, million-dollar-a-year ALV grants. . . . My role in it was to basically drop out. I didn't believe in the project; I didn't think it was possible. What was eventually achieved [shows] pretty much [that] my intuition was right: it really was premature. I didn't think with the current speed of computing you could do that job adequately. . . . You really need to look at a few million pixels every few seconds and to evaluate them under several different hypotheses [such as] "This could be an edge or it could not be." You have to carry both those hypotheses through for quite a while until confirming or negative evidence builds up to some level of confidence. Nowadays you've got . . . to run with a low level of confidence, in which case your system will fail every hundred feet or so: this is the sort of numbers they have been getting.[40]

By 1987, it became clear that the ALV project goals could never be reached with the expected delays. According to the schedule, the proto-type (a van crammed with video and computer equipment) should by then have traveled without incident across six miles of open desert; moving at up to three miles an hour, it should have avoided bushes and ditches. In fact, the longest outing it ever did off-road was a six-hundred-yard stroll, at about two miles an hour.[41] The ax fell in 1989, when the Pentagon ended the main project work at Martin Marietta Corporation.

Research projects failed not only in vision and not just in the United States. At the same time as the Smart Truck, and on a much grander scale, the $850-million Japanese Fifth Generation Project was likewise fizzling out. In 1981, the Japanese government had brashly invited seventy foreign observers to the official project kickoff in Tokyo. Profes-sor Moto-Oka of Tokyo University, chairman of the Japanese Ministry of Trade and Industry (MITI) committee that had drafted the plan, laid out the project's objectives to the audience. Fifth Generation machines would carry on casual conversations, translate languages, interpret pictures, and reason like human beings. Users wishing to set up a particular application would need no knowledge of arcane computer languages. The computer would literally interview them to understand their needs, and ferret out of them any information required to correctly specify the task; the machine would then program itself accordingly. Moreover, the computers would be inexpensive enough for everyday use in home, office, and factory.[42]

As I write this book ten years after the launching of the project, no computer, Japanese or other, approaches human reasoning power. Translation machines remain experimental,[43] and computer vision is impractical outside of well-defined factory applications. Computer programmers fluent in C, Pascal, or FORTRAN are more in demand than ever. A researcher at the Japanese External Trade Organization recently said of the Fifth Generation Project, "It's dated, forget about it."[44] Japan's Institute for New Generation Computer Technology, responsible for administering the project, has revised its goals. ICOT now aims at the development of a congenial, enhanced Macintosh-like machine, and a computerized encyclopedia.[45]

RECOVERY

By the end of the 1980s, both the vision and the AI industries were on the road to recovery and making more realistic pitches about the abilities of their products. Yet one can still see psychological scars in the reluctance of many companies to use the "expert system" label. "We tend not to use even the term AI," said Palo Alto–based Aion's president Harry Reinstein.[46] The tendency now is for AI companies to embed expert systems into conventional products to build up a functional unit. They strive at becoming known as successful solution suppliers, rather than AI technology enterprises. A typical example of this covert approach is a sales support program for a retail company that takes orders by telephone. In its standard form, the program would simply check the presence of a requested item in inventory, record the sale, prepare the invoice, and advise shipping to act on it. The new-wave AI touch consists in "embedding" an expert system into this program. To the sales clerk it looks exactly the same, but for one exception: for sold-out items, suggestions for alternative choices pop on screen.[47] As a result, the retail company polishes its reputation for good service and increases its sales. "Not as glamorous as prescribing a cure for meningitis," some would say—yet such modest feats form the bread and butter of the new, battle-tested AI industry. Hidden applications are also building a firm foundation upon which to erect higher achievements. The next version of the preceding program may well provide a list of the advantages of the proposed item and advice on how to close the sale. Patrick Winston, director of MIT's AI Laboratory, summarized for me the 1991 state of the AI industry:

> I think it's getting increasingly difficult to draw a circle around it. Like everybody else, I have started a company and as I go out into the real world, the scales fall from my eyes. One of these scales had been the belief that AI could be sold to anybody by itself. It really must be blended with other more standard technology in order to be useful. The new enterprise of AI is to combine with people to produce something that neither can produce alone. It means your programs don't even have to be really smart. If all you do is save a $200-million blunder once in a while by asking somebody to look at something, that's good enough to be very important. I think we are going to enter into a new era with respect to applications of AI that's quite different from the 1980s. This was the age where expert systems were replacing people, whereas the 1990s will be the age of what we could call "raisin bread systems" for making people smarter. AI is now embedded in systems like raisins in raisin bread. It doesn't have to occupy much volume and may carry a lot of the nutrition. You can't have the raisin bread without the raisins, and there can be different kinds of raisins. That's the way I think the 1990s will benefit from AI: raisin bread systems for making people smarter.

Indeed expert systems, embedded or not, are now helping people make better decisions in all branches of industry. Despite their limitation to specialized fields of application and inferiority to the best human experts, such systems can drastically improve the performance of non-experts. Often developed in a few months' time through modern knowl-edge engineering software, expert systems will usually run on PC's. As Winston pointed out: "Now that you can get a fifty-million-instruc-tions-per-second workstation for less than ten thousand dollars, AI applications that had been hopelessly impractical when they had to run on a million-dollar computer are within reach."

As for the future of AI research, Winston was optimistic:

> The number of AI researchers is still growing, but more slowly than in the early 1980s. This in spite of the fact that the number of researchers in computer science in general has stabilized: according to some sources, computer hardware, software, and services now amount to 10 percent of GNP. It's hard to imagine it going to 20 percent. Plus the fact that demographics are such that there are far fewer students than there used to be. Those two factors together have led to a numeric decline in the number of computer science students in the last five to ten years: enrollments in many computer science programs are down by 50 percent. But all that means is a slowdown in the rate of growth of people doing AI research.

NEURAL NETWORKS REVISITED

Another factor contributing to this slowdown may be the resurgence in the mid-1980s of neural network technology, which Marvin Minsky and Seymour Papert had forced underground with the publication of their 1967 book *Perceptrons* (see chapter 4). As I explained, Minsky and Papert had thoroughly debunked the simple neural networks studied in the 1960s under the name of Perceptrons, which consisted of a single layer of McCulloch-Pitts neurons sandwiched between input and output units. The authors showed that many fundamental classification operations would remain forever beyond the reach of Perceptrons. It so happened that around 1974, not seven years after the appearance of Minsky and Papert's book, a Harvard graduate student named Paul J. Werbos discovered a way out of the impasse.[48] It had long been known that Perceptrons could acquire new abilities if additional layers of artificial neurons were inserted between the input and output units. For example, adding a single such "hidden unit" to a Perceptron allowed it to perform the XOR operation, which Minsky and Papert had shown ordinary Perceptrons could not do. In the simple XOR network, the weights could be adjusted by trial and error to achieve the desired result. The problem, however, was that Rosenblatt's Perceptron Learning Rule did not apply to such networks, and no one knew how to train multilayer networks with many neurons to perform complicated operations. Werbos discovered a procedure called the back-propagation algorithm, which allowed him to train those souped-up Perceptrons. Perhaps because of the lethargy into which neural network research had fallen in the 1970s, however, his discovery made no splash at all.

The revival of the field had to await two events which occurred in the next decade. In 1982, physicist John Hopfield published a paper in which he showed how networks of simple neurons could acquire the ability to calculate, and explained this behavior with a mathematical theory similar to thermodynamics.[49] The second event was the independent rediscovery of back-propagation in the early 1980s by David E. Rumelhart and David B. Parker, who were then respectively at the University of California at San Diego and Stanford University. Rumelhart and psychologist James McClelland of Carnegie Mellon then persuaded interested colleagues (including Nobel Prize–winner Francis Crick) to gather into a team which they called the Parallel Distributed Processing Study Group. In 1986, the group published a two-volume collection of ground-breaking papers[50] that are now considered the "Bible" of connectionists, as the new generation of neural network researchers call themselves. Neural networks soon successfully tackled such tasks as artificial speech generation,[51] learning to play backgammon,[52] and even driving a vehicle.[53] According to McClelland, in 1991 approximately ten thousand people were involved in neural network research in the United States alone.[54]

It is not yet clear whether this headway of neural networks is a victory or a defeat for artificial intelligence as a field of scientific inquiry. Even though neural nets fall under the umbrella definition of AI as "the science of making machines do things that would require intelligence if done by people" (see chapter 1), they certainly do not share the fundamental paradigm of conventional AI, which purports to achieve intelligence in machines throughout the manipulation of symbols. Rather than a specialty of AI, many connectionists consider their field a new science of its own. Indeed, connectionists meet in different conventions, express themselves in different journals, and speak a technical dialect different from that of AI researchers. Yet, there are signs that the two fields may be converging: as I'll explain in chapter 10, conventional AI now recognizes the need for extensive parallel computation, and new AI theories postulate the existence of large numbers of cooperating "agents" within a mind: intelligence would then be the result of a "network" of interacting entities.

One would think, however, that the past difficulties of expert systems would moderate pretensions about other technologies for making machines intelligent. Yet as I write this, the buildup of the neural-network industry looks like an exact replay, a decade later, of the expert-system drama. The press expounds on the new technology, and the military announces a $400-million supporting fund for it. All concerned admit that neural nets are still in their infancy, but predict a billion-dollar market by the end of the century. In 1989, three hundred companies, most of them startups founded by researchers, competed for this market.[55]

Beyond this second boom, forecasters see the beginnings of a third. Like expert systems, it will concern a technology that has been around for many years. It also reminds one of how the Japanese Fifth Generation effort spurred U.S. government funding of expert systems. Sudden enthusiasm in Japan for the rediscovered fuzzy logic is now rekindling interest for this technology on this side of the Pacific, where it started.[56] Fuzzy-logic computers, built into microchips, may be capable of decisions under uncertainty, much as humans are.

There is a measure of truth in these assertions, and both the neural networks and fuzzy-logic technologies inject much-needed fresh air into the stale room of symbol-manipulating AI. Will success happen as fast as the new entrepreneurs expect, and will it be as dramatic as they claim? If past blunders in forecasting by AI researchers are any indication, the apostles of these new faiths may be in for rough times.

Meanwhile, all through the 1980s, AI researchers who managed to keep at least one step removed from the industry, realizing the deficiencies of first-generation expert systems, have been taking steps to remedy them. As we'll see in chapter 10, this research led to unexpected and deep insights into what makes us human. But first, let us look at a branch of artificial intelligence that also knew many exciting successes in the 1980s.

9

GAME PLAYING:
CHECKMATE FOR
MACHINES?

Getting computers to win games against humans has been one of the earliest goals in AI. As we've seen, the main objective of AI is to let machines perform tasks that, if done by humans, would be said to require intelligence. Playing such complicated games as backgammon, checkers, and chess certainly qualifies. Game playing also has provided AI researchers with a convenient set of well-defined problems against which to pit the developing mental powers of their machines. Contrary to most problems we meet in life, games come with clear definitions and involve only a small number of basic elements. They are, however, complex enough to require nontrivial solution techniques. Also, one can easily assess the value of a particular game-playing program: either it wins games, or it doesn't. Game playing therefore sidesteps the thorny issue of determining, in a general context, whether a given program behaves intelligently.

THE GAMES

Game-playing programs have equaled, and at times bettered, human performance in board games. The successes of these programs, and the nature of their reasoning processes, affect our understanding of what intelligence is.

Backgammon

Luigi Villa had, just the previous day, won the world championship. He was now in danger of becoming history's first world champion to be defeated by a machine. The three-foot-high metallic opponent facing him across the board was leading five games to one. The robot had played with accuracy and imagination. It consistently deployed the kind of gambit computers are not supposed to know, like making sacrificial moves which bring greater rewards over the duration of the game. Later, experts who did not know which side the machine had played attributed its sparkling ploys to the human opponent. By the robot sat the stocky, white-haired American professor who had written the program controlling the machine. He was smiling expectantly, as if already sure of the final kill. The ax fell quickly. One last sensational move by the robot, and the tournament drew to an end, assuring Villa of his place in a footnote of history. A crowd of stunned spectators, having watched from outside through television monitors, flooded the quiet room. Flashes erupted, experts congratulated the white-haired professor, and reporters sought to interview him. Villa was crestfallen.

Science fiction, you think? These events occurred in July 1979, at the Monte Carlo Winter Sports Palace. The game was backgammon. Involving both skill and chance, it attracts twenty million adepts in the United States and a total of seventy million around the world. The computer program that beat the Italian champion, Luigi Villa, was the brainchild of a researcher, Hans Berliner, from Carnegie Mellon University. Connected to the robot by satellite, the program had been running on a computer located in Pittsburgh.[1]

Like most board games, backgammon is a sublimated version of human warfare, its name deriving from the Welsh *bac* and *gamen*, "little" and "war." The backgammon board has twenty-four spaces, or landing places. Each player commands a small army of fifteen pieces, or men, originally placed at preordained starting positions. In the game, each player must move his or her pieces to a portion of the board called the "inner table," and then take them (or bear them, in the game's parlance) off the board. The first player to complete the process wins. Rolling a pair of dice decides the number of landing places a player can advance a particular piece. The two dice remain separate: one should not think of a 6–1 roll as a 7. It is a 6 and a 1, and one can play it with one man or with two. The fun and challenge lie in deciding which man or men, and where to land them. The board configuration is such that the two armies of men must pass each other and mingle to get to their destinations. This is where fights erupt on the board. Opponents pouncing on a solitary piece force it back to the starting position. Conversely, if a player has two or more men on a landing place, they can blockade the opponent's progress by preventing him or her from alighting there en route. Since in any single game, because of the dice, luck counts for about as much as know-how, backgammon matches always consist of several games.

In the late 1970s, Hans Berliner, a psychologist turned AI researcher at Carnegie Mellon University, was studying the so-called evaluation, or scoring, method for playing games with computers. This method is the counterpart of the search method, which assesses a given play by searching branching chains of moves and countermoves. Evaluation, by contrast, lies perhaps closer to how humans plan their play. It consists of defining various criteria, or features, that measure the goodness of a move. In backgammon, for example, a useful feature to consider would be blockading. It measures the extent to which one's men impede the opponent's progress by occupying landing places. Other factors might include the safety of the pieces and the degree to which either side is ahead in the race to bear pieces off. Having evaluated the features for all possible moves, one then selects the most appropriate play accordingly, without searching beyond the next move.

Backgammon was ideal for experiments with the evaluation method because of the random aspect of the game, which generates too many possibilities for the search method to work. Since there are 21 possible rolls of the dice for each move, and some 20 ways of playing each roll, rating possible countermoves in backgammon involves the consideration of 20 × 21, or 420 possible results per move. In chess, where the search method works, this number is only 35.

The outcome of Berliner's program surprised backgammon adepts and, to a certain extent, the program's author. One reason was that the robot, in Berliner's terms, "gave a semi-comic impression during the event, rolling around, controlled by a remote radio link, and occasionally speaking and bumping into things." During the opening ceremonies of the tournament, "the overhead lights dimmed, the orchestra began playing the theme of the film *Star Wars* and a spotlight focused on an opening in the stage curtain through which Gammonoid [as the robot was dubbed] was supposed to propel itself onto the stage. To my dismay the robot got entangled in the curtain and its appearance was delayed for five minutes."[2] Nevertheless, there was a $5,000 winner-take-all stake in the match between the robot and Villa. Even a world champion would play seriously for that much money. The spectators had come to laugh. Instead, the robot treated them to steady, even brilliant, play. Toward the end of the last game, the machine conducted an apparently reckless attack. It left several men standing alone, vulnerable to being sent home. It did not mind exposing them, however, because this adventurous assault, coupled with its already fine defensive position, meant two chances of winning instead of one. It was a highly imaginative and correct judgment, which the watching experts approved.

Checkers

A less successful plan for defeating a human world champion with a computer goes back to 1947. It involved the game of checkers and Arthur Samuel, then a professor at the University of Illinois. The university was willing to finance the construction of an "electronic brain," as computers were known in those days. Samuel, having become an expert in vacuum tubes at Bell Labs during the war, found himself in charge of the design and construction of the machine. Since he believed that the $110,000 of internal funds assigned to the project would not be enough, Samuel looked for ways of drumming up support from the private sector. He decided that a world checker championship, which the neighboring town of Kankakee would host a few months afterward, was the occasion he needed. Samuel wrote thirty-five years later: "[I]t seemed quite reasonable at the time for us to put together some sort of computer in a few months, and for me to write a checker program . . . that could challenge and beat the new world checker champion at the conclusion of this match. This would give us the publicity we needed. How naive can one be?"[3] In those days, Samuel knew nothing of programming or checkers, a game he did not like. Of course, the checkers championship went on without his contribution.

It eventually took Samuel fifteen years to write a computer program that could play checkers at the championship level. In 1962, the program beat Robert Nealy, ex-Connecticut state champion. In a revenge match, Nealy, however, defeated the program several times.

Samuel developed his program mostly at IBM, which he joined in 1949. As would be the case for most later researchers developing game-playing programs, Samuel had to moonlight his way through it. His main duties consisted of helping to develop IBM's first generation of general-purpose computers, the 701 series. When Samuel half jokingly suggested that the machine's architecture was, in fact, designed to ease the modeling of a checkerboard, IBM did not appreciate the remark.[4] Even if it tolerated Samuel's activities, the company did not encourage or publicize them.*

Samuel's program found its match in a program developed at Duke University in 1977 by the researchers Eric C. Jensen and Tom R. Truscott. The Jensen-Truscott program won two consecutive games against the Samuel program, proving to be "dramatically superior," in Truscott's words. Truscott claimed his program to be the tenth strongest player in the world.[6] Nevertheless, AI circles still fondly remember Samuel's program because of its genuine contributions to the field: today's powerful chess programs embody some of the techniques implemented by Samuel. Here is how Samuel coaxed his program to beat a champion.

Like Berliner's backgammon program, Samuel's program relied on an evaluation function. The function's features included the number of men and kings, occupation of the center squares, advance of the men, and number of moves available. Samuel even developed statistical techniques that let the program determine for itself, by analyzing many games, which weight to attribute to each factor. Samuel's program thus learned to play checkers better than its author, whom it beat regularly.

Samuel's program contained another distinguishing feature: the ability to model the game as a tree and search it for judicious moves. Contrary to backgammon, the evaluation function alone does not guarantee a good play in checkers. A search procedure must complement it. Picture the starting position (or the current position, in an ongoing game) as the

---

*This attitude is typical of the ambivalence with which IBM, as I have already discussed in chapter 3, has always regarded artificial intelligence: on the one hand, the company has a vested interest in endowing computers with more powers; on the other, its public relations arm is embarrassed by the fears that the prospects of thinking machines create in the public. "Artificial Intelligence," said a company spokesperson, Kathleen Keeshen, in 1982, "is not a term generally used at IBM."[5] This attitude may be changing. IBM is now a driving force behind the development of chess-playing machines.

root of a tree. From this root, draw lines (or branches) representing all legal moves for the player whose turn it is to play (player A). The ends of those lines, known as "nodes," will correspond to the board positions after each of the moves. From each of these nodes, draw lines representing all legal countermoves by player B. One can then draw the counter-countermoves of player A at the end of these last nodes and, in principle, continue drawing branches and nodes until a winning position occurs. In practice, one must stop the exploration after a very few moves, because the number of nodes to explore grows out of bounds. Since the complete tree for checkers contains about 10^{40} nodes, it would take the fastest computer in existence longer than the age of the universe to explore them all.

The game tree for ticktacktoe, down to the third move, appears in figure 9.1. Following usual practice, I have drawn it upside down, with the starting position on top. Note how for even that simple-minded game the bare beginnings of the tree take up most of a printed page.

If one can't follow the tree down to the conclusion of the game, what is it good for? The answer is that, having drawn the tree for a limited depth, one can use it to decide upon a move. This is where the scoring function becomes useful. If one knows how to interpret them, the function values for the deepest positions explored in the tree provide good indications on how to conduct the game. The classical procedure for interpreting them is called "minimaxing"—first clearly described in 1947 by the mathematician Claude Shannon, also famous for his application of Boolean algebra to switching networks (see chapter 1).[7] In figure 9.1, I have planned the opening of a ticktacktoe game through minimaxing. If you are mathematically inclined and enjoy elegant strategies, you'll probably want to read through the caption of this figure in detail. If not, you won't lose much of what follows. Just remember that this relatively simple procedure accounts for much of the success of the most powerful checkers and chess programs.

Chess

In recent years, most AI researchers interested in game playing, including Berliner of backgammon fame, have forsaken other games to the benefit of chess. They have channeled the logical abilities of their machines toward the stylized version of medieval warfare viewed as the king of games in Western civilization. Beyond the prestige and challenge of chess, one reason for this enthusiasm is the existence of an elaborate rating system to assess the strength of chess players. Progress is thus measurable, and researchers can isolate the strongest techniques with fewer chances of error.

Claude Shannon was the one to publish the first paper on computer chess in 1950.[8] Alan Turing followed suit in a 1953 article describing the games of a hand-simulated program.[9] The first actual computer programs appeared between 1955 and 1958.[10] Two were written by groups of researchers at Los Alamos Laboratories and IBM. The AI pioneers Newell, Simon, and Shaw wrote a third program. All three programs played mediocre chess, and none ever won a game against a human player. Ominously, another program, started at MIT and continued at Stanford University, lost the first computer chess match played by mail—its opponent a program from the Institute of Control Sciences in Moscow.

It was only in 1967 that chess programs became meaningful opponents to human players. The originator of the first such program was Richard Greenblatt, then studying under Marvin Minsky at MIT. Somewhat against the advice of his professor, Greenblatt wrote the first chess program to compete successfully against human players in a chess tournament. Greenblatt called his program MacHack. (In those pre-Apple days, the prefix *Mac* referred to the program's affiliation with project MAC at MIT.)

Following the lead of previous chess programmers, Greenblatt tried to limit the amount of searching required for good play. The chess game tree is indeed a formidable structure. On the average, chess players must select a move among 35 options each time they play. Game theorists call this number the "branching factor." Its value of 35 shows that at the third level, the tree will have sprouted 35^3, or 42,875, branches! By contrast, the three-level ticktacktoe tree in figure 9.1 has only 61 branches, some being even duplicates of others. Shannon, in his 1950 paper, estimated 10^{120} to be the number of nodes of the complete chess tree.[11] The Hitech computer, one of the most recent chess machines, testing 175,000 moves per second, would take about 10^{107} years to explore the entire tree!

Searching even a minor part of it remains a tremendous undertaking. Greenblatt tried to prune the branches of the game tree by selecting only

FIGURE 9.1
Part of the Game Tree for Ticktacktoe

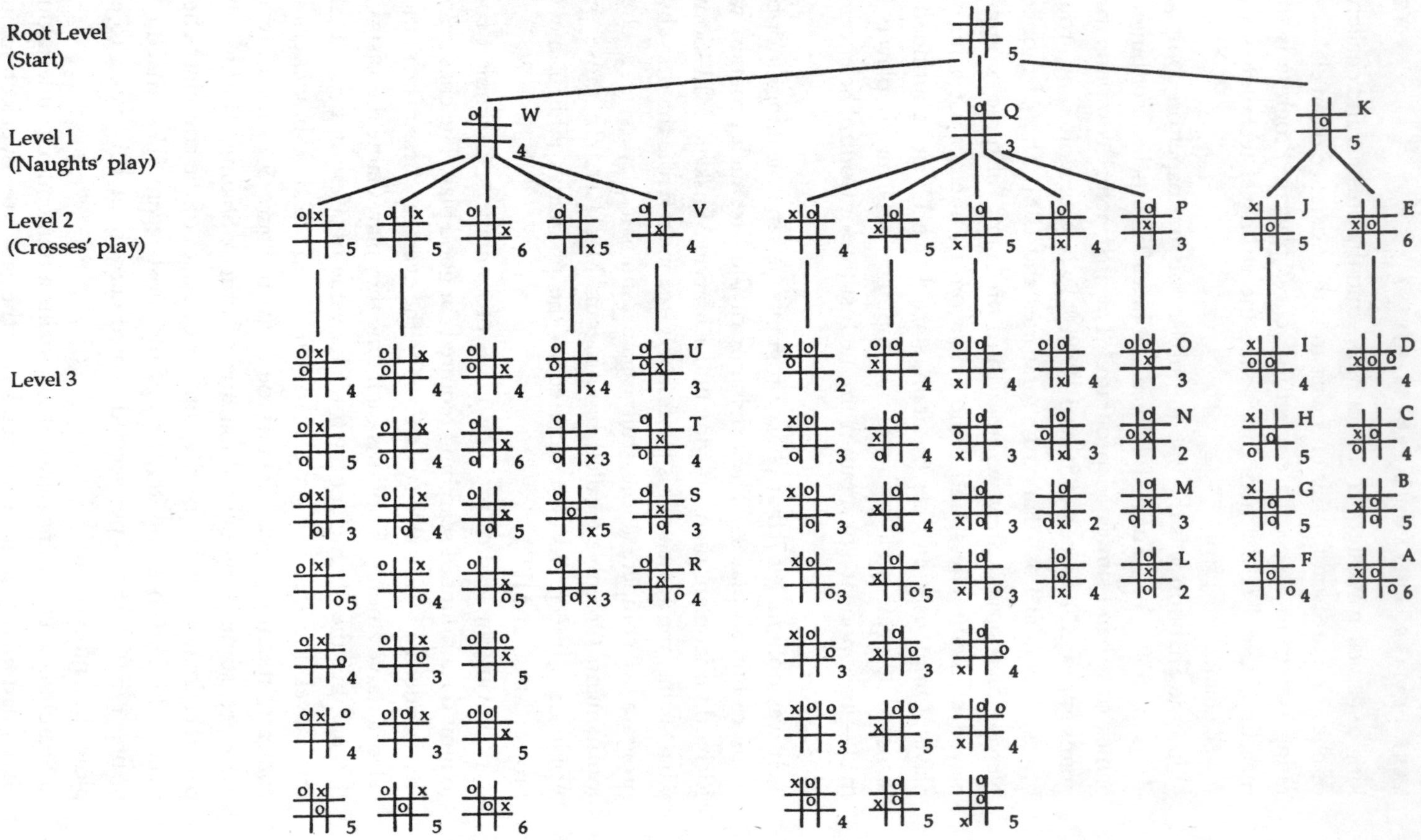

Root Level
(Start)
Level 1
(Naughts' play)
Level 2
(Crosses' play)
Level 3
W
Q
K
V
P
J
E
U
T
S
R
O
N
M
L
I
H
G
F
D
C
B
A

Figure 9.1 (*continued*)

To help keep the drawing on one page, I have taken symmetries into account. You can reduce missing ticktacktoe grids to one of those appearing in the figure by appropriate rotations. The sets of grids corresponding to the first level (first move by naughts) and second level (countermove by crosses) are laid out horizontally. To save space, I have laid out the third level vertically.

To illustrate how computers search a game tree, I have devised the following evaluation, or scoring, function. Its aim is to measure, at any stage of the game, how close the naughts side is to winning. You can calculate its value for any of the grids as follows:

—Start at zero.
—For each way of completing a straight line of naughts by adding one naught to the grid, add 2 to the score.
—For each way of completing a straight line of naughts by adding two naughts to the grid, add 1 to the score.

I have calculated the scores for each of the third-level grids in the figure: they are the numbers by the grids. For the second and first levels, the scores appearing are the so-called backed-up values of the scoring function. Naughts can use them to plan their first move. The letters appearing by some of the grids are labels to clarify these explanations.

To see how naughts can plan their first move, let us start at grid E on the rightmost branch of the tree. This grid corresponds to the (as-yet) hypothetical situation where naughts have taken the center position, and crosses have just played the middle of the left column. Naughts must now decide upon their second move. Excluding symmetries, there are only four choices. The largest scoring function (6) occurs for naughts playing the lower-right corner (grid A). Naughts would therefore take that position in an actual game. At the planning stage, naughts can say: "If crosses play the middle of a row on second level, I can always achieve a six on third level." Naughts will therefore assign a value of 6 to grid E. This is the value appearing by this grid in the figure. Note that 6 is the *largest* of the values associated with the daughters of grid E (grids A to D). Similarly, if crosses played a corner on second level (grid J), naughts would achieve at most only a 5-score on the third level (grids F to I). They will thus assign this value to the corresponding second-level grid (grid J).

The trick now for naughts is to assume that the cross-player is also clever and will conduct a similar analysis. Crosses will therefore know that if they play a corner on second level (grid J), naughts will be able only to achieve a five in the next move. If crosses play the middle of a row (grid E), naughts will achieve the higher score of 6. Obviously then, crosses will play a corner on second level. Assuming this worst-case play by crosses, naughts can thus assign a score to taking the center position on the first level (grid K). Since it leads to a 5 in the third level, this is what the first-level score should be. Note that 5 is the *smaller* of the scores of the daughters of grid K (grids E and J).

Naughts will then carry out a similar analysis for other first-level moves (either the middle of a row or a corner: grids Q and W). They will discover that if crosses play correctly, these moves will lead only to a 3 and a 4. The winning opening move is therefore to play center, which leads to a 5.

How can we summarize what we have done? Start at the deepest level laid out in the tree, calculate the scoring functions, and move up one level. If it's your move, assign the *maximum* score of the deeper positions to the parent position. If it's your opponent's move, assign the *minimum* score of the deeper positions to the parent. Back up along the tree in this way until you reach the present position. The procedure's name, minimax, shows that it alternately minimizes and maximizes along the tree. In principle, one can use this strategy to back up from any depth of analysis.

the most promising moves for further evaluation. A section of Greenblatt's program contained information on chess strategy and how to generate moves.

MacHack's rating, as evaluated by the U.S. Chess Federation, stood between 1,400 and 1,500[12]—tantalizingly close to the 1,537 mean rating of UCSF members. Greenblatt's program inspired many AI researchers to take up computer chess. Conversely, chess experts also took up an interest in AI. Among them was Hans Berliner, who won the world correspondence chess championship in 1968 and was for some fifteen years one of the top twelve players in the United States. His fascination with computers and chess led him to quit industry to seek higher education in the field of artificial intelligence.

Among other successes, Greenblatt had the pleasure of seeing his program trounce Hubert Dreyfus,[13] who had recently put out his vitriolic RAND paper against AI[14] and insisted that no chess program could play even amateur chess.

By 1970, there were enough chess programs for the Association of Computing Machinery to schedule a tournament. It drew six entries and made up one of the main attractions of the association's annual meeting. Seeing this, ACM organizers decided to hold tournaments annually: the next year there were eight entries. Other countries followed suit; and by 1974, contenders for a world chess championship convened in Stockholm under the auspices of the International Federation for Information Processing (IFIPS). Kaissa, the Russian program that had won the mail match against Stanford, won the title.

Meanwhile, computer programs started actively participating in human tournaments, and climbed their way up chess ratings. The first battle of wits between humans and artificial minds was on. Spurring this competitive spirit, bets and prizes for programs that could defeat chess champions proliferated. A Scottish international master with a penchant for computers, David Levy, threw the first challenge. In a now-celebrated 1968 wager, Levy bet that no computer could beat him at chess for ten years. The AI researchers John McCarthy, then at Stanford, and Donald Michie, of the University of Edinburgh, took him up on it, for £250 each. In 1971, Seymour Papert, of MIT, and Ed Kozdrowicki, of the University of California at Davis, raised the ante by similar amounts. Levy collected in August 1978 at the Canadian National Exhibition in Toronto. He held up for humankind by trouncing the world computer champion Chess 4.5, a program created at Northwestern

University. Levy won the match 3½ to 1½, and estimated that computers would not reach the international grand-master level for many more years. He thus renewed the bet for another six years. In a 1984 rematch against Cray Blitz, the world computer champion of the day, Levy again won handily. Emboldened, he issued a challenge to the world at large: he was ready to wager £100,000 that no computer would defeat him, or a chess player he would appoint, for ten years. So far no one has taken him up on it.[15]

In general though, impoverished AI researchers are unwilling to wager large sums of their own money on the abilities of their programs. Prizes, however, do get their attention. In 1979, a Dutch software company, Volmac, offered $50,000 to the author of any program that could beat the former world champion Max Euwe by 1 January 1984.[16] The prize remained unclaimed. In 1979 also, Edward Fredkin, a wealthy inventor and MIT professor, set up three prizes with no time limit on them: $5,000 for the first chess program to earn a master level in tournament play against humans; an intermediate prize of $10,000 for the first program to reach the level of international grand master; more significantly, for $100,000 the authors of the first program to beat the world champion. Fredkin thinks, as most AI researchers do, that computer chess is a kind of benchmark for progress in AI research. As an example of the positive impact of prizes, he cites the one that got Lindbergh to fly solo across the Atlantic in 1927: "Prizes are a wonderful thing and there should be more of them."[17]

Spurred by the competitive spirit of the tournaments, and later attracted by the prizes, AI researchers designed programs that scored ever higher in the human chess ratings. Their steady progression is depicted in figure 9.2.

The undisputed computer champion of the early 1970s was Chess 3.0. Written at Northwestern University, this program followed the model of Greenblatt's MacHack and tried to simulate human play. Such programs did not stay at the top for long: they had one crippling weakness. Despite the competence of most of their moves, they were likely to make outright blunders. This happened when they overlooked either obvious or subtle plays defying the general principles of chess embodied in their rules or evaluation functions. Conversely, these very rules would at times lead them to dumb maneuvers that cost them a game. The authors of these so-called selective search programs have been able to formalize the principles that guide human playing only to

FIGURE 9.2

Representative Ratings of Computer Chess Tournament–Winning
Programs in Their Times of Glory

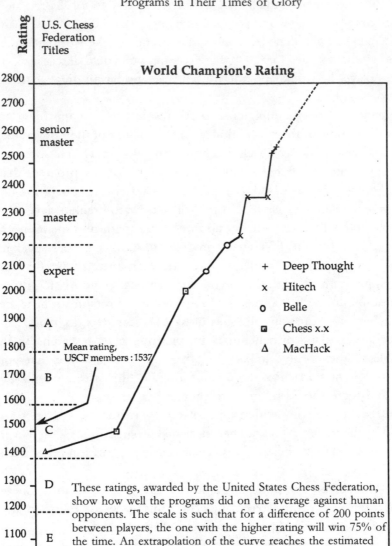

These ratings, awarded by the United States Chess Federation, show how well the programs did on the average against human opponents. The scale is such that for a difference of 200 points between players, the one with the higher rating will win 75% of the time. An extrapolation of the curve reaches the estimated rating of world champion Boris Kasparov (2800) in 1993.

an extent. They have captured some aspect of competent play, but excellence remains beyond their grasp.

In 1973, the authors of Chess 3.0, Davis Slate and Larry Adkin, realizing this weakness of their early strategy, redesigned their program around the so-called brute force approach. Relying on efficient search procedures and ever faster computers, the new program searched the game tree to new depths. In fact, the "brute force" appellation is a misnomer since the technique still relies on subtle strategies to reduce the search effort. Surprisingly, it is possible to prune the game tree (that is, limit the number of moves considered) by means that do not require any knowledge of the game itself. One of these strategies, called "alpha-beta pruning," consists of abandoning the investigation of a move when the opponent can respond with a countermove better than the best response to a move already examined.

In the ticktacktoe example of figure 9.1, alpha-beta pruning would work as follows: Assume the search proceeds from right to left. We, the naughts player, have already examined the rightmost branch and assigned a value of 5 to playing center on the first move (this situation corresponds to grid K in the figure). We then proceed to examine the value of playing the middle of a row on the first move (grid Q). Proceeding from right to left at level 2, we would immediately discover that for crosses to play center results in a scoring function of 3 (grid P). Consider now that the scoring function at level 1 will correspond to the smallest of the level 2 scores and, thus, can be no larger than 3. Yet we already know (grid K) that since playing center on the first move is worth 5 for naughts, it is thus a better move than the one we are considering, and there is no point to rating the other daughters of grid Q. Alpha-beta pruning has saved us about 75 percent of the work in rating the branch. If we had explored the branches in a different order (say, from left to right), the search would have taken longer. Modern chess programs have ways of optimizing the search order to make the most of alpha-beta pruning. One of them is the "killer heuristic": the computer gives precedence to investigating opponent responses that killed, or refuted, other moves the computer has already considered. In the example, the killer move was for crosses to play center (grid P). In investigating the leftmost branch of the tree, the computer would look for this opponent's move first (grid V). It would then discover that this play also leads to a weak position for naughts, and immediately assign a weak rating to the entire branch following grid W.

An obvious strategy for tree pruning consists in keeping track of duplicate boards, as follows: If a move leads to the same situation as a combination of moves already examined, use the corresponding known value for the scoring function. If the previous situation is one that led, through a sequence of moves, to the present one, we are in a loop. Label this branch "draw," and move on to another branch.

One problem with straightforward searches is the "horizon effect," which enables knowledgeable opponents to sandbag the computer by dangling a juicy capture leading to a deathly trap, lying just beyond the machine's search horizon. Even in the absence of traps, this effect could lead the computer to give up an eventual large gain for a small immediate advantage. For this reason, computer chess often looks impatient and hungry for material. The chess programmers' response to the horizon effect was the "quiescence search": they let the machine search to deeper levels for moves leading to the capture of pieces.

These not-so-brutish search methods paid off for the Northwestern University researchers, who were able to recapture the world and North American computer chess championships, which they had both lost in 1974. A unique arrangement with Control Data Corporation allowed them free use of the mighty Cyber series of computers during tournaments and exhibitions. The Cyber's power allowed the Northwestern team to hold on to the annual North American championship until 1977 and to the world championship until 1980. Other participating programs, such as Duchess from Duke University, also ran on very large machines. According to one participant, the value of the computers used by the sixteen entrants to the 1977 Toronto tournament exceeded $100 million.[18] The Northwestern program could rate about 3,600 chess moves per second. The resulting high level of play made it the first program to gain the title of "expert," awarded to tournament players who attain a U.S. Chess Federation rating of 2,000.

Chess 4.7 eventually lost both its titles to a hardware version of itself. The researchers Ken Thompson and Joe Condon of Bell Laboratories implemented algorithms similar to those of the Northwestern program into special-purpose silicon chips. The result was a dedicated, portable chess computer that could beat any other machine in sight—or, rather, connected to any telephone in sight, since the bulkier machines it battled pretty much had to stay in their laboratories. The portability of Belle (as Bell Lab's researchers had called their machine) was at times a source of mishaps. As the machine and Ken Thompson were supposed to board a plane for a Moscow tournament, the U.S. Customs Service called Bell Labs' security department, claiming that someone had stolen one of their computers. They were trying to ship it to Moscow. "Not to worry," Customs said, "our Exodus team has seized the computer." (Exodus was a special project to prevent illegal exports of high technology to the Soviets.) Meanwhile, Thompson was flying to Moscow, unaware that the computer was not in the plane's cargo hold. Belle remained lost in the bowels of the federal administration for two weeks and could not participate in the tournament.[19] On another trip, this time to the 1983 world chess tournament in New York, Belle had a car accident. Many people blamed its loss of the world title to the resulting "electronic concussion."[20] A few weeks before, in August 1983, Belle had nevertheless raised its chess rating to the master level. It was the first computer ever to earn this title, which requires a rating of 2,200 on the U.S. Federation scale. It also earned Belle the first Fredkin prize of $5,000. Belle could then look at 150,000 chess positions per second.

In New York, Belle had lost to Cray Blitz, a 28,000-line-long computer program that ran on a general purpose Cray XMP-48 supercomputer. No simple minded brute, the program had required 32,000 hours of its authors: Bob Hyatt and Albert Gower, from the University of Southern Mississippi, and Harry Nelson, of Lawrence Livermore Laboratory.[21] Cray Blitz was the only chess program to reap the world title twice: it won the 1983 New York championship against Belle and twenty-one other teams from eight countries and, three years later, successfully defended its title in Cologne, Germany. Cray Blitz, though, also marked the swan's song of general-purpose computers in chess championships. After its demise, all world championships went to dedicated machines like Belle who were, so to speak, to the trade born.

Cray Blitz first bit the dust at the North American chess championship of 1985. Its victor was a machine conceived by none other than Hans Berliner of Carnegie Mellon University. The computer's designation, Hitech, celebrated the days when CMU went under the name of Carnegie Tech. Berliner's creation combined the innovative elements of Belle and Cray Blitz: its dedicated circuits let it process 175,000 chess positions per second, yet it did so in a manner that could take elaborate chess knowledge into account. Berliner's experience as world mail chess champion provided the source for most of this savvy. In contrast to the $14,000,000 machine required to run Cray Blitz, the Hitech system consisted of a special breadbox-sized contraption called the Searcher, connected to a $20,000 Sun microprocessor. The Searcher contained sixty-four dedicated processor chips, one for each square of the chess board, which the processors monitored. Before each move, the processor detected all moves that could land a piece on its square, and analyzed them. Meanwhile, other chips were doing the same thing for their squares, which considerably increased the machine's speed. Yet Hitech didn't entirely rely on hardware to select its moves: the sixty-four processors fed summaries of their observations to a program called Oracle, which contained much of Berliner's chess knowledge and decided upon which move to make. In this way, Hitech managed an average look ahead of eight levels but could, on occasion, pursue interesting moves to a depth of fourteen levels.[22] In 1986, Hitech raised its chess rating to well over 2,300, which made it the world's first computer international master.

The next quantum leap in computer chess also came from Carnegie Mellon, but involved different people. Aside from any personal rivalries, the new machine probably disappointed Berliner. Its designers did not believe in enhancing chess computers' performances by endowing them with humanlike chess knowledge. They were a team of CMU graduate students who knew little about chess. Deep Thought, as they called their creation, relied on speed and clever search methods. It made absolutely no pretense at imitating human play. And deeply did the machine probe: it could analyze 700,000 chess moves per second[23] (four times as many as Hitech) and project 15 to 20 moves ahead along the most promising lines of play.[24] In 1987, a prototype of Deep Thought, containing only half as many dedicated computer chips as the final version, won the North American Computer Chess championship. In 1988, Deep Thought raised its chess rating over the benchmark of 2,500. This made it the first computer international grand master and qualified its designers for the intermediate Fredkin prize.[25] Being a better chess player than all but some two hundred people in the world, Deep Thought was now in the same league as the human world champion.

And, indeed, the reigning champion felt compelled, for the first time in history, to accept an official challenge from a nonhuman opponent. On the afternoon of 22 October 1989, a two-game match opposed Boris Kasparov and Deep Thought in the New York Academy of Art.[26] The computer and the human champion faced off in front of an audience of hundreds of reporters and aficionados, most of them in a mood to see the upstart machine put in its place. Meeting their expectations, Kasparov won both games handily. This defeat did not much disappoint the machine's designers. Even though they had hoped to at least draw one game, their underdog status put them in a no-loss situation. Kasparov, for his part, was clearly taking no chances. He had prepared for the match by studying fifty of his opponent's previous games and avoided the daring moves that constitute his trademark.

Elated as the audience was at Kasparov's victory, its knowledgeable members could not shake off a feeling of doom. As one commentator put it: "In the rapidly evolving relationship between people and their machines, this match is an acknowledgement of a new, and inherently short-lived state—one of essential parity on the board."[27] Said the match's organizer, Shelby Lyman, "The real drama here is that Gary is facing his fate."[28] Kasparov thought he could beat computers "perhaps to the end of the century."[29] Lyman gave him five to ten years; and Berliner, four. The history of computer chess supports Berliner's view. Kasparov's chess rating, the highest in the world, is about 2,800. The curve in figure 9.2 portrays the steady climb of computers through human chess ratings. A straight line extrapolation of it reaches Kasparov's level by 1993.

Which computer will beat the world champion and win the $100,000 Fredkin prize? It may very well be a direct descendant of Deep Thought. IBM hired most of the machine's design team, who are, as of this writing, working on a new version of Deep Thought at the company's Yorktown Heights laboratory. The new system will deploy chips one thousand times faster than the current ones and look at roughly a billion chess positions per second. Kasparov is willing to take it on: "I would have to challenge it to protect the human race," said the champion.[30]

THE IMPLICATIONS OF COMPUTER CHESS

The fun and challenge of computer chess should not make one lose sight of its deeper implications. The computer's performance raises penetrating questions that may help us understand how our minds differ from other potential intelligences, and help us forecast the future of AI.

Are Chess-Playing Computers Intelligent?

Deep Thought plays chess better than 99.9 percent of human players. Does that performance make it intelligent? To this question, there are no simple answers.

I have already said that Deep Thought and other winning chess programs and machines do not play chess as humans do. In the three minutes allowed per move in tournament play, Deep Thought considers 126 million moves. By contrast, the studies of the Dutch psychologist Adrian de Groot show that human master players ponder only an average of 1.76 moves per play.[31] They use up most of their three minutes verifying that these one or two moves are indeed the judicious ones. As Herbert Simon noted, expert players have an instantaneous understanding of chess positions and a compelling sense of the winning move. Simon believes that chess masters are familiar with thousands of patterns involving small groups of pieces in certain relationships to each other. Simon calls these patterns "chunks." Each chunk would suggest a desirable move or strategy, which would cut the need for extensive simulations of later moves.[32] Hans Berliner has investigated the application of chunking to computer chess.

According to the AI critic Hubert Dreyfus, the difference between human and machine play is even more basic. Expert chess players, claims Dreyfus, respond to whole board positions, not component chunks.[33] An expert player practicing fast play, or carrying out forty games at a time, is not simply showing off. He is developing his ability to rate board positions instantly and intuit the winning move in any given situation. Topflight masters can play a very strong game when given only five seconds per move. Gary Kasparov is reported to have said that the intuitive chess player somehow takes all resulting games into account when planning a move. While certainly exaggerated, this claim agrees with Dreyfus's assessment that our major intellectual leaps are *a*rational.

Some, like the computer-trouncing chess master David Levy, offer a negative view of the intelligence of chess-playing computers. Tree searching, Levy says, "produces a kind of monkey/typewriter situation. . . . [The computer] appears to play moderately well, whereas it is actually playing very weak chess so much of the time that its best results resemble the moves of strong players."[34] The fact remains, however, that computers play games and win them. "Intelligence," says Edward

Fredkin, "is having a problem and solving it."[35] Chess machines certainly do that.

Holders of Levy's opinion could also argue that chess computers know nothing but chess, while intelligent human beings can reason about a large variety of subjects. Yet aren't human chess champions somewhat limited in their world views also? General-purpose game programs could, in any case, learn games other than chess. It took only a few weeks to train Deep Thought to play grand-master chess, a lifetime endeavor for any human being. Programs similar to Deep Thought could master other games, like checkers, in a snap.

In the opinion of many researchers, it is reasonable to claim that chess computers are intelligent, but in a way different from us. Many investigators now believe in a knowledge-search continuum, within which computers make up for a lack of chess knowledge by an ability to do more searching. Much as airplanes do not fly by flapping their wings, chess computers do not imitate human thought processes to win games.

Computer Chess and AI

This pattern may well reappear in future AI developments. When machines do perform mental tasks of a depth and diversity similar to our own, they may rely on principles different from the ones that govern our brains. If such is the case, interesting and familiar as their behavior might appear, the machines would be foreign to us inside—and sometimes, this difference would show.

Chess computers already provide us with some inklings of these differences. A popular distraction during AI meetings, which could be called "Turing chess," consists of pitting human chess players against hidden opponents, some of them machines, some of them humans. The fun, for audience and players, comes from guessing which opponents are machines. Even when humans and machines play at the same strength, knowledgeable observers can usually tell them apart from play styles: computer chess often looks ugly and inelegant. The computer, says Dave Slate of Northwestern University, "is like a shark sitting around. It's not very bright, but once it gets a taste of blood, it's right there and goes munch, munch, crunch. . . . If you allow any slight chink in your armor, then you suddenly find this thing coming after you, and all your nicely laid plans go astray."[36] Unencumbered by traditional strategies, computers also often drag their opponents into situations human players find bizarre. "They are always original," says Belle's designer, Ken Thompson. "They're not enslaved by what's been done in the past."[37]

Computer chess might model future AI progress in yet another manner: success came about because of hardware advances; computers did not equal human champions at chess before they achieved a certain processing power. The fact that Deep Thought could in 1989 examine roughly two hundred times as many positions per second as the comparatively pedestrian Chess 4.7 could in 1978, even though their software was similar, shows that speed is at the root of better performance. As I will discuss later, AI's present failure at modeling certain aspects of human thought, such as common sense, stems in part from the weakness of our present hardware (see chapter 11). Researchers may overcome them when, and only when, their machines overcome the speed bottleneck.

This demonstration that machines can equal the human mind in playing certain games also demolishes an argument that many people oppose to the final success of AI. "Computers can do only what they are told," this objection goes. "They will never produce more than what their creators put into them. Computers will never create and will remain forever dumb in situations unforeseen by their programmers." Yet, as I mentioned, Samuel's checker program used to beat him regularly. The creators of Deep Thought know little chess and would never dream of trying to win against their machine. "The fascination," says the Deep Thought designer, Thomas Anantharanam, "was writing a computer program that can do something I can't do."[38] During computer chess competitions, such programmers find it hard to tell whether a puzzling computer move is a subtle piece of strategy or a downright blunder.

Yet, in one significant way, computer chess failed the expectations of early researchers: it failed to meet their hope of learning about the human mind. By getting computers to play chess, the reasoning had gone, investigators could discover how people think and decide. Sometimes labeled the "drosophilia" of artificial intelligence, computer chess would play the role in developing AI that fruit flies played in genetic research. This did not happen. Carried away by sheer competition, many researchers started designing programs that won games instead of thinking like people. That it nevertheless led them to discover thinking processes different from our own is an illustration of the serendipity of science. In the next chapter, I'll examine how other approaches have enabled AI researchers to model their programs on the human mind.

10

SOULS OF SILICON

Long before we became concerned with understanding how we work, our evolution had already constrained the architecture of our brains. However, we can design our new machines as we wish, and provide them with better ways to keep and examine records of their own activities—and this means that machines are potentially capable of far more consciousness than we are.   —Marvin Minsky

The significant forward leaps AI made during the 1980s did not make the front pages. Much more than an era of commercial ventures, this was the decade when AI looked in the eye the problem of endowing computers with common sense and attacked it on a grand scale. The industrial debacle of the late 1980s painfully emphasized the urgency of this task. Making computers see, understand the spoken word, and communicate in English became a priority. As a result, approaches more basic and daring than those permitted by the comparatively puny budgets and primitive computers of earlier decades produced AI projects involving person-centuries of effort, some of them claiming to account for the whole of human cognition. These original approaches threw a new light on the nature of awareness, and researchers started to consider seriously the possibility that their machines might some day wake up to conscious thought and feelings. Interesting debates followed a philosopher's objection to the emergence of what amounts to a soul in mere assemblages of electronic chips made of silicon metal.

THE COMMON-SENSE QUESTION

It all started with the common-sense question. Needless to say, the various chapels into which the AI community had subdivided all addressed the problem in different ways. Some of these approaches still doggedly depended on logic. Others, as we'll see, would have no truck with it.

Logical and Not-So-Logical Solutions

Recognizing that a crucial element of common sense resides in the ability to change one's mind when circumstances require, a large part of the neat, or logic-oriented, community in AI research is now busy investigating ways out of McCarthy's qualification problem (see chapter 5): How can one tell a computer that something is true, except when there are good reasons why it should not be?

To achieve this discernment, the neats discovered they had to revamp their logical calculus, lifted almost intact from Russell and Whitehead's 1910 edition of *Principia Mathematica*. They outfitted good old First Order Predicate Calculus (FOPC, if you are on familiar terms with it) with extensions called "default," "nonmonotonic," or "modal" logic to deal with exceptions.

John McCarthy calls his own technique for dealing with the potentially infinite exceptions to a general rule "circumscription."[1] His idea is to circumscribe, or delimit, the set of possible exceptions to a statement. In the river-crossing example (see chapter 8), circumscription would isolate in the knowledge base, or minimize, the set of possible obstacles. If none exist in a given situation, then it would be safe to infer that one can cross the river.

As a result of these efforts, the new generation of expert systems is equipped with a monitoring mechanism called a Truth Maintenance System, or TMS. Returning to Minsky's duck challenge (chapter 8), knowing that Charlie is a duck, and that ducks normally fly, the expert system will conclude that Charlie flies. Upon learning of poor Charlie's passing away, the TMS will normally undo this inference. The amount of computation required tends, however to grow exponentially with the size of the knowledge base, and the millions of facts needed for true common-sense reasoning would still snow a logic-based TMS.

Other investigators are exploring reasoning techniques that owe less to logic. A prominent example is Janet Kolodner: after modeling the mind of former secretary of state Cyrus Vance as a doctoral project for Roger Schank in 1980, she was among the first to use a technique called "case-based reasoning."[2] Kolodner's idea is to stop painstakingly trying to distill the knowledge of experts into rules and, instead, record it directly as the experts do, in the form of a series of well-documented cases. Confronted with a new case, such as a set of symptoms in a patient or the salient points of a legal argument, the computer would then search its knowledge banks for a similar case, adapt it to the new situation, and conclude accordingly.

David Waltz, of constraint propagation fame in the blocks world (see chapter 4), is now pursuing a goal similar to Kolodner's with the super-computers of Thinking Machines, Inc., a late-1980s vintage commercial spinoff of MIT's AI Lab. Waltz, who is director of information systems at Thinking Machines, calls his approach "memory-based reasoning."[3] It consists of feeding each one of the possibly sixteen thousand different processors of his company's Connection Machine with memories of a recorded case or situation. When a new situation comes up, the Connection Machine compares it to all its records simultaneously, identifies the closest match, and uses it to define a possible solution. Janet Kolodner has recently spent a sabbatical at Thinking Machines on a first try at implementing case-based reasoning into the Connection Machine: the results are encouraging.

However, the most dramatic AI project aimed at instilling common sense into computers, and certainly the best-funded one, owes little to logic. It is Douglas Lenat's Cyc effort at MCC.

An Ontology for Common Sense: Cyc

Lenat had, in his quest for ways to make computers learn (see chapter 7), met with some spectacular successes. His Automated Mathematician program learned by discovering mathematical concepts; and its successor, EURISKO, learned by inventing new heuristics for such activities as playing games and designing computer chips. In 1984, Lenat was approached by MCC, a consortium that made up America's answer to the Japanese Fifth Generation Project. Short for Microelectronics and Computer Technology Corporation, MCC was chartered by such heavy-weights as the Digital Equipment Corporation, Control Data Corporation, Kodak, and National Cash Register to carry out large, high-risk decade-sized projects. And so it was that in September 1988, Lenat began an MCC research report as follows: "I would like to present a surprisingly compact, powerful, elegant set of reasoning methods that form a set of first principles which explain creativity, humor, and common sense reasoning—a sort of 'Maxwell Equations'* of thought." Although such a discovery would have been a logical outcome of Lenat's previous work in programming computers to figuratively go out into the world and make sense of what they saw, he continued: "I'd like very much to present [those reasoning methods], but, sadly, I don't believe they exist. So, instead, this paper will tell you about Cyc, the massive knowledge base project that we've been working on at MCC for the last four years."[4]

Stemming from an admission of defeat, Cyc (short for encyclopedia) is a $25-million research project that will last for two person-centuries. Lenat had become convinced that no amount of finessing and fancy footwork would ever let a machine discover by itself such elementary facts as "Nothing can be in two places at once," or "Animals don't like pain," and "People live for a single solid interval of time."[5] The most salient discovery in AI since the Dartmouth conference is that we need to know a colossal number of these common-sense assertions to get by in the world. Lenat convinced his MCC sponsors that the woes of the new discipline stemmed from repeatedly trying to wriggle out of the need to encode this knowledge manually, tedious fact after painful assertion, in machine-usable form.

"Fifteenth century explorers couldn't discover new land without long voyages," claimed Lenat and his team.[6] And thus in 1984, they embarked on their own excursion over the ocean of knowledge: during a ten-year period, they were to encode about ten million assertions like the ones in the previous paragraph into a gigantic knowledge base amounting to over a billion bytes of information. Ad-hoc inferencing mechanisms will allow

---

*Derived in the nineteenth century by Scottish physicist James Clark Maxwell, the equations Lenat refers to explain virtually all of electromagnetism in a few crisp lines of algebra.

a computer to reason from that knowledge and understand natural language. Like an iceberg, Cyc will have a small visible part corresponding to the contents of the one-volume *Concise Columbia Encyclopedia*. Below the waterline, and much larger, will loom the behemoth collection of "self-evident" facts that children know when they enter grade school, and that are never included in reference books. Lenat's first challenge was to impose a workable structure onto this amorphous jumble of knowledge. To work out an adequate set of ontological categories for carving up the universe, MCC researchers started by lifting pairs of sentences at random from newspapers, encyclopedias, and magazine articles. They then programmed into Cyc the basic concepts inherent in each sentence, so that the program could "understand" their meanings.[7]

The first two sentences took Lenat's team three months to code. They were: "Napoleon died on St. Helena. Wellington was saddened." Through a complex hierarchy of interlocking frames, the researchers were able to impart to Cyc the knowledge that Napoleon was a person. To Cyc, a person is a member of a set denoted by the frame Individual-Agent. Persons make up a subset of the larger category of Composite-Objects: those objects that have a physical extent (mass) and an intangible extent (such as a mind). The set CompositeObject also comprises such things as books, which have mass and meaning. A slot in the frame IndividualAgent states that the members of this set have the unfortunate habit of dying. Death, in turn, is a subset of the frame Event, which has as one of its properties TemporalExtent (indefinite, in the case of death: this means that when a person is dead, he or she stays dead). Going back to Wellington, other properties of IndividualAgents are those of harboring beliefs and emotions. Sadness is an element of the set Emotion and frequently accompanies death. Invoking further combinations of frames, the researchers could also convey to Cyc that if the time of doing battles is long over, even the death of one's archenemy can sadden. This involved talking about war, France, and England (which are CollectiveAgents), and news media (Wellington probably learned about Napoleon's death through the newspapers). A description of islands was needed to explain St. Helena, which in turn required spelling out the nature of land, sea, and water.

For a while it appeared to Lenat's team that they would be stumped by the philosophical objections of Hubert Dreyfus: every sentence required the definition of a new and arbitrarily long chain of related categories, and reality seemed to branch out into an infinitely large number of unrelated concepts. In September 1987, though, Cyc reached a stage that Lenat calls "semantic convergence": it became possible to define systematically new concepts in terms of other concepts. Cyc researchers (or "Cyclists," as Lenat dubs them) could by then enter new knowledge in Cyc by locating similar knowledge, copying it, and slightly modifying the copy. As a result, said Lenat, knowledge could be entered faster than originally estimated.[8] Lenat hopes that "around the mid-1990s, we can transition more and more from manual entry of assertions to (semi-)automated entry by reading on-line texts; the role of humans in the project would transition from that of brain surgeons to tutors, answering Cyc's questions about difficult sentences and passages."[9]

Lenat is upbeat about the future of Cyc, and believes that it has a good chance of serving "as the foundation for the first true AI agent. . . . No one in 2015 would dream of buying a machine without common sense, and more than anyone today would buy a personal computer that couldn't run spreadsheets [or] word processing programs."[10]

The opinions of other AI researchers about Cyc vary considerably. When I discussed Cyc with him, Marvin Minsky was enthusiastic about the project. He agreed that Lenat was on the right path, and regretted that there were no other projects like Cyc. Himself a part-time Cyclist, Minsky travels from time to time to the MCC facility in Austin, Texas.

Most other researchers just don't believe that Cyc is going to work, but can't help being fascinated with it. Witness a technical presentation on Cyc I attended at the 1990 American Association for Artificial Intelligence meeting in Boston: it was scheduled in an otherwise-dull session on knowledge representation which attracted few listeners. Yet the AAAI organizers are sticklers for punctuality, and everybody knew that the talk about Cyc would start at 3:15 P.M. sharp. Just as Cyc's co-director, Ramanathan V. Guha, was climbing the podium, the small auditorium suddenly filled to capacity with about two hundred deserters from other simultaneous presentations. After listening to Guha and using up the question period to throw several barbs at Cyc's method for representing default knowledge, they promptly filed out of the room again.

The problem is that Cyc is the quintessential scruffy AI project, and Lenat and Company make no bones about it. "We differ from the rest of the AI community," said Lenat, ". . . in that we have refrained from agonizing over the myriad subtleties of, for example, the different formalisms for representing pieces of time; instead, we have concentrated on using the formalisms we have for actually encoding information about various domains."[12] What he meant was that instead of worrying about why Cyc couldn't be done, they just went ahead and did it. "Most AI people are spending their research lives creating bumps on logs," Lenat said elsewhere.[13]

Hans Moravec, who was a graduate student with Lenat at Stanford, said to me that Cyc has been labeled in the grapevine as a "half-serious attempt."[14] Randall Davis, another of Lenat's fellow graduate students, doesn't grant Lenat more than an "outside chance" of capturing a substantial body of common-sense knowledge.[15] David Waltz and Allen Newell both pointed out to me the ad-hoc character of the representation mechanisms in Cyc:[16,17] as a result, two Cyclists may not encode related concepts in the same way, which could make it impossible for the knowledge base to associate them afterward. Lenat intends to correct the situation by having learning programs crawl over the knowledge base at night and set it right, but Newell was pessimistic about the outcome.

But the attitude of the artificial intelligentsia toward Cyc is not one of total rejection, as Randall Davis summed it up for me:

> Cyc is not a rocket ship that is going to make it to the moon or not. It is a vast experiment in absolutely hard-core empirical AI. Something important will come out of it. . . . There are people in the field whose overarching goal is to get the theory right. That's important, but there have to be people whose fundamental goal is to get the thing to work. . . . Philosophers have been dealing in theories of time, space, and causality for millennia, and they are still arguing about it. Now you can take the attitude that until they get the answer right, we're not going to be able to build an intelligent system. Or you can look around and see that the planet is populated by semi-intelligent systems [ourselves], who have only the barest theory about time, space, causality, and so forth. You can justify Cyc by saying: "Maybe if we just build it in a way that is good enough for the time being, we'll learn a lot!" This is what Lenat is doing.

AI AND PSYCHOLOGY

Where Cyc embodies the pragmatic, blue-collar approach to the common-sense problem, other avenues of investigation have a much more humanistic flavor. From early on, AI researchers have maintained relations with their psychologist colleagues, sometimes with productive results. The examination of human thought processes occasionally helped scientists design replicas of them into machines. Conversely, findings made without reference to human cognition have helped psychologists understand the human mind better. A science of universal psychology, regrouping both people and machines, may well be in the making. It might help us answer such questions as: When machines finally think and manipulate their environment, will our minds and theirs have anything in common? Will our basic drives and purposes share any ground with theirs?

Modeling Human Problem Solving

We saw in chapter 3 how Newell and Simon implemented into their General Problem Solver reasoning techniques abstracted from tape recordings of actual problem-solving efforts by human subjects.

Another early example of psychological modeling was the work of Edward Feigenbaum, who later pioneered commercial expert systems (see chapter 6). His program EPAM (an acronym for Elementary Perceiver And Memorizer) simulated the mechanism by which we memorize meaningless syllables.[18] By so doing, Feigenbaum hoped to unearth principles applicable to the entire learning process. Perhaps still under the influence of behaviorism (see chapter 2), Feigenbaum studied the phenomenon as a stimulus-response situation. An experimenter presented a subject with pairs of monosyllables. The experimenter stated the first member of the pair (the stimulus), and the subject tried to answer with the second member (the response). Behaviorist theories did not properly account for some of the phenomena that occurred in such experiments, like oscillation: a subject learned a sequence of syllables correctly, and then forgot them and learned them again many times. Neither could behaviorists explain why learning new associations made the subject forget previous ones, a phenomenon called "retroactive inhibition."

Explaining these phenomena through a procedure a behaviorist would never contemplate, Feigenbaum postulated a complex information structure in the subject's mind and proceeded to build a computer model of it. This structure, called a "discrimination tree," grew with the learning process. Feigenbaum worked out of a very simple idea: he assumed that subjects didn't bother remembering entire syllables but, instead, extracted salient features of the syllables (for example, the first letters) and built up associations between these features. The discrimination used no more features than those required to associate the pairs already learned. Feigenbaum found out that by implementing these assumptions in his program, he could reproduce the inexplicable phenomena. For example, suppose the program had learned to associate the syllable pair JIR-DAX by simply remembering "any time I see a syllable starting with *J,* I must respond with DAX." Then, if presented with the new pair JUK-PIB, the program suffered from retroactive inhibition for the following reason: Since the discrimination rule could no longer tell JIR and JUK apart, the program had to develop a new one. For this, more syllable presentation were needed. During this time, the response syllable was "forgotten" because access to it was lost.

Generalization

Yet another common ground between psychology and AI concerns the problem of generalization, about which psychologists have always speculated. How do we manage to extract global concepts out of the torrent of specific instances we constantly face? How do we learn about furniture and plants, when we see only individual chairs or trees? On a more abstract level, how do we identify a given instance of interpersonal behavior—for example, a conflict or a betrayal? AI made a direct use of psychology's response to these questions.

We make sense of the world, some psychologists assumed, by structuring our knowledge in the form of prototypes, or schemata. For example, the prototype for a chair was an information structure containing a generalized description of it. It somehow corresponded to the statement: "A chair is something to sit on, usually including four legs, a seat, and a back." Similar descriptions existed for more abstract concepts. Although the philosopher Immanuel Kant first used the word *schema* in his *Critique of Pure Reason,* published in 1787, the idea remained in the realm of philosophy until the twentieth century, when the new science of psychology took it up.[19] Sir Frederick Bartlett, a British psychologist, used *schemata* in his 1932 studies on remembering to describe how we recall the essence of a story.[20] According to Bartlett, we first remember outline features, which are common to several stories. For example, a fairy tale corresponds to one schema ("Valiant prince frees princess from bewitchment"). The main sequence of events typical of a Western make up another. One remembers a given story as a superposition of its schema and the particular traits that made it stand out. The Swiss psychologist Jean Piaget elaborated on the idea and used it in his theory of mental development.[21] The German philosopher and psychologist Max Wertheimer incorporated schemata into the Gestalt theory of perception.[22] The concept remained vague, however, and experimental psychologists could never make any concrete use of it.

When Marvin Minsky introduced schemata into AI in his 1975 paper "A Framework for Representing Knowledge," he called them "frames" in order to freshen up the slightly stale psychological notion.[23] As we saw earlier (chapter 7), a Minskyan frame looks like an income tax form, its main feature being a set of slots to fill in. In a generic frame, some slots are empty, and others contain default entries corresponding to usual or necessary characteristics of a concept. For example, the frame for chair has slots labeled *seat* and *back*. The slot *number of legs* holds the number 4. The slot *purpose* contains the mention *to sit on*. Another slot shows that a chair is a specific case of a more general frame called *piece of furniture*. In the generic case, other slots—such as *color, weight, material, height, position*—remain empty. One fills them with appropriate values when applying the frame to a specific instance of a chair.

In AI programs, frames serve several purposes. One can use them to recognize objects or concepts ("It has four legs, a seat, and a back: what is it?"). Frames can keep track of where objects are. They can help reach goals ("Need to rest your legs? Look for something with four legs, a seat, and a back"). Frames allow AI programs to make inferences ("It's a chair, but I can see only two legs: the table corner probably hides the other two"). Schank's scripts (chapter 7) are frames designed for the express purpose of inferring what stories leave untold ("If John ordered a hamburger in a restaurant, he probably ate it, even if the story doesn't say so.")

Not by coincidence, studying the role of prototypes in intelligent behavior has developed into a growing new field of psychology. *Categori-*

zation and *prototypicality effects* are now new research avenues in this science.

Tools for Psychological Investigation

The influence of AI on psychology extended beyond providing general insights about the workings of intelligence. AI has also influenced the everyday practice of psychological investigation. Because of AI, psychologists now have new instruments for prying open the secrets of the mind.

The first one is a tool for expressing many of their theories in unambiguous terms: the computer program. Formulating a hypothesis so precisely that it will run on a computer forces crystal clarity on it. Computers tolerate neither hand waving nor fuzzy thinking and keep you honest. Unrealized, implicit, or unspoken assumptions are mercilessly weeded out. Weaknesses of construction appear as if under a magnifying glass.

Second, running theories on a computer allows psychologists to evaluate them better. The computer has a substantial edge over the laboratory rat. As MIT's Patrick Winston facetiously pointed out to Pamela McCorduck, a computer requires little care and feeding and does not bite.[24] As a more considerable advantage, computers give psychologists a capability so far restricted to the hard sciences: the ability to isolate phenomena. Physicists and chemists have always been able to set up their experiments so as to study only one factor at a time. You want to investigate gravity? Plot the impact speeds of objects as a function of their falling heights; see whether heavier objects fall faster. You want to cut air friction? Carry out the experiments in a vacuum. You think temperature might have an influence? Keep it constant! Before computers, one could hardly apply similar methods in psychology. It was extremely difficult to isolate a particular aspect of a mind and study it independently of all other mental activities.

Yet this isolation of factors is precisely what Feigenbaum did for the memorization of meaningless syllables. He could study how minute variations in a hypothesized discrimination procedure affected learning. He never had to worry about subject fatigue or random fluctuations. The writer Pamela McCorduck aptly captured the advantage by calling AI programs "parts of intelligent behavior cultured in silicon."[25]

Cognitive Science

Through ever-increasing intermingling, the boundaries between artificial intelligence and psychology have grown fuzzy. The blurred line along which the two fields blend into each other is even starting to emerge as a discipline of its own, under the name "cognitive science." With help from other fields (anthropology, linguistics, philosophy, and neuroscience), cognitive science aims to explore the nature and functioning of the mind. The Sloan Foundation favored the emergence of cognitive science through a multimillion-dollar financing effort in the 1980s. The main cognitive science research centers are MIT, Berkeley, and San Diego. Others exist at Stanford, Carnegie Mellon, and the University of Pennsylvania.

How does one distinguish between the disciplines of AI, cognitive science, and psychology? At the risk of offending researchers in all three fields, here is a try at telling them apart. Roughly speaking, AI is about building thinking machines, while psychology studies how people act and feel. Cognitive psychology tries to learn how people think. Cognitive science is a meeting ground between AI and psychology.

These differences in goals frequently correspond to differences in methodology and philosophy, often with misunderstanding, distrust, and even contempt between workers in different disciplines. Psychologists, for example, mostly interpret the workings of the mind through meaning. AI workers, instead, look to the mechanism of the process involved as an explanation. The psychologist Sherry Turkle of MIT gives the example of a typical Freudian slip, in which a chairperson opens a meeting by declaring it closed.[26] Into this lapse, psychologists would read feelings of uneasiness and the chair's hidden wish for the meeting to be over. An AI worker, on the other hand, may remark that computers often encode meanings and their opposites in similar ways: the brain may proceed in the same manner. Minute errors in reading the symbol back, like flipping the sign bit from positive to negative, may turn "open" into "closed."

The psychologists Noel Sharkey from Stanford and Rolf Pfeifer from Zurich University point out another difference: AI and psychology section cognition differently.[27] Psychologists investigate long, horizontal sections of cognition. Sharkey and Pfeifer cite as a typical example the psychologist Morton's *logogen* model or word recognition. Morton postulated that each word of our vocabulary corresponds in our mind to a specific word detector, or *logogen*. Elaborating on the structure of these detectors, Morton applied them to the phenomenon of word perception in several contexts and explained a wide range of experimental effects from many different sources. For example, the model applied to written and spoken word perception: it explained in both cases why we can recognize a word faster after a recent exposure to it. An AI worker might complain about the lack of generality of this work, since it concentrates on only one part of our understanding processes: the word.

For an AI researcher, generality involves processing a deep, vertical section of cognition that would look very thin to a psychologist. For example, Roger Schank's story-understanding programs involve everything from parsing sentences to explaining the behaviors described. Yet a psychologist may find this work too restrictive because it handles only stories in a limited field of understanding.

AI workers and psychologists frequently emerge from different backgrounds and pursue different goals. They often deeply mistrust each other's work and apply adjectives like "naïve," "slipshod," and "irrelevant" to work performed in the other discipline. Psychologists often decry AI workers as amateur psychologists, and vice versa. Cognitive scientists try to reconcile opposing viewpoints, often to the disapproval of both sides.

Despite these differences, an uneasy alliance has formed between AI and psychology in specific fields. Researchers recognize that work on sensory perception can be good experimental psychology and good AI. They can match computer program results and the experimental behavior of subjects with such accuracy that little argument is possible. In many instances, researchers even know the workings of the pertinent neuroanatomical structures in enough detail to permit specific hardware modeling. Higher-level cognitive activities like conscious thought or language processing, on the other hand, are too remote from experimental test to allow such research. It is there that AI may have to precede psychology. Hypotheses formed through computer modeling could then enable the design of experiments specifically aimed at testing them.

Is the Human Mind Unique?

If computers can model our mental activity in different ways, have we proved that our minds are not unique? Could processes radically different from the ones in our brains lead to cognition? Such speculations led cognitive scientists to investigate the question of mind in general. Even if minds can differ from each other, are there general principles that apply to all of them, whatever their make up? Is it possible to extract mental properties common to humans, thinking computers, or even aliens from other stars? The investigation of this question has barely begun, and scientists can offer few conclusions. However, the very questions they are asking expose the flavor of the research.

The more abstract question deals with the continuity of the space of minds. Can one say that the set of all possible minds forms a smooth slope? Is there an unbroken rise starting at bacteria and thermostats and leading to the human mind or intelligent computers? The sketchy results available point to a negative answer. From what we see, the path to higher minds involves long stretches of flat ground broken by soaring cliffs. In the 1950s, John von Neumann identified one of these cliffs and called it the "complexity barrier." Beyond this level of organization, he said, a being can make another one more complex than itself.[28] Yet another step-increase in mind power is the phenomenon of cognitive convergence, which Douglas Lenat claims to have achieved with the Cyc project. Cyc's designers have now fed into it enough basic concepts to be able to explain most new entries in terms of earlier ones.[29]

Other questions cognitive scientists ask are: To what extent is intelligence inherited? How much can one develop it after birth? One partial answer stems from the position that intelligence is mostly knowledge: the very act of reasoning requires the application of techniques and steps that humans have had to learn. Some speculate that the structure of the brain somehow determines what we can learn, and experience determines what we do learn. If this is the case, we would mostly inherit intelligence. Others claim that we are all born with the same basic abilities. The specially bright people are those who, accidentally or otherwise, learn in their youth ways of making their learning more efficient.

Yet another issue concerns domain limitation. This weakness plagues all AI programs, limiting their fields of competence to narrow domains. For example, an expert system for electric locomotive repair knows nothing about diesel engines or railroad cars. Perhaps in self-defense, AI workers claim that in practice people are also severely domain-restricted. Some point out that we even label each other according to our domain restrictions, or specialties: salesman, accountant, lawyer, cook, and so on. From making this observation to claiming domain restriction as a general property of intelligence is a small step, and many have taken it. Were they right? The future will tell.

Anyone who has had a hand at programming computers knows about program loops. They occur when a weakness in programming logic causes the computer to repeat the same steps endlessly. AI programs are not immune to loops, and debugging one is often a process of keeping it from going into ever wider loops. First, one identifies trivial errors that induce the repetition of short sequences of instructions: these are easy to fix. One then discovers that sometimes a subtle conjunction of circumstances makes the program jump back to an earlier step after executing many instructions. The reasons for this behavior often lie deep in the structure of the program. Devising additional program tests to detect offending circumstances and prevent looping when they occur may be a major undertaking.

We all know people who endlessly repeat the same, often self-destructive, pattern of behavior. This phenomenon is so common that psychologists interpret it as a compulsive acting out of unconscious wishes. Freud made one such classical diagnosis of a woman who managed to marry not one, not two, but three cancerous husbands whom she attended on their death beds.[30] Granted the pathological character of such extreme cases, couldn't the common occurrences be just program loops? Often the cycles last several years. Their victims may well act out of healthy and natural inclinations. Since one's basic disposition remains the same, it will sooner or later place one in the same kinds of situations. Like the computer program above, these people may simply lack an appropriate loop-detection mechanism—like a little man on one's shoulder, for example, who at the beginning of a new loop would detect analogies with the present situation and its equivalents in past cycles. But since each loop is slightly different from the one before, and similar situations may occur only at intervals of several years, it might take a very clever little man indeed to say, "Look, there you are! You're doing it again! Stop it!" As we shall soon see, Marvin Minsky surmises that such monitoring and error-prevention activities make up the major part of our mental processes. Like discontinuities, domain restriction, and the tendency to loop, they could be attributes of all minds, natural or artificial.

Invoking such a little man to explain mental processes is deeply unsatisfying. For what accounts for the thought processes of this little man? Another little man within *his* mind? Since the eighteenth-century philosopher David Hume first implied this threat of infinite regress in his essays on human understanding,[31] the modern philosopher and AI fan Daniel Dennett has called it "Hume's problem."[32] Other investigators called it the "homunculus problem," after the Latin word for "little man."[33] A startling conclusion of AI research is that "little men" may not be such a bad idea after all: all minds may, in fact, consist of myriads of them.

To understand this aboutface, let me first consider the all-pervasive technique of recursive computer programming. Very simply, it consists in defining programs in terms of themselves. This procedure is now standard in computer science. Programmers long ago discovered an effective technique for tackling complicated assignments. First, write a simple procedure to take care of obvious tasks and special cases; call this program A. Then, anything that is not obvious or a special case is entrusted to another program named B, to be called by A. Thus, execution of program A consists of carrying out simple instructions and then calling program B to handle the rest. It turns out that one can often neatly solve the problem by using a duplicate of A for B. A takes care of obvious or special cases and then calls itself to deal with the rest. For example, to count the number of words in a sentence, A would set its counter to zero (no words), and then count the first word. Counting the rest of the words would consist of applying A as many times as required (until it had completed all of the counting in this operation). Recursivity gave rise to an entire mathematical culture which defines concepts and procedures in terms of themselves. This policy emphasizes how one can break up complex activities into the recursive application of simpler functions.

One can therefore use little men to describe thinking as long as they do less work than the activity they purport to explain. This "ability of thought to think,"[34] represented by the little man, opens up pathways once forbidden on pain of regress. It allows me to add a last item to a potential list of universal mind properties: the building blocks of all minds may be just smaller subminds.

Subminds

Yet another trend in computer science led to the decomposition of programs into semi-independent components: it started out with down-to-earth bookkeeping problems in simulation programs. Carl Hewitt (author of the MicroPlanner language, itself an early experiment in decomposition), recalled it for me:

> Kristen Nygaard and Ole-Johan Dahl* were inspired to develop more modular ways to program simulation than existing ways using languages like FORTRAN. . . . If you were going to simulate a car wash, you needed an array of variables over here to keep track of which cars had been washed or not, you'd have an x-y-z coordinate array over there that kept track of what the positions of the automobiles were, and this spaghetti piece of code to put it all together. So they said, "Hey, we've got objects out there: automobiles and car-washing stations. So let's have each object keep track of itself. Let an automobile keep track of whether it's clean or dirty, of what its position is, of how long it is. Each washing station will keep track of how much soap and water it has." . . . [In this way], they were able to do simulations in beautiful, elegant fashion.[35]

Special-purpose programming languages like SIMULA and Small-Talk appeared, which implemented these concepts. Their basic philosophy was for the programmer to describe not what the objects did by using computer data structures, but who they were; specialized mechanisms built into the languages then let these creatures interact as their natures dictated.

The advent of computer networks provided the clinching motivation for developing software-enabling multiagent interactions. Instead of concentrating all their data processing in a single mainframe, large corporations found it more practical in the 1970s to have minicomputers, and later microcomputers, perform whatever operations they could locally. The machines then transmitted only the required information to each other. Pretty soon they themselves started gossiping over telecommunication lines like unquenchable busybodies: air traffic control information, airline reservations, and electronic fund transfers now make up a sizable fraction of long-distance communications. Protocols such as Message-Passing allow the orderly and error-free cooperation of many processors. Carl Hewitt formalized their analysis in a new branch of computer science called "Actor Theory."

By coincidence, at about the same time, the idea of multiple cooperating minds within a mind was also gaining ground in psychology—owing

*Inventors of the language SIMULA at the Norwegian Computing Center in Oslo.

in part to psychologists' shift from Freud's model of the brain to that of Norbert Wiener in his theory of cybernetics (see chapter 2). Information, he and psychologists after him believed, better describes the stuff of thought than energy does, and this is what the brain receives from outside. Information, contrary to energy, does not build up pressures. In fact, the law of conservation does not even apply to information: if necessary, one can destroy data, and the brain can receive more information than it releases. The brain's main drive, concluded these psychologists, was to organize information into coherent objects and form relationships between them. Thus was born the psychology of internal-object relations.

Freud, to his credit, had already described a process by which we "take in" people to form inner objects. He first conceived of it as a pathological phenomenon—the reproaches of an internalized father, for instance, leading to melancholia. Eventually, Freud came to think of internal-object formation as a part of normal development. Later theorists, like the Austrian psychoanalyst Melanie Klein, widened this view, setting up as a base for mental life the relationships we have with our inner images of people as entities within the mind.[36] In the words of the psychologist Thomas Ogden, these agents were "microminds . . . unconscious suborganizations of the ego capable of generating meaning and experience, i.e. capable of thought, feeling and perception."[37] Even though many psychologists do not accept this view in its entirety, most admit that one does build up one's personality by identifying with other people or fragments of their personalities.

A Society of Mind

In 1986, Minsky published *The Society of Mind,* in which he built the concept of subminds into a sweeping attempt at explaining human intelligence.[38] In a sense, *The Society of Mind* represents the full blooming of the scruffy movement away from pure logic as an explanation of the mind. The scruffies hold that, in the words of Daniel Dennett, the mind is

> a gadget, an object that one should not expect to be governed by deep mathematical laws, but nevertheless a designed object, analyzable in functional terms: ends and means, costs and benefits, elegant solutions on the one hand, and on the other, shortcuts, jury rigs, and cheap ad hoc fixes. . . . The mix of elegance and Rube Goldberg found elsewhere in nature . . . will be discernible in the mind as well."[39]

Minsky's own mix of elegance and ad-hoc fixes is reminiscent of the hive-mind theme of science fiction. Our minds, claims Minsky, are made up of a billion entities, which he calls "agents." Individual agents are dumb and know only one function. They constantly monitor inflow from the senses or signals produced by other agents. They perform whatever action they are capable of upon recognizing their own activation signals. Mind results from the simultaneous and often tangled, conflicting, and disorderly action of agents. Structured as a loose hierarchy, agents make up specialized systems called "services." A high-level service may be capable of quite advanced tasks, and terms usually reserved for a whole person might apply to it.

In an example strikingly suggestive of the block-manipulating robot in the Micro Worlds project, Minsky describes how agents might operate in the mind of a child building block towers. The highest agent in this hierarchy (call it BUILDER) knows only how to call three subordinate functions: BEGIN decides where to place the tower, ADD piles up the blocks to build it, and END decides whether the tower is high enough. Each one of these functions depends on its own subordinates: those of ADD, for example, will FIND a new block, GET it, and PUT it into place. FIND, GET, and PUT, in turn, activate their own subagents, and so on down to the agents that eventually control eye movements or activate the muscles causing the child to pick up the blocks.

Some find this model too formal a description for the diffuse and ill-defined tissue of interlocking meshes of neurons in the brain. It is not clear that one can isolate individual neural structures corresponding to Minsky's agents. Yet the model provides a surprisingly faithful account of many mental phenomena. Here is a brief sampling of some of the questions it answers:

Why do babies suffer sudden and drastic changes in humor? We have all seen a baby move in seconds from a contented smile to tears of rage or hunger. Answer: early minds consist of few independent services geared to satisfy our basic needs. When control passes from one to the other, sudden changes in mood result. More complex, tightly linked services make up the adult mind: mood shifts are less drastic and take longer.

How does the mind grow? How do we learn? Answer: we form new agents and services and include them in existing hierarchies. However, when a structure becomes too large, it can no longer expand into crowded nearby tissue. In addition, other services come to depend on it, and further changes might disturb their activities. The solution? Copy the structure with any required improvements into another part of the brain. When it is ready, transfer control to the new structure. This explains why we learn new skills in bursts of rapid progress separated by stretches of slow development, or "learning plateaus." A plateau corresponds to the construction and testing of a new structure. The bursts of progress occur when a new structure is suddenly switched on.

How do remembering, recall, and associations occur? Some agents act as links between other agents, activating specific aspects of a concept in several services. These "knowledge lines," as Minsky calls them, arise when we have a new experience. For example, our first sight of an apple might activate the agents for *round, fist-sized, smooth-skinned,* and *red.* The knowledge line associated with the new concept of *apple* will afterward link, framelike, these properties together.

Like Freud's, Minsky's model of the mind assigns an important role to unconscious mechanisms. In Minsky's view, avoiding mistakes is as important as learning new skills. Special agents, called "censors" and "suppressors," come into being when we blunder. The suppressor created when we first put our fingers in a flame detects our intention to do so the next time around and prevents the action. With time, this suppressor evolves into a censor, which prevents us from even thinking of touching a flame. Censors speed up our mental processes: to reach an object on the other side of a flame, we don't lose time considering the option of going straight for it.

Censors are exceptional agents for two reasons. First, they remain by definition invisible. Faithful to their purpose of unburdening the field of our consciousness, they stay carefully outside it. Second, they are large, in the sense of requiring much knowledge and processing power. For example, the censor against touching flames should catch much more than our intention of touching a flame: it must detect the many more circumstances that might lead us to even think of touching a flame. This watchdog activity requires a close monitoring of the many agents that might give rise to such thoughts. If new circumstances occur that lead us to think about touching a flame, the censor must learn to recognize them also. Invisible, large, and growing, censors are the black holes of thought.

Unlike Minsky's previous contributions about Perceptrons and frame theory, the Society of Mind was given a cold shoulder in AI circles. Some thought Minsky—as was his right as one of the originators of the idea—had simply renamed and repackaged object-oriented programming.[40] As Minsky pointed out to me, though, there is a fundamental difference between the two concepts: it has to do with communication, which objects-oriented programs typically handle through a protocol called "message passing":

> Message passing is basically a foolproof logical way of making sure that nothing gets lost. If a message is not accepted, the system locks up. However, a Society of Mind will tolerate errors through heuristics: agents acting as managers have their own knowledge about how you express progress, and may decide that some other agency is having a bad day and should be made to go away.

Another of the Society of Mind's problems has to do with Minsky's strategy of leaving plenty of work to do for those who climb onto one of his bandwagons: it did marvels for frames but backfired when he applied it to the Society of Mind. This time, potential followers thought they just didn't have enough to go on. "I do not consider the Society of Mind to be a serious proposal," Allen Newell told me.

> It's too soft. . . . The problem is that Marvin wants to talk about his agents in metaphoric language, so you are never able to feel how limited they are or whether they are really a whole bunch of little kids in there with all the apparatus of a human. There isn't any constraint in that design proposal to enable you to pin it down.

Many critics feel that Minsky does not adequately explain how the interaction of many simple components results in very complex behavior. Terry Winograd accused Minsky of engaging in "sleight of hand by changing from 'dumb' agents to 'intelligent' homunculi communicating in natural language at the point of Wrecker versus Builder in a child."[41]

Minsky, for his part, is leery about becoming more specific. When I asked him whether there were ongoing efforts to implement the Society of Mind into hardware, he answered, "No, not anymore. People want to but they keep asking me how to do it. I'm unable to make design decisions like that. I might mislead them."

Patrick Winston, Minsky's successor at the head of MIT's AI Laboratory, conceded the theory's incompleteness but cautioned against hasty judgments:

Marvin's Society of Mind is not a single idea, but a vast potpourri of ideas. I've sometimes compared it to a diamond or gold mine. There's lots of gold in it, and there are diamonds and there are duds. None of it is exactly in gem form yet, half of it is hidden in rocks, some of it is fool's gold, some of it is too low-grade to mine for a long time. There's material for lots of Ph.D. theses there. So as time goes on the Society of Mind will become in many respects even more of a land-mark than it is today.[42]

Unified Theories of Cognition

So far in this chapter I may have given the impression that researchers have definitely abandoned the dream of accounting for mind through a handful of simple mechanisms, the "Maxwell's equations of thought" upon which Doug Lenat has turned his back. Even though the logicians have attacked the common-sense problem with renewed and more powerful logical techniques, it is not at all clear that a single kind of logic can account for all of thought. Scruffies, through the Cyc project, have in fact broken logic down into many special-purpose inferencing mech-anisms, whose main purpose is to sift through the mountain of hand-coded knowledge where the real power of Cyc will reside. Marvin Minsky's Society of Mind makes up yet another *dis*-integrated effort to explain mind, relying as it does on the sheer proliferation of interacting special-purpose functions.

Other schools of AI researchers are, however, still pursuing the original goal in all its purity and finding in psychology the basis for the powerful, general-purpose mechanisms with which they hope to explain thought. The 1980s saw the emergence of theories with the colorful names of Act* (pronounced "Act Star"), Soar, and Prodigy, which have much in common in methodology and share the ambitious goal of accounting for all of cognition. Indeed, Allen Newell, showing no sign of the cancer that would kill him a year later, all but swept me out of my chair in his enthusiasm for Soar: "In Herbert [Simon]'s and my stuff is . . . always the concern for artificial intelligence . . . right there with the concern with cognitive psychology. Large parts of the rest of the AI field believe that this is exactly the wrong way to look at it: you ought to know whether you're being a psychologist or an engineer. Herb and I have always taken the view that maximal confusion between those is the way to make progress."

The roots of Soar go back to the 1960s and the shift from search to knowledge that Newell and his followers never quite bought. Although they believe in the power of knowledge, they don't see it as a final solution to the problem of intelligence. Further, they point out, dealing with mountains of knowledge complicates the search problem by making it harder to identify the pertinent pieces of knowledge. As Newell put it: "There were attempts to move out of search, to say 'It's all knowledge now!' but as soon as one deals with difficult problems, you'll find—lo and behold—the search efforts continue."

Throughout the 1960s, Newell and Simon continued the experiments that had led them to discover means-ends analysis late in the previous decade: they conducted psychological tests to find out how people solve problems, and tried to embody their reasoning techniques in software. The experimenters learned much by asking people to prove theorems in logic and later studying how other subjects played chess. The crucial discovery occurred, however, when Newell and Simon asked their subjects to identify digits corresponding to the different letters in puzzles known as "cryptarithmetic problems":

```
    SEND
  + MORE
  ──────
   MONEY
```

Newell and Simon observed that their subjects started by trying out different numbers more or less at random: this corresponded to pure search behavior. After a while, the subjects discovered shortcuts that speeded up their searches. For example, they would realize that if the result of the addition had more digits than the numbers being added, then the first digit of the result had to be the number 1 (thus, the letter *M* stands for 1 in this problem). Learning how to solve cryptarithmetic puzzles, Newell and Simon discovered, simply consisted of acquiring more of these little pieces of knowledge and finding out how to make efficient use of them. In fact, Newell and Simon discovered that the behavior of their subjects gradually moved over a continuum in which they traded search for knowledge. They would start off with pure, time-consuming searches, which became shorter as the subjects acquired more knowledge. Experienced problem solvers hardly performed any searching at all and arrived at a solution quickly by the routine application of knowledge. Newell and Simons's key discovery pertained to how the subjects stored their different pieces of knowledge. One could give a detailed account of a subject's performance, they found out, by assuming that he or she kept available knowledge fragments in long-term memory, more or less independent of each other, in the form of IF . . . THEN rules (as I formulated the knowledge I applied in reaching the solution for *M*). It was precisely this observation that led Edward Feigenbaum, a former student of Newell and Simon, to implement IF . . . THEN rules into the first expert system over at Stanford (see chapter 6).

At the beginning of the 1970s, Newell and Simon had analyzed thinking into two basic abilities: the ability to search—that is, try out different solutions to problems; and the ability to store and retrieve pertinent fragments of knowledge as IF . . . THEN rules, in order to speed up the searches. In 1972, Newell and Simon published their findings about the strong role of production systems (another name for sets of IF . . . THEN rules) in a one-thousand-page book called *Human Problem Solving,* which had taken fourteen years to write. ("I'm glad I didn't have to earn a living as a writer!" Herbert Simon confided to me upon remembering this period.)[43] From then on, as Simon pursued different interests, it was left to Newell to refine the theory of cognition that would become Soar. As often happens in science, Soar came about in a fairly roundabout manner. "The Soar effort is an outgrowth of another project called the Instructible Production System," Newell told me.

That's one of the few efforts I've been associated with that turned into an out-an-out total failure. The idea was that very large production systems would have to be educated from the outside rather than programmed. We addressed the issue of how to build a production system which could be instructed without knowing in detail all that was in it. The project never went anywhere at all—but as it disintegrated, it gave birth to some major achievements.

These include the OPS-5 production system language; John McDermott's XCON, the first commercial expert system; and Soar, which Newell assembled with two graduate students, John Laird and Paul Rosenbloom. "What was missing in the Instructible Production System was an organization for putting tasks together," continued Newell.

We needed to identify knowledge relevant to particular situations, and do things like implementing operators and computing evaluation functions. This was when we discovered the gimmick that turned out to be central in making Soar: it was the realization that we could represent all these other tasks simply as searches in their own problem spaces. We implemented this through the principle of universal sub-goaling: it's a device for recognizing when you run out of gas and providing a new opportunity for more knowledge.

As a simple example of subgoaling, suppose Soar is playing ticktack-toe against a human opponent. A set of IF . . . THEN rules within Soar's memory would tell it what moves are legal and perhaps suggest useful moves like blocking the opponent whenever possible. At some stage in the game, though, Soar may have to choose between two or more allowed moves, without its rules expressing a preference for any move in particular. Soar rises to this situation, called a "tie impasse," by setting up as a new goal the selection of the best move among the alternatives available. This selection becomes a separate subproblem, upon which the full problem-solving power of Soar can be brought to bear.

"You see, that's the magic of production systems," Newell said. "They are self-selecting systems, in which the rules themselves say, 'I'm relevant to that situation.' " Soar contains standard rules for resolving tie impasses, which come into play as soon as a situation has been tagged as an impasse. In this case, the rules would tell Soar to look ahead—that is, try out all the moves and see which leads to the most desirable situation. This strategy would remain the same whether Soar were playing chess, checkers, or ticktacktoe: therefore, universal subgoaling potentially allows Soar to play any game.

Universal subgoaling was the subject of John Laird's doctoral disser-tation;[44] Paul Rosenbloom's thesis initially concerned not Soar, but the mechanism for learning called chunking suggested by the Harvard psy-chologist George Miller during the 1950s in his famous paper on short-term memory.[45] Chunking consists of tying existing notions into a new bundle that itself becomes a single notion: we do it for example when we chunk seven digits under the heading of a person's phone number. In his thesis, Rosenbloom was able to provide substantial evidence for the presence of chunking at the heart of learning.[46]

He did it as follows. We all know that the only way to improve a new skill—whether it's typing, skating, or speaking a new language—is through practice. Since the 1960s, experimental psychologists had been able to determine that the speed with which we perform the new task increases as some fractional power (say, the square root) of the number of times we've done it before. They called this phenomenon the "power law of practice" but were at a loss to explain it. Rosenbloom showed that if learning occurs by chunking, and if we perform this chunking at a constant rate, then skill will improve in a manner dictated by the power law of practice.

When these results were in, Newell, Laird, and Rosenbloom realized, somewhat to their surprise, that Soar provided a ready-made mechanism for incorporating chunking. It was only necessary to exploit impasses. As I indicated, these happened only in situations where no direct piece of pertinent knowledge was available. In the ticktacktoe example, Soar reached an impasse when none of its rules could tell it which move to make. Even more to the point, Soar already had the means for discovering the missing piece of knowledge. After evaluating the available tick-tacktoe moves, for example, it knew which one was best. Thus, in order for Soar to have the ability to learn, it had to be enabled to remember this knowledge by means of a new IF . . . THEN rule. This rule described the situation that had given rise to the impasse (the IF part), and prescribed the action taken as a result of the ensuing search in the THEN part. For example, a new ticktacktoe rule might say: "IF you can play either a corner or the center, THEN take the center." In later games, Soar would know which move to make, and no impasse would occur.

Newell still couldn't believe how easy it turned out to be; as he recalled to me:

I was out of town when John and Paul decided to try and program-in learning for one little task. And when they implemented it, they discovered how to make it general. So when I came back after two or three days, chunking was in and working in a general fashion through all of Soar. I've had a few breakthroughs in my career, but that was the most dramatic one. It brought everything into a very tight knot in which problem spaces, production systems, impassing, and chunking are just one ball of wax. All of a sudden Soar became a complete cognitive engine.

These events happened in January 1984. Since then, Soar has evolved into a multidisciplinary research program involving more than a hundred researchers on both sides of the Atlantic. Newell, in a book of the same title, has proposed it as a "unified theory of cognition."[47] Much as Maxwell in his equations explained all of electromagnetism in terms of four quantities (charge, current, electric and magnetic fields), Newell hopes to eventually account for the whole of human cognition through the four fundamental mechanisms implemented in Soar.

Among other architectures similar to Soar, most notable are John Anderson's Act*[48] and a system called Prodigy by Steven Minton, Jaime Carbonell, and others.[49] Both Act* and Prodigy posit a learning mechanism similar to Soar's, which is called "explanation-based learning." Contrary to Soar, which can learn only from its successes, Prodigy can also learn from its mistakes. Since Anderson is a Carnegie Mellon psychologist, and Carbonell one of Newell's colleagues at that university's computer science department, these projects obviously sprouted off the same intellectual branch. Together, they make up a substantial chapel of AI research.

The Question of Awareness: Could Machines Love?

Whether through the worldly knowledge of a Cyc-like data base or architectures modeled on our own minds, intelligent machines of the future may comprehend the world in a manner not totally unlike our own. This raises the question whether they will share other mental attributes with us: Will such machines be aware of themselves? Will they feel pain, love, and anger?

On a philosophical level, one can study emotions as one studies intelligence. I have already discussed the human inability to define intelligence in absolute terms: the only way to establish its presence in an artificial system is to compare its behavior with human behavior. Further, intelligence seems to disappear when we succeed in embodying aspects of it in machines, since relatively simple logic or association mechanisms can make a system behave as if it did contain a piece of intelligence. There are two ways to consider this phenomenon. One stems from the position that intelligence is in essence different from matter, a kind of immaterial fluid breathed into a being. The logical consequence of this position is to dismiss as pure mimicry our partial successes at imitating intelligence. If intelligence is in essence different from matter, and we don't put any into our mechanism, then it can only be imitating intelligence. In this case, much as we can't imitate all aspects of life with mechanical dolls, we probably couldn't build a more complex mechanism to imitate the entire mind.

The other interpretation of the seeming disappearance of intelligence takes a reverse view of the matter. The fact that one can build pieces of mind out of nonmind substance like computer circuitry may just show that mind naturally emerges out of properly organized matter. Indeed, it is a widespread property in nature that complex phenomena emerge out of simple interactions and components. The simple forces between ice molecules, for instance, induce an infinite variety of intricate snowflake structures. Further, groups of interacting components often exhibit properties totally absent in individual components. For example, it doesn't make sense to talk about the temperature, entropy, and pressure of an individual molecule, yet these properties emerge out of the collective behavior of large numbers of gas molecules. This interpretation is much more encouraging for the future of AI; and, indeed, most AI researchers subscribe to it. Many of them claim that one good reason we can build a thinking machine is that we all carry one in our skulls— hence, the "meat machine" quality of the brain Marvin Minsky is fond of invoking.

Is the brain truly a machine? Aren't one's conscience, one's thoughts, one's immortal soul if it comes to that, essentially different from one's physical body? A consensus is building among scientists and philosophers that they are not. Most of these experts subscribe to the opinion that the mind is essentially an emanation of the brain. In other words, physical processes occurring in the brain explain our mental processes in their entirety. Many arguments justify this opinion.

One is anatomical evidence for the association of mind and brain. Damage to the brain disturbs our thinking. Damage to specific areas even gives rise to specific kinds of disorder. Particular brain structures correspond to abstract abilities, such as language. For example, damage to either Broca's or Wernike's area, both located below the left temple, can produce permanent and specific language disabilities. And isn't one problem of our drug-abusing society precisely that specific chemical changes in the brain correlate with changes of moods and emotions?

Another argument for mind-brain association stems from the history of science. We have not, so far, discovered anything in nature which physical law cannot explain. It would be surprising if the mind were an exception. If fact, the entire history of science is one of explaining phenomena previously thought to be governed by forces extraneous to the physical universe. Wind, lightning, volcanoes, and earthquakes are no longer expressions of the whims of gods, but strictly material phenomena governed by natural law. We can now make mathematical models of the evolution of the universe, all the way to the primordial big bang. The laws of physics and chemistry, together with the mechanisms of natural evolution, explain the appearance of life on earth. They also appear to account for the evolution of humans.

In a parallel phenomenon, science has gradually displaced humans and their physical environment from their special status in the world. Copernicus started the movement by moving the earth from its central position to being a satellite of the sun. Later Darwin displaced the human body from its pedestal and proved its lineage with nonhuman ancestors. Biochemistry showed that the life processes in this body are natural phenomena. Freud, without proving the natural origin of the human mind, showed that it was at least amenable to scientific study. AI would be the last step in this revolution: its success would show that even our minds have purely material origins.

If such is the case, shouldn't it be possible to re-create, out of inert matter, beings with not only thought but also awareness, feelings, and emotions? Although the opinions of philosophers and AI researchers cover the usual spectrum of diverging views, I have been hard put to find any creditable expert who would answer a clearcut no to this question. Most responded with a qualified yes; and in the past decade, most debates on the subject did not oppose the partisans of yes and no answers. The action centered on the yes part of the spectrum, with factions arguing over whether they should qualify their positive answers, and how.

The closest approximation to an uncompromising no comes from Berkeley's Hubert Dreyfus, who simply claims that truly intelligent machines cannot be made in the first place. And even on that point, Dreyfus's objections stop at symbol-manipulating machines: he is non-committal about machines based on artificial neural nets, presumably closer to the way our brains are built.[50]

Taking a somewhat less hard line, MIT's Joseph Weizenbaum, author of the anti-AI book *Computer Power and Human Reason,*[51] summarized his position for me:

> I don't see any way to put a limitation to the degree of intelligence that [a machine] could acquire. The only qualification I make, and I can't understand why it's resisted, is that the intelligence that will develop in this way will always be alien to human intelligence. It will be at least as different as the intelligence of a dolphin is to that of a human being.[52]

Weizenbaum points out that dolphins are different—not unfeeling. This comparison leaves open the possibility of creating a machine with feelings. As he himself said, "I don't understand what [my position] takes away from any ambition that the AI people might have."

For an all-out yes, consider Carnegie Mellon's Hans Moravec, who believes that early in the next century we will be served by successive generations of gradually more intelligent robots. He views these machines as anything but unfeeling aliens. "On the contrary, I think robots in general will be quite emotional about being nice people," Moravec told me. He explained this character trait as the result of evolutionary forces:

> Imagine these robots being made in a factory, and the main purpose of the factory, which is the reproductive unit of the robots, is to cause robots to sell well. The best-selling robots will bring in profits to their companies, which will then build more factories. Then it is customer response that will mostly shape the character of these robots. So when you bring one into your house, it will understand that you're the person it's there for, and that it had better keep you happy, or at least induce you to buy another one of it. It should somehow estimate whether you're happy or not, and receive [from its internal make-up] a positive conditioning if it does something that makes you happy. It will care how you feel about its actions. It will try to please you in an apparently selfless manner because it will get a thrill out of this positive reinforcement. You can interpret that as a kind of love.

Moravec's point is that emotions are just devices for channeling behavior in a direction beneficial to the survival of one's species. The most basic emotions are love, which stirs us toward certain goals, and fear, which keeps us out of harm's way. Moravec believes robots will experience fear also. Tongue in cheek, he imagined a minor emergency for his future household robot:

> It can't let its batteries run down to nothing, because then all its memories will erase and it will forget all sorts of important things with terrible, terrible consequences. So if it gets locked out of the house, it may try desperate measures to obtain a recharge somewhere. Its emergency modules would come into play, it would express agitation, or even panic, with signals that humans can recognize. It would go to the neighbors and ask them to use their plug saying, "Please! Please! I need this! It's so important, it's such a small cost! We'll reimburse you!"

He also sees in the maneuvers by which his robot carts calibrate their vision sensors the forebears of playful behavior in young animals: such activities serve to sharpen the skills on which will depend the life-saving fights or flights of adult life. Marvin Minsky has, in *The Society of Mind,* carried out a deeper analysis of emotions in which he explains them as special-purpose cognitive devices. Fear, anger, and pleasure act as short-term attention focusers. For longer time spans, "liking" holds us to our choice: "Liking's job is shutting off alternatives; we ought to understand its role since, unconstrained, it narrows down our universe."[53] Minsky even sees a clear cognitive role for humor and laughter, which play "a possible essential function in how we learn": "When we learn in a serious context, the result is to change connections among ordinary agents. But when we learn in a humorous context, the principal result is to change the connections that involve our censors and suppressors."[54]

Freud had already understood the role of censors and suppressors as inhibitory agents responsible for preventing harmful or socially unacceptable behavior, but Minsky extends their action to the cognitive realm: in common-sense reasoning, censors and suppressors must recognize trains of thought that lead to absurdity or infinite recursion, and make us avoid them in the future. This is why, to our subconscious, the absurd is almost as touchy as sex. Absurd and sexy jokes are funny because their punchlines surprise us with forbidden outcomes, and laughter is the mechanism during which censors against these new approaches are built. "In order to construct or improve a censor," Minsky explains, "you must retain your records of the recent states of mind that made you think the censored thought. This takes some time, during which your short-term memories are fully occupied."[55] For Minsky, laughter's function is to keep your attention focused on these memories and ensure that nothing interrupts the censor-formation process. If all works well, surprise is avoided the next time around, and the joke is no longer funny.

To all this, one might object that emotions are biochemical phenomena, that mood-altering drugs can induce depression or ecstasy, and that biochemists have demonstrated that emotions are related to minute variations of neurotransmitters in the brain. How, then, can a machine made of transistors and wires feel anything like an emotion? The answer is that neurotransmitters are just handy devices for inducing special electrical behavior in the brain. As their name implies, neurotransmitters are chemicals that selectively alter the conductivities of synapses, the connections between neurons. Relaxants like Valium function by switching on whatever brain circuits or patterns of brain activity make you feel relaxed. Dedicated hardware or software controls could achieve similar effects in machines: this is what Moravec meant by switching on an "emergency module" to induce panic in his discharging robot.

"All right," the skeptic might say at this point, "I'll believe that you can make a machine behave, when observed from outside, as if it were acting in an emotional manner. I will even admit that such behavior is necessary for a machine's intelligent interaction with the world. However, I absolutely refuse to admit that when Moravec's home robot pampers you, it feels anything like love or even affection. We have no business assigning human mental states to machines that cleverly simulate human behavior modes."

This position is known to the philosophically inclined artificial intelligentsia as "weak AI," and they have fought believers in "strong AI" in many private and public debates over the last two decades. Adepts of strong AI hold that intelligent machines can be imbued with self-awareness, consciousness, and true feelings. The issue may remain forever uncertain since, contrary to behavior, internal states of mind cannot be assessed objectively.

Although at first the reasonable reaction seems to be "Who cares?" one could argue that for moral reasons such questions should be addressed and resolved before we ever build truly intelligent machines. For example, what should be the fate of your future loving but battered robot nanny? Wouldn't it be murder to junk her? We should, in fact, ponder such issues at the design stage: it may turn out to be cruel to mass-produce robot brains and wire them all with the same basic motivations. Wouldn't a robot personality fit to perform as a tour guide be quite unhappy in repetitive factory work?

The most vivid attack against strong AI came from the Berkeley philosopher John R. Searle, who claims that computer simulations of awareness are no closer to the real thing than their simulations of thunderstorms, which never made anyone wet. He drove the point home in his now classic 1980 "Chinese Room" paper,[56] which described a thought experiment in which he simulated a computer passing Turing's test in Chinese. Searle, who is totally ignorant of the Chinese language, would sit in a closed room and receive the judge's questions as Chinese ideograms on pieces of paper. He would then consult a set of English-language instructions (a "program") telling him how to compose appropriate responses, all in terms of Chinese symbols unintelligible to him. After working out his answers in this way, he would hand them out as ideograms on paper. Now, to one observing the procedure from outside the room, the being inside it would clearly appear to understand Chinese. Searle, however, would have been merely following formal rules: he would have remained totally ignorant of the meaning of his answers and unaware of the mental processes involved in working them out. He concluded that mere symbol manipulations, even were they to generate outwardly intelligent behavior, could not induce awareness in the mechanism performing them.

Searle's opponents answered by claiming that a new awareness might indeed emerge from these activities, but that it would be associated with the system consisting of the room, the program, and the man's symbol-processing activities. Since this consciousness would be external to him, the man in the room would remain unaware of it. As Searle was quick to point out, it does seem a bit ridiculous to argue that a person could create a new consciousness by merely shuffling around bits of paper. In practice, however, the instructions explaining how to generate the answering ideograms would amount to a million pages of printed text, which is the quantity of knowledge a full-fledged common-sense data base would contain. Further, in order to carry out the simulation at a speed approaching real time, the poor mug in the room would have to perform long-hand calculations at the rate of one hundred billion operations every second, the speed at which our brains process information for us. Outside of its sheer physical impossibility, this whirlwind of activity makes the appearance of an awareness somewhat less preposterous.

My favorite counterargument to the "Chinese Room" paper was offered by the philosophers Paul and Patricia Churchland in 1990.[57] Suppose that, instead of trying to show that symbol manipulation and awareness are unrelated, the man in the room were attempting to demonstrate, falsely, that light and electromagnetic waves have nothing to do with each other. He could achieve this by darkening the room and pumping a magnet up and down at arm's length, thereby generating electromagnetic waves of a very low frequency. The pitch-darkness still permeating the room would let him infer the desired conclusion. The catch here is simply that to generate any light (that is, electromagnetic waves of a frequency perceptible to the eye), the man would have to speed up his pumping rate by about fifteen orders of magnitude—or just about the same factor by which he would have to accelerate his paper shuffling in order to generate an observable awareness in the Chinese Room.

What of Searle's claim about the difference between simulations and the real thing? What difference is there between a computer performing operations that appear to endow it with awareness, and the same computer simulating a storm in a weather-forecasting center? Is the computer's awareness any more real than the storm? Well, for one thing the computer's intelligence certainly is. The "essence" of a storm is to whirl around raindrops, air molecules, and lightning, which the computer surely isn't doing. However the "essence" of intelligence is to manipulate information, and this is precisely what the computer does. Now is the "essence" of awareness also the manipulation of information? No one really knows, but this argument doesn't show us otherwise, any more than the Chinese Room does.

Indeed, neither Searle nor other proponents of weak AI have provided a definition of the nature of awareness that would satisfy anyone. For their position begs the question: If the manipulation of information by a digital computer cannot generate true awareness, then what does it take to do it? Searle himself answers that "cognition is a biological phenomenon: mental states and processes are caused by brain processes. This does not imply that only a biological system could think, but it does imply that any alternative system, whether made of silicon, beer cans or whatever, would have to have the relevant causal capacities equivalent to those of brains."[58] What these mysterious causal capacities consist of exactly, Searle refuses to specify, except to add the further claim that parallel computers or artificial neural-net systems would not possess them either.

On this point, an argument proposed by the philosopher Zenon Pylyshyn raises puzzling questions on the boundary between biological and electronic systems. In this thought experiment, Pylyshyn supposed that as a person is talking, more and more of her brain cells are replaced by electronic components with identical input-output functions, until the entire brain consists of integrated circuit chips. In all likelihood, the person would keep on acting in just the same way except that if Searle is right, she would at some point have lost her awareness and stopped "meaning" anything with her words. Somehow that doesn't sound quite right.[59]

Daniel Dennett drew yet another argument for strong AI from the theory of evolution: if systems with and without Searle's mysterious causal powers for awareness can't be told apart by their behavior, then they have exactly the same survival value. In this case, evolution would have absolutely no incentive for developing such a superfluous mechanism as "true" awareness. If so, how did it come about and maintain itself? Indeed, if some chance mutation had robbed our ancestors of awareness, we would be acting exactly as we are now, claiming to be aware, except we wouldn't be.[60] Wouldn't that be downright silly?

Assuming, then, that one can define "true" awareness in terms of pure functionality, what are the specific functions a system should embody in order to qualify? If the proponents of strong AI are right, these would be the same functions that would let a machine pass Turing's test. But can some of the philosophical steam generated in the weak-strong AI debate allow us to point out some feature of those mechanisms? In other words, can philosophers provide engineers with design guidelines for conscious machines?

Perhaps they can. As I've hinted, philosophers draw a strong link between awareness and the ability to give meaning to symbols. Indeed, John Searle rests his whole case on the fact that symbols manipulated by a computer acquire a meaning only when interpreted by humans. In Searle's parlance, symbol-manipulating computers possess syntax but no semantics. Hans Moravec, for his part, was trained as an engineer, and his bottom-line conclusions on machine awareness are entirely opposite to Searle's. Yet Moravec agrees with Searle on this point. "Today's reasoning programs require humans to front for them," Moravec admitted to me. "They need somebody to tell them what's in the world, and to act on what the programs say. In essence, to give meaning to the abstract symbols the programs manipulate." Moravec however sees a straightforward engineering solution to this philosophical quagmire: "If we could graft a robot to a reasoning program, we wouldn't need a person to provide the meaning anymore: it would come from the physical world." Moravec also believes that some kind of sensory reference to the world is required for a machine to pass Turing's test:

> Human communication is only language on the surface. What's below the language are these perceptual models of the world containing mythical allusions and pictures and emotions. There is much nonverbal machinery in our heads. A really insightful Turing judge would be probing for these things, asking, "How do you feel about this," or "Here is a situation, how does it strike you?" And I believe there is no more compact way of encoding that machinery than something analogous to the actual structures we have in our brains, including our brain stems and limbic systems.

And, indeed, since the mid-1980s, for reasons not unrelated to the issue raised by Moravec, an influential faction of the AI research world has concerned itself with coupling their programs ever more closely with the physical world. Moravec belongs to this school of thought, and Rodney Brooks of MIT is its most colorful figure. He, in fact, takes the extreme position that reasoning is not necessary for intelligence, and that mechanisms akin to those of reactive or inborn behavior in animals suffice to explain it. His tiny six-legged robots, which mimic much of the behavior of insects, are Brook's first step in proving his point of view.[61]

In respect to design rules, philosophers also point to self-consciousness as another crucial component of awareness. Daniel Dennett notes, though, that "self-awareness can mean several things. If you take the simplest, crudest notion of self-consciousness, I suppose that would be the sort of self-consciousness that a lobster has: When it's hungry, it eats something, but it never eats itself. It has some way of distinguishing between itself and the rest of the world, and it has a rather special regard for itself."[62]

That kind of bodily awareness has been instilled into robots from the beginning. For example, Marvin Minsky's first hand-eye robot pretty well had to have it, in order for the camera to tell the hand from the blocks it was manipulating. When the robot thought it had identified its hand in the image, it would move it slowly in front of the camera to see whether it really was itself (see chapter 4).

A higher level of self-consciousness corresponds to introspection: the ability to inspect some of one's own mental states. Most AI programs require this ability in various degrees, if only to justify their recommendations to their users. All medical expert systems, starting with MYCIN (see chapter 6) have had the ability to explain why they prescribe a certain treatment: for this, they have to examine their own motivations by retracing their reasoning. As a further example, Terry Winograd's SHRDLU could explain why it had manipulated certain blocks: after exhausting a long list of intermediate objectives, it gave "Because you asked me to" as the ultimate justification to a sequence of moves (see chapter 4). Marvin Minsky, for one, turns the table around and points out that we could design machines better equipped than our brains to monitor themselves, thus making them more conscious than we are.[63]

Perhaps the major disappointment of AI research to those of us schooled in traditional Western values was to evacuate the substance out of intelligence: if you take apart an AI program and try to trace the source of its cleverness, you'll see it disappearing into a maze of interlocking subprocesses, in themselves all quite trivial. Recent forays into cognitive architectures indicate that our consciousness and sense of identity may well participate in the same disappointing evanescence. When I came across the following paragraphs in *The Society of Mind*, I couldn't help but feel that Marvin Minsky was letting me down. These sections appear far apart in the book, but together make up devastating left-right punches against consciousness and identity:

[W]hat we call "consciousness" consists of little more than menu lists that flash, from time to time, on mental screen displays that other systems use. It is very much like the way the players of computer games use symbols to invoke the processes inside their complicated game machines without the slightest understanding of how they work.[64]

[O]ur brains appear to make us seek to represent dependencies. Whatever happens, where or when, we're prone to wonder who or what's responsible. ... But what if those same tendencies should lead us to imagine things and causes that do not exist? Then we'll invent false gods and superstitions and see their hand in every chance coincidence. Indeed, perhaps the strange word "I"—as used in *"I just had a good idea"*—reflects the selfsame tendency. If you're compelled to find some cause that causes everything you do—why, then, that something needs a name. You call it *"me."* I call it *"you."*[65]

Consciousness as an arcade player and the "I" as a figure of speech, indeed! In person, Minsky wouldn't give me any reprieve. When I asked whether he thought the self is an illusion, he answered:

It's a complicated set of illusions, there are many different processes involved in it. One is just the inference of correctly recognizing that people are also objects. So at first the I is a body, and when the child is about two years old it usually gets this wonderful idea that it is a person. . . . By the time you're adult, you have a dozen different concepts of self.

But Minsky considers these concepts as illusory, superficial explanations of processes too complex to be accounted for in a convenient way. Daniel Dennett, the very same philosopher who believes that machines can have emotions, dismayed me by agreeing with Minsky:

I call the "I" the Center of Narrative Gravity. Now consider the center of gravity of this object [a stapler on his desk]. It's not an atom, it's not a particle, it's an abstract point in space. But you can use it to explain why the stapler tipped back when I tilted it: because the center of gravity was still over a point in the supporting base. Now, are centers of gravity real? In one sense they are, in another sense they aren't. That is, the center of mass of an object is just a very convenient way of organizing what would otherwise be hopelessly messy data, but where would we be without it! Now the self, the "I," is the center of narrative gravity for [our discourse about human beings]. And, boy, does it help! We see a human body flinging about, talking: it would be incomprehensible, just so much [random] motion, if we couldn't posit a sort of center of narrative gravity, that agent who is responsible for these words the body is uttering. It's a mistake to think this agent is a point in the brain. There's not any one thing in the brain which is the self, and it's a mistake to look for the President in the Oval Office in the brain. But the idea of there being a single agent is a wonderful way of organizing psychology.

True enough, I reflected, but being useful doesn't necessarily make a figure of speech wrong. Instead of trying to follow the self down through its myriad mechanisms, why not try to trace it in the more constructive upward direction? As the separate notes of many instruments blend into a single symphony, couldn't the self truly exist as an entity emerging from the concerted activities of a multitude of agents? I put the question to MIT's Minsky and to Tuft's Dennett. Minsky wasn't encouraging:

> That's what many people believe, and I don't think so. I think the self just doesn't emerge. In fact, we make it: it's not an emergent; it's an afterward construction. In general, emergents don't produce anything that clever. . . . If it were an emergent, you couldn't attach properties to it, like "I'm handsome." Because to do so you need a small representation, a little symbolic "I" that you can attach properties to. You can't attach them to a vague emergent: it doesn't have any hooks. There is something generally wrong with the idea of emergence: if a beehive starts to swarm in a certain direction, that's an emergent, but you can't attach to it. It can't store any knowledge because it doesn't actually exist: it's just a solution to a differential equation.

Although Daniel Dennett was willing to label our feeling that there's "somebody home" in our heads as an emergent phenomenon, he hastily qualified his opinion:

> Some people use the term *emergence* in a mystical way. Emergent properties are supposed to be very mysterious and special properties that you can't explain with science. [Dennett privately calls this view "Woo Woo West Coast Emergence."] I mean *emergent* in the much more pedestrian, but I think more useful, sense of a convenient level of description. In this sense, a traffic jam is an emergent phenomenon: many different people make semi-independent decisions to get into their cars, and suddenly you get the "traffic jam" phenomenon. And you really want to talk about it at that level. Don't try to "reduce" talk about traffic jams to talk about behaviors of just individual motorists, even though that's all they really are. A traffic jam is just one god-awful combination of individual motorist behaviors. But it is also emergent in the sense that there are regularities about traffic jams which are best described at the "traffic jam" level.

As it turned out, then, what Dennett means by calling the self an "emergent entity" is in fundamental agreement with Minsky after all: the concept of self is a convenient figure of speech—so convenient as to be indispensable.

On this question, I found more solace in Pittsburgh than in Boston. Somehow, I had expected to meet the less down-to-earth attitude in the ivy-green Tufts campus and MIT's lofty hallways, the latter once described as a cross between the Pentagon and the Vatican.[66] Yet I was surprised and somewhat comforted by the attitude of researchers in Carnegie Mellon University, Andrew Carnegie's utilitarian former Carnegie Tech. At least, they didn't make any case for reducing human awareness to a figure of speech. I put the question to the psychologist James McClelland who, with a group of San Diego colleagues in the mid-1980s, resurrected neural-net research by publishing a two-volume collection of groundbreaking papers called *Parallel Distributed Processing.*[67] PDP showed how, by extending Rosenblatt's Perceptrons to many-layered structures, they could be made to overcome most of the failings Minsky and Papert had pointed out in their 1967 book.[68] Bearded and relaxed, John McClelland is a slow speaker. He enters a state of deep reflection when a question requires consideration. Eyes closed, he tends to hold his head with both hands and, slowly intoning, appears painfully to force his answer through as if hauling it out of a deep well. He discussed the Society of Mind's relevance to neural networks:

> Minsky's notion that the I is an illusion misses the point that there is a fundamental coherence to the mental state. There are two hundred and fifty million people all going about their daily business in the United States, and you don't get a sense of a collective mind out of that. So I think the Society of Mind is missing something, which might be that the states of a neural network are actually quite coherent. When you have large numbers of simple computational elements that are massively interconnected with each other, they can't just go about doing whatever they damn well please. What each one does is basically governed by what all the others are doing at the same time. So the human mind is much more coherent than the distributed population of a country.[69]

Over in Carnegie Mellon's computer science department, Allen Newell made similar remarks. I tried out on him a notion of mine that one could draw parallels between Soar and Minsky's Society of Mind. Weren't Soar's complicated IF . . . THEN rules somewhat equivalent to Minskyan agents, all interacting in their own specialized ways?

"I think you're just plain wrong," Newell answered in a vehement manner all his own, which I found disconcerting after McClelland's slow pronouncements.

A production—a rule, if you will—is much too simple to be a Minskyan agent. Minskyan agents are in fact little homunculi all by themselves. Also, productions don't directly communicate with each other: they just all look at the same data. The only way a production could talk to another is by making a change that the other could perceive in this common data: this places a lot of restrictions on communication between productions. So the Society of Mind and Soar are profoundly different in two ways. First, the grain size of the agents is much larger in the Society of Mind. Second, the ability of agents to communicate with each other is much smaller in Soar. It's absolutely unclear to me how you can produce in that Society of Mind any sort of integration.

The paradigm on Soar is much more how you get the communication rate high enough so that you don't have the problem of separate little agents knowing separate different things. A community of scientists, all with telephones in their hands, cannot produce an integrated intelligence. The available rate of communication between them relative to what they've each got in their memories is too small. The problem of producing beings like you and me, which are highly integrated, requires an architecture that's very responsive to that communication problem. I believe that Marvin is on the wrong side of this chasm, in the wrong region of the communication space with respect to the integration issue. Marvin's view is that there are a lot of ways in which we are dis-integrated, unintegrated. And he is certainly right, but I think that he just doesn't even come close to accounting for the huge amount of integration that we have.

I don't have any objections to being shown wrong. If making awareness more than an illusion required the victory of an army of productions marching in lockstep over a rabble of individualist agents, I am all for it.

AI AND RELIGION

Most of us are perfectly willing to accept scientific explanations in all matters physical, yet feel uncomfortable with the idea of an essentially material origin for our minds. One reason, as I've said, is the potential erosion of human values inherent in this belief, which led some researchers to dismiss consciousness and feelings as illusions. Another of our discomforts with the concept arises from its potential conflict with religious beliefs. Doesn't the materialistic view of the mind contradict the existence of an immortal soul, different in substance from the body? Perhaps, but as I shall show, this opinion doesn't clash with Western religions.

These verses, for example, from the Old Testament,[70] seem to imply that Judeo-Christian tradition is not inconsistent with an intimate association of mind and body:

Your dead will come to life, their corpses will rise; awake, exult, all of you who lie in the dust, for . . . the land of ghosts will give birth. Isaiah 26:19

Of those who lie sleeping in the dust of the earth many will awake, some to everlasting life, some to shame and everlasting disgrace. Daniel 12:2

I prophesied as I had been ordered. While I was prophesying, there was a noise, a sound of clattering; and the bones joined together. I looked, and saw that they were covered with sinews; flesh was growing on them and skin was covering them. Ezekiel 37:7–8

And you will know that I am Yahveh, when I open your graves and raise you from your graves, my people. Ezekiel 37:13

And this from the New Testament:[71]

It is the same with the resurrection of the dead: the thing that is sown is perishable but what is raised is imperishable. . . . Howbeit that was not first which is spiritual, but that which is natural; and afterward that which is spiritual. 1 Corinthians 15:42–46

These verses strongly suggest bodily resurrection in the afterlife, which indicates a belief that the mind cannot exist independently of the body;

and Christianity preaches that a human being's soul and body are sub-stantially united.[72] Resurrected Christians live after death not as disem-bodied spirits, but in a new body—as the Gospels claim that Christ resurrected the body. The soul as an entity separate from the body is an influence from Eastern faiths, and Christian religions do not make it a tenet of their doctrines.

Other religions do, however, erect soul-body dualism as a dogma. The doctrine of reincarnation, for example, does indeed appear to conflict with the materialistic view of the mind, since for the same soul to live in several successive bodies implies a dichotomy between body and soul. And then there are the near-death experiences, as reported by Raymond A. Moody[73] and a growing body of other researchers. Patients revived after approaching or reaching a state of clinical death recount strange experiences, claiming to have stepped out of their bodies and observed the efforts of the medical team to bring them back to life. Many recall traveling through a dark tunnel and emerging in a bright and peaceful light where they meet deceased friends and relatives. These accounts cannot be dismissed lightly. For one thing, there are too many of them: a Gallup poll performed in 1982 indicated that as many as eight million adult Americans may have undergone a near-death experience.[74] Further, NDE subjects are often in possession of knowledge they could not have acquired by conventional means: many who were unconscious during the revival attempts can afterward describe those attempts in great detail. Some subjects can even provide faithful accounts of events occurring in other rooms, which they claim to have visited in their disembodied state.

It is still possible to argue that the AI view of a materialistic origin for the mind is not incompatible with near-death experiences or reincarna-tion. First, no dualist would deny the essential unity of mind and body during life: otherwise, why would damage to the brain (such as a head wound or cerebrovascular accident) result in damage to the mind? The problem is what happens at the moment of death, and the AI folklore contains interesting speculations on that very issue.

These concern the gradual and eventual replacement of brain cells by electronic circuits with identical input-output functions. Although the philosopher Zenon Pylyshyn used this thought experiment as a philo-sophical argument in 1980,[75] the idea had been the subject of intense debate in the AI grapevine for some years beforehand, under the name of "downloading." In 1988, Hans Moravec gave a dramatic description of the process in his book *Mind Children.*[76] Assume you are a critically ill patient in a twenty-first-century operating room, says Moravec in substance. A robot surgeon equipped with micromanipulators opens your skull under local anesthesia and sets to work on your brain. You remain fully conscious. The surgeon first concentrates on a small clump of neurons located in the periphery of your cortex. He severs the nerve-cell connections linking this assembly of cells to the rest of your brain, and replaces them with two-way connections. These link your brain either to the clump or to an artificial model of it made of microscopic components, which the surgeon proceeds to build. He reproduces the structure of the cell clump in the artificial model, and tunes it so as to duplicate the exact behavior of the biological clump. By activating the switch that connects the rest of your brain to either the original cluster or its electronic replica, you can verify for yourself the accuracy of the modeling. When you no longer feel any difference between the two positions of the switch, the biological clump is removed, and the surgeon sets to work on another clump. In a large number of similar stages, he replicates your entire brain in an artificial construction; yet at no point do you experience an interruption of your awareness. At the end, your mind has been transferred to an artificial neural net.

This (so far) imaginary process strongly suggests the possibility of transferring a mind from one support to another. Near-death experiences and the survival of the "soul" after death could be explained by a similar transfer process. In this case, the receiving support would not be matter as we know it, and the transfer would involve mechanisms we do not yet understand. It is certain, though, that some kind of support would be required for the information and organization that constitutes our minds. Indeed, in this regard, some of those who underwent near-death experiences insist that in the disembodied state, they were not pure spirits; rather, they inhabited another kind of "body" which, though invisible to living humans, did possess a definite structure.[77] This is, of course, pure speculation to show that religious beliefs, and particularly the belief in survival after death, are not incompatible with the idea that the mind emerges from physical phenomena.

11

HOW MANY BULLDOZERS FOR AN ANT COLONY?

It should be clear by now that intelligence defies the heartiest effort to define it. Yet it is equally clear that an essential ingredient of an intelligent system is its ability to manipulate information. Indeed, this is the only function common to brains and computers. The essential ingredients of information are bits. Just as matter ultimately consists in atoms, all the information that reaches us through our senses can be broken down into little pieces of "yes" and "no." These particles make up any conversation, scenery, spanking, or caress we experience. To see how this is possible, consider the spectacle of the sun setting into the ocean. Delicate hues play on clouds and water; a royal alley of gold leads to the sun, and waves twinkle like stars in the reflected light. Yet our brain, which lets us appreciate this beauty, has no direct contact with it. Locked up inside our skull, our thinking organ is just as removed from the sea as would be a computer shuttered in the basement of the Pentagon. In order to appreciate this scene, our brain must reassemble the raw elements of data that our senses supply it as nerve impulses corresponding to yes or no bits of information.

In the case of sight, perception happens as follows: The cornea, a transparent lens on the front of the eye, projects an image of the scene onto the back of the ocular globe. In this respect, the eye works much like a camera, where a lens projects the image on photographic film. The retina, which plays the role of film in our eyes, is a sheet of nervous tissue covering the back of the ocular globe. It contains many light-sensitive nerve cells called "receptors." Some of these receptors tell other neurons, through a sequence of nerve pulses, how bright the projection of the image is at the location of the receptor. Some other receptors signal how much red, green, or blue the image contains at their locations. (All the delicate hues of pink, orange, and indigo in the sunset correspond to varying mixtures of these three primary colors.) The image is turned into discrete pulses in two ways: first, spatially, by becoming an array of dots, with each dot corresponding to the location of a receptor cell; second, in the domain of brightness and color. Colors become mixtures of discrete hues, and brightnesses translate into more or less rapid firings of nerve cells (the larger the brightness, the faster the firing rate). In similar ways, nerve cells in our ears turn the sounds we hear into pulse trains. Sensor cells in our skin do the same for sensations of heat, cold, and pressure.

Thus, our brain is constantly bombarded with trains of pulses telling it what our senses perceive. Intelligence has to do with our ability to manipulate these bits of information and use them to make sense of the world. Animals manipulate the information from their senses in a manner that does not let them generate more than immediate reactions to perceived threats or inducements. We, however, get more mileage out of the information we extract from our surroundings. We can refine it into *knowledge* and use it for long-range planning and abstract reasoning.

Nevertheless, our brains do work on the same principles as those of animals. Dissection shows that any differences between our brains and those of most mammals lie in the size of the structures present and in their complexity. Thus, one can logically conclude that our capabilities for planning and abstract thought are built on the same basic skills that allow animals to react to their environment. Further, this extra power probably stems from the additional abilities for processing information that the more elaborate structure of our brains allow.

Thus, intelligence has to do with how much information one can manipulate in a given time (say, per hour or per second). Since one measures information in bits, one aspect of intelligence, in its most elementary form, is bits per second of raw processing power. If one compares the brain to a telephone switching station, this power would correspond to the number of phone lines the station can switch in a given time. Of course, there is more to intelligence than raw power, but let us not worry about this aspect of the problem right now. Let us just recognize that no matter how superbly structured and programmed the switching station is, it will simply not do its job if it can't process enough connections in a given time.

In the first part of this chapter I shall try to answer the following questions: How many bits of information can the brain manipulate per unit of time, and how close do our present computers come to this benchmark? I shall then look back at the history of computer development, and try to extrapolate how long it will take for our machines to rise to the level of our brains. Finally, I shall acknowledge that raw processing power is not the only ingredient required for intelligence, and discuss whether software powerful enough to emulate the human mind can be developed for the computers of the future.

THE HUMAN CORTEX AS CIRCUIT BOARD

The exposed human brain is certainly not an impressive sight: about three pounds of soft, jellylike, grayish tissue. This mushy texture long prevented anatomists from cutting the brain into clean thin slices suitable for microscopic observation. Further, the uniform color of the material kept them from seeing structural details. It was only in the late nineteenth century that different hardening and coloring processes, among them the still-used Golgi stain, enabled anatomists to study the fine texture of neural tissue.

It came as no surprise that, like other organs, the brain is made up of cells. They come in varying sizes and shapes, and neuroanatomists called them "neurons." One feature of the neurons, however, did astonish early researchers, including the Spaniard Santiago Ramón y Cajal and the Italian Camillo Golgi, developer of the staining process. They were astonished by the intricacy and extensiveness with which these cells connected to each other, each sending out literally thousands of tendrils that link it to as many other neurons. They make up a network of such Byzantine complexity that Golgi, for one, firmly believed it formed one continuous tissue extending throughout the brain. He defended this point of view, called "reticularism," in his 1906 Nobel address.[1] Later observations—as science progressed in its usual tedious, prodding path—proved him wrong. Indeed, as we will see, the gaps between neurons play a crucial role in the workings of the brain.

Early in this century, researchers started to distinguish elements of order in the apparent chaos of brain structure. First, investigators realized that, although neurons can differ from each other as much as a honeysuckle bush does from a sequoia tree, they come in a small number of different shapes and sizes. Only seven kinds of cells with similar exterior morphology exist throughout the cortex (the largest structure in the brain). Moreover, cells very similar to these make up the brains of mammals, from the higher primates down to the puny mouse. The nuts and bolts of our most abstract thoughts are thus the same ones that support the mouse's instinctive reactions.

The cortex, the brain structure responsible for our perceptions, motor responses, and intellectual functions, is a thin sheet of nerve cells, about six millimeters (a quarter of an inch) in thickness. Its surface area is that of a square twenty inches on a side: roughly the space that IBM's first personal computers used to take up on a desk. To fit it into our skulls, Nature has had to fold the cortex; hence, the furrowed look of the naked brain. The cortex comprises six distinct layers, caused by an uneven distribution of neurons of different types. The thicknesses and makeup of the layers vary over the area of the cortex. However, except in the visual part, the number of cells per unit area remains fairly constant at 146,000 per square millimeter. (Multiplying this figure by the area of the cortex produces an estimated total number of neurons in it of about 30 billion, or 3×10^{10}.) The average distribution of types of cells throughout the cortex also remains constant. The density of cells per unit area is likewise the same for all mammals. What distinguishes us from the mouse is the area of our cortex, and not the kinds or density of the cells in it.

To an engineer's eye, the cortex presents striking similarities with a structure universally present in computers: the printed circuit board, a flat, thin support holding integrated circuit chips, which serve as processing elements. The board allows the chips to talk to each other through conductive paths buried in distinct layers over its thickness. Strangely enough, a typical board comprises six layers, just like the cortex. Each chip on the board is made up of microscopic elements (transistors, capacitors, diodes) of about the size of a neuron, and performs a specific function within the computer. It turns out that one can also divide the cortex into chips, after a fashion. Experiments conducted on animals by probing the sensory cortex with a microelectrode can detect firing impulses from single neurons. If you move the electrode to and fro, in a direction perpendicular to the surface of the cortex, you will meet only nerve cells that process one kind of stimulus. For example, if buried into the visual part of the cortex, the probe may only respond if you shine a light in the left eye, and not on the right. However, if you probe in a nonperpendicular direction by slanting the needle, you will meet neatly separated regions which respond to the left or the right eye, alternatively. It is as if the cortex were divided horizontally into different *modules,* each extending throughout its depth.

Why did Nature design our cortex as a circuit board? We can conjecture that, in both brain and board, it is necessary to separate the closely interacting processing elements from the cabling connecting faraway parts of the network. As in a circuit board, the cabling of the brain lies underneath the computing units. Large neurons present in the cortex, called "pyramidal cells," send nervous fibers downward, out of the cortex, toward other regions of the brain or cortex. Covered with an insulating greasy layer of myelin, these fibers make up a whitish tissue, very different in appearance from the gray color of the cortex itself. Only about one cell in a hundred extends beyond the cortex, yet the volume of white matter in the brain is larger than that of gray matter. Having the "white cables" travel through the gray matter would have interfered with the direct communication between adjacent gray cells: this is probably why Nature kept them out of the cortex. The similarity in structure between the cortex and a circuit board may have yet another reason, related to ease of design. It is already quite complicated to lay out the chips and connecting paths on a flat surface. Doing it in three dimensions would be a combinatorial problem of monstrous proportions. Perhaps Nature was no more willing to face this difficulty than human engineers are! Whatever the reason for it, one cannot contemplate the convergent evolution of brain and circuit boards without wondering.

Let us go back to the basic building block of the brain, the neuron. Its anatomy can tell us more about the amount of computing performed by the brain. Extending from the cell body of the neuron are different appendages. On the input side, the dendrites look like the branches of a tree. They connect with sensor cells, or other neurons, and receive their electric pulses. The meeting points between dendrites and appendages of other cells are actually gaps, called "synapses." Although researchers had long suspected their existence, they could not prove it before the invention of electron microscopy in the 1950s. Direct observations of synapses then struck a final blow to the theory of nervous system continuity, or reticularism, which Golgi had defended until his death in 1926.

When strong enough, nerve pulses can cross the synaptic gap between cells. Pulses usually increase the electric potential of the receiving cell, which encourages this cell to generate a pulse of its own, or "fire." Sometimes, however, arriving pulses decrease this potential, and discourage the receiving cell from firing. The cell body sums (or otherwise combines) the membrane potentials and fires at a rate that is an *s*-shaped function of this sum. The pulses generated by the cell body travel along a wire-like appendage of the neuron called the "axon." It may be short or very long: axons sometimes bundle together to form a nerve, which can be as long as your arm. They also form the "white cabling" of the brain I have mentioned. The axon eventually branches out into another treelike network of fibers. These pass along signals to other cells, or activate muscles.

The input and output ramifications of the neuron are its most striking characteristic. Extrapolations from counts on electron micrographs show there are from 10^{14} to 10^{15} synapses in the cortex. This means that, on the average, each neuron receives signals from about 10,000 other cells and sends its own messages to as many others. In this respect, the brain differs markedly from electronic circuits: on a circuit board, one component typically makes contact with fewer than five others. However, what computers lose in connectivity, they make up for in speed. In the brain, the pulses traveling from neuron to neuron are local imbalances in salt concentrations moving at relatively low speed— exactly how fast depends on the diameter of the nerve fibers, but it is in the order of 100 feet per second. This is why sensory stimuli take from 10 to 100 milliseconds to reach the cortex. In a computer, however, pulses moving from chip to chip are pure electromagnetic fields. They travel at two thirds of the speed of light—about seven million times faster than nerve pulses!

The Brain's Processing Power

Although our knowledge of the brain's structure is progressing, it remains sketchy. Recently bold-hearted scientists have tried to use this scanty evidence to estimate the amount of raw computing going on in the brain. I shall examine two such tries—by Jacob T. Schwartz at New York University and by Hans Moravec at Carnegie Mellon University. It will come as no surprise that these professors achieved wildly different results. In fact, the very divergence of these estimates is a good illustration of how little we really know about the brain. Yet, because of the accelerating pace of technological development, even guesses as poor as these provide useful estimates of when we will be able to beat Nature at brain building.

I shall start with the work of Jacob T. Schwartz, a professor at NYU's Courant Institute of Mathematical Sciences.[2] Schwartz estimates that since a neuron can fire about one hundred times per second, it sends information to other neurons at a rate of about one hundred bits per second. The amount of information processed inside the neuron is, however, much larger. To decide, every one hundredth of a second, whether to fire, the average neuron has first to combine all the signals it receives from ten thousand other neurons. The cell must then establish whether this total is large enough for it to fire. The decision to fire is complex, especially since some of the messages received from other neurons may inhibit firing rather than promote it. Schwartz estimates that to reach this decision, the neuron must—for each firing, at each synapse—perform the equivalent of calculations involving forty bits. Since these operations involve intermediate steps, let's assume that to simulate them, we have to manipulate one hundred bits of information per synapse, per firing. It is then a straightforward affair to work out the overall amount of information processed by one neuron in one second: 100 bits per synapse per firing per neuron $\times$ 100 firings per second per synapse $\times$ 10,000 synapses per neuron $=$ 100 million bits per second per neuron. From there, we get an estimate for the processing power of the entire cortex: 100 million bits per second per neuron $\times$ 3×10^{10} neurons in the cortex $=$ 3×10^{18} bits per second of information processing. Extrapolating to the entire brain, a total of about 10^{19} bits per second results. Thus we have our first estimate: Schwartz's estimate of brain power: 10^{19} bits per second.

Schwartz, however, puts a very strong qualifier on this figure. He points out that computation rates, many orders of magnitude lower, might suffice to represent the *logical* operations of the brain. Indeed, it is fairly safe to suppose that what really matters to our thought processes is not the internal mechanics of a neuron, but how it looks like to other neurons. This may be considerably more simple than the neuron's internal structure would show. Thus, stick-figure models of neurons may be enough to simulate the brain accurately. Moreover, our brain is built to accommodate a very large amount of redundancy, and much of its complexity may be due to the constraints limiting its growth and evolution (see the section entitled "Avoiding Nature's Mistakes" later in this chapter).

Hans Moravec calculates the information-processing power of the brain in a manner different from Schwartz's, concentrating on the retina, the paper-thin layer of nerve cells and photoreceptors in the back of the eye.[3] After performing a certain amount of massaging on the information provided by the receptors, the nerve cells send the results of their calculations to the brain through the optic nerve. Such is the structure of the retina that, in effect, it makes up an extension of the brain. Yet, contrary to most brain structures, the functions the retina performs are well understood. They are similar to those of artificial vision systems processing TV images. Of course, we know exactly how much computing power these operations require. Further, and by no coincidence, the resolution (number of receptors) of the fovea, the high-resolution part of the retina, is about equivalent to that of a television image. On that basis, Moravec estimates the processing power of the retina at about one billion operations per second.

He then proceeds to extrapolate from this figure the computing power of the entire brain, and is faced with a dilemma. The brain has about 1,000 times as many neurons as the retina, but its volume is 100,000 times as large. Which figure correctly accounts for the larger computing power of the brain? We can attribute the excess volume to three factors. First, the connections between neurons in the brain are longer: the required cabling takes up most of the space in the brain. Next, there are more connections per neuron in the brain. Finally, the brain contains nonneural tissues, such as the greasy myelin sheath of many nerve fibers. Of these three factors, only one—the excess of connections per neuron—entails an increase in complexity. Following Moravec, we shall thus take the Solomonic decision of awarding the brain a computing power 10,000 times that of the retina. There follows an information-processing capability on the order of 10^{13} calculations, or about 10^{14} bits, per second—which is Moravec's estimate of brain power.

According to him, the brain is thus 100,000 times slower than

Schwartz's estimate of 10^{19} bits per second. Moravec's procedure has one crucial advantage: since it sidesteps the need to rate the unknown factors required to adjust Schwartz's estimate, we no longer need to guess the effective ("stick figure") processing power of an individual neuron, and we are also spared the need to assess the unnecessary complexity with which evolutionary constraints burdened our brains. Moravec's estimate probably lies closer to the truth.

How do computers fare compared with the processing power of the brain? Not well at all. The fastest computer in existence in 1989, the Cray-3, could process only 10^{11} bits per second. By Moravec's estimate, it is therefore 1,000 times weaker than the human brain, or at about the level of the laboratory rat, with its brain of 65 million neurons. Further, the Cray-3 is much too expensive to serve in AI work. Researchers must make do with machines like the Sun-4 workstation. At 2×10^8 bits per second, the Sun-4 is 500,000 times less powerful than a human brain— but it would evenly match the 100,000 neurons of a snail!

The Size of Human Memory

As any computer enthusiast knows, the rate at which a given machine calculates is but one measure of its power. Another crucial question is, How much information can the computer hold in memory? Similarly, in respect to the human mind, how well we *think* is very much a function of how much we *know*. As it turns out, it is possible to estimate how much memory we need to function in the world.

There are three ways to go about this.[4] One is to repeat what I have just done for the brains calculating power: that is, examine the brain's anatomy and work out estimates from hardware considerations. A more direct method is to survey the knowledge of an average adult. Third, we could also deduce how much adults know from how fast they can learn, and how long they live.

To start with the first approach, what happens in our brain when we remember something? Scientists are still very much in the dark about memory. They know plenty about the periphery of brain operation, such as how we perceive the world through our senses, or how we activate our muscles to act on the world. What happens between, though, remains very much a conjecture. Researchers do not really know how we settle on one particular response to a perception, or how we store the memories on which we base this decision. One can make plausible assumptions, though. Consider a mouse that flees in response to the snarl of a cat: this instinctive reaction mechanism probably resembles our own. First, sensor cells in the mouse's ears send nerve pulses to other neurons in the brain, which start firing in response. Thus, an activation pattern of neurons assembles in the mouse's brain. Eventually, further waves of activation reach the neurons controlling the legs, which send the mouse running.

The snarl of the cat thus corresponds to an activation pattern of neurons in the mouse's brain. A human brain would represent it in the same way. What happens, then, when we remember the snarl of a cat in response to another cue, such as the sight of an angry cat? It is logical to assume that at least some of the neurons that fired when we last perceived a snarl become active again. By this token, a memory is also a neural activation pattern.

Can we identify in the brain the elements responsible for eliciting such an activation? What can cause a certain group of neurons, among the billions present in the brain, to become active all of a sudden? All evidence points to the synapses, these microscopic gaps between neural terminations. The average neuron makes contact with ten thousand others through synapses of various conductivities. A synapse can let through more or less of the nerve pulses emitted by the source neuron. Of the ten thousand downstream neurons, those that are more likely to fire in response are those with the more conductive synapses. Thus, one can assume that highly conductive synapses connect the neurons representing an angry cat to those representing the snarl of a cat. Hence, *synapses* probably store the information causing the recall of memories.

If this is the case, we can estimate the capacity of the brain for encoding memories as follows: Assume that the degree of conductivity of a synapse can have sixteen values. Then the synapse can store four bits of information, since a sequence of four bits can represent the numbers from 0 to 15. The 10^{15} synapses in the brain would then hold room for 4×10^{15} bits.

Does this mean the brain can actively use that many bits of information? Probably not. Synapses are just the mechanism that induces patterns of neural activation in response to stimuli or other activation patterns. There are, however, many fewer neurons than synapses. If a memory item corresponds to a group of neurons firing together, then there will be fewer such items than synapses also. In the past few years, AI researchers have devoted much attention to studying networks of artificial neurons. Experimental results, as well as mathematical theory, show that the number of bits one can store in such a net depends on the number of neurons in it. Further, an artificial net can store typically fewer bits than there are neurons in it. For example, a type of neural net known as a Hopfield network, containing n neurons, has a storage capacity of $0.15n$.[5] Assuming a similar ratio for the brain, we end up with a capacity of about 15 billion bits of usable memory.

A more direct way of finding out how much each of us knows is the game of twenty questions. It involves two people. Player A thinks of a subject, and player B must find out what it is by asking questions that A will only answer with yes or no. A wins if B can't guess the subject in twenty questions or less. The target item must be clearly identifiable and known to both players. Facts that one must deduce from other primary information—like "300,286 is the product of 482 by 623"—do not count. It turns out that a good player can usually come to the answer in just about twenty questions—this fact reveals how many items you have to sift through. The first question lets you partition the other player's memory in two groups: the items corresponding to a yes answer, and those corresponding to no. The next question divides one of these groups in two again, and so on. Since twenty partitions are required for you to end up with a single fact, the number of items to choose from is clearly 2^{20}, or about 1,000,000. We must, however, correct this figure because players will typically limit their choices to neutral items of mutual knowledge, such as Marilyn Monroe or the Eiffel Tower. Items known to A only, or too sensitive for casual evocation, will be avoided. It is not farfetched to multiply by another factor of 2 to compensate for this effect: we are now up to 2,000,000 items.

A knottier issue concerns the hidden information corresponding to unconscious or informal knowledge. For example, how much memory does a recipe for how to tie shoelaces, say, take up? What about the knowledge that enables us to interpret body language or voice inflections in people? Such knowledge will never appear as an item of the game. Psychologists consider that most of our mental activities occur at the unconscious level. Are most of our memories, then, also unconscious? Not necessarily. There are two reasons for a mental activity to remain unconscious: one is the repression of painful associated emotions ("I desire mother, but it is forbidden!"); the other reason, which probably accounts for many more cases, is that there is simply not enough room in a person's awareness for all his or her mental activities.

For example, consider your behavior when you drive while carrying on a conversation. You will steer left or right, watch for other cars, slow down or speed up as required without any conscious decision. That does not mean you are ignorant of the technicalities of driving, such as being able to stop by stepping on the brake pedal. You are simply too busy to pay attention to these details. Thus, much unconscious behavior uses facts that could come to full awareness in the twenty-question game. So one might reasonably argue that it is not most of our memories that are unconscious, merely just a good deal! Let us boldly "guesstimate" again and multiply by 2 to compensate for this effect: we are now up to 4,000,000 items of memory in a typical human being.

An important question remains. What I have called an "item" represents much more than one bit. Typically, it would correspond to an entire data structure: if player A says, for example, "I was thinking of Abraham Lincoln," to how many bits of information does the Abraham Lincoln structure correspond? First, the sequence "Abraham Lincoln" contains 14 characters plus 1 blank, which probably requires the equivalent of 15 bytes of storage space in the brain. (A byte is a set of eight bits. Digital computers use bytes to represent characters.) The sequence of phonemes corresponding to the pronunciation of the name probably requires about as much. A few years after history classes, most of us probably remember only a sketchy biography of the sixteenth president: "He taught himself law and campaigned against slavery as a congressman. His election as president caused the Civil War. Lincoln led the North to victory, emancipated the slaves, and delivered the Gettysburg Address. He was assassinated in 1865 when attending a play." Our internal representation of this information is certainly very different from the string of 265 characters it takes to write it down or store it in a computer. There is no reason, however, to believe that this representation requires much less information in our brain. If this were so, we would probably have developed a much more concise language and writing. Similarly, if we needed much more information than a few hundred bytes to store these characters, it would mean that our speech is much more efficient than our thinking: this is hard to believe. Let us, therefore, accept that this short biography of Lincoln requires the equivalent of about 265 bytes of storage in our brain.

What about Lincoln's face? Even if we cannot visualize him precisely in our mind's eye, we could certainly recognize his photograph among thousands of others. How many bits of information does one need to store a recognizable likeness of a face? Not much, it turns out. Digitizing TV images into arrays of numbers, with varying resolutions, shows that an image of 20 × 20 pixels (dots) of varying gray levels provides a very recognizable likeness. With 4 bits per dot, it would take 200 bytes to store such a picture, which brings the size of our Lincoln data structure to 495 bytes.

Yet another item of our internal representation of Lincoln is the emotional aura surrounding assassinated presidents. Something in the data structure must be pointing to the emotions *awe* or *sadness*. We also require pointers to other items of information: the words *congressman* or *Civil War* refer us to other complete data structures. Further, we know that Lincoln was a *man* and a *politician*—categories that contain still more information we could tap if required. We can estimate how many bytes these relations require by reference to conventional computer data bases. Some kinds of them, such as relational data bases or the data structures used by the LISP language, require pointers between data items. These pointers serve much the same purpose as in our human memory model above. In a LISP data structure, as much memory is reserved for the pointers as for the data. Thus, let us assume that in the brain, the amount of memory required for relationships between items is equal to the memory required for the data items themselves.

How much information does one require, finally, for the data structure "Abraham Lincoln"? The 495 bytes above correspond to about 4,000 bits of direct information. Doubling this for pointers brings us to 8,000 bits for one item of the twenty-question game. For the 4 million items of information the game and other considerations show we hold in memory, the total would amount to about 32 billion bits. In view of the number of approximations and informed guesses involved, this figure is in surprising agreement with the one we got by assuming 0.15 bits per neuron, or 15 billion bits.

Looking at how we gather information provides yet another cross-check on this figure. As witnessed by the helplessness of a newborn baby, little of our abilities are inborn. From walking to the multiplication table, we must painfully learn virtually all of the skills and knowledge we need to function in the world. Yet, in less than twenty years, we learn the basic material that will support us in life. If we knew how fast we can absorb new information, we could estimate how much of it the basic "human knowledge base" contains.

Certainly, we do not commit new information to memory as fast as our senses feed it to us. The optic nerve, for one, sends over a hundred million bits of information to the brain at each second. Yet we interpret and remember only a tiny fraction of this information. Consider what happens when you try to learn a page of text by heart. At a resolution equivalent to 300 dots per inch, your optic nerve can send over to the brain the entire contents of that page in about a second. Yet, if you glance at an open book for a second, and then read the page in your mind's eye, you'll discover that you can retain at most a few words. Further, rather than corresponding to the image of the words, which requires thousands of bits per letter to describe, your memory will be a highly abstracted description of the words you recognized while glancing at them. This encoding probably requires only a few bits to store a letter. In fact, experiments on memorizing random sequences of syllables show that we can absorb new information only at rates of 100 bits per second.[6] Learning at 100 bits per second means memorizing an entire page of text (about 400 words) in less than three minutes. At that rate, an actor could memorize his lines by reading them once aloud! Yet, even at such breathtaking speed, twenty years of continuous learning at eight hours a day would let you digest only 21 billion bits of information.

We thus have four estimates of the size of human memory. Assessing it from the number of synapses leads to the astronomical figure of 4 million billion bits. But as I pointed out, there is no direct link between the capacity of synapse storage and the number of explicit items represented in the brain. The other three estimates give much lower values: considerations from the number of neurons in the brain and neural-net theory yield 15 billion bits. The twenty-question game leads to 32 billion bits. Learning rate and duration give 21 billion bits. The relatively close agreement of these three estimates lets one hope that the true value lies somewhere in the range they define. Thus, I shall settle on 20 billion bits (2.5 gigabytes) as an estimate of the memory capacity of the brain. This is still a lot of information: it corresponds to slightly more than a million pages of printed text or twenty-five hundred books like this one.

Can computers store that much information? Yes: by this yardstick, our machines have already overtaken us. The Cray-2 supercomputer, built in 1985, already had 32 billion bits of memory capacity.[7] Even AI research budgets allow scientists to come close: As I write this the typical AI workstation offers about 200 million bits of random access memory, only 100 times less than the brain. As we saw in chapter 10, the Cyc common-sense knowledge base will be slightly smaller than our estimate of the brain's capacity (about 8 billion bits instead of 20). AI workstations will have that much random access memory at their disposal in a very few years.

REACHING HUMAN EQUIVALENCE

Despite this essential parity of the board in memory, machines still process information thousands of times more slowly than we do. Because of its myriads of cells working together, it is tempting to compare the brain to an ant colony. Computer engineers, by contrast, like to think of their mainframe machines as bulldozers shoveling about mountains of data through their unique central processors. Puny bulldozers, indeed, since it would take thousands of them to match the ant colonies in our skulls. This fact certainly explains many of the disappointments AI researchers have met. If the brain is a jet engine, they have to make do with the equivalent of bicycles! Rather than uncover the secrets of intelligence, they must spend most of their time programming around the weaknesses of their machines. Yet, as we will see next, engineers are closing the gap. Soon computers will approach the power of the human brain.

The Fifth Generation of Computers

As I described in chapter 1, the first generation of computers was based on vacuum tubes: orange-hot filaments glowed in various computing machines from 1943 to 1959. Even during those years, progresses in vacuum tube technology cut down by a factor of 20 the time needed to perform an addition. The gain in cost per unit of computing power was even more impressive. In 1943, it cost about one hundred dollars to buy one bit per second of computing power. Sixteen years later, it cost less than ten cents.

Generation 2, based on single transistors, accounted for most of the new machines until 1971. From then on, computers were built out of integrated circuits: silicon chips containing first a few, then hundreds, and finally thousands of microscopic elements. These formed the third generation of computers, and lasted until 1980. Around that year, it became possible to put the entire processing unit of a computer on a single chip; and by 1985, these microprocessor chips contained up to a quarter of a million elements. Thus was born the fourth generation of computers.

As I write this in the early 1990s, the upward spiral of computer power continues to accelerate. If you've ever pondered the economics of replacing an aging computer, you may have felt a kinship with the future space traveler faced with the star ship problem: a better time to leave is always next year, because by then ships will be faster and will get you to your destination sooner. So is it with computers: next year's machine will, on the average, offer 50 percent more computing power than this year's for the same price.

Let me demonstrate this tendency by focusing on two particular machines.[8] The Zuse-2, the first electromechanical computer built in 1939 by the German engineer Konrad Zuse, would then have cost about $90,000 in today's money and took 10 seconds to multiply two numbers. By contrast, the Sun-4 workstation, introduced in 1987, cost $10,000 and can multiply two numbers in 400 nanoseconds.

In raw power, measured by the admittedly crude yardstick of the time required to multiply two numbers, the Sun-4 is 25 million times faster than its predecessor. If we consider the cost per unit of computing power, the comparison is even more favorable: it costs 225 million times less to do a multiplication with the Sun-4 than with the Zuse-2.

To understand the staggering implication of these figures, consider what similar improvements would bring about if applied to automobiles. A luxury car of 1938—say, a Cadillac—would have cost about $30,000 in today's money. It reached a top speed of 60 miles an hour and traveled about 15 miles on a gallon. If today's Cadillac were to the 1938 car what the Sun-4 is to the Zuse-2, it would cost only $3,300, run at twice the speed of light, and do 3 billion miles per gallon!

No fairy waved a wand suddenly to induce these changes. If one compares the relay-activated Zuse-2 to electronic machines introduced right after it, and progresses on to the Sun-4, there are no abysmal drops in price or dramatic improvements in performance anywhere. Instead, a smooth evolutionary process is revealed. Hans Moravec courageously calculated and plotted the cost per unit of computing power of sixty-seven consecutive machines, starting with a mechanical calculator built in 1891.[9] These data points clearly show that, for the past sixty years, the cost of computing has decreased by a constant factor of 2 every other year. As a result, the mainframes of the 1970s are the desktoppers of today. Mainframes of the 1960s can now be stored in a single chip, and many electronic wristwatches contain more elements than these early machines did!

Although speculators who blindly extrapolate stock prices from past tendencies usually end up broke, there are sound arguments for applying yesterday's trends to tomorrow's computers. The staggering progress of the past sixty years stems from profound structural processes in the evolution of the technology. Since we are also dealing with the behavior of an industry, many of these arguments are economic rather than technical. In fact, one could even argue that the brain-equivalence problem is essentially economic. Indeed, it is now technically possible to build a machine with the raw computing power of the brain if we connect a thousand Cray-3 supercomputers. And, even though managing such interconnection, and programming it to perform like a human brain, would still raise formidable problems, the raw power would be available for us to experiment with. Before we could do that, however, we would have to deal with the small matter of finding the twenty billion dollars this network would cost. Thus, the problem of building human-equivalent hardware boils down to reducing the cost of processing power to affordable levels. Let me examine, therefore, why we can expect the sixty-year-old trend of decreasing prices to continue.

First, the regularity of the price curve is to a large extent the result of a self-fulfilling prophecy. Manufacturers, aware of the tendency, plan the introduction of new products accordingly; hence, the absence of drastic jumps in cost/performance ratios. Manufacturers introducing a product well ahead of the competition in performance have no incentive to reduce prices drastically, even if their costs are much lower. Instead, they pamper their profits for a while, until competition forces them to accept lower prices.

Competition in the computer industry is fierce. To grab a share of a $150-billion world computer market, companies are willing to scramble.[10] For this reason, the number of people developing computers, and the resources at their disposal, are on the rise. Since computer companies spend a constant fraction of their revenues on research and development, resources for computer development grow about as fast as the computer market. They pushed ahead by about 15 percent a year since 1960. Since this growth is much faster than that of the economy, it will slow down eventually. (Otherwise, a continued growth would lead to the impossible situation of everybody developing or building computers.)

Even if the number of people and dollars devoted to computer development levels off, the total intellectual resources available for this activity would still increase exponentially. The reason is because computers are largely designed by other computers. Indeed, involving computers in their own conception can have dramatic effects. Consider the problem of planning the paths of metallic traces on printed circuit boards. In the assembled board, these traces connect together the pins of different processing chips. They all have to fit in the restricted area available on the board, while maintaining minimum distances between each other. Typically, out of a multitude of possible combinations of paths, only a few satisfy these constraints. In the 1960s and 1970s, laying out these paths with pencil and ruler used to take months. Worse, changing a design after testing took almost as long as starting anew. Nowadays, computers perform this layout automatically in a matter of hours. Similar gains occurred in implementing those procedures at the chip level: integrated circuits are also designed by computers. In coming years, computers ever more powerful will gradually assume a larger part of the design and construction of their successors, further speeding up the design (or, reproduction) cycle.

Economies of scale should also speed up the rate of price decrease. Present computers typically contain only one, expensive, processing unit. Future machines, however, will consist of thousands, and eventually millions, of identical components which will serve as both memory and processors. Manufacturing these components in such large quantities will give rise to economies of scale comparable to those affecting memory chips. Since there are many memory chips in a computer, they come down in price faster than processing chips. Recognizing these new economics, the Defence Advanced Research Projects Agency's goal is to double the pace of cost reductions in coming years. From now on, instead of multiplying computer power by 2 every other year, the U.S. government hopes to double it every year.

But even if we devote ever larger resources to perfect electronic components, little will result if Nature does not cooperate. Aren't we coming up against basic natural barriers that cannot be overcome? Won't we soon bump our noses on the outer limits of computation?

One obvious boundary which is fast approaching is that of the speed of light—or, as computer scientists sometimes call it, the "Einstein

bottleneck." In a conventional computer equipped with a single processing unit, information flows between the memory and the lone processor
as acrobats leap-fly between swings. Infinitesimal errors in timing lead
to murderous crashes, and the entire computer must operate like a finely
tuned clock. Indeed, an electronic master clock beats time, keeping all
components in lockstep, as inexorably as the drummer in a slave ship.
For the drummer to be obeyed, there should be time enough for one
beat to reach all parts of the computer well before the clock generates
the next beat. The beats are electric signals: the fact that they travel at
close to the speed of light, but no faster, imposes a limit on the
frequency of the clock. For example, the time required for light to travel
the entire width of a 1-foot-wide computer is 1.76 nanoseconds. This
implies a maximum clock frequency of 568 million beats per second
(megahertz, in computerese). Many desktop computers already operate
within a factor of 10 of that limit.

One solution would be to keep walking on the path we have so
profitably followed since the invention of the transistor: that of miniaturization. Let us make the components smaller and cram them in a
tighter space. The signals will have less distance to travel, and we can
then speed up the clock. Alas, this approach immediately bumps into
another obstacle: heat removal. Not only will crowding more components in a smaller space increase the amount of heat generated, but
having them work faster will also increase the heat generated per component. Evacuating this extra heat to keep the machine from melting
down requires—when it is possible at all—technological prowesses.
These complications just about cancel any economies brought about by
the extra miniaturization.

Nature herself presents us with a way out of this blind alley. Compared with those of computers, the components of the human brain
operate at positively slumbering rates. A neuron will generate about a
hundred impulses per second, as opposed to the millions of beats per
second of a digital computer's clock. Being so sluggish, each neuron
generates little heat, and we normally find it easy to keep a cool head.
Yet the brain packs about a thousand times the information-processing
capability of our fastest computers. This performance is due to the
different mode of operation of the brain.

Von Neumann's suggestion to break up computers into a memory
and CPU initially offered obvious advantages. It was possible to manufacture the memory as many low-cost, identical cells. Since there was

only one processor, it could be as complex as required to perform a variety of logic or arithmetic functions. Further, this layout reduced programming to the relatively simple task of issuing a single string of instructions to the one processing unit. Unfortunately the setup also introduced a major inefficiency that became clear when memories increased in size to billions of bits. So huge is the memory of a modern computer that it compares to a large city. (Indeed, it could store the names and addresses of all inhabitants of New York or Los Angeles.) A metropolis of its own, the processing unit also houses millions of elements. The problem is that only one road connects these two cities. It takes a long time to travel and allows through only a very few bits of information at a time.

Running a program in a von Neumann computer is like moving your household from New York to Los Angeles in the following senseless fashion. First load the TV set in your car, drive it to Los Angeles, and come back. Take the laundry iron, drive to LA, and come back. Take the coffee pot, drive to LA, and so on. To enhance matters a bit, computer manufacturers have recently tried flying between the cities instead of driving: they have improved the data-transfer rates between the parts of a computer. Unfortunately, this amounts to speeding up the circuitry, and soon bumps into the speed-of-light and heat dissipation limitations I mentioned. An analogue to the obvious solution—using a van to move all items of your household at once—is not possible in a computer. Each bit transferred between processing unit and memory requires a separate wire, and there is a limit to how many of these can be crammed into a machine. Over the years, manufacturers have widened the data path from 8 bits at a time to 32, and even to 128 for large machines. A small improvement, this amounts to little more than letting you move both the coffee pot and laundry iron together!

In terms of my two-city analogy, the solution adopted by our brains is surprising. It consists in moving Los Angeles to New York and mingling the two cities so you don't have to move at all! In my fable, New York plays the role of processing unit, and Los Angeles, that of memory. It turns out that the brain does not make any difference between these two functions: each neuron serves as both a memory and a processing unit. In the brain, there is indeed no clearly identified center of intelligence comparable to the processing unit of a von Neumann computer. For example, despite long-standing efforts, neurologists have never been able to pinpoint a center of consciousness. The neurosurgeon Wilder Penfield suggested it might lie in the combined action of the upper brain stem and various areas of the cerebral cortex.[11] Others pointed out that consciousness has to do with laying down and recalling memories of the world. In this case, the hippocampus, which plays a central role in this function, might qualify for the seat of consciousness.[12] Another view holds that our ability to communicate makes up our most obvious mark of intelligence: the language centers, located in the left cerebral cortex, would then bear the palm.[13] There are, however, good reasons to believe that, although various parts of the brain handle special functions, consciousness arises from the combined operation of many areas.[14] Likewise, long-term memories, once laid down, appear distributed throughout large areas of the brain.

What are the advantages of this distributed configuration over the von Neumann architecture? For starters, it allows the brain to perform a myriad of operations concurrently. This is how your brain can analyze the torrent of information your eyes send it (millions of bits per second), and let you instantly recognize what you're looking at. Roughly speaking, your brain separates the image into hundreds of thousands of dots, each separately analyzed by several neurons. A pure von Neumann machine would, by contrast, slowly process each dot in succession.

Computer scientists call "parallel processing" the simultaneous application to a single task of many processors, be they neurons or computers. In addition to the speedup inherent in getting more workers on the job, applying parallel processing to computers offers another potential advantage: it amounts to nothing less than breaking the light-speed barrier. Since processors in a parallel machine work separately, they are no longer enslaved to the drumbeat of a central clock. These semi-independent units could now be made as small and quick as we want them.

Through such parallelism, Nature will allow us to keep on increasing the power of our computers at a steady rate for a long time to come. Eventually, individual processors will reach microscopic dimensions. The emerging science of nanotechnology[15] will soon let us build structures in which every atom plays its assigned role.

By common agreement among computer scientists, fifth-generation machines are those that implement parallel processing in an extensive way. A few of these machines are now in existence: for example, the Connection Machine, built by Thinking Machines, Inc., of Cambridge, Massachusetts, with 250,000 processors. As I said in chapter 8, machines based on neural networks, in which microscopic components will emulate the neurons of our brains, are being contemplated.

Duplicating the Brain's Processing Power

I can now attempt to answer the question raised earlier: How long before we close the gap in processing power between computers and the human brain? I have summarized in tables 11.1 and 11.2 the earlier estimates about the brain's computing power and information-storage capacity.

Since we still know little about how the brain works, different avenues of investigation lead to extremely different results. The two estimates I cited for the information-processing capacity of the brain (table 11.1) differ by a factor of 100,000. My estimates for the memory capacity of the brain (table 11.2) do not fare any better, being six orders of magnitude apart.

Our mightiest computers offer only an insignificant fraction whichever value we adopt for the brain's processing power. How long will it take for the upward spiral of hardware progress to close this gap? Various answers appear in tables 11.3 and 11.4. Despite the arguments for a speedup in the rate of computer improvement, I have taken the conservative view that the sixty-year-old tendency of doubling every other year persists.

I have taken for benchmarks in tables 11.3 and 11.4 the Cray-3 supercomputer, built in 1989, and the Sun-4 workstation, built in 1987.

TABLE 11.1 *Two Estimates of the Computing Power of the Brain*

Argument	Estimate
Detailed modeling of neurons (Schwartz)	10^{19} bits per second
Comparison of the retina with similar hardware	10^{14} bits per second

TABLE 11.2 *Various Estimates of the Information Storage Capacity of the Brain*

Argument	Estimate
Raw synapse storage	4×10^{15} bits
Neural-net theory and number of neurons	15×10^9 bits
20-question game	32×10^9 bits
Human learning rate and duration	21×10^9 bits

TABLE 11.3 *Estimates for the Year in Which Supercomputers Will Reach Human Equivalence*

	Best Case	Worst Case
Processing power	2009	2042
Memory	1989	2023

TABLE 11.4 *Estimates for the Year in Which Desktop Computers Will Reach Human Equivalence*

	Best Case	Worst Case
Processing power	2025	2058
Memory	2002	2037

These tables list the years in which machines of a cost equivalent to the Cray-3 (about $10 million) and the Sun-4 (about $10,000) should reach human equivalence. The "best case" columns correspond to the weaker estimates of brain-processing power and memory in tables 11.1 and 11.2; the "worst case" columns correspond to the stronger estimates.

The large discrepancies between estimates make remarkably little difference on dates. According to table 11.3, if the weak estimate is right, supercomputers will attain human equivalence in the year 2009. If the strong estimate holds, this sets us back only thirty-three years, to 2042! Indeed, if computer power doubles every other year, thirty-three years is all it takes to improve by a factor of 100,000. Also, as is clear in both tables, the roadblock is processing power, since we will always reach the required memory about twenty years earlier. From the first line of table 11.3, supercomputers will attain human equivalence around 2025,* give or take seventeen years. According to table 11.4, desktop machines will have to wait until 2041, with the same error margin.

After these dates, we can expect our machines to become more clever than we are. We have already done Nature one better for all physical abilities of the human body. Our machines are stronger, faster, more

*Recent developments indicate that this date may be advanced: the September 1992 issue of *Spectrum* (the journal of the Institute of Electrical and Electronic Engineers) noted that "engineers . . . expect teraflops machines by 1996. . . . Price estimates exceed U.S. $100 million" (page 40). A teraflops is the approximate equivalent of our weaker estimate for brain power. This power, however, will come at ten times our target price of $10 million. Further, the degree of specialization of these early teraflops machines makes it unlikely that any amount of programming could endow them with intelligence.

enduring, and more accurate than we are. Some of them have sharper eyesight or hearing. Others survive in environments that would crush or suffocate us. Shouldn't we expect to improve upon our mental abilities just as well?

Avoiding Nature's Mistakes

Not only can we build into our machines the strength of our minds, with eventually much to spare, but we can also avoid duplicating the many weaknesses and inefficiencies of our brains. Indeed, when building artificial minds, we enjoy much more freedom that Nature had in building us.

First, we are free of the limitations on material and structure imposed on biological organisms. Living cells must grow, reproduce, repair themselves, and move over to their proper positions in the body early in life. They must constantly absorb nutrient material from their environment and evacuate waste. Most of their internal structure and functions serve these ends. An artificial neuron, however, would not have to perform any of these tasks. Its function would reduce to generating electric signals similar to those of a biological neuron. Thus, we can expect the structure of an artificial neuron to be much more simple than that of a natural one. Further, it could use materials that transmit impulses millions of times faster than protoplasm and process signals that much faster.

Yet another limitation our machines will dispense with has to do with blueprints. Nature's blueprint for our bodies, the DNA molecule, does not contain enough information to specify the connections of each neuron. Instead, Nature must make do with general instructions issued to entire classes of brain cells. What we know of neuroembryology shows that in the early stages of life, brain cells emit filaments that travel through brain tissue. These filaments eventually form the dendrites and axon of the adult cell. They travel more or less at random, until their ends meet cells of a kind that chemically attracts them. The filaments then bind to the cells in connections that become synapses. To understand the limitations this mode of construction places on the brain's performance, consider the following fable, which I have called "Harry's Plight."

Harry, an electronics engineer, has just taken charge of a new computer assembly plant in the remote country of Ogomongo. Harry has accepted a mission no one else in the company wants: to design a computer that the unskilled workers of Ogomongo can assemble easily from component chips. To Harry's dismay, it soon becomes clear that the Ogomongans are incapable of reading a connection diagram. Neither can they tell apart chip models, except by their colors. Since differentiating the pins on the chips is also a little hard for Ogomongans, Harry has to settle for mounting instructions that typically read: "Connect any pin of a green chip to any pin of a yellow chip." It is now Harry's considerable challenge to design chips of a kind that will, when connected in this haphazard way, produce a computer. To increase the chance that compatible pins on different chips will connect, Harry first increases the number of pins per chip. Second, he adds some intelligence inside the chips and decrees that each newly assembled computer will undergo a "running in" period of a month. During this time, each chip sends out, through each of its pins, exploratory, low voltage pulses. It also listens to pulses emitted by other chips. Each pin of each kind of chip emits a characteristic pulse pattern, enabling chips on each side of a connection to check the validity of this link. Specially designed internal mechanisms break off connections of the wrong kind. Connections of the right kind are maintained and strengthened.

Much to the surprise of Harry's colleagues, and somewhat to his own, this Rube Goldberg procedure eventually does produce a working computer. There is only one snag: the machine is a hundred times bulkier and more expensive than a conventional number cruncher. Harry's company wants to close the plant. The Ogomongans, however, feel it improves their international image, and insist on buying it. Since Ogomongo sits on newly discovered oil fields amounting to half the world's reserves, they can well afford to.

This is all fantasy, of course—but any resemblance to existing biological processes is intentional!

In addition to the indiscriminate assembly of its parts, the brain suffers from their lack of reliability. A neuron is a complex, delicately balanced mechanism, and we all lose hundreds of thousands every day. Yet we do not feel any the worse for this loss because the brain compensates for it by having a large amount of redundancy in its circuits. Computers also benefit from redundancy, and engineers are now finding ways to let their machines tolerate minor component failures. Yet they must pay a price: making computers more resilient requires more components. For this reason, building an intelligent machine out of parts more simple and robust than neurons would increase its performance.

The brain evolved through a process of small-scale, local changes spanning millions of years. It embodies many elegant features that an intelligent designer would not disown. The layered, circuit-board—like structure of the cortex is a prime example. Yet the brain's overall architecture expanded gradually, without benefit of advance planning, and it shows. In many respects, the brain is like a Midwestern country schoolhouse turned into a major city high school. It started with a one-room cabin with a wood stove, spacious enough to accommodate the children of the first few settlers. Then came the railway station: the school needed another room to handle the suddenly doubled population. Over the years, classrooms multiplied. To keep a studious atmosphere, workers had to pare precious square feet from each room to set up linking corridors. Later, installing indoors plumbing and electricity required major surgery, which gave the principal a severe headache. When it became necessary to add a second floor on a structure never meant for one, the mayor and the city engineer almost came to blows. The aldermen, leery of raising taxes for a whole new building, finally overruled the engineer and hired a contractor themselves. Twenty years later, congested plumbing and air conditioning, corridor traffic jams, and wavering lights prevented any further expansion of the school. The city council voted the site into a park and erected a new school elsewhere.

Evolution does not have the option of starting over, and our brains still contain the original cabin *cum* wood stove. Lemon-sized, it grows out of the upper end of the spinal cord. The *reticular formation*[16] is in fact the brain of our reptilian ancestors. Programmed to stake out a territory and attack prey or enemies, it holds our darker instincts. Wrapped around the reptilian brain is the *limbic system,* or old mammalian brain: this is the school's second floor. Developed from centers that govern smell in primitive mammals, the limbic system is the seat of emotions. It enabled our warm-blooded ancestors of a hundred million years ago to care for their young. Its programming often contradicts the reptilian brain, and many of our internal conflicts have no other origin. The *cerebral cortex* holds our higher reasoning functions and forms the outer layer of the brain. It talks to the inner parts through many nerve fibers, which somehow coordinate its action with theirs. The cortex has no equivalent in our fictional country school. At that level, a human architect trying to design a better brain probably would have started over.

Our old friend the retina offers a striking example of how Nature evolves impressively elaborate fixes to make up for no longer adequate structures. Evolution hit upon the retina's peculiar layout early in the development of vertebrates, and its unthinking mechanisms later locked it into place. As you recall, the retina includes photoreceptors, which turn light into nerve pulses, and layers of nerve cells that preprocess the image. These cells pack the number-crunching power of a modern mainframe computer. Nature made the early mistake of placing them up front, so light must pass through the cell layers to reach the photorecep- tors. This arrangement put a major design constraint on the data- processing part of the retina: just imagine IBM trying to make their computers perfectly transparent. Yet Nature rose to precisely that chal- lenge in evolving our eyes: the nerve cells in the retina *are* transparent. There is yet another difficulty: the nerve cells' position forces the optic nerve to pass *through* the photoreceptive layer to reach the brain, creating a blind spot in our field of vision. We do not see it because, through more sleight of hand, our brain interpolates from neighboring parts of the image and covers up the blind spot.

"What if it wasn't an early blunder?" you may ask. "Couldn't a constraint we do not realize make this roundabout design the only possible one?" It seems not, because the independently evolved octopus and squid do have their photoreceptors up front. In a classic paper in *Science,* the eminent biologist François Jacob maintained that evolution is not a rational designer but a thinker. He illustrated his point with many more examples of biology mixing slapdash foundations with prodigies of workmanship.[17]

Many find this iconoclastic view of evolution shocking. Indeed, im- perfection in Nature's creations contradicts many an ecologist's view of cosmic order. Personally, I find Nature's ability to make up for its mistakes and keep forging ahead more impressive than the blunders themselves. And who knows: perhaps creating our brains was a crucial step in this self-correcting process? Now that we realize our imperfec- tions, we may help weed them out of the next batch of intelligent beings.

As in our other duplications of natural functions, we will probably discover in building artificial minds that it pays to design a little differ- ently than Nature. Much as airplanes have wings but do not flap them, intelligent machines will operate on the same principles as their natural equivalents, but exploit these principles better. Streamlined, robust, and faster, they may well surpass our minds the way airliners do sparrows.

SOFTWARE: THE STRUGGLE TO KEEP UP

So far I have compared the brain to a telephone switching station and looked only at how fast it can switch lines. I have neglected the fact that the switching station has to be wired to make the right connections. Since there is a lot more to intelligence than simple line switching, it is time to ask this question: If we do develop, in the early part of the next century, hardware powerful enough to process as many bits per second as the brain does, will we be able to program intelligence into this hardware? In other words, will software progress follow hardware development?

If the past is any indication, hardware and software development are closely linked. In general, software needs can provide the motivation for and point the way to appropriate directions in hardware development. Conversely, weaknesses in hardware can not only act as a powerful brake on software development but also divert it into blind alleys. There is no question that the relative inadequacy of early computers hindered early progresses in artificial intelligence. Marvin Minsky recalled for me how early researchers (himself included) would toil for years over a program, only to see it founder over lack of memory.[18] For example, Ross Quillian, the inventor of semantic nets, never could test his theory on word disambiguation simply because the computers of the mid-1960s couldn't hold enough word definitions (see chapter 4). We also saw in chapter 6 that the advent of expert systems had to await the availability of computers with enough memory to hold large amounts of knowledge and the programs needed to quickly sift through it. Early AI work was deliberately performed in toy task that did not require much special knowledge.

This mind-set became so ingrained that researchers didn't always realize that they were programming around their machines' weaknesses instead of addressing the real issues. Consider SHRDLU, the talkative block-manipulating program that made up the wonder hack of the early 1970s (see chapter 4). Carl Hewitt, who invented the PLANNER language used for SHRDLU, pointed out the following to me:

> PLANNER performed so well because, *and we weren't so conscious of it in those days,* by working on only one aspect of a problem at a time it

accommodated itself to the very small machine memories we had then. When it explored possible solutions to a problem, it went down one single branch and only used the amount of storage needed for that one branch. If that solution didn't work out, it would backtrack, recover all the storage, and try another branch.[19]

Despite such craftiness, Marvin Minsky told me, SHRDLU still required a formidable amount of memory by the standards of the time. Without belittling the role of MIT's researchers, I might add, DARPA's financial largesse probably counted as much as their genius in the success of such projects. "The MIT AI Laboratory," Patrick Winston remembered, "took delivery of the first megabyte memory. It cost us a million dollars, a dollar a byte." He added ruefully, "It is strange to think that I carry ten megabytes in my portable PC these days."[20]

Re-examining the history of AI in the light of unrealized hardware constraints can lead to interesting revisions of accepted explanations for why the field took certain orientations. For example, although the demise of neural networks in the 1960s is widely attributed to Minsky and Papert's implacable criticism of Perceptrons in their book of that same title, Carnegie Mellon's James McClelland, a major contributor to the revival of this field in the mid-1980s, suggested an alternative explanation to me. He pointed out that most research on neural networks involves simulating them on digital computers:

> I don't believe it was that book per se which discouraged Perceptron research in the 1960s. I think what actually happened is that the world wasn't ready for neural networks. A certain scale of computation is necessary before simulations show that neural networks can do some things better than conventional computers. The computing power available in the early sixties was totally insufficient for this.[21]

Patrick Winston also believed that hardware limitations have often led researchers to make the wrong turns in their paths towards progress: "We are discovering that a lot of ideas we once rejected on the grounds of computational impracticality have become the right way after all." He explained how conventional robots control their movements by constantly recalculating the control signals they send to their arms. Recent experimental robots, however, can use their increased memories and parallel processors to learn gradually by experience which efforts to exert under given circumstances. "This idea had been rejected twenty years ago," continued Winston, "and a lot of the efforts that went into motion dynamics and the mathematical approach now seem somewhat misplaced. In my view, one of the milestones of AI research over the last five years is the realization that we can do things on vastly parallel computers that we couldn't do before."

However, Winston was quick to point out that hardware progress will not solve all of AI's problems. Raising a cautioning finger, he added:

> Don't infer from what I said that we should just stop software research for twenty years and wait for the hardware to catch up. In fact, I'm a little schizophrenic on the subject of hardware. I'm saying, on the one hand, that the availability of better hardware allows the discovery of new ways of doing things. At the same time, I think we could do a whole lot more with the hardware we've got. In fact, I believe it would take us ten years worth of current software research to do hardware bad.

Minsky was, for his part, convinced that if hardware had constituted a bottleneck until the 1970s, the shoe was now on the other foot: that, in the 1980s, software turned into a millstone around AI's neck: "The machines right now could be as smart as a person if we knew how to program them." Minsky's former student David Waltz later elaborated on this point for me:

> In the old days, machine memories were too small to hold the knowledge researchers wanted to pour into them. Now it's the other way around: you aren't ever going to fill the new machines with hand code. Nowadays almost all research on learning is really aimed at making use of hardware in a better way. Ideally, you should only have to hand-code certain initial circumstances into the machine. You would then feed it experience in some form, which would allow the computer to acquire new knowledge on its own.[22]

CONCLUSION

Thus it would appear that AI software scientists have stepped into seven-league boots too large for them. Their hardware colleagues have outfitted them with machinery they can't quite handle. Will AI software developers, then, remain hopelessly behind? Probably not: throughout the history of computer science, hardware and software development have kept leapfrogging each other. Software developers, periodically overwhelmed by hardware suddenly grown ten times as powerful, soon push it to its limits and start clamoring for more speed and memory. Because of the subject matter's complexity, it hadn't happened before in AI. Yet there is no reason to believe that AI software won't take the lead again, and it may already have happened in areas of AI other than symbolic reasoning. For example, in the Autonomous Land Vehicle project, which fell short of its objectives (see chapter 8), more powerful vision hardware might have made all the difference.

Finally, although most of the AI programs described in this book ran on computers with about as much processing power as a snail's brain, these programs appeared much brighter than any snail. If AI software researchers could cajole that much performance out of such puny hardware, what will they not achieve with machines a million times as powerful?

And, when this day arrives, what may lie in store for humankind? How will we fare in a world containing machines intellectually equal, if not superior, to most human beings is the subject of my next, and final chapter.

12

THE SILICON CHALLENGERS
IN OUR FUTURE

If, indeed, early in the next century, machines just as clever as human beings appear, the question arises of how we will interact with them, and how they will affect our society. Perhaps the new machines will simply relieve us of tedious chores, expand our intelligence, and bring about universal peace and prosperity. But will not the sight of a lifetime of human experience embodied into a few thousand dollars of electronics strike a fatal blow to our self-esteem? Will these machines not create a massive unemployment problem as they replace us first in factories, and then in business, science, and the professions? Even if we do find ways to redistribute the wealth generated by automated factories and businesses, what will be left for humankind to do? Having taken control of our lives through the economy, how do we know that machines will act in our best interests? If such comes about, how do we know that later generations of today's smart weaponry will not take forceful control of our world? In order to bring out these issues, I have drawn up three scenarios which run the gamut from paradise on earth to apocalypse. As we shall see, our future with our silicon progeny will become largely what we make it to be.

THE COLOSSUS SCENARIO

Let's take the bad news first, and consider the worst possible outcome. I have borrowed this scenario's name from the 1969 movie *Colossus: The Forbin Project,* based on a novel by D. F. Jones.[1] It tells how a future United States entombs an intelligent computer (Colossus) into an impregnable vault, and gives it control of the nation's nuclear missiles in the belief that the computer will react to enemy attack faster than any human strategist. As soon as it takes charge, Colossus discovers the existence of its previously unsuspected Soviet equivalent, with which the silicon commodore has more affinity than with its human creators. The two machines soon electronically merge, and the resulting composite digital superpower dictates its will to humanity.

Farfetched, you think? Despite the end of the cold war and the obvious foolishness of ever letting control of the nuclear button slip from human hands, two of the experts I have interviewed fear that we are tottering dangerously close to such a chasm. Their fear stems from the fact that AI research is, at least in the United States, first and foremost a military affair. It all started with the launching of Sputnik in the 1950s: American backwardness in launching rockets generated a crying need for miniaturization, and turned NASA and the military into avid consumers of the first integrated circuits. The chips soon found their way into smart bombs* and missile heads. As a result, the military, through its civilian funding arm of the Defense Advanced Research Projects Agency, became the most ardent supporter of innovation in electronics and computer science. The United States owes its position as a world leader in computer technology, as well as the breathtaking progress in this field since the 1950s, to DARPA's support. Some observers have even commented that the computerization of society is but a side effect of the computerization of warfare.[2] AI departments and laboratories in American universities owe their birth and continued existence to DARPA's funding. Although the agency has a history of stressing open, unclassified basic research, it has in the past several years begun to seek a return on its investment. Starting in 1983, a program known as the Strategic Computing Initiative has focused much AI

---

*"Smart bombs" are equipped with controls that allow the bombs to steer themselves toward their target under the guidance of a computer.

research on three clearly identified military achievements. One of these undertakings, the Automated Land Vehicle, fell by the wayside in 1989 (see chapter 8). The other two projects—an R2D2-like electronic co-pilot known as the Pilot's Associate, and a ship-borne strategic knowledge base called the Battle Management System—seem to fare somewhat better as I write this.

The military may on occasion set its research goals too high; but, as the 1991 Persian Gulf War showed, it can hardly be faulted on field results. The allied forces in the gulf owed their overwhelming superiority largely to sophisticated computer technology. AI played no small part in this success. "Some of the things we did did have a significant impact in Saudi Arabia," Patrick Winston of MIT told me, "but these were not necessarily the things we thought they would be."[3] In addition to cruise missiles and smart bombs, much of the success of Desert Storm stemmed from prosaic AI applications, as Hans Moravec of Carnegie Mellon explained to me:

> Computer mail* grew out of AI: there was a lot of that in use in the Gulf War. Everybody had workstations, even field troops. The American command was coordinated through E-mail: it was a very substantial contribution, but not a spectacular one. The planning and logistics also owed a lot to AI techniques. I mean simple things like: How do you pack a transport plane? How do you physically arrange the supplies? That's a dynamic programming problem, which at one point was considered an AI problem. Also, scheduling is actually an expert-systems problem. You can do simple scheduling using numerical algorithms, but when you face a complicated scheduling problem like the timing and coordination of Desert Storm, you need an expert system to solve it.[4]

It is extremely difficult in AI research, Moravec later complained, to guess which of one's insights will turn into a weapon. Even the most outwardly anodyne ideas sometimes find their way into the war effort. He remembered how he spent part of his youth as a Stanford graduate student looking for ways of making a robot cart cross a cluttered room without colliding with the furniture. Moravec was surprised to find that

*Computer mail (or E-mail) allows computer users to send messages to each other over telephone or radio links, and display the messages on their terminals.

some of his fellow graduate students later went to work for a Lockheed research center in Palo Alto. They adapted his methods to let a cruise missile find its way to its target. Since Lockheed eventually lost the cruise missile contract to another firm, Moravec's technique wasn't used in the Gulf War, but he expects the idea to resurface in a later generation of cruise missiles.

This example illustrates wherein lies the danger: in spite of the desires of many in the AI research community, modern weaponry is constantly increasing its speed and savvy. This evolution, in turn, imposes new, relentless constraints on field combatants, which make them dependent on information and advice provided by machines. The frenzy of modern battlefield activity often leaves the human link in the military control loop no choice but that of blind obedience to its electronic counselors. Daniel Dennett of Tufts University drove the point home to me when I asked him whether he thought that, when machines become truly intelligent in the next century, they might seize control of our weapons systems:

> I think you're looking too far down the line. The dangers will come sooner. Long before we build really serious and complicated intentions into weapons systems, we're already in deep trouble. Consider the movie *Wargames* [1983], where a child hacker almost causes World War Three by breaking into the missile defense system. I think the most chilling part of that movie happens during the opening credits. You see a fire drill of a mock Soviet attack, of which the personnel is informed by computer displays. But it's a serious drill. You're shown that the officers who are putting their keys in the missile launching locks believe that this is the real thing. And there is this one guy who won't turn his key. The conditions are such that he's supposed to turn his key and he won't do it. He's under tremendous pressure, and collapses. The chilling bit is the reaction of the superiors as they go through a postgame analysis of the fire drill. They decide to eliminate the man because he couldn't perform the job he was supposed to.
>
> Well look. If we only give those keys to people who will simply take whatever the machine says and do it, let's not kid ourselves. Throw away the keys and just put a wire in. What role is human judgment playing if it can't stand up against computer judgment? Let's just admit it and not delude ourselves about still having human beings in

the loop. We are already at a point in the standoff between machine judgment and human judgment where it sometimes takes heroic or even pathological chutzpah to say, "Well, I know better than the computer." And this is long before we've got intentions really built into computers.[5]

MIT's Joseph Weizenbaum was of a similar opinion, when asked about the possibility of computers taking control of our armaments:

To a certain extent we have crossed that threshold. For one thing, I believe the eagerness with which the American military jumped into the Gulf War was intimately related to their fascination with computerized weapons. In that sense, the weapons control the behaviors of their owners. As another case in point, consider the shooting of the Airbus in the gulf about a year before the Gulf War itself. An American cruiser thought itself to be under attack by an airplane coming from Iran and shot it down. It turned out to be an Airbus with two hundred and thirty people on board. Had the ship's captain known the plane to be an airliner, he would, of course, never have ordered it to be fired at. One of the reasons for this accident is that the captain didn't have time to gather evidence and evaluate it. He was forced to make a decision, and made the wrong one. What the technocrats learned from such events is that in these cases the weakest link in the chain is always the human being: consequently, the role of humans ought to be even further reduced. I don't think that holds water. The reason that the captain was the weakest link in the chain is just that he had to make the ultimate decision. Had the system been fully automatic, it probably would have made the same decision.[6]

If humans can no longer alter the outcome of such crisis situations, then we have already lost to computers much control over our armaments. The problem for now is that machines cannot be counted on to react any better than a human being under stress, and would certainly perform far worse than a person with enough time to consider the options. The chilling angle is that it is often the frantic rhythms forced upon us by the machines that bring about crises in the first place. Yet if we are not careful, this situation may develop into a much grimmer scenario. As machines become smarter, we may be tempted to give them more control in situations where time is of the essence. We might even extend their dominion over circumstances more complex or without the time limitation of the relatively simple knee-jerk situations considered so far. Assuming that such smarter machines might indeed perform better than time-pressed, or even comparatively inept, humans, we would still be faced with two dangers. The first one we could label the "Hal syndrome," after the paranoid computer in Stanley Kubrick's 1968 movie *2001: A Space Odyssey*. An intelligent computer in control of a space ship bound for Jupiter, Hal turns psychotic and kills the ship's human crew when faced with conflicting mission goals. Such behavior should be expected from early intelligent programs. To see why, consider the parallel I drew earlier between Norbert Wiener's feedback principle, and Newell and Simon's means-ends analysis method (see chapter 3). Feedback, when first introduced into gun-control mechanisms, produced wild mechanical oscillations that initially baffled engineers. They later explained this behavior as a side effect of the amplification of the error signal between the actual and the desired aims of the guns. Means-ends analysis, just like feedback, uses the difference between perceived and desired states of affairs to decide how to reach a goal: this kind of reasoning is frequent in AI systems. One could think of an AI program as a complex network of such interlocked symbolic feedback loops. Just like gun-control mechanisms, AI programs are subject to unforeseen and wild behavior; and the more complex they are, the more vulnerable.

This difficulty is not peculiar to gun control or AI programs. In large artificial systems, stability problems are the norm rather than the exception. Designing a structure that will withstand its own weight or a mechanism that performs its basic function is comparatively easy. The problem is that huge systems tend to amplify small, naturally occurring vibrations to a point where they tear the structure apart. Large bridges are more susceptible to the infantry lockstep problem* than small ones; supersonic aircraft have an unsettling tendency to nose dive and vibrate. The generators in large electric power utilities have a positively unnerving way of going into spontaneous oscillations that can tear the interconnection apart, at times blacking out entire countries. The first machines to approach human intelligence will be incomparably more complex

---

*When many soldiers cross a bridge in lockstep, they can set up resonances that would tear the bridge apart. This is why armies break step when they cross a bridge on foot.

than any aircraft, bridge, or electric utility, and will bring about stability problems correspondingly more difficult to handle.

If AI systems hold true to the venerable engineering tradition of instability, a typical encounter with the phenomenon in a new program will run more or less like this: After a series of normal program runs, the computer will suddenly generate wildly inappropriate results. Checking individual program steps will reveal nothing; the engineers will discover no faulty internal connections, and the programmers, no misplaced commas. All individual events within the machine will have remained within specifications. And yet the results of these faultless steps will amount to irrational and imbalanced behavior: madness.

Like bridge builders and electric power system engineers before them, the AI researchers involved will probably be taken by surprise. They will have devoted a great deal of thought to the instability problem beforehand, and probably weeded the obvious failure modes out of their design. And yet this particular behavior will baffle them at first. After days or weeks of head scratching, a bright young specialist will finally discover how the combination of a specific set of operating parameters resulted in this unique failure mode, and a new chapter will be added to the long (and unending) book on intelligent-system instability. With luck, such problems will be spotted before the program assumes whatever responsibilities its designers planned for it. It may not always be so. We can expect that, in their first decades of functioning, artificially intelligent systems will be much more susceptible to the analogues of paranoid or psychotic tendencies than human beings are. After all, evolution has had a million years to stabilize our design. And yet we remain highly tuned and critically balanced systems: barely measurable deficiencies in neurotransmitters throw us out of kilter; emotional traumas or deprivations lead us to depression or suicide. For a long time, intelligent machines will tend to go mad, just as people do and perhaps even for similar reasons. We will thus have to take into account the possibility of madness and irrationality before handing over responsibilities to future intelligent machines.

Yet if one is willing to consider all the implications, an even more unsettling possibility comes to mind. As I said earlier, an intelligent machine will probably develop its analogues of human feelings. In order to deal with the world efficiently, it will also have the ability to learn new knowledge by drawing its own conclusions from events. (To see why, consider two household robots: one doesn't recognize your friends as they come to visit, and is unable to inform them of your whereabouts if you are absent. The other learns to recognize your friends' faces, is able to distinguish them from unwanted solicitors, and learns their names if they come regularly; if the robot sees you step out to walk the dog, it can infer that you will be back in a few minutes and tell your friend. Which robot is more useful?) Furthermore, in order to perform its functions properly, a robot will, as I have noted, feel its equivalent of satisfaction with well-done work, and frustration when obstacles prevent it from acquitting itself or its mission.

Such a machine would be constantly absorbing new knowledge from its environment and, in effect, forever modifying itself. Thus, a robot (or missile-control program) certified sane and well meaning at the factory might well go crazy after confronting the contradictions and mysteries of real life. Or, like Colossus, it might come to the conclusion that the original goals programmed into it ("keep the house clean" or "protect thy nation") are inappropriate to its own growth and well-being.

Indeed, programming in good intentions may not turn out to be as simple as it seems. In this respect, the parallel between minds and bureaucracies, which both Herbert Simon and Marvin Minsky have exploited in their theories, provides sobering food for thought. The spontaneous organization modes observed in bureaucracies, contend both Simon[7] and Minsky,[8] provide insightful models of how minds, either natural or artificial, organize themselves. In democratic nations, government bureaucracies are set up with the common good in mind—tantamount, in computer parlance, to "programming in" good intentions. Yet it is a common place that a bureaucracy will inevitably, unless held under very tight leash, grow out of all proportions to further its own power. In former communist countries, bureaucracies, in fact, sucked all life out of the very nations they were supposed to pamper. The reason is probably that in order to stay alive and proficient in a competitive world, any active entity—animal, bureaucracy, or machine—must possess a minimum of self-assertion and aggressiveness. This places it in perpetual danger of running amuck. Thus, a machine that, whether through oversight of its builders or sheer force of merit, acquires some control over human affairs can be expected to strive for more influence.

From these arguments, the Colossus scenario of gross military takeover by computers does not appear so implausible after all. To summarize, there is a real danger inherent in putting AI machinery in control of armaments, especially of nuclear weapons. Yet the unrelenting logic of the battlefield is pressing our military technicians ever further into this direction. Today's artificial intelligences are simply too dumb to avoid the mistakes that fast-paced modern combat situations render probable. With the intelligence that will eventually let them handle these conditions better than human beings, will come other uncertainties about the machines' behavior and motivation. At present, we simply do not know enough about such matters to entrust the power of modern weapons to intelligent computers.

The time to prevent the gradual handing over of military power to machines is now, when we still have a large measure of control over them. For this reason, it may be more urgent to work into disarmament agreements anti-AI clauses than antinuclear ones. The present world-wide reduction in superpower military tensions offers an ideal occasion to do just that.

THE BIG BROTHER SCENARIO

Less sensational, but equally grim takeovers might result from AI power running amuck. Computers, either alone or in cooperation with a human technical ruling class, may come to exert a more insidious and dehumanizing control than gross military takeover.

Such a situation would ultimately result from the potential for privacy invasion which is inherent in modern information technology, and which AI could amplify without bounds. Daniel Dennett had the following thoughts to offer about the matter:

> It is trivially easy now with high tech to eavesdrop on people, simply by recording their telephone or private conversations. There is, however, a bottleneck: you need trained, qualified, secure personnel to listen to those hundreds of hours of tape that you'll gather. It must be horribly mind-numbing: thank God for that bottleneck! I'm sure that in the CIA and other organizations the problem is finding people who will do the work. As Joe Weizenbaum pointed out years ago, AI speech-recognition systems [similar to those investigated by DARPA during the SUR program; see chapter 5] would provide a way out. Long before you can make a speech-recognition system that could

replace a stenographer, you could make a system which could act as a good filter. It could be tuned to listen for a few hundred key words, which would increase the effective surveillance power of any single human monitor by orders of magnitude. By letting the system filter out the tedious bits, an AI-assisted listener could process four hundred hours of tape in, say, two hours. There is some evidence that it has actually happened. In England, certainly, and probably in the National Security Agency, and the CIA.

There are other equally dangerous aspects of AI. Consider its possible application to electronic-funds transfer [which allows you to pay for your purchases by credit or debit cards]. What if EFT proceeds to such a point that paying in cash becomes anomalous? Suppose that it becomes a presumption that if you are paying in cash, you must have something to hide. If the anonymity of cash disappears, we will leave our fingerprints all over the world in machine-readable form, as we do business electronically. It's hard to imagine a better system of surveillance than the elimination of cash. It might be time to start a political movement for the use of cash whenever possible, simply to preserve this political anonymity.

Other opportunities for electronic snooping include the two billion messages that Americans annually send to each other by electronic mail. Largely unprotected over the computer networks, they are a secret police's dream. A young German demonstrated their vulnerability in 1988 by perusing the correspondence of United States military officers worldwide.[9] Yet another danger to our privacy is that of data-base mining and matching by government agencies and private companies alike. These organizations are increasingly drawing together from multiple data sources information about people; and these sources include credit ratings, voters' lists, magazine subscription lists, and lists of customers of various stores, together with their purchases. (Have you noticed how many stores ask for your name and address after you make a purchase?) Telephone bills, bank, medical and criminal records, and even Internal Revenue Service files have also been known to be so pilfered.

The personal records reassembled from these various sources can state what your style of living is, what you eat, where you travel, and whom you associate with. By way of example, in 1988 the files of the credit information company TRW, Inc., contained information on more than 138 million people, including their income, marital status, sex, age, telephone number, number of children, and type of residence.[10] Moreover, companies such as TRW often offer what they call "predictive" services. These are based on statistical techniques allowing the companies to predict a person's likely behavior (such as defaulting on a loan or purchasing certain goods) from the characteristics in their data-base entries. Such procedures force the persons so assessed into arbitrarily defined categories which take little account of true individuality. As this is usually done without a person's knowledge or consent, it opens the door to political repression and social abuse.

Despite attempts by concerned legislators to erect legal barriers against this sort of activity, the U.S. federal government has a long history of using data bases to gather information about its citizens without their consent. As early as the 1960s, it was using IRS files against political dissidents. The Justice Department then created a special computer network to keep track of presumed agitators during the ghetto revolts that erupted across the continent from Washington to Los Angeles. The department later added New Left activists and antimilitary protestors to this target group. At the peak of the cold war, the CIA launched Operation CHAOS to unearth links between American pacifist movements and communist powers. The project at one point handled computer files on more that three hundred thousand individuals.[11] For twenty years, the National Security Agency, with twice the budget of the CIA, attempted to penetrate and control the world communication network. It eventually gained access, with the help of RCA, Western Union, and ITT, to all telegrams received or sent from the United States. The Watergate investigations eventually interrupted these operations in the early 1970s, but by no means brought an end to the government's electronic snooping. According to the American Civil Liberties Union, the number of data matches performed by the government tripled between 1981 and 1984. During this period, eleven cabinet-level departments and four independent agencies carried out 110 computer matching operations, comparing more than two billion records.[12]

The AI researcher Roger Schank raised the issue of AI and privacy in his *The Cognitive Computer*. He facetiously remarked that if worse comes to worse, the means exist for the IRS to find out about a taxpayer's math grades in school and audit people who were poor at addition. Schank then went on to explore a more unnerving possibility:

It used to be difficult to find out who reads what. But today books are ordered from general warehouses of booksellers who tend to keep their records on computer. How hard would it be to determine which bookstores sold the most copies of *Slaughterhouse Five* last year? Change *Slaughterhouse Five* for *Das Kapital* or any other book associated with a clear radical movement and suddenly the idea of surveillance of this kind doesn't seem so far-fetched. And if some bureaucracy decided to audit the property taxes paid by the bookstore in an effort to close it down? How hard would it be to get a copy of every single check or credit card transaction used by the customers of that bookstore? Not hard at all: all this information is on computers. The Nazis began by simply telling Jews to register. After registration, it became more and more difficult to escape the chain of events that the identification process made possible. Access to information is a powerful thing.[13]

Nowadays we are all registered with countless data banks, whether we like it or not. It is not clear that legislation will suffice to prevent government bureaucracy from using AI to acquire, in the interests of efficiency, more control over our lives than any previous dictatorship would have dreamed of.

If the programs that now collate data-base information for their human masters one day accede to intelligence and acquire desires of their own, even nastier possibilities emerge. Unimpeded by legal constraints, such a program (or programs: a multitude of them may come to haunt the computer networks) could gather information at will. They could use this information (such as through blackmailing) to increase their power and resources. If exposed, a program could simply send a copy of itself to another computer in the network, and start over again. Using software viruses akin to those that can wreak havoc in your PC if you insert into it a diskette of uncertain origin, such a program could disseminate enough copies of itself as to become virtually ineradicable.

How could such free-lance programs come into existence? One possible mechanism would stem from the need for secrecy in the development of AI programs: Security considerations make secrecy necessary in military applications, and competitive pressures require it in commercial environments. At present, the single largest impediment to keeping the lid perfectly closed on how an AI program works is the need to thoroughly document the code. This is mandatory to permit orderly development of a program by human beings and for maintenance purposes afterward. Programs that learn by themselves, such as Allen Newell's Soar, could one day acquire target characteristics under loose human supervision, without a person's ever having to write a single line of code. Such programs would most conveniently sidestep human threats to secrecy, since they would be self-developing and self-maintaining. If they come into existence, it will be against the interests of the military or corporate authorities concerned to let human beings monitor their innards too closely. This lack of scrutiny could let deviant harmful traits in a program's "personality" go undetected.

It has also been feared that, in addition to spying upon their human victims, AI programs and robots could deprive them of their livelihood. It might start in the factories where, as has already happened in Japan, fifty-year-old machinists would sweep around the robots that replaced them. As robots become more versatile, most of the twenty-five million Americans working in production plants may fall victim to a similar fate. Their computerized replacements would work twenty-four-hour shifts, never strike or call in sick, and entail amortization and running costs much lower than a human's wages.

The management and service sectors of the economy will be in no position to absorb displaced plant employees, because automation will wreak havoc in these activities also. Conventional computer applications have already drastically changed the nature of clerical and secretarial work. Nowadays most technical and office workers enter their reports or correspondence on word processors, greatly reducing the need for typists. Future speech-understanding systems should eliminate typists altogether. Sales and accounting clerks fare no better: in most stores, recording a sale is now reduced to scanning a bar code affixed to the goods, thus generating an invoice or cash receipt which proceeds automatically to an accounting computer. Gone are the laborious ledger entries of yesteryears! In many organizations, all transactions involving goods or money are recorded electronically: the paperless office will soon be reality. With accounting programs to process the resulting automated records, generating a company's financial statements requires an ever smaller fraction of the work it used to.

What run-of-the-mill programs are doing to clerical work, expert systems will soon do to middle management functions. Middle managers are typically those executives who gather and interpret information for their superiors. Middle managers will also make recommendations on the basis of such information and implement them after their bosses' approval. More and more, computerized management information systems can take care of the data-gathering part of a middle manager's job.

For example, in GM's fully automated Saturn division, upper management can instantly discover through their computers what color or model of car is selling—something it used to take a market analyst three to six weeks to find out.[14] As for the interpretation and recommendation responsibilities of a middle manager, expert systems are beginning to take them over. For example, an expert system could correlate sales with advertising campaigns and formulate adjustments to the ad schedules or even revisions to their contents. Likewise, a scheduling expert system could reorganize production runs to better follow sales. In this case, the system could also, to a large extent, implement its recommendations. In the Saturn type of manufacturing, all parts and supplies are ordered automatically. The expert system simply sends orders for the proper parts to the plant's suppliers, together with a delivery schedule. It is then the supplier's responsibility (or that of their own scheduling expert system) to arrange for the parts to show up at the plant at the right day and hour. After unloading, the plant's automated machine tools and robots process these parts as specified by the plant's scheduling expert system.

Other encroachments into middle management can be found in banks as more and more simple clerks, using expert systems and data bases holding borrowers' financial statements, perform loan analyses that formerly required the services of experienced loan officers. In other industries, specialized technical personnel are also feeling the pinch of AI. Just as GE's DELTA (see chapter 8) expert system allows a technician to carry out repairs to electric locomotives which used to require a highly skilled engineer, Edward Feigenbaum's DENDRAL (see chapter 6), the first expert system ever produced, allows any graduating chemist to perform certain highly specialized analyses that were formerly the province of Ph.D. scientists.

Up to now, though, AI has affected only highly specialized areas of technical and managerial work; and most people have never been exposed to an expert system. In particular, the professional and service sectors, which account for two thirds of the economic activity of Western countries, have been largely immune to the encroachment of AI. There are several reasons for this state of affairs, but they may not keep AI at bay for long.

First, the fact that AI programs still cannot converse in human languages tends to restrict their applicability to areas where they interact with the environment through highly stylized symbols (such as bar codes or inputs from measuring instruments), or in domains so narrow as to be circumscribed by answers to relatively few standard questions. A second and related problem is the common-sense bottleneck, which can lead a medical expert system to such ludicrous behavior as to prescribe antismallpox drugs to a car showing rust spots. As we saw, continued research should gradually erode these restrictions during the next thirty years.

In truth, though, these difficulties should not prevent the immediate application of expert systems to many professional activities: for example, since a medical expert system would operate in a clinic, not a garage, it should have no reason to confuse human and car bodies. The true reasons we don't see more expert systems in everyday life have nothing to do with technology. One of these is the blurring of responsibilities that expert systems entail. Who is to blame for a professional fault involving an expert system? In a medical context, the physician who uses the system, and the hospital that employs him, probably bear primary responsibility for a patient. With an expert system, it is likely that these parties would turn around and sue its programmers, along with the original expert who embodied into it his or her knowledge, and the company that distributed the program. What with lawyers' tendency to sue everyone in sight, such a lawsuit might also target the operators of the computer system or network on which the expert system ran. According to some authorities, even the theoretical scientists who originally developed the computer science principles implemented in the expert system might be held liable under some circumstances.[15]

Medical authorities (or the ruling body of whichever concerned profession) might eventually appoint committees to certify the soundness of the rules in expert systems bearing upon their respective trades. It is not clear, however, how such evaluations could account for interactions between the rules, which might lead to faulty behavior even if all the rules were sound in themselves. The problem would worsen if, as all human experts do, the program were allowed to learn (that is, modify itself) as a result of its experiences. Not surprisingly, all professional and technical people involved in the potential implementation of expert systems in professional activities shy away from such a legal Damocles' sword. In the early 1990s, medical expert systems remain confined to experimental or educational applications: virtually none are put into clinical use.

Doctors also object to expert systems on other grounds. One is data entry: typing in symptoms during an examination would be time consuming and unseemly. Further, since expert systems just embody the knowledge of human experts in the first place, they cannot exceed the competence of individual physicians in their areas of expertise and are thus of little use to them, except perhaps in a watchdog role to prevent errors of fatigue or distraction. Many physicians would resent such scrutiny. Further, even if expert systems were to increase the competence of some physicians in certain areas, such programs would merely automate away the challenging and intellectual parts of a physician's job. Issues of lesser scientific import, like easing anxiety, or the tedious routine of physical examinations ("smelling" the patient, as a surgeon friend put it to me), would remain the physician's responsibility.

Although these difficulties might seem to preclude the penetration of expert systems into hospitals or doctor's offices for the foreseeable future, there is a way in which expert systems may force themselves upon the medical (or other) professions in an undesirable manner. This has to do with the exploding costs of medical malpractice suits. One way to curb them would be to define the standards of good medical practice in a flexible and easily accessible medium, and to provide means for a physician to maintain records that would conclusively show for each patient whether such standards had been followed. Expert systems, acting in a watchdog capacity, could probably accomplish this function. This solution might lead to situations where physicians would make themselves more vulnerable to law suits by not using an expert system than by using one.

After being forced to rely on such an external standard of good practice, some physicians might abdicate their responsibility and blindly follow the expert system's advice. Some observers of the AI scene are already worried that AI might affect our intellectual élites as the industrial revolution affected craftsmen.[16] The last century's proud class of blacksmiths, cabinetmakers, tinsmiths, and assorted glassblowers gradually lost their specialized know-how as they became operators of ever more sophisticated mass-producing machinery. Some of them moved on to become our modern designers and engineers, while a much smaller number kept on working as before, the product of their skills now being considered a luxury. By and large, though, those craftsmen, who used to embody humanity's technical knowledge in earlier periods, have seen their skills taken over by machinery. This process, called "de-skilling," may now threaten to blunt many of our intellectual abilities. The effect certainly is not limited to those élites whose expertise can be embodied into expert systems. When calculators became common-place fifteen years ago, didn't we all stop bothering about manipulating numbers in our heads? Now that your typewriter can check your spelling, isn't there much less pressure to worry about the intricacies of orthography? Such simple applications of computers have already taken away the incentive to learn some kinds of knowledge: expert systems will surely carry on the process at a much higher intellectual level.

Embodying human skills into machines may bring about other adverse effects. Seeing knowledge acquired by one person over several years of hard work bottled up into a few thousand dollars' worth of hardware does not bolster one's respect for the value of human effort. Not only can the availability of machine standins lead to a decline in the number of human experts, but such a discouraging equivalence might reduce the morale of our entire species. The British philosopher and psychologist Margaret Boden compared the potential effect of this mechanistic analogy to the traumatic implications of cremation feared by the Catholic Church in past centuries:

It was difficult enough for the faithful to accept the notion of bodily resurrection after having seen a burial (knowing that the body would eventually decay into the ground). But the image of the whole body being consumed by flames and changing within a few minutes to a heap of ashes was an even more powerful apparent contradiction of the theological claim of body resurrection at the Day of Judgment.[17]

Likewise, an abstract belief in the physical origins of thought processes differs altogether from the gut feeling of the presence of a "meat machine" in one's skull. Seeing our very thought processes routinely replicated in a desktop computer can be expected to undermine our image of ourselves and devaluate our sense of responsibility and individuality.

As AI programs take over many human functions, they may bring about a gradual ossification of society into undesirable patterns. Most people occupying what we now call "white-collar jobs" may gradually see their skill requirements reduced, together with the control they have over their work. Their pay level may go down accordingly, and their jobs turn into insecure, monotonous, and stressing chores. Meanwhile, a group of professionals—scientists and managers lucky enough to commune with the AI programs and participate in high-level decisions—

may see their work enriched, together with their power and living standards. Such social polarization evokes the image of a police state where law enforcement mainly consists in keeping down a massive and permanent underclass.

The élite itself, however, might soon yield to another kind of petrification, brought about by the high cost of developing expert systems. Once in place, there is a strong incentive to use such a system as long as possible, despite progresses in its specialty or changes to the social context in which it is applied. By thinning out the ranks of human experts and scientists, expert systems might also slow down the creation of new knowledge, further reinforcing this intellectual stagnation.

The British philosopher Blay R. Whitby pointed out one puzzling way in which AI could damp human progress even further: so far the pioneering work in AI has been performed by people who, growing up without exposure to computers, introspected some of their thinking processes and implemented them into machines.[18] The home-micro generation, by contrast, may have grown up thinking like computers. After the changing of the guard, can artificial intelligence continue to progress?

THE BLISSFUL SCENARIO: LIFT-OFF?

At one point when doing the research for this book, I contemplated these discouraging conclusions and despaired of the suicidal consequences of trying to instill intelligence into machines. I was at the time interviewing Gerald Sussman at MIT, and his answer to an apparently unrelated question provided my first inkling that there might be rosier prospects for humankind's future after all.

"Centuries from now," I asked Sussman, "what do you think will be remembered as the most salient aspect of AI research in the latter half of this century?"

After thinking a while, Sussman replied at some length:

To understand the answer I'll give you, it's necessary to look back at the intellectual history of humanity. Five thousand years ago, in ancient Egypt, people started inventing geometry. As the myth goes, waters of the Nile overflowed every year and wiped out the land boundaries. It was necessary to reconstruct them for taxation purposes and for telling people where to plant their seeds. So the Egyptians invented geometry and surveying. Later the Greeks understood this vision and gave it a linguistic basis. Their words for describing measurements and relationships among spatial objects provided new ways for people to explain themselves to each other. Because of what these Greeks and Egyptians did thousands of years ago, you can now tell a ten-year-old child that, if you want to make a rigid framework, you build it out of triangles: unlike a square, you cannot deform a triangle. And the child can understand those words, now.

The next breakthrough occurred around two thousand years ago when the Arabs and Hindus developed algebra, which is just a language to talk about generic numbers and relations among them. Because of what they did then, we can now say things like "The following is true of all numbers."

The third advance happened about five hundred years ago. It was the invention by Descartes, Galileo, Newton, and Leibnitz of continuous variables and functions involving them. Calculus, in particular, allowed them to account for motion in mathematics and made modern science possible. And, again, because of what those people did five hundred years ago, you can now tell a child that a car crashed against a tree at thirty miles an hour, and the child at least has an idea of what that might entail. That idea was not clear six or seven hundred years ago.

I believe that the same kind of blossoming is happening in the late twentieth century. We are witnessing a breakthrough in how people can express complex ideas. For example, one can now specify very complex algorithms, or procedures. The earliest algorithms were quite simple; and until recently, no one had ever written down any very complex algorithms because the means for expressing them did not exist. The fun part of such algorithms is that they allow you to solve problems, rather than just specify the properties of the answer. Let's take the idea of square root, for example. You can say: "The square root of y is the number x such that x times x is equal to y." But that statement doesn't tell you how to find x. It is just a mathematical description of a square root. An algorithm for finding x is more complicated to explain; and a few decades ago, mathematicians had trouble getting such ideas across. Now we can easily specify algorithms much more complicated than the calculation of a square root.

You might think it's no big deal, but I found out otherwise while teaching electrical engineering. Typical textbooks about electrical engineering contain plenty of formulas and explanations on how to build sets of equations to solve network problems. These explanations are long-winded, poorly described, and ambiguous. You don't usually understand them on first reading. Further, if you look at how a real engineer finds out from a schematic what a circuit does, you'll discover that hardly any equation writing is done. The engineer performs lots of rather subtle mental operations, and until recently it was nearly impossible to write down what it was that she was doing.

Well, as a professor of electrical engineering, I thought it was my job to figure out what a professional does, so I could tell my students. It turned out that by using the language of artificial intelligence [Sussman was referring to the SCHEME language, a dialect of LISP that he developed specifically for explaining complex procedures], I could explain to my students a simple qualitative method for finding the properties of an electric circuit: it tells them precisely how a professional goes about it. I couldn't have carried these concepts across fifty years ago: the words didn't exist.

I believe that this new capability will have a profound influence on humanity over a long period of time and will be the thing that's remembered many years from now.[19]

Sussman's view of AI as the Great Simplifier of complex ideas seems to carry promise. In fact, AI is a mode of expression, and it is even possible to draw a parallel between the advent of AI and the invention of writing. Indeed, some of the very misgivings expressed nowadays about the effect of AI on moral values were voiced thousands of years ago about writing. In *Headrus*, Plato quoted the Egyptian god-king Thamus as complaining that those who practice writing will stop exercising their memory and become forgetful: they might start believing that wisdom dwells in writings, objected Thamus, when it resides in the mind. Socrates even made a remark that Hubert Dreyfus might not disallow: "You might suppose that written words understand what they are saying; if you ask them what they mean by anything they simply return the same answer over and over again."[20]

The analogy between AI and writing should help dispel our fears about our eventual replacement by thinking machines, for the written word already accomplishes some of this function. In a sense, a book substitutes for its author; and, to take effect, written laws or regulations do not depend on the presence of legislators. AI might affect our culture much as writing did as it gradually took on the role of general-purpose intelligence amplifier in society. By endowing factual reports with new permanence and allowing ideas to be expanded in a degree of detail impossible in a single person's memory, writing made history, mathematics, and philosophy possible. It also allowed commerce and law to take on a new dimension in both space and time. Writing did not simply replace the verbal activities that had gone on before; it increased their power and made new undertakings possible.[21]

A similar power of innovation can be expected of AI, imbued as it is with a magic absent from mere inscriptions. In the world of computers, the power to spell out wishes is tantamount to making them happen. Incredible as it may sound to the profane, this notion is so ingrained into computer scientists that, latter-day spiritualists, they casually talk of *evoking* a program to induce its execution. The aptness of the word is revealed as one types out "Eliza" in luminous letters on a dark screen, and presto!, Joseph Weizenbaum's mischievous creation appears to chat and entertain. Spelling out complex procedures in the limpid language of AI does more than allow us to understand them: it lets a computer execute these orders or control other machinery embodying these complex processes. Not only can AI simplify complex ideas, as Sussman pointed out: it can also simplify complex machines or complex activities. Indeed, Donald Michie, the British dean of AI research, has called AI a remedy to "complexity pollution": "AI is about making machines more fathomable and more under the control of human beings, not less. Conventional technology has indeed been making our environment more complex and more incomprehensible, and if it continues as it is doing now, the only conceivable outcome is disaster."[22] The increasing complexity of our machines and administration is probably the major cause of the economic stagnation affecting developed countries. Solving the problem would require "a complete reversal of the approach traditionally followed by technology, from one intended to get the most economical use of machinery to one aimed at making the process of the system clearly comprehensible to humans. For this, computers will need to think like people."[23]

For example, data bases, although a threat to privacy, have better uses as well. They can be invaluable in aiding a scientist carrying out a literature search, a businessman investigating market trends before launching a new product, and even to anyone planning a vacation or in search of a good deal on certain goods. Anyone with a modem and a personal computer could tap hundreds of data bases if it weren't for one rub. In order to query a data base, one must be familiar with its overall contents and the way these are structured inside the data banks. Further, since many data bases come with their own query languages, one is forced to formulate questions in a different dialect of computerese every time one switches to a new data base. These requirements turn away anyone (and that turns out to be most of us) who doesn't have plenty of time and patience for searching through thick manuals. AI will soon replace the thick manuals with programs that will understand questions in a close approximation of English, and find out what we want.[24]

By the turn of the new century data bases, coupled to expert systems, should make possible services that are much more individualized. Those of us so inclined may have access to our very own personal automated librarian. It may, for example, inquire about what you feel like reading on a particular day, combine these hints with its knowledge of your personal taste, acquired over many such interactions with you, and come up with selections to suit your mood. Should you be interested in researching a particular subject (say, fishing), this librarian will review with you the contents of the various books available and help you select the one most appropriate to your needs. Or, how about a resident silicon chef, available at beck and call to whip up recipes and menus combination, matching your tastes to the contents of your refrigerator or pocketbook? Kristian Hammond's CHEF program came close to these objectives in 1986, but required a hardware platform much more powerful than the home computers of the day.[25] The exponential increase in power of these machines will soon make CHEF an affordable option for most households.

Automated travel and insurance agents are obvious extensions of this concept. Likewise, an expert system acting as a souped-up and interactive home medical encyclopedia might make for a healthier population and even save lives in emergencies. Home legal advisers might inform you of your responsibilities and options in a particular situation, and help you decide whether the expense of consulting a human lawyer is warranted. A home financial planner could help you invest a few hundred dollars with almost as much wisdom and savvy as you might get from a human adviser if you had tens of thousands of dollars to invest. In most cases, though, expert systems will not replace people in their areas of competence. Instead, they will expand the qualifications of their users and simplify their tasks. As I've said earlier, expert systems will not, for many years to come, exceed the savvy of the human experts they model.

Expert systems will also need—for the right information to be entered and their recommendations interpreted—the help and common sense of someone already familiar with their domain of knowledge. Hence, an expert system's main function will be to enhance the knowledge and performance of non-experts. For example, the dearth of medical specialists in remote areas might be alleviated by expert systems allowing general practitioners to perform as specialists. Furthermore, we already have expert systems allowing nurses to perform cardiorespiratory resuscitation in the absence of a physician. Unfortunately, as I've mentioned, such systems have never been implemented in emergency wards: such artificial extensions of the human intellect lie ahead of our present legal means of defining and certifying competence.

In the long run, however, the pattern of our culture should rearrange itself to accommodate them. At the root of the problem lies our understanding and use of innovations in the context set forth by older practices. The earliest automobiles, for instance, looked very much like carriages. It took years for paved roads, mass production, and service stations to turn the automobile into a universal means of transportation; to begin with, early drivers had to make do with few outlets for fuel and a dearth of qualified mechanics. Likewise, AI will have to find its place and shape both itself and its environment in order to bloom. Today's expert systems are akin to the early Phoenician writings that just recorded a ship's cargo and the products of a sale: early scripts did not engender history, philosophy, and mathematics overnight.

To what equivalents of mathematics and philosophy, then, will AI give birth to? Much as the scribe-accountants of early Phoenicia could not have predicted these disciplines, today's practitioners of AI are hard put to answer this question. Donald Michie, for one, made the following prediction:

We can foresee a whole industry arising . . . based around a novel type of industrial plant, the "knowledge refinery," which would take in specialist knowledge in its existing form and debug it, pull it together, carry out creative gap-filling whenever the need becomes evident, and turn out knowledge that is precise, tested, and certified correct. . . . The boon to mankind would be significant if even a fraction of the world's accumulated practical wisdom could be sifted, brought together, and turned into accurate usable knowledge in this way.[26]

Roger Schank, in *The Cognitive Computer,* explored how the new expressive power of AI may affect the sciences and professions. For the first time, we will be able to "develop understanding systems in various particular fields." Stating exactly how doctors go about making their diagnoses and lawyers assess a case, and what kinds of knowledge structure economists use to make decisions, will endow these fields of knowledge with unequaled investigative powers. "AI will encourage a renaissance in practically every area it touches," claims Schank.[27]

The main impact of writing, in addition to creating new ways of thinking, was to revolutionize social organization. The same may well hold true of AI. There are potential positive effects of AI in this respect as well as the negative ones. First, consider the effect of automation in both the blue- and the white-collar worlds. It turns out that blue-collar unions are usually supportive of robotics for two reasons: robots often replace workers in tedious, uncomfortable or hazardous jobs; and most unions acknowledge the need for productivity improvements which robots effect. AI and robotics just might relieve us of the repetitive and tedious parts of our work brought about by the first industrial revolution. Consider loom operators: two hundred years ago, they were skilled manual workers enjoying definite professional respect. Then came the Jacquard loom, which automated the weaving of figured fabrics and reduced the operator's job to one of feeding in materials and activating the machine: this new job description required no education and little skill. Thanks to automation, the loom operator's profession has now taken a turn for the better. I recently visited a carpet manufacturing plant where the looms mostly take care of themselves. Their overseers are engineers with the competence to suggest major design changes to the equipment if needed, and submit written reports to this effect to the company's board of directors. Their eighteenth-century counterparts would envy them their professional status.

But isn't one such loom engineer replacing scores of mechanical loom attendants and hundreds of earlier manual loom operators? Haven't these or their descendants gone on to swell the ranks of the unemployed? Since fewer than 10 percent of the population are unemployed in most industrialized countries, the answer to this question is an obvious no. Indeed, today's workers typically match the combined production of many of their Victorian predecessors, but they also enjoy an incomparably superior standard of living. By and large, producing the additional goods and services consumed by the average person occupies the displaced workers. Also, in spite of the current tightness of the *job* market, there is plenty of *work* to be done.[28] Given enough resources, education, health care, and psychological counseling provide an infinite source of employment for people displaced by AI from other sectors. Even though it may take years to retrain them, and the problem may often not be resolved until the next generation, the key point is that, in the long run, the employment problem is self-correcting. The reason plant engineers are replacing workers by robots, and managers are substituting computers for clerks, is not to reduce production but to increase it. Thus, automated economy will keep on generating an ever-growing amount of goods and services. Since computers don't buy cars, there will still be plenty of supplies around to meet the needs of humans. Those people displaced by automation (or, if retraining is impractical, their offspring) will be available to educate the young, take care of the sick, or help developing countries along the road to the good life. Twice in the past hundred years, we've developed mechanisms for redistributing goods whose production required a drastically dwindled fraction of the population. During the first industrial revolution, manufacturing jobs absorbed workers freed from farm work, which before had occupied 80 percent of the American work force. Agriculture now accounts for only 9 percent of total employment, and the services sector is taking up the slack from an ever-shrinking supply of manufacturing jobs. In the United States, the service sector occupies two thirds of the work force. Surely we will invent means of spreading around the wealth generated by our emerging automated economy. At worst, we will end up with more time on our hands than we can occupy with full-time jobs. If this happens, then we'll just have to learn to place less moral value on work.

Indeed, AI will profoundly influence our values, including our perception of ourselves. We must weigh any fears about the potential de-skilling induced by AI against the fact that AI programs will make their embodied intellectual skills available to humans. Further, it is beyond anyone's natural ability to acquire all the skills one would wish for. For example an

AI-assisted layperson of thirty years hence may well, in the same morning, reach a considered opinion on the authenticity of an antique piece of furniture brought to her attention (thoroughly understanding every step of the reasoning involved), decide (wisely) whether to invest in a new lunar mining venture, and repair her disabled domestic robot. Is such a person likely to feel de-skilled?

As for the negative impact of AI on our self-image, Marvin Minsky has pointed out that the meat-machine aspect of AI could, in fact, boost our self-respect.[29] Seeing our mental powers embodied in mere machines needs not be debasing if one realizes the stupendous complexity of such machines. His fellow AI researchers are in almost unanimous agreement with Minsky. Roger Schank declared:

> Over the past decade AI has caused a wide range of people to ask some very interesting questions about language, reading and understanding. . . . In trying to model our thought processes on computers, we continually learn more about what it means to be human. Far from dehumanizing us, AI research has compelled us to appreciate our human qualities and abilities.[30]

And one of Minsky's colleagues at MIT, Michael Brady, has remarked: "In a real sense, studying AI has precisely the opposite effect [to that of stripping us of self-respect]: one becomes much more appreciative of the ordinary qualities of being human, and de-emphasizes such relatively minor differences as . . . getting the Nobel Prize."[31]

Far from ossifying society, the codification of knowledge into expert systems, and their participation in routine decision making, may smoothe social intercourse. Having an objective, neutral agent recommend actions may eliminate the strife, rivalry, ad-hominem charges, and bickering that mar decision processes in most organizations. On a wider scale, AI could act as an instrument to further democracy. Just as public libraries were initially conceived as an inducement to the democratic process, so will the advent of personal librarian and intelligent data-base browsing programs help maintain an informed citizenry. Nowadays, many serious books and journals that might better inform us are ignored simply because they are often difficult to locate, or too diffuse in their coverage (for example, I am seldom interested in more than one article in an entire issue of *Scientific American*). An intelligent, automated reading assistant might help correct that situation. The hatching of a population fully educated and informed on public issues could be AI's gift to democracy.

At the same time, AI could help in the fight for privacy rights, presently eroded by uncontrolled access to data banks containing private information on individuals. It would be possible to have an AI program sit as a watchdog over a data bank, allowing information to be copied only after thoroughly probing an inquiring system's right to know. Security measures implemented in present networks through passwords act like the combination of a safe: once the door is opened, one loses all control over what is taken out of the chamber. An AI watchdog program could subdivide the safe into many smaller boxes and look over an inquirer's shoulder as it takes items out.

But it is a mistake to interpret the potential effects of AI as simple extensions of present tendencies—as Seymour Papert put it:

> Faced with a computer technology that opens the possibility of radically changing social life, our society has responded by consistently casting computers in a framework that favors the maintenance of the status quo. For example, we typically think of computers making credit decisions in an otherwise unchanged banking system, or helping to teach children to read in an otherwise unchanged school system. We think of computers as helping schools in their task of teaching an existing curriculum in classrooms instead of confronting the fact that the computer puts the very idea of school in question.[32]

Thus, as AI seeps into our daily lives, we will be faced with upheavals comparable in magnitude to those faced by our hunter-gatherer ancestors when they switched over to agriculture, or by our peasant-artisan forebears during the first industrial revolution. During these periods, human beings had continually to review their vision of themselves and of their role in the universe. Artificial intelligence will induce such changes again.

Hans Moravec of Carnegie Mellon proposes an intriguing strategy to keep humankind in the flow of things after the critical period when machines surpass us in intelligence. His basic theme amounts to: "If you can't beat them, join them." First, Moravec points out the possibility of making human-machine interfaces much better than the familiar mouse-*cum*-color-screen combination. Already, virtual reality setups are starting to replace the single screen by means of goggles displaying computer-generated, high-resolution stereo images. A glove equipped with electronic sensors substitutes for the mouse, allowing you to grasp objects in the electronic universe portrayed in the goggles. Soon tiny electric motors will provide sensory feedback for the glove, enabling you to feel the solidity of the computer-evoked objects you will seize. Additional enhancements, such as sound and perhaps a sensor-equipped suit covering the entire body, will later add to the vividness of the illusion. In what Moravec calls "bare-hands programming," a programmer will be able to perceive in such artificial environments the elements of a program (files, variables, pieces of a program) as physical substitutes.[33] For example, your C-language programming environment might look like a grassy yard sprinkled with boxes of various shapes and with attachments for them. These would correspond to the functions you would assemble to build your program, which would look like a piece of abstract sculpture in this sunny meadow.

To peer further into the crystal ball, technologies called "molecular electronics" and "bio-chips" might make possible direct brain-to-computer connections. K. Eric Drexler, the mercurial author of the bestselling *Engines of Creation,* has described how such methods, which he refers to as "nanotechnology," might one day permit the manufacture of supercomputers small enough to be carried as biological implants.[34] You don't believe he's serious? The last time I looked, Drexler was working on a doctoral thesis at MIT, with no less than Marvin Minsky and Gerald Sussman as supervisors.

Such gambits would bring about a gradual synthesis of human and machine intelligence, which would let us participate in the evolution of the machines Moravec calls our "mind children."[35]

The ultimate technological prowess—referred to as "downloading" in AI circles—that he envisions would let us become full-fledged members of the new artificial life and also ensure us of immortality. Downloading is the hypothetical process of transferring the architecture of a person's brain into computer circuits replicating the neural connections of the original organ. As I discussed in chapter 10, Moravec has convincingly described how the procedure could be accomplished in steps, without a subject's ever losing consciousness. This gradual transition from carnal existence to embodiment into electronic hardware would guarantee the continuity of an individual's subjective experience, and would make it harder to argue that the subject had really died, leaving behind a mere electronic simulacrum. The resulting artificial brain could be outfitted with a body providing full sensory perception. The mental powers of the continuing electronic personality could even be enhanced by speeding up the embodying circuitry or adding new hardware modules to it. Thus, AI may lift us into a new kind of existence, where our humanity will be not only preserved but also enhanced in ways we can hardly imagine.

CONCLUSION

Which of these three scenarios will be fulfilled is hard to say. Attempting to predict our future as intelligent machines become part of our lives is like trying to make out the features of a fog-shrouded landscape. Our probably adaptation over the next decade can be made out with some detail; and the path to follow, if pitfalls are to be avoided, is fairly clear. We need not fear the Colossus scenario if we do not put AI in control of military hardware. We should also take advantage of the present reduction in military tensions to work AI-control clauses into disarmament agreements.

The means to steer away from the Big Brother scenario include an insistence on always programming expert systems to explain the reasons for their recommendations in a manner clearly understandable to humans. The designers of expert systems should take special care that these be used to help their users reach decisions, instead of deciding for the users. Legislation against both uncontrolled information dissemination, and the use of AI technologies for gathering intelligence on citizens, is also indispensable.

It is encouraging that AI researchers are starting to realize the social implications of their work. Computer Professionals for Social Responsibility, a Palo Alto–based group founded in 1981, originally regrouped members of the computer professions wanting to address the role of computer technology in the field of nuclear weaponry and arms control. Many AI researchers belong to CPSR, which has since expanded its interests to cover the threats to civil liberties posed by overcomputerization.

I believe that for the next decade or two we will follow the "Lift-Off" script. AI will gradually seep into all human activities, with mostly beneficial effects. Since, during that period, machines will remain less intelligent than people, we should keep the upper hand on them without too much difficulty.

In the longer term, however, AI remains immensely threatening. The machines will eventually excel us in intelligence, and it will become impossible for us to pull the plug on them. (It is already almost impossible: powering off the computers controlling our electric transmission networks, for instance, would cause statewide blackouts.) Competitive pressures on the businesses making ever more intensive use of AI will compel them to entrust the machines with ever more power. Such pressures will extend to our entire social and legal framework. For instance, proposals already exist for legally recognizing artificial intelligence programs as persons in order to solve the issues of responsibility posed by the use of expert systems.[36]

When machines acquire an intelligence superior to our own, they will be impossible to keep at bay. Episodes where a deputy rises and becomes the effective ruler of a nation have happened countless times in history. The evolution of life on earth is itself nothing but a four-billion-year-long tale of offspring superseding parents. The unrelenting progress of AI forces us to ask the inevitable question: Are we creating the next species of intelligent life on earth?

At the very least, human society will have to undergo drastic changes to survive in the face of artificial intelligences. Such changes may be for the best, but the possibility of evil will always be lurking in the silicon innards of our new allies. Their arrival will threaten the very existence of human life as we know it. Whatever the outcome, we will have to radically re-examine our values and ask ourselves such questions as: Is intelligence what humanity is about? Whether it is or not, where do our loyalties belong—to humanity or to evolution? Can nonbiological life achieve a higher spiritual evolution than humanity can?

It is neither possible nor desirable to outlaw AI. We should not, however, expect the main battles of the twenty-first century to be fought over such issues as the environment, overpopulation or poverty. No, we should expect the fight to be about how we cope with the creations of our own human ingenuity; and the issue, whether we or they—our silicon challengers—control the future of the earth.

Notes

PREFACE

1. Grant Fjermedal, *The Tomorrow Makers: A Brave New World of Living Brain Machines* (New York: Macmillan, 1986), pp. 67–68.

INTRODUCTION. PROBING THE MYSTERY OF HUMAN INTELLIGENCE

1. A. Chapuis and E. Droz, *Les Automates: Figures artificielles d'hommes et d'animaux. histoire et technique* (Neuchatel: Editions du Griffon, 1949; and Paris: Dunod, 1949).
2. J. C. Beaune, *L'Automate et ses mobiles* (Paris: Flammarion, 1980), p. 38.
3. G. L. Simons, *Are Computers Alive? Evolution and New Life Forms* (Hemel Hemstead: Harvester Press, 1983), ch. 2.
4. Beaune, *L'Automate,* p. 55. See also Chapuis and Droz, *Les Automates,* pp. 35–38.
5. Simons, *Are Computers Alive?*
6. Chapuis and Droz, *Les Automates,* pp. 43–49.
7. Ibid., pp. 240–43.
8. Herbert A. Simon, *The Sciences of the Artificial* (Cambridge, Mass.: MIT Press, 1969), p. 4.
9. Interview with Herbert Simon, 23 May 1991.
10. Interview with Berthold Horn, 15 May 1991.

CHAPTER 1. ENGINEERING INTELLIGENCE:
COMPUTERS AND PROGRAMMING

The epigraph is from Alan Turing, "Computing Machinery and Intelligence," in E. A. Feigenbaum and J. Feldman, eds., *Computers and Thought* (New York: McGraw-Hill, 1963), p. 19.

1. Margaret A. Boden, *Artificial Intelligence and Natural Man* (New York: Basic Books, 1972), p. 4.
2. Stan Augarten, *Bit by Bit: An Illustrated History of Computers* (New York: Ticknor & Fields, 1984), ch. 2.
3. Claude E. Shannon, "A Mathematical Theory of Information," *Bell System Technical Journal* 27 (1948): 379–423, 623–56; and "Programming a Computer to Play Chess," *Philosophy Magazine,* March 1950, pp. 256–75. See also Andrew Hodges, *Alan Turing: The Enigma of Intelligence* (New York: Simon & Schuster, 1983), ch. 8; Morris W. Firebaugh, *Artificial Intelligence: A Knowledge-Based Approach* (Boston: Boyd & Fraser, 1988), p. 17; Anthony Liversidge, "Interview. Claude Shannon," *Omni* 9 (August 1987): 60–66; and John Horgan, "Profile. Claude E. Shannon," *Scientific American,* January 1990, pp. 22–22B.
4. H. Goldstine, *The Computer from Pascal to von Neumann* (Princeton, N.J.: Princeton University Press, 1972).
5. Hodges, *Alan Turing,* ch. 8.
6. J. Cohen, *Human Robots in Myth and Science* (London: Allen & Unwin, 1966); and P. McCorduck, *Machines Who Think* (San Francisco: W. H. Freeman, 1979), p. 69.
7. McCorduck, *Machines Who Think,* p. 69.
8. Philip Wiener, ed., *Leibnitz, Selections* (New York: Charles Scribner, 1951), p. 18.
9. Emilienne Naert, "Leibnitz," in Denis Huisman, ed., *Dictionnaire des Philosophes* (Paris: Presses Universitaires de France, 1984).
10. Arturo Sangalli, "From the Laws of Thought to Computer Logic," *New Scientist,* 19 August 1989, pp. 48–52.
11. Gottlob Frege, *Conceptual Notation and Related Articles,* trans. and ed. by Terrell Ward Bynum (Oxford: Clarendon Press, 1972).
12. Ibid., p. 105.
13. K. Gödel, "On Formally Undecidable Propositions in Principia Mathematica and Related Systems I," *Monatshefte für Mathematik und Physik* 38 (1931): 173–98.
14. J. R. Lucas, "Minds, Machines and Gödel," *Philosophy* 36 (1961): 112.
15. Donald Michie and Rory Johnston, *The Knowledge Machine—Artificial Intelligence and the Future of Man* (New York: William Morrow, 1985), pp. 149–50.
16. Hodges, *Alan Turing,* ch. 5.

17. Alan Turing, "Computing Machinery and Intelligence," in E. A. Feigenbaum and J. Feldman, eds., *Computers and Thought* (New York: McGraw-Hill, 1963), p. 22.

18. Ibid., p. 19.

19. David Ritchie, *The Binary Brain: Artificial Intelligence in the Age of Electronics* (Boston: Little, Brown, 1984), ch. 9.

CHAPTER 2. THE FIRST AI PROGRAM: DEFINING THE FIELD

1. N. Wiener, *Ex-Prodigy: My Childhood and Youth* (New York: Simon & Schuster, 1953); N. Wiener, *I Am a Mathematician* (Toronto: Doubleday, 1956); and R. Levinson et al., "Norbert Wiener 1894–1964," *American Mathematical Society Bulletin* 72(1) [1966]:1–145.

2. C. Reid, *Hilbert* (New York: Springer Verlag, 1970).

3. A. Rosenblueth, N. Wiener, and J. Bigelow, "Behavior, Purpose and Teleology," *Philosophy of Science* 10 (1943): 18–24; and N. Wiener, *Cybernetics: Communication and Control in the Animal and the Machine* (New York: John Wiley, 1948), 2nd ed. (Cambridge, Mass.: MIT Press, 1961).

4. Interview with Marvin Minsky, 13 May 1991. All other personal quotes of Minsky's in this chapter are from this interview.

5. W. S. McCulloch, "What Is a Number, That a Man May Know It, and a Man, That He May Know a Number?" in W. S. McCulloch, *Embodiments of Mind* (Cambridge, Mass.: MIT Press, 1970), p. 2.

6. Ibid., p. 2.

7. Grant Fjermedal, *The Tomorrow Makers: A Brave New World of Living Brain Machines* (New York: Macmillan, 1986), p. 73.

8. W. S. McCulloch and W. H. Pitts, "A Logical Calculus of the Ideas Immanent in Nervous Activity," *Bulletin of Mathematical Biophysics* (Chicago: University of Chicago Press) 5 (1943): 115–33, reprinted in McCulloch, *Embodiments of Mind,* pp. 19–39.

9. Rosenblueth, Wiener, and Bigelow, "Behavior, Purpose and Teleology."

10. P. McCorduck, *Machines Who Think* (San Francisco: W. H. Freeman, 1979), p. 59.

11. Ibid., p. 78.

12. Andrew Hodges, *Alan Turing: The Enigma of Intelligence* (New York: Simon & Schuster, 1983), ch. 8.

13. McCulloch, *Embodiments of Mind,* p. 35.

14. Ibid., p. xviii.

15. D.O. Hebb, *The Organization of Behavior* (New York: John Wiley, 1949).

16. J. Bernstein, "Profiles: Marvin Minsky," *New Yorker,* 14 December 1981, p. 50.

17. McCorduck, *Machines Who Think,* p. 84.

18. C. Holden, "Profile. Herbert A. Simon: the Rational Optimist," *Psychology Today,* October 1986, pp. 54–60.

19. G.A. Miller, "The Magical Number Seven," *Psychological Review* (1956): 63:81.

20. Bernstein, "Profiles," p. 66.

21. Ibid., p. 70.

22. Marvin Minsky, "Memoir on Inventing the Confocal Scanning Microscope," *Scanning* 10 (1988): 128–38.

23. Part of the background material on John McCarthy was extracted from the following sources: Philip J. Hilts, "The Dean of Artificial Intelligence," *Psychology Today*, January 1983, pp. 28–33; Philip J. Hilts, *Scientific Temperaments: Three Lives in Contemporary Science* (New York: Simon & Schuster, 1982); Time-Life editorial staff, *Artificial Intelligence* (Alexandria, Va.: Time-Life Books, 1986), ch. 3; McCorduck, *Machines Who Think,* pp. 216–23, 351.

24. C. Shannon and J. McCarthy, eds., "Automata Studies," *Annals of Mathematical Studies* (Princeton University Press) 34 (1956).

25. Interview with Hans Moravec, 21 May 1991.

26. Philip J. Hilts, "Interview: John McCarthy," *Omni*, April 1983, pp. 101–26.

27. Interview with Herbert Simon, 23 May 1991. All other personal quotes of Simon's in this chapter are from this interview.

28. N. Rochester et al., "Tests on a Cell Assembly Theory of the Action of the Brain Using a Large Digital Computer," *IRE Transactions on Information Theory,* September 1956, p. 80.

29. See the following sources for information on the Dartmouth conference: F. Rose, *Into the Heart of Mind* (New York, Harper & Row, 1984), p. 35; M.M. Waldrop, *Man-made Minds: The Promise of Artificial Intelligence* (New York: Walker, 1987), p. 11; M. W. Firebaugh, *Artificial Intelligence: A Knowledge-Based Approach* (Boston: Boyd & Fraser, 1988), p. 18; McCorduck, *Machines Who Think,* pp. 93–109.

30. O.G. Selfridge and U. Neisser, "Pattern Recognition by Machine," in E. A. Feigenbaum and J. Feldman, eds., *Computers and Thought* (New York: McGraw-Hill, 1963), pp. 237–50.

31. O.G. Selfridge, "Pandemonium: A Paradigm for Learning," in D.V. Blake and A.M. Uttley, eds., *Proceedings of the Symposium on Mechanization of Thought Processes* (National Physical Laboratory, Teddington, England; London: H.M. Stationery Office, 1959), pp. 511–29.

32. Background information on Herbert Simon was extracted from the following sources: T. Nicholson and P.L. Abraham, "Economics: Simon Says," *Newsweek,* 30 October 1978, p. 70; R. Goodell, "A Nobel Gadfly," *Psychology Today,* January 1979, p. 6; "Decision Doctor," *Time,* 30 October 1978, p. 51; C. Holden, "Profile. Herbert A. Simon: the Rational Optimist," *Psychology Today,* October 1986, pp. 54–60; "Simon, Herbert," *Nobel Prize Winners* (New York: Wilson, 1987), p. 978; J. G. March, "The 1978 Nobel Prize in Economics," *Science,* November 1978, pp. 858–61; and H. A. Simon, "Herbert A. Simon," in G. Lindzey, ed.,

A History of Psychology in Autobiography (San Francisco: W. H. Freeman, 1980), vol. VII.

33. Herbert A. Simon, *Administrative Behavior* (New York: Macmillan, 1947).
34. George Polya, *How to Solve It* (Princeton, N.J.: Princeton University Press, 1945).
35. McCorduck, *Machines Who Think,* p. 134.
36. Herbert A. Simon, *Models of My Life* (New York: Basic Books, 1991), pp. 206–7.
37. Ibid., p. 190.
38. Ibid., p. 209.
39. Ibid., p. 209.
40. Ibid., p. 212.
41. Ibid., p. 211.
42. McCorduck, *Machines Who Think,* p. 98.

CHAPTER 3. THE DAWN OF THE GOLDEN YEARS: 1956–63

1.   O. K. Moore and S.B. Anderson, "Modern Logic and Tasks for Experiments on Problem Solving Behavior," *Journal of Psychology* 38 (1954): 151–60; and "Search Behavior in Individual and Group Problem Solving," *American Sociological Review* 19(6) [1954]: 702–14.
2.   Interview with Herbert Simon, 22 May 1991. All other personal quotes of Simon's in this chapter are from this interview.
3.   A. Newell and H.A. Simon, "GPS: A Program That Simulates Human Thought," in E. A. Feigenbaum and J. Feldman, eds., *Computers and Thought* (New York: McGraw-Hill, 1963), pp. 279–93.
4.   G. Ernst and A. Newell, *GPS: A Case Study in Generality and Problem Solving* (New York: Academic Press, 1969).
5.   Edward A. Feigenbaum, "The Simulation of Verbal Learning Behavior," in Feigenbaum and Feldman, *Computers and Thought,* pp. 297–309.
6.   Robert K. Lindsay, "Inferential Memory as the Basis of Machines Which Understand Natural Language," in Feigenbaum and Feldman, *Computers and Thought,* pp. 217–35.
7.   H. Gelernter, "Realization of a Geometry-Theorem Proving Machine," proceedings of an International Conference on Information Processing, Paris, UNESCO House, 1959, pp. 273–82; reprinted in Feigenbaum and Feldman, *Computers and Thought,* pp. 134–52.
8.   H. Gelernter, J.R. Hansen and D. W. Loveland, "Empirical Explorations of the Geometry-Theorem Proving Machine," in Feigenbaum and Feldman, *Computers and Thought,* p. 155.
9.   A. Bernstein and M. de V. Roberts, "Computers vs. Chess Player," *Scientific American,* June 1958, pp. 96–105.
10. Pamela McCorduck, *Machines Who Think* (San Francisco: W. H. Freeman, 1976), pp. 158–9.

11. Oliver G. Selfridge and Ulrich Neisser, "Pattern Recognition by Machine," *Scientific American,* August 1960, pp. 60–68.
12. Oliver G. Selfridge and Ulrich Neisser, "Pattern Recognition by Machine," in Feigenbaum and Feldman, eds., *Computers and Thought,* p. 250.
13. D. G. Bobrow and B. Raphael, "A Comparison of List-Processing Computer Languages," Comm. ACM, April 1964; and V.H. Yngve, *COMIT Programmer's Reference Manual* (Cambridge, Mass.: MIT Press, 1961).
14. John McCarthy, "Programs with Common Sense," in *Mechanization of Thought Processes* (London: Her Majesty's Stationery Office, 1959), pp. 75–84; reprinted in M. Minsk, ed., *Semantic Information Processing* (Cambridge, Mass.: MIT Press, 1968), p. 404.
15. McCarthy, "Programs with Common Sense," p. 403.
16. Alonzo Church, "The Calculi of Lambda-Conversion," *Annals of Mathematical Studies,* no. 6 (Princeton, N.J.: Princeton University Press, 1941).
17. Herbert A. Simon, *Models of My Life* (New York: Basic Books, 1991), p. 213.
18. Interview with Berthold Horn, 15 May 1991. All other personal quotes of Horn's in this chapter are from this interview.
19. Jeremy Bernstein, "Profiles," *New Yorker,* 14 December 1981, p. 13.
20. Interview with Marvin Minsky, 13 May 1991. All other personal quotes of Minsky's in this chapter are from this interview.
21. Interview with Joseph Weizenbaum, 16 May 1991.
22. *Boston Herald,* 28 June 1963.
23. Ibid.
24. J. R. Slagle, "A Heuristic Program That Solves Symbolic Integration Problems in Freshman Calculus: Symbolic Automatic Integration (SAINT)," Report No. SG-0001, Lincoln Laboratory, MIT (Cambridge, Mass.), 1961; reprinted in Feigenbaum and Feldman, eds., *Computers and Thought,* pp. 191–205.
25. J. Moses, "Symbolic Integration," Report No. MAC-TR-47, Project MAC, MIT (Cambridge, Mass.), 1967.
26. Interview with Patrick Winston, 15 May 1991.
27. Interview with David Waltz, 15 May 1991. All other personal quotes of David Waltz's in this chapter are from this interview.
28. Interview with Gerald Sussman, 14 May 1991. All other personal quotes of David Sussman's in this chapter are from this interview.
29. Stewart Brand, *The Media Lab* (New York: Penguin Books, 1987), p. 136.
30. Interview with Randall Davis, 17 May 1991.
31. Joseph Weizenbaum, *Computer Power and Human Reason* (San Francisco: W.H. Freeman and Company, 1976).
32. Brand, *The Media Lab,* p. 56.
33. Sherry Turkle, *The Second Self: Computers and the Human Spirit* (New York: Simon & Schuster, 1984), pp. 210–11.
34. Brand, *The Media Lab,* p. 57.

35. Turkle, *Second Self*, p. 213.
36. Turkle, *Second Self*, p. 28.

**CHAPTER 4. THE CONQUEST OF MICRO WORLDS:
1963–70**

1. T. G. Evans, "A Heuristic Program to Solve Geometric Analogy Problems," doctoral diss., MIT, 1963. Reprinted in Marvin Minsky, ed., *Semantic Information Processing* (Cambridge, Mass: MIT Press, 1968), pp. 271–353.
2. Daniel G. Bobrow, "Natural Language Input for a Computer Problem-
Solving System," report TR-1, Project MAC, MIT, Cambridge, Mass.,
1964. Reprinted in Minsky, *Semantic Information Processing*, p. 189.
3. Bertram Raphael, "SIR: A Computer Program for Semantic Information
Retrieval," report TR-2, Project MAC, MIT, Cambridge, Mass., 1964.
Reprinted in Minsky, *Semantic Information Processing*, pp. 33–34.
4. Raphael, "SIR," p. 58.
5. Interview with Herbert Simon, 22 May 1991. All other personal quotes
of Simon's in this chapter are from this interview.
6. R. F. Simmons et al., "Toward the Synthesis of Human Language Behavior," *Behavioral Science* 7 (3 [1962]): 32–33; and R.F. Simmons, "Synthetic
Language Behavior," *Data Processing Management* 5 (1963): 45.
7. Noam Chomsky, *Syntactic Structures* (The Hague, Netherlands: Mouton,
1957).
8. M.R. Quillian, "Semantic Memory," doctoral diss. no. AFCRL-66-189,
Carnegie Mellon University, Pittsburgh, 1966. Reprinted in part in
Minsky, *Semantic Information Processing*, pp. 227–70.
9. Quillian, "Semantic Memory," p. 253.
10. Marvin Minsky, ed., *Semantic Information Processing* (Cambridge, Mass.: MIT
Press, 1968).
11. H. A. Simon and L. Siklossy, eds., *Representation and Meaning: Experiments
with Information Processing Systems* (Englewood Cliffs, N.J.: Prentice-Hall,
1972).
12. Herbert A. Simon, *Models of My Life* (New York: Basic Books, 1991), p.
230.
13. Interview with Joseph Weizenbaum, 16 May 1991. All other personal
quotes of Weizenbaum's in this chapter are from this interview.
14. R. Schultz, "Interview: Seymour Papert," *Omni* 8 (October 1985): 98–
104; B. Carpenter, "On the Trail of Nintendo's Magic," *U.S. News &
World Report*, 16 July 1990, pp. 56–57; P. Angiolillo and M. Bluestone,
"Now Even Lego Is Going High-Tech," *Business Week*, 17 August 1987,
p. 40; and P. McCorduck, *Machines Who Think* (San Francisco: W. H.
Freeman, 1979), pp. 288–99.
15. A.B. Bass, "Computers in the Classroom," *Technology Review*, April 1987,
pp. 52–64.

16. Interview with Marvin Minsky, 13 May 1991. All other personal quotes of Minsky's in this chapter are from this interview.

17. Interview with Gerald Sussman, 14 May 1991. All other personal quotes of Sussman's in this chapter are from this interview.

18. Interview with Berthold Horn, 15 May 1991. All other personal quotes of Horn's in this chapter are from this interview.

19. Interview with David Waltz, 15 May 1991. All other personal quotes of Waltz's in this chapter are from this interview.

20. L. G. Roberts, "Machine Perception of Three-dimensional Solids," in J. Tippett, ed., *Optical and Electro-optical Information Processing* (Cambridge, Mass.: MIT Press, 1965).

21. A. Guzman, "Computer Recognition of Three-dimensional Objects in a Visual Scene," Ph.D. thesis no. AI-TR-228, Artificial Intelligence Laboratory, MIT, Cambridge, Mass., 1968.

22. M. B. Clowes, "On Seeing Things," *Artificial Intelligence* 2 (1 [1971]): 79–112; D. A. Huffman, "Impossible Objects as Nonsense Sentences," in B. Meltzer and D. Michie, eds., *Machine Intelligence* 6 (Edinburgh: Edinburgh University Press, 1971), pp. 295–323.

23. Patrick H. Winston, "Learning Structural Descriptions from Examples," doctoral diss., published as Project MAC Report MAC TR-76, MIT, Cambridge, Mass., 1970.

24. Interview with Patrick Winston, 15 May 1991. All other personal quotes of Winston's in this chapter are from this interview.

25. Bertram Raphael, *The Thinking Computer: Mind Inside Matter* (San Francisco: W. H. Freeman, 1976). See also Pamela McCorduck, *Machines Who Think* (San Francisco: W. H. Freeman, 1979), pp. 232–34; and Howard Rheingold, "The Well-Tempered Robot," *Psychology Today,* December 1983, p. 44. I also discussed Shakey with Hans Moravec of Carnegie Mellon.

26. Nils J. Nilsson, *Principles of Artificial Intelligence* (Palo Alto, Calif.: Tioga Publishing Co., 1980), pp. 275–311.

27. Brad Darrach, "Meet Shakey, the First Electronic Person," *Life,* 20 November 1970, pp. 58–68.

28. Minsky quoted in ibid.

29. Terry Winograd, *Understanding Natural Language* (New York: Academic Press, 1972).

30. Hubert L. Dreyfus and Stuart E. Dreyfus, *Mind Over Machine: The Power of Human Intuition and Expertise in the Era of the Computer* (New York: Free Press, 1985), p. 212.

31. Winograd, *Understanding Natural Language,* pp. 8–15 (comments and portions of dialogue were left out).

32. Interview with Carl Hewitt, 13 May 1991. All other personal quotes of Hewitt's in this chapter are from this interview.

33. C. Hewitt, "Descriptions and Theoretical Analysis (Using Schemata) of PLANNER: A Language for Proving Theorems and Manipulating Models in a Robot," doctoral diss., AI Lab, report AI-TR-258, MIT, Cam-

bridge, Mass., June 1971; and G. Sussman, T. Winograd, and E. Charniak, "Micro-Planner Reference Manual," AI Memo 203a, MIT, Cambridge, Mass., 1970.

34. Y. A. Wilks, "Natural Language Understanding Systems Within the AI Paradigm: A Survey and Some Comparisons," in A. Zamponelli, ed., *Linguistic Structures Processing* (Amsterdam: North-Holland, 1977), pp. 341–98.

35. Marvin Minsky, *The Society of Mind* (New York: Simon & Schuster, 1985).

36. Terry Winograd, "What Does It Mean to Understand Language?" in Donald Norrnan, ed., *Perspectives on Cognitive Science* (Norwood, N.J.: Ablex Publishing, 1981), p. 240.

37. "Human Brains Replaced?" *Science,* 21 July 1958, p. 50.

38. "Rival," *The New Yorker,* 6 December 1958, p. 45.

39. "Machine Learns Alphabet," *Science News Letter,* 2 July 1960, p. 7.

40. Frank Rosenblatt, *Principles of Neurodynamics* (New York: Spartan Books, 1962), p. 596.

41. Wilfrid K. Taylor, "Electrical Simulation of Some Nervous System Functional Activities," in E. C. Cherry, ed., *Information Theory* (London: Buttersworths, 1956), p. 3.

42. Bernard Widrow and M. E. Hoff, "Adaptive Switching Circuits," *WESCON Convention Record* 4 (1960): 96.

43. Karl Steinbuch, "Die Lernmatrix," *Kybernetik* 1 (1 [1961]): 36; and Karl Steinbuch, Piske U.A.W., IEEE Transactions EC-12 (1963), 846.

44. Marvin Minsky and Seymour Papert, *Perceptrons—An Introduction to Computational Geometry* (Cambridge, Mass.: MIT Press, 1969). An expanded edition was published in 1988.

45. Rosenblatt, *Principles of Neurodynamics,* p. 596.

46. Minsky and Papert, *Perceptrons,* p. 242.

47. Seymour Papert, "One AI or Many?" in Stephen R. Graubard, ed., *The Artificial Intelligence Debate* (Cambridge, Mass.: MIT Press, 1988), p. 8.

48. J. Bernstein, "Profiles: Marvin Minsky," *New Yorker,* 14 December 1981, p. 18.

CHAPTER 5. CLOUDS ON THE AI HORIZON

The epigraphs are, respectively, from Hubert L. Dreyfus, *What Computers Can't Do* (New York: Harper & Row, 1979), p. 86; and Herbert A. Simon, *Models of My Life* (New York: Basic Books, 1991), p. 274.

1. H. A. Simon and Allen Newell, "Heuristic Problem Solving: The Next Advance in Operations Research," *Operations Research* 6 (January–February 1958): 7–8.

2. Allen Newell, J. C. Shaw, and H. A. Simon, "The Processes of Creative Thinking," RAND Corporation, report P-1320, 16 September 1958, p. 6.

3. H. A. Simon, *The Shape of Automation for Men and Management* (New York: Harper & Row, 1965), p. 96.

4. M. Minsky, *Computation: Finite and Infinite Machines* (Englewood Cliffs, N.J.: Prentice-Hall, 1967), p. 2.

5. Hans Moravec, *Mind Children* (Cambridge, Mass.: MIT Press, 1988), p. 20.

6. John R. Pierce, "Language and Machines: Computers in Translation and Linguistics," publication 1416, National Academy of Sciences/National Research Council, Washington, D.C., 1966.

7. For an indication of how low GPS had sunk in popular opinion, see D. McDermott, *SIGART Newsletter* 57 (April 1976): 4.

8. M. Minsky and S. Papert, "Draft of a Proposal to ARPA for Research on Artificial Intelligence at MIT, 1970–71," p. 39; quoted in Hubert L. Dreyfus, *What Computers Can't Do,* rev. ed. (New York: Harper Colophon, 1979), p. 9.

9. Terry Winograd, "Understanding Natural Language," *Cognitive Psychology* 3 (New York: Academic Press, 1972): 26; quoted in Dreyfus, *What Computers Can't Do,* p. 12.

10. Eugene Charniak, "Toward a Model of Children's Story Comprehension," Ph.D. thesis, MIT, 1972, p. 6.

11. Ibid., p. 96.

12. Ibid., p. 97.

13. Patrick H. Winston and the staff of the MIT AI Laboratory, AI Memo no. 366 (May 1976), p. 22; quoted in Dreyfus, *What Computers Can't Do,* p. 14.

14. Interview with Hans Moravec, 21 May 1991. All other personal quotes of Moravec's in this chapter are from this interview.

15. Mark Stefik, "Strategic Computing at DARPA: Overview and Assessment," *Communications of the ACM* 28 (7 [July 1985]): 698.

16. Ibid.

17. Interview with Raj Reddy, 20 May 1991. All other personal quotes of Reddy's in this chapter are from this interview.

18. Morris W. Firebaugh, *Artificial Intelligence, a Knowledge-Based Approach* (Boston: Boyd & Fraser, 1988), p. 474.

19. Jonathan Jacky, "The Strategic Computing Program," in D. Bellin and G. Chapman, eds., *Computers in Battle: Will They Work?* (New York: Harcourt Brace Jovanovich, 1987), p. 191.

20. James Lighthill, "A Report on Artificial Intelligence," unpublished manuscript, 1972, Science Research Council, U.K.; quoted in Howard Gardner, *The Mind's New Science: A History of the Cognitive Revolution* (New York: Basic Books, 1985), p. 164.

21. Donald Michie, with Rory Johnston, *The Knowledge Machine—Artificial Intelligence and the Future of Man* (New York: William Morrow, 1985), p. 232.

22. J. McCarthy and P. J. Hayes, "Some Philosophical Problems from the

Standpoint of Artificial Intelligence," in B. Meltzer and D. Michie, eds., *Machine Intelligence,* vol. 4 (Edinburgh: Edinburgh University Press, 1969), pp. 466–67.

23. Ibid., p. 487.
24. Ibid., p. 489.
25. Mortimer Taube, *Computers and Common Sense: The Myth of Thinking Machines* (New York: Columbia University Press, 1961).
26. Richard Bellman, *Artificial Intelligence: Can Computers Think?* (Boston: Boyd & Fraser, 1978).
27. Pamela McCorduck, *Machines Who Think* (San Francisco: W. H. Freeman, 1979), p. 193.
28. Greenberger, ed., *Management and the Computer of the Future* (Cambridge and New York: MIT Press and John Wiley, 1962).
29. Quoted in McCorduck, *Machines Who Think,* p. 193.
30. Ibid.
31. Hubert L. Dreyfus and Stuart E. Dreyfus, *Mind Over Machine: The Power of Human Intuition and Expertise in the Era of the Computer* (New York: Free Press, 1985), p. 5.
32. Hubert L. Dreyfus, "Alchemy and AI," RAND Corporation, December 1965.
33. Dreyfus and Dreyfus, *Mind Over Machine,* p. 8.
34. McCorduck, *Machines Who Think,* p. 194.
35. W. Ross Ashby, *Design for a Brain* (New York: Wiley, 1952).
36. W. Ross Ashby, "Review of Feigenbaum's Computers and Thought," *Journal of Nervous and Mental Diseases,"* 1964
37. McCorduck, *Machines Who Think,* p. 195.
38. Dreyfus and Dreyfus, *Mind Over Machine,* p. 8.
39. Interview with Joseph Weizenbaum, 16 May 1991. All other personal quotes of Weizenbaum's in this chapter are from this interview.
40. Interview with David Waltz, 15 May 1991. All other personal quotes of Waltz's in this chapter are from this interview.
41. "Talk of the Town," *New Yorker,* 11 June 1966.
42. Seymour Papert, "The Artificial Intelligence of Hubert L. Dreyfus: A Budget of Fallacies," AI Memo 154, MIT AI Laboratory.
43. McCorduck, *Machines Who Think,* p. 187.
44. Hubert L. Dreyfus, *What Computers Can't Do* (New York: Harper & Row, 1972; rev. ed. 1979), p. 307, n. 6.
45. Dreyfus and Dreyfus, *Mind Over Machine,* p. 13.
46. Dreyfus, *What Computers Can't Do,* pp. 194–95.
47. Hubert and Stuart Dreyfus, "Making a Mind versus Modeling the Brain," in Stephen R. Graubard, ed., *The Artificial Intelligence Debate: False Starts, Real Foundations* (Cambridge, Mass.: MIT Press, 1988), p. 37.
48. Ibid., p. 196.
49. Ibid., p. 128.

50. Ibid., p. 163.

51. Ibid.

52. Claude E. Shannon, "The Mathematical Theory of Communication," in C. E. Shannon and W. Weaver, eds., *The Mathematical Theory of Communication* (Urbana: University of Illinois Press, 1962), p. 3; quoted in Dreyfus, *What Computers Can't Do,* p. 165.

53. Ulrich Neisser, *Cognitive Psychology* (New York: Appleton-Century-Crofts, 1967), p. 4.

54. Dreyfus, *What Computers Can't Do,* pp. 183, 181.

55. Ibid., p. 175.

56. Ibid., p. 190.

57. J. Bar-Hillel, "The Present Status of Automatic Translation of Language," in F. L. Alt, ed., *Advances in Computers* (New York: Academic Press, 1964), p. 158.

58. Dreyfus, *What Computers Can't Do,* p. 222.

59. Dreyfus, "Alchemy and AI."

60. Dreyfus, "Making a Mind versus Modeling the Brain," p. 32.

61. Dreyfus, *Mind Over Machine,* p. 77.

62. Dreyfus, *What Computers Can't Do,* p. 166.

63. Joseph Weizenbaum, *Computer Power and Human Reason* (San Francisco: W. H. Freeman, 1976).

64. Ibid., p. 188.

65. Ibid., pp. 3–4.

66. Daniel Bobrow, *ACM SIGART Newsletter,* December 1968.

67. Grant Fjermedal, *The Tomorrow Makers: A Brave New World of Living Brain Machines* (New York: Macmillan, 1986), pp. 109–110.

68. K. M. Colby et al., "Artificial Paranoia," *Artificial Intelligence* 2 (1972) 1–26; and K. M. Colby et al., "Turing-like Undistinguishability Tests for the Validation of a Computer Simulation of Paranoid Processes," *Artificial Intelligence* 3 (1973): 47–51.

69. K. M. Colby, J. B. Watt, and J. P. Gilbert, "A Computer Method of Psychotherapy," *Journal of Nervous and Mental Disease* 142 (1966): 151.

70. McCorduck, *Machines Who Think,* p. 254.

71. Colby et al., "Computer Method of Psychotherapy," pp. 148–52.

72. McCorduck, *Machines Who Think,* p. 311.

73. Herbert A. Simon, *The Sciences of the Artificial* (Cambridge, Mass.: MIT Press, 1969), p. 25.

74. Simon and Newell, "Heuristic Problem Solving," p. 6.

75. Weizenbaum, *Computer Power and Human Reason,* p. 201.

76. Ibid., p. 212.

77. Ibid., p. 213.

78. Ibid., p. 222.

79. Ibid., p. 210.

80. Ibid., pp. 226–27.

81. Ibid., p. 127.
82. Ibid., p. 269.
83. Ibid.

CHAPTER 6. THE TREE OF KNOWLEDGE

The epigraph is from an interview with Marvin Minsky, 13 May 1991.

1.   J. H. Breasted, *The Edwin Smith Surgical Papyrus* (Chicago: Chicago University Press, 1930).
2.   C. A. Elsberg, "The Anatomy and Surgery of the Edwin Smith Surgical Papyrus," *Journal of Mt. Sinai Hospital* 12 (1945), 141–51.
3.   Michel Gondran, *Introduction aux systèmes experts* (Paris: Eyrolles, 1983), p. 88.
4.   Interview with Herbert Simon, 22 May 1991. All other personal quotes of Simon's in this chapter are from this interview.
5.   Interview with Marvin Minsky, 13 May 1991. All other personal quotes of Minsky's in this chapter are from this interview.
6.   Edward A. Feigenbaum and Julian Feldman, eds., *Computers and Thought* (New York: McGraw-Hill, 1963).
7.   R. Lindsay et al., *DENDRAL* (New York: McGraw-Hill, 1980).
8.   Edward A. Feigenbaum and Avron Barr, eds., *The Handbook of Artificial Intelligence,* vol. II (Reading, Mass.: Addison-Wesley, 1982), pp. 106–15.
9.   Edward A. Feigenbaum and Pamela McCorduck, *The Fifth Generation—Artificial Intelligence and Japan's Computer Challenge to the World* (Reading, Mass.: Addison-Wesley, 1983), pp. 61–62.
10. Interview with Bruce Buchanan, co-developer of DENDRAL, in H.L. Dreyfus and S. E. Dreyfus, *Mind over Machine: The Power of Human Intuition and Expertise in the Era of the Computer* (New York: Free Press, 1985), p. 111.
11. Interview with Allen Newell, 23 May 1991. All other personal quotes of Allen Newell's in this chapter are from this interview.
12. Allen Newell and Herbert Simon, *Human Problem Solving* (Englewood Cliffs, N.J.: Prentice-Hall, 1972).
13. Emil Post, "Formal Reductions of the General Combinatorial Decision Problem," *American Journal of Mathematics* 65 (1943): 197–215.
14. Noam Chomsky, *Syntactic Structures* (The Hague: Mouton, 1957).
15. Edward H. Shortliffe, *MYCIN: Computer-based Medical Consultations* (New York: Elsevier Press, 1976); and Bruce G. Buchanan and Edward H. Shortliffe, eds., *Rule-based Expert Systems—The MYCIN Experiments of the Stanford Heuristic Programming Project* (Reading, Mass.: Addison-Wesley, 1984).
16. Feigenbaum and Barr, *Handbook,* p. 93.
17. Victor L. Yu et al., "Antimicrobial Selection by a Computer," *Journal of the American Medical Association,* 21 September 1979, pp. 1279–82.

18. Interview with Randall Davis, 17 May 1991. All other personal quotes of Davis's in this chapter are from this interview.

19. Quoted in Gondran, *Introduction,* p. 92.

20. R. Davis, "Applications of Meta-knowledge to the Construction, Maintenance, and Use of Large Knowledge Bases," doctoral diss., Computer Science Department, Stanford University, 1976; reprinted in R. Davis and D. Lenat, eds., *Knowledge-based Systems in Artificial Intelligence* (New York: McGraw-Hill, 1982), pp. 229–490.

21. Barr and Feigenbaum, *Handbook,* p. 100.

22. Morris W. Firebaugh, *Artificial Intelligence: A Knowledge-Based Approach* (Boston: Boyd & Fraser, 1988), p. 356.

23. Edward A. Feigenbaum, Pamela McCorduck, and Penny Nii H., *The Rise of the Expert Company* (New York: Vintage Books, 1988), pp. 218–20.

24. Judith Bachant and John McDermott, "R1 Revisited: Four Years in the Trenches," *AI Magazine,* Fall 1984, p. 21.

CHAPTER 7. COMING OF AGE

1. Morris W. Fircbaugh, *Artificial Intelligence: A Knowledge-Based Approach* (Boston: Boyd & Fraser, 1988), p. 239.

2. Charles Fillmore, "The Case for Case," in E. Bach and R. Harms, eds., *Universals in Linguistic Theory* (New York: Holt, Rinehart & Winston, 1968).

3. W. A. Woods, "Transition Network Grammars for Natural Language Analysis," *Communications of the ACM* 13 (1970): 591–606.

4. Frank Rose, *Into the Heart of Mind* (New York: Harper & Row, 1984), p. 46.

5. Roger C. Schank, *The Cognitive Computer: On Language, Learning and Artificial Intelligence* (Reading, Mass.: Addison-Wesley, 1985), pp. 137–38.

6. Ibid., p. 93.

7. For discussions on logical atomism and AI, see, for example, Daniel C. Dennett, "When Philosophers Encounter Artificial Intelligence," in Stephen R. Graubard, ed., *The Artificial Intelligence Debate: False Starts, Real Foundations* (Cambridge, Mass.: MIT Press, 1988), pp. 203–55; and Douglas Hofstadter, "Waking Up from the Boolean Dream, or Subcognition as Computation," in his *Metamagical Themes* (New York: Basic Books, 1985), pp. 631–65.

8. R. C. Schank and R. P. Abelson, *Scripts, Plans, Goals, and Understanding* (Hillsdale, N.J.: Lawrence Erlbaum, 1977).

9. Schank, *Cognitive Computer,* p. 104.

10. Schank, *Cognitive Computer,* pp. 101–2.

11. Ibid., pp. 95–96.

12. Interview with Marvin Minsky, 13 May 1991. All other personal quotes of Minsky's in this chapter are from this interview.

13. Schank, *Cognitive Computer,* p. 122.

14. This script is a summarized version of the one appearing in Schank, *Cognitive Computer,* pp. 119–21.
15. Schank, *Cognitive Computer,* p. 143.
16. Ibid., p. 125.
17. Ibid., p. 146.
18. Ibid., p. 156.
19. Ibid, p. 161.
20. Marvin Minsky, "A Framework for Representing Knowledge," in Patrick H. Winston, ed., *The Psychology of Computer Vision* (New York: McGraw-Hill, 1975), pp. 211–79.
21. Ibid., p. 211.
22. Ibid., p. 212.
23. Personal communication from Marvin Minsky, 3 September 1992.
24. Interview with Herbert Simon, 23 May 1991.
25. Minsky, "A Framework," p. 213.
26. Interview with Gerald Sussman, 14 May 1991. All other personal quotes of Sussman's in this chapter are from this interview.
27. E. B. Hunt, J. Marin, and P. Stone, *Experiments in Induction* (New York: Academic Press, 1966).
28. D. Michie and R. Johnston, *The Knowledge Machine—AI and the Future of Man* (New York: William Morrow, 1985), p. 136.
29. R. S. Michalski and R. L. Chilauski, "Learning by Being Told and Learning From Examples: An Experimental Comparison of the Two Methods of Knowledge Acquisition in the Context Of Developing an Expert System for Soybean Disease Diagnostic," *International Journal of Policy Analysis and Information Systems* (2 [1980]): 125–61.
30. D. B. Lenat, "AM: An Artificial Intelligence Approach to Discovery in Mathematics as Heuristic Search," in R. Davis and D. Lenat, eds., *Knowledge-Based Systems in Artificial Intelligence* (New York: McGraw-Hill, 1981).
31. Time-Life Editorial Staff, *Artificial Intelligence* (Alexandria, Va.: Time-Life Books, 1986).
32. Interview with Randall Davis, 17 May 1991. All other personal quotes of Davis's in this chapter are from this interview.
33. D. B. Lenat, "The Role of Heuristics in Learning by Discovery: Three Case Studies," in Ryszard Michalski et al., eds., *Machine Learning—An AI Approach* (Palo Alto, Calif.: Tioga Publishing, 1983).
34. Lenat, "The Role of Heuristics," p. 236.
35. George Johnson, *Machinery of the Mind—Inside the New Science of Artificial Intelligence* (New York: Times Books, 1986).
36. Interview with Patrick Winston, 15 May 1991. All other personal quotes of Winston's in this chapter are from this interview.
37. David Marr, "A Theory of Cerebellar Cortex," *Journal of Physiology of London* 202 (1969): 437–70.
38. Marvin Minsky and Seymour Papert, *Perceptrons: An Introduction to Computational Geometry* (Cambridge, Mass.: MIT Press, 1969).

39. David Marr, "A Theory for Cerebellar Neocortex," *Proceedings of the Royal Society* (London) B176 (1970): 161–234; and David Marr, "Simple Memory: A Theory for Archicortex," *Philosophical Transactions of the Royal Society of London* B262 (1971): 841.

40. David Marr, *Vision* (New York: W. H. Freeman, 1982), p. 15.

41. Ibid., p. 35.

42. Berthold K. Horn, "Obtaining Shape from Shading Information," in Patrick H. Winston, ed., *The Psychology of Computer Vision* (New York: McGraw-Hill, 1975), pp. 115–55.

43. Allen Newell, "The Knowledge Level," 1980 Presidential Address to the American Association for Artificial Intelligence, reprinted in *AI Magazine* 2 (2 [1981]): 1–20.

44. Daniel Dennett, "Précis of the Intentional Stance," *Behavioral and Brain Science* 11 (3 [1988]): 495–546.

45. David Marr and Tomaso Poggio, "Cooperative Computation of Stereo Disparity," *Science* 194 (1976): 283–87.

46. Marr, *Vision,* p. xvii.

47. Interview with Hans Moravec, 21 May 1991.

48. Marr, *Vision,* p. xvii.

49. J. Alan Robinson, "A Machine-Oriented Logic Based on the Resolution Principle," *Journal of the Association for Computing Machinery* 12 (1 [January 1965]): 23–41.

50. Patrick Henry Winston, foreword to Ivan Bratko, *Prolog* (Reading, Mass.: Addison-Wesley, 1990), p. vii.

51. Interview with Carl Hewitt, 13 May 1991.

52. Robert Kowalski and Donald Kuehner, "Linear Resolution with Selection Function," *Artificial Intelligence* 2 (1971): 27–260.

53. Alain Colmerauer, "Les Systèmes-Q, ou un formalisme pour analyser et synthétiser des phrases sur ordinateur," Internal Report no. 43, Computer Science Department, Université de Montréal, September 1970.

54. Michel van Caneghem, *L'Anatomie de Prolog* (Paris: Interéditions, 1986), p. 16.

55. Winston, foreword.

CHAPTER 8. THE ROLLERCOASTER OF THE 1980S

1. Daniel G. Bobrow, Sanjay Mittal, and Mark J. Stefik, "Expert Systems: Perils and Promise," *Communications of the ACM* 29 (9 [September 1986]): 880–94.

2. E. Feigenbaum, P. McCorduck, and H. P. Nii, *The Rise of the Expert Company* (New York and Toronto: Vintage Books, 1988).

3. P. Harmon and D. King, *Expert Systems: Artificial Intelligence in Business* (New York: John Wiley, 1985), pp. 160–63.

4. Andrew Kupfer, "Now, Live Experts on a Floppy Disk," *Fortune,* 12 October 1987, p. 70.

5. Ruth Simon, "The Morning After," *Forbes,* 19 October 1987, p. 164.

6. "Artificial Intelligence Is Here," *Business Week,* 9 July 1984, p. 54.

7. Donald A. Waterman, *A Guide to Expert Systems* (Reading, Mass.: Addison-Wesley, 1986).

8. Emily T. Smith, "A High-Tech Market That's Not Feeling the Pinch," *Business Week,* 1 July 1985, p. 78.

9. Mitchell M. Waldrop, *Man-Made Minds: The Promise of Artificial Intelligence* (New York: Walker and Co., 1987), p. 155.

10. Raj Reddy, presidential address to AAAI, 1988.

11. Kupfer, "Now, Live Experts," p. 70.

12. Ibid., p. 78.

13. Alex Kozlov, "Rethinking Artificial Intelligence," *High Technology Business,* May 1988, p. 19.

14. Waldrop, *Man-Made Minds,* pp. 147–49.

15. Ibid., pp. 44–49.

16. Morris W. Firebaugh, *Artificial Intelligence: A Knowledge-Based Approach* (Boston: Boyd Fraser, 1988), p. 437.

17. "Machine Vision Systems: A Summary and Forecast," Tech Tran Corporation, Naperville, Ill.

18. Interview with Patrick Winston, 15 May 1991. All other personal quotes of Winston's in this chapter are from this interview.

19. Mitchell M. Waldrop, "Artificial Intelligence Moves into Mainstream," *Science,* 31 July 1987, p. 484.

20. Kupfer, "Now, Live Experts," p. 69.

21. Smith, "A High-Tech Market."

22. Tom Alexander, "Why Computers Can't Outthink the Experts," *Fortune,* August 1984, p. 106.

23. Drew McDermott et al., "The Dark Ages of AI: A Panel Discussion at AAAI–84," *AI Magazine,* Fall 1984, pp. 122–34.

24. Simon, "The Morning After," p. 166.

25. "Maintenance Keeps AI Software Alive," *High Technology Business,* September 1988, p. 52.

26. John McCarthy, "Mathematical Logic in Artificial Intelligence," in R. S. Graubard, ed., *The Artificial Intelligence Debate. False Starts, Real Foundations* (Cambridge, Mass.: MIT Press, 1987), p. 304.

27. Marvin Minsky, presidential address to the American Association for Artificial Intelligence. Available from AAAI, 445 Burgess Drive, Menlo Park, CA 94025.

28. Simon, "The Morning After," p. 164.

29. Firebaugh, *Artificial Intelligence,* p. 378.

30. Hubert L. Dreyfus and Stuart E. Dreyfus, *Mind Over Machine: The Power of Human Intuition and Expertise in the Era of the Computer* (New York: Free Press, 1985), pp. xv, 118.

31. Alexander, "Why Computers Can't Outthink the Experts."

32. Dreyfus and Dreyfus, *Mind Over Machine,* p. 120.
33. "The US Market for Artificial Intelligence Products," report no. A1951/J, Frost & Sullivan Inc., New York, Summer 1988.
34. Andrew Pollack, "Setbacks for Artificial Intelligence," *New York Times,* 4 March 1988, p. 1, col. 3.
35. Simon, "The Morning After," p. 164.
36. Ibid., p. 166.
37. Gregory Pope, "Machine Vision Focuses on Profits," *High Technology Business,* January 1989, p. 14.
38. Lise Olson, "Machine Vision Industry Works to Regain Focus," *Detroit News,* 8 June 1987, p. 1D.
39. Waldrop, *Man-Made Minds,* p. 179.
40. Interview with Hans Moravec, 21 May 1991.
41. Andrew Pollack, "Pentagon Sought Smart Truck But It Found Something Else," *New York Times,* 30 May 1989, p. 1, col. 1.
42. For more information on the Fifth Generation project see, for example, Waldrop, *Man-Made Minds,* p. 166; and Howard Ullman, "Machine Dreams," *The New Republic,* July 17 and 24, 1989, p. 12.
43. Jim Impoco, "Computers That to Translate Good Enough," *U.S. News & World Report,* 5 December 1988, p. 72.
44. Ullman, "Machine Dreams," p. 12.
45. Ibid.
46. Alex Kozlov, "Rethinking Artificial Intelligence," *High Technology Business,* May 1988, p. 20.
47. Ibid., p. 18.
48. Geoffrey E. Hinton, "How Neural Networks Learn from Experience," *Scientific American,* September 1992, p. 146.
49. John J. Hopfield, "Neural Networks and Physical Systems with Emergent Collective Computational Abilities," *Proceedings of the National Academy of Sciences, USA,* Vol. 79, 1982, pp. 2554–58.
50. David E. Rumelhart, James L. McClelland, and the PDP Research Group, *Parallel Distributed Processing: Explorations into the Microstructure of Cognition, Volumes 1 and 2* (Cambridge, Mass.: MIT Press, 1986).
51. Terrence J. Sejnowski and C. R. Rosenberg, "Parallel Networks That Learn to Pronounce English Text," *Complex Systems* 1 (1987): 145–68.
52. G. Tesauro and Terrence J. Sejnowski, "A Parallel Network that Learns to Play Backgammon," *Artificial Intelligence* 39 (1989).
53. D. Pomerleau, "ALVINN: An Autonomous Land Vehicle in a Neural Network," in D. Touretzky, ed., *Advances in Neural Information Processing Systems I* (San Mateo, Calif.: Morgan Kaufman, 1989), pp. 305–13.
54. Interview with James McClelland, 20 May 1991.
55. For more information on the neural networks industrial segment see, "Neurocomputing," Technology Impact Report No. T003, Frost & Sul-

livan Inc., New York, Spring 1989; and "Neural Network Sales to Mature in Mid-90s," *Computer Dealer News,* 29 June 1989, p. 17.

56. On fuzzy-logic industry, see Philip Elmer Dewitt, "Time for Some Fuzzy Thinking," *Time,* 25 September 1989, p. 85; and "Fuzzy Computing," Technology Impact Report No. T023, Frost & Sullivan Inc., New York, Summer 1989.

CHAPTER 9. GAME PLAYING: CHECKMATE FOR MACHINES?

1. Hans J. Berliner, "Backgammon Computer Program Beats World Champion," *Artificial Intelligence* 14 (1980): 205–20.
2. Hans J. Berliner, "Computer Backgammon," *Scientific American,* January 1980, p. 68.
3. Arthur L. Samuel, "AI, Where It Has Been and Where It Is Going," *Proceedings of the Eighth International Joint Conference on AI,* Karlsruhe, West Germany, 8–12 August 1983, p. 1155.
4. Time-Life editorial staff, *Artificial Intelligence* (Alexandria, Va.: Time-Life Books, 1986), p. 74.
5. *Science Digest,* May 1982, p. 55.
6. *Scientific American,* July 1984, p. 14.
7. Judea Pearl, *Heuristics: Intelligent Search Strategies for Computer Problem Solving* (Reading, Mass.: Addison-Wesley, 1984).
8. Claude E. Shannon, "Programming a Computer for Playing Chess," *Philosophy Magazine,* 41 (March 1950): 356–75.
9. Alan M. Turing, "Digital Computers Applied to Games," in B. V. Bowden, ed., *Faster Than Thought* (London: Pitman & Sons, 1953).
10. Hans J. Berliner, "A Chronology of Computer Chess and Its Literature," *Artificial Intelligence* 10 (1978): 201–14.
11. Shannon, "Programming a Computer to Play Chess," p. 26.
12. Berliner, "Chronology," p. 202.
13. Hubert L. Dreyfus and Stuart E. Dreyfus, *Mind Over Machine* (New York: Free Press, 1985), p. 112.
14. Hubert L. Dreyfus, "Alchemy and Artificial Intelligence," RAND Corporation Paper P-3244, December 1965.
15. *Scientific American,* February 1986, p. 14.
16. Arthur L. Robinson, "Tournament Competition Fuels Computer Chess," *Science,* 29 June 1979, p. 1397.
17. *Science,* 17 October 1980, p. 293.
18. Robinson, "Tournament Competition," p. 1397.
19. *Science,* 25 June 1982, p. 1392.
20. *Science News,* 5 November 1983, p. 303.
21. *Science Digest,* March 1985, p. 8.

22. Hans Berliner, "Hitech Wins North American Computer Chess Championship," *AI Magazine,* Winter 1986, p. 30.
23. *US News & World Report,* 13 March 1989, p. 64.
24. *Time,* 27 February 1989, p. 56.
25. *Science News,* 17 December 1988, p. 396.
26. *Science,* 3 November 1989, pp. 572–73.
27. *New York Times Magazine,* 14 January 1990, p. 33.
28. *Science,* 3 November 1989, p. 572.
29. *Science News,* 28 October 1989, p. 276.
30. *Time,* 6 November 1989, p. 100.
31. *Science Digest,* June 1986, p. 75.
32. Herbert Simon, *Models of Thought* (New Haven: Yale University Press, 1979), pp. 386–403.
33. Dreyfus and Dreyfus, *Mind over Machine,* p. 34.
34. *Byte,* 24 March 1984, p. 294.
35. *Science,* 17 October 1980, p. 294.
36. *Science News,* 8 October 1983, pp. 236–37.
37. Ibid., p. 236.
38. *Discover,* May 1989, p. 30.

CHAPTER 10. SOULS OF SILICON

The epigraph is extracted from Marvin Minsky, *The Society of Mind* (New York: Simon & Schuster, 1986), p. 160.

1. John McCarthy, "Circumscription, a Form of Nonmonotonic Reasoning," *Artificial Intelligence* 13 (1 [1980]): 27–39.
2. Janet L. Kolodner, R. L. Simpson, and K. Sycara, "A Process Model of Case Based Reasoning in Problem Solving," *Proceedings of the Ninth International Joint Conference on Artificial Intelligence,* Menlo Park, California, 1985, pp. 284–90.
3. Craig Stanfill and David L. Waltz, "Towards Memory-Based Reasoning," *Communications of the ACM* 29 (12 [December 1986]): 1213–28.
4. Douglas B. Lenat and R. V. Guha, "The World According to CYC," MCC Technical Report no. ACA-AI-300-88, September 1988, pp. 2–3.
5. R. V. Guha and Douglas B. Lenat, "Cyc: A Midterm Report," *AI Magazine* 1 (3[Fall 1990]): 33.
6. D. B. Lenat, M. Prakash, and M. Shepherd, "Cyc: Using Common Sense Knowledge to Overcome Brittleness and Knowledge-Acquisition Bottlenecks," *AI Magazine* 6 (Winter 1986): 65–85.
7. M. Leibowitz, "Brain Trusts," *Omni,* June 1988, pp. 44–46.
8. Guha and Lenat, "Cyc: A Midterm Report," p. 53.

9. Ibid., p. 34.

10. Ibid., p. 57.

11. Interview with Marvin Minsky, 13 May 1991. All other personal quotes of Minsky's in this chapter are from this interview.

12. Guha and Lenat, "Cyc: A Midterm Report," p. 33.

13. Leibowitz, "Brain Trusts," p. 44.

14. Interview with Hans Moravec, 21 May 1991. All other personal quotes of Moravec's in this chapter are from this interview.

15. Interview with Randall Davis, 17 May 1991. All other personal quotes of Davis's in this chapter are from this interview.

16. Interview with David Waltz, 15 May 1991. All other personal quotes of Waltz's in this chapter are from this interview.

17. Interview with Allen Newell, 23 May 1991. All other personal quotes of Newell's in this chapter are from this interview.

18. Edward A. Feigenbaum, "The Simulation of Verbal Learning Behavior," in E. A. Feigenbaum and J. Feldman, eds., *Computers and Thought* (New York: McGraw-Hill, 1963).

19. Immanuel Kant, *Critique of Pure Reason* (1787).

20. Frederick C. Bartlett, *Remembering* (Cambridge: Cambridge University Press, 1932).

21. Jean Piaget and B. Inhelder, *The Child's Conception of Space* (New York: Humanities Press, 1956).

22. Max Wertheimer, *Productive Thinking* (New York: Harper & Row, 1959).

23. Marvin Minsky, "A Framework for Representing Knowledge," in P. H. Winston, ed., *The Psychology of Computer Vision* (New York: McGraw-Hill, 1975), pp. 211–77.

24. Pamela McCorduck, *Machines Who Think* (San Francisco: W. H. Freeman, 1979).

25. Pamela McCorduck, "Artificial Intelligence: An Aperçu," in Stephen R. Graubard, ed., *The Artificial Intelligence Debate* (Cambridge, Mass.: MIT Press, 1988), p. 67.

26. Sherry Turkle, "Artificial Intelligence and Psychoanalysis: A New Alliance," in S. R. Graubard, ed., *The Artificial Intelligence Debate: False Starts, Real Foundations* (Cambridge, Mass.: MIT Press, 1988), p. 249.

27. N. E. Sharkey and R. Pfeifer, "Uncomfortable Bedfellows: Cognitive Psychology and AI," in M. Yazdani and A. Narayanan, eds., *Artificial Intelligence: Human Effects* (Chichester, England: E. Horwood, 1984), p. 166.

28. John von Neumann, "Lecture at the University of Illinois, 1949," in Arthur W. Burks, ed., *Theory of Self-Reproducing Automata* (Urbana, Ill.: University of Illinois Press, 1966).

29. Guha and Lenat, "Cyc: A Midterm Report," p. 53.

30. Sigmund Freud, *Beyond the Pleasure Principle,* James Strachey, ed., vol. 18 in *Standard Edition of the Complete Psychological Works of Sigmund Freud* (London: Hogarth Press, 1957–74; originally published, 1920).

31. David Hume, *Philosophical Essays Concerning Human Understanding* (1748).
32. Interview with Daniel Dennett, 17 May 1991. All other personal quotes of Dennett's in this chapter are from this interview.
33. Douglas Hofstadter and Daniel Dennett, *The Mind's I* (New York: Basic Books, 1981), p. 473.
34. Turkle, "Artificial Intelligence," p. 264.
35. Interview with Carl Hewitt, 13 May 1991. All other personal quotes of Hewitt's in this chapter are from this interview.
36. Turkle, "Artificial Intelligence," pp. 256–61.
37. Thomas H. Ogden, "The Concept of Internal Object Relations," *International Journal of Psycho-Analysis* 63 (1983): 227.
38. Marvin Minsky, *The Society of Mind* (New York: Simon & Schuster, 1986).
39. Daniel C. Dennett, "When Philosophers Encounter Artificial Intelligence," in Graubard, ed., *Artificial Intelligence Debate,* p. 287.
40. David M. West and Larry E. Travis, "From Society to Landscape: Alternative Metaphors for Artificial Intelligence," *AI Magazine* 12 (2 [Summer 1991]): 71, 83.
41. T. Winograd, "Thinking Machines: Can There Be, Are We?" presented at Stanford University Centennial Conference, 23–27 April 1987, Stanford, California; quoted in West and Travis, "From Society to Landscape."
42. Interview with Patrick Winston, 15 May 1991. All other personal quotes of Winston's in this chapter are from this interview.
43. Interview with Herbert Simon, 23 May 1991.
44. John E. Laird, "Universal Subgoaling" (Ph.D. diss., Department of Computer Science, Carnegie Mellon University, May 1984).
45. G. A. Miller, "The Magical Number Seven," *Psychological Review* 63 (1956): 81.
46. Paul S. Rosenbloom, "The Chunking of Goal Hierarchies: A Model of Practice and Stimulus-Response Compatibility" (Ph.D. diss., Computer Science Department, Carnegie Mellon University, August 1983).
47. Allen Newell, *Unified Theories of Cognition* (Cambridge, Mass.: Harvard University Press, 1990).
48. J. R. Anderson, *The Architecture of Cognition* (Cambridge, Mass.: Harvard University Press, 1983).
49. S. Minton et al., "Explanation-Based Learning: A Problem Solving Perspective," *Artificial Intelligence* 40 (1–3 [1989]): 63–118.
50. Hubert L. and Stuart E. Dreyfus, "Making a Mind versus Modeling the Brain," in Stephen R. Graubard, ed., *The Artificial Intelligence Debate: False Starts, Real Foundations* (Cambridge, Mass.: MIT Press, 1988), p. 37.
51. Joseph Weizenbaum, *Computer Power and Human Reason* (San Francisco: W. H. Freeman, 1976).
52. Interview with Joseph Weizenbaum, 16 May 1991. All other quotes of Weizenbaum's in this chapter are from this interview.
53. Minsky, *The Society of Mind,* sec. 9.1, p. 94.
54. Ibid., sec. 27.6, p. 279.

55. Ibid., sec. 27.7, p. 280.

56. John R. Searle, "Minds, Brains and Programs," *Behavioral and Brain Sciences* 3 (3 [1980]): 417–58.

57. Paul M. Churchland and Patricia Smith Churchland, "Could a Machine Think?" *Scientific American,* January 1990, pp. 32–37.

58. John R. Searle, "Is the Brain's Mind a Computer Program?" *Scientific American,* January 1990, p. 29.

59. Zenon W. Pylyshyn, "The Causal Power of Machines," *Behavioral and Brain Sciences* 3 (1980): 442–44.

60. Daniel C. Dennett: "The Role of the Computer Metaphor in Understanding the Mind," in Heinz R. Pagels, ed., *Computer Culture: The Scientific, Intellectual and Social Impact of the Computer* (New York: New York Academy of Sciences, 1984).

61. Pattie Maes and Rodney A. Brooks, "Learning to Coordinate Behaviors," in *Proceedings of the Eighth National Conference on Artificial Intelligence* (Menlo Park, Calif.: AAAI Press, 1990), pp. 796–802.

62. Daniel C. Dennett, "Can Machines Think?" in Michael Shafto, ed., *How We Know* (San Francisco: Harper & Row, 1985), p. 143.

63. Minsky, *Society of Mind,* sec. 15.10, p. 160.

64. Ibid., sec. 6.2, p. 57.

65. Ibid., sec. 22.7, p. 232.

66. David Ritchie, *The Binary Brain: Artificial Intelligence in the Age of Electronics* (Boston: Little, Brown, 1984), chap. 16.

67. D. E. Rumelhart, J. L. McClelland, and the PDP Research Group, *Parallel Distributed Processing,* vols. I and II (Cambridge, Mass.: MIT Press, 1986).

68. Marvin Minsky and Seymour Papert, *Perceptrons* (Cambridge, Mass.: MIT Press, 1969).

69. Interview with John McClelland, 20 May 1991.

70. Old Testament verses taken from *The Jerusalem Bible* (Garden City, N.Y.: Doubleday, 1966).

71. New Testament verse taken from *The Holy Bible, King James Version* (Biblehouse, N.Y.: American Bible Society).

72. Louis Roy, *La Foi en quête de cohérence* (Montreal: Bellarmin, 1988), p. 136.

73. Raymond A. Moody, *Life After Life* (Covington, Ky: Mockingbird Books, 1977).

74. Raymond A. Moody, *The Light Beyond* (New York: Bantam Books, 1988).

75. Pylyshyn, "Causal Power of Machines."

76. Hans Moravec, *Mind Children: The Future of Robot and Human Intelligence* (Cambridge: Harvard University Press, 1988). See also Hans Moravec, "Today's Computers, Intelligent Machines and Our Future," *Analog,* February 1979, p. 59. For a discussion of the effect of this thought experiment on the AI research community, see Grant Fjermedal, *The Tomorrow Makers: A Brave New World of Living Brain Machines* (New York: Macmillan, 1986).

77. Moody, *Life After Life.*

CHAPTER 11. HOW MANY BULLDOZERS
FOR AN ANT COLONY?

1. Jean Pierre Changeux: *L'Homme neuronal* (Paris: Fayard, 1983).
2. Jacob T. Schwartz, "The New Connectionism: Developing Relationships Between Neuroscience and Artificial Intelligence," in Stephen R. Graubard, ed., *The Artificial Intelligence Debate: False Starts, Real Foundations* (Cambridge: MIT Press, 1988), p. 126.
3. Hans Moravec, *Mind Children: The Future of Robot and Human Intelligence* (Cambridge and London: Harvard University Press, 1988), pp. 57–60.
4. W. Daniel Hillis, "Intelligence as Emergent Behavior; or, The Songs of Eden," in Graubard, *Artificial Intelligence Debate*.
5. J. J. Hopfield, "Neural Networks and Physical Systems with Emergent Collective Computational Abilities," *Proceedings of the National Academy of Sciences, U.S.A.,* vol. 79, April 1982, pp. 2554–58.
6. Allen Newell and Herbert Simon, *Human Problem Solving* (Englewood Cliffs, N.J.: Prentice-Hall, 1972), p. 793. In this section of their book, Newell and Simon estimate the time it takes to store knowledge into long-term memory at five to ten seconds per chunk, but leave undefined the *size* of a chunk in bits. However, Newell's Soar program models the psychological mechanism of learning by chunk creation: Soar encodes chunks as if-then rules which occupy about 1000 bits of memory. Putting these two figures together yields a human learning rate of about 100 bits per second.
7. IEEE Scientific Supercomputer Subcommittee, "Supercomputer Hardware: An Update of the 1983 Report's Summary and Tables," *IEEE Computer,* November 1989, p. 64.
8. Moravec, *Mind Children,* pp. 174–77.
9. Ibid., p. 64.
10. Data extrapolated from IEEE Scientific Supercomputer Subcommittee, "The Computer Spectrum: A Perspective on the Evolution of Computing," *IEEE Computer,* November 1989, p. 57.
11. W. Penfield and H. Jasper, "Highest Level Seizures," *Research Publications of the Association for Research and Mental Diseases, New York* 26 (1947): 252–71; quoted in R. Penrose, *The Emperor's New Mind* (New York: Oxford University Press, 1989), p. 493.
12. H. O'Keefe, "Is Consciousness the Gateway to the Hippocampal Cognitive Map?" in D. A. Oakley, ed., *Brain and Mind* (London and New York: Methuen, 1985); quoted in Penrose, *Emperor's New Mind,* p. 495.
13. J. C. Eccles, *The Understanding of the Brain* (New York: McGraw-Hill, 1973); quoted in Penrose, *Emperor's New Mind,* p. 496.
14. Penrose, *Emperor's New Mind,* pp. 492–500. See also Francis Crick and Christ of Koch, "The Problem of Consciousness," *Scientific American,* September 1992, pp. 152–9.
15. K. Eric Drexler, *Engines of Creation: The Coming Era of Nanotechnology* (New York: Anchor Books [Doubleday], 1986).

16. David Ritchie, *The Binary Brain: Artificial Intelligence in the Age of Electronics* (Boston: Little, Brown, 1984).
17. François Jacob, "Evolution and Tinkering," *Science* 196 (1977): 1161–66.
18. Interview with Marvin Minsky, 13 May 1991. All other personal quotes of Minsky's in this chapter are from this interview.
19. Interview with Carl Hewitt, 13 May 1991.
20. Interview with Patrick Winston, 15 May 1991. All other personal quotes of Winston's in this chapter are from this interview.
21. Interview with James McClelland, 20 May 1991.
22. Interview with David Waltz, 15 May 1991.

CHAPTER 12. THE SILICON CHALLENGERS IN OUR FUTURE

1. Dennis Feltham Jones, *Colossus* (New York: Putnam, 1967).
2. Frank Rose, *Into the Heart of Mind* (New York: Harper & Row, 1984), p. 43.
3. Interview with Patrick Winston, 15 May 1991. All other personal quotes of Winston's in this chapter are from this interview.
4. Interview with Hans Moravec, 21 May 1991. All other personal quotes of Moravec's in this chapter are from this interview.
5. Interview with Daniel Dennett, 17 May 1991. All other personal quotes of Dennett's in this chapter are from this interview.
6. Interview with Joseph Weizenbaum, 16 May 1991. All other personal quotes of Weizenbaum's in this chapter are from this interview.
7. Herbert Simon, *The Science of the Artificial* (Cambridge, Mass.: MIT Press, 1969), pp. 84–118. (See also chapter 2 of this book.)
8. Marvin Minsky, *The Society of Mind* (New York: Simon & Schuster, 1985), p. 34. (See also chapter 10 of this book.)
9. John Markoff, "More Threats to Privacy Seen as Computer Links Broaden," *New York Times,* 1 June 1988, Vol. 1, p. 1, col. 3.
10. Ibid.
11. Rose, *Into the Heart of Mind,* pp. 156–57.
12. Markoff, "More Threats."
13. Roger C. Schank, *The Cognitive Computer: On Language, Learning, and Artificial Intelligence* (Reading, Mass.: Addison-Wesley, 1985), pp. 239–40.
14. Mitchell M. Waldrop, *Man-Made Minds: The Promise of Artificial Intelligence* (New York: Walker, 1987), p. 220.
15. John A. Campbell, "The Expert Computer and Professional Negligence: Who Is Liable?" in M. Yazdani and A. Narayanan, eds., *Artificial Intelligence—Human Effects* (Chichester, England: E. Horwood, 1986), p. 44.
16. M. Yazdani and A. Narayanan, "Intelligent Machines and Human Society," in Yazdani and Narayanan, *Artificial Intelligence,* pp. 64–65.
17. Margaret A. Boden, "AI and Human Freedom," in Yazdani and Narayanan, *Artificial Intelligence,* p. 196.

18. Blay R. Whitby, "AI: Some Immediate Dangers," in Yazdani and Narayanan, *Artificial Intelligence,* p. 240.

19. Interview with Gerald Sussman, 14 May 1991. All other personal quotes of Sussman's in this chapter are from this interview.

20. Quoted in Donald Michie and Rory Johnston, *The Knowledge Machine—Artificial Intelligence and the Future of Man* (New York: William Morrow, 1985), p. 74.

21. Robert Sokolowski, "Natural and Artificial Intelligence," in S. R. Graubard, ed., *The Artificial Intelligence Debate: False Starts, Real Foundations* (Cambridge: MIT Press, 1988), p. 48.

22. Michie and Johnston, *Knowledge Machine,* p. 244.

23. Ibid., p. 10.

24. Schank, *Cognitive Computer,* p. 240.

25. K. Hammond, "CHEF: A Model of Case-Based Planning," Proceedings of the 1986 AAAI Meeting.

26. Michie and Johnston, *Knowledge Machine,* p. 148.

27. Schank, *Cognitive Computer,* p. 22.

28. As pointed out in Michie and Johnston, *Knowledge Machine,* pp. 223–24.

29. Marvin Minsky: *The Society of Mind,* sec. 2.6, p. 30.

30. Schank, *Cognitive Computer,* p. 216.

31. J. Michael Brady, "The Social Implications of AI," in Yazdani and Narayanan, *Artificial Intelligence,* p. 71.

32. Seymour Papert, "Computers and Learning," in Michael L. Dertouzos and Joel Moses, eds., *The Computer Age: A Twenty-Year View* (Cambridge: MIT Press, 1980), p. 73.

33. Hans Moravec, *Mind Children: The Future of Robot and Human Intelligences* (Cambridge, Mass.: Harvard University Press, 1988), p. 93.

34. K. Eric Drexler, *Engines of Creation: The Coming Era of Nanotechnology* (New York: Anchor Books [Doubleday], 1986).

35. Moravec, *Mind Children,* pp. 108–12.

36. See, for example: Margaret Boden, chairperson, "Panel: Artificial Intelligence and Legal Responsibilities," *Proceedings of the International Joint Conference on Artificial Intelligence,* Los Angeles, Calif., 1985, pp. 1267–8; Yoris Wilks, "Responsible Computers?" ibid., pp. 1279–80; and Marshal S. Willick, "Constitutional Law and Artificial Intelligence: The Potential Legal Recognition of Computers as 'Persons,'" ibid., pp. 1771–3.

Index